D0641908

ARC WELDED
PROJECTS

Volume II

THE JAMES F. LINCOLN ARC WELDING FOUNDATION
CLEVELAND, OHIO

Published As An Aid To Teaching Shop Skills
And To Designing And Fabricating Arc Welded Projects

By

The James F. Lincoln Arc Welding Foundation

First Printing—20,000 May 1978
Second Printing—15,000 August 1979
Third Printing—15,000 September 1981
Fourth Printing—5,000 September 1987

Printed in U.S.A.

Library of Congress Catalog Card Number 78-54347

The serviceability of a product or structure utilizing this type of information is and must be the sole responsibility of the builder/user. Many variables beyond the control of The James F. Lincoln Arc Welding Foundation affect the results obtained in applying this type of information. These variables include, but are not limited to welding procedure, plate chemistry and temperature, weldment design, fabrication methods and service requirements.

Important—Read Before Using These Plans

The plans, suggestions and instructions for making the projects included in this book were prepared by students as entries in The James F. Lincoln Arc Welding Foundation Award Programs. The material has been edited and some of the drawings improved, but neither the projects nor drawings and instructions have been reviewed for accuracy or safety. The Foundation will welcome the comments of persons who, in making a project, uncover an error or fault. This will permit correction in the next printing of the book.

The projects are included because they appear to be interesting, and, in some respects, propose novel applications. However, since the Foundation has not tested the material, nor verified the computations or other aspects described, The James F. Lincoln Arc Welding Foundation cannot, and does not, assume responsibility for the accuracy of the plans or safety of the projects. The projects are submitted for such use as may appear feasible, but those making the projects must assume full responsibility for the results of their efforts to make or use the projects described.

The name of the student, school and teacher that produced the original material is given for each project. Further information about a project, if needed, should be sought from the teacher involved.

Note To Teachers

The projects described in this book are representative of the range of entries submitted in the Lincoln Arc Welding Foundation's Award Programs both as to type and size of project and the nature of the descriptive information included. Many similar projects are made each year by students. Relatively few of these are submitted to the Foundation in competition for cash awards. The reason for this may be that teachers have not used the opportunities afforded by the Programs as incentives to student endeavor.

The planning, designing and execution of a project, and then the preparation of a written and illustrated description of how it was accomplished provided a student with:

(1) an involvement in something of his own choosing and desire; (2) a challenge to complete the work successfully, using many different shop skills that will be used in industry and business; (3) an experience in report writing and communications that is as important in business as other skills; (4) the satisfaction and recognition that come from participation in a national competition.

The Lincoln Arc Welding Foundation annually sponsors Award Programs for high school students, post high and career students, and four year college students. If you would like a copy of the rules brochure for a current Award Program please write indicating your level of interest.

TABLE OF CONTENTS

SECTION A
TABLE OF CONTENTS
AGRICULTURAL EQUIPMENT

A Scraper Grader

Author: Stanley R. East
William J. Langley
Instructor: Gary Fuchs
School: Opelika State Tech. Coll.
City & State: Opelika, AL

This scraper is conventional in design, except that wherever possible heavier material was used in construction. The finished weight of 350 pounds attest to the heavier than normal construction. The scraper can be used in the usual forward position or can be rotated to either of three positions to the left or right of center. It can also be used in the reverse position, with one position to the left or right of center.

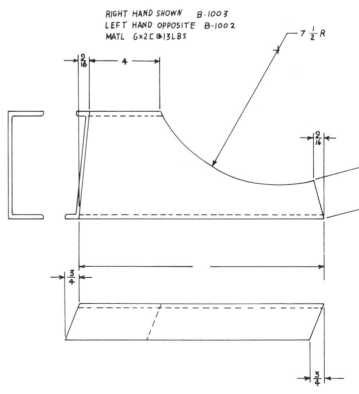

RIGHT HAND SHOWN B-1003
LEFT HAND OPPOSITE B-1002
MATL 6×2⊏@13LBS

7 ½ R

9/16

4

9/16

3/4

3/4

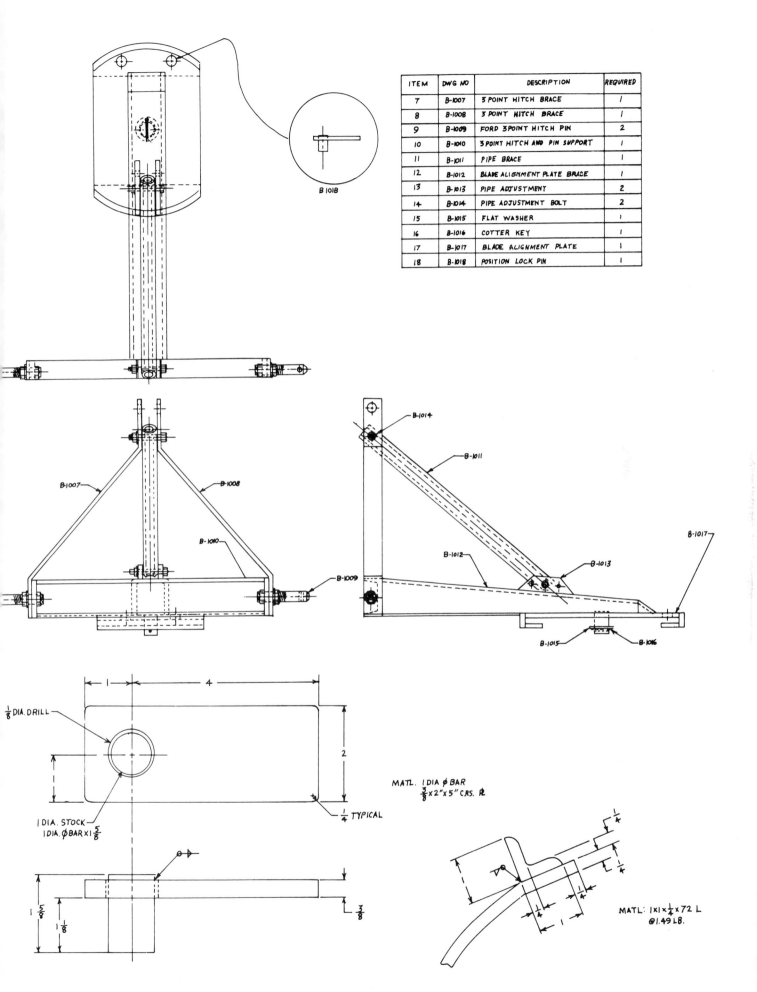

ITEM	DWG NO	DESCRIPTION	REQUIRED
7	B-1007	3 POINT HITCH BRACE	1
8	B-1008	3 POINT HITCH BRACE	1
9	B-1009	FORD 3 POINT HITCH PIN	2
10	B-1010	3 POINT HITCH AND PIN SUPPORT	1
11	B-1011	PIPE BRACE	1
12	B-1012	BLADE ALIGNMENT PLATE BRACE	1
13	B-1013	PIPE ADJUSTMENT	2
14	B-1014	PIPE ADJUSTMENT BOLT	2
15	B-1015	FLAT WASHER	1
16	B-1016	COTTER KEY	1
17	B-1017	BLADE ALIGNMENT PLATE	1
18	B-1018	POSITION LOCK PIN	1

B-1018

B-1014
B-1011
B-1012
B-1013
B-1017
B-1009
B-1015
B-1016

B-1007
B-1008
B-1010

$\frac{1}{8}$ DIA. DRILL

1 DIA. STOCK
1 DIA. ϕ BAR X 1$\frac{5}{8}$

$\frac{1}{4}$ TYPICAL

MATL. 1 DIA ϕ BAR
$\frac{3}{8}$ X 2" X 5" C.R.S. R.

MATL: 1 X 1 X $\frac{1}{4}$ X 72 L
@ 1.49 LB.

3

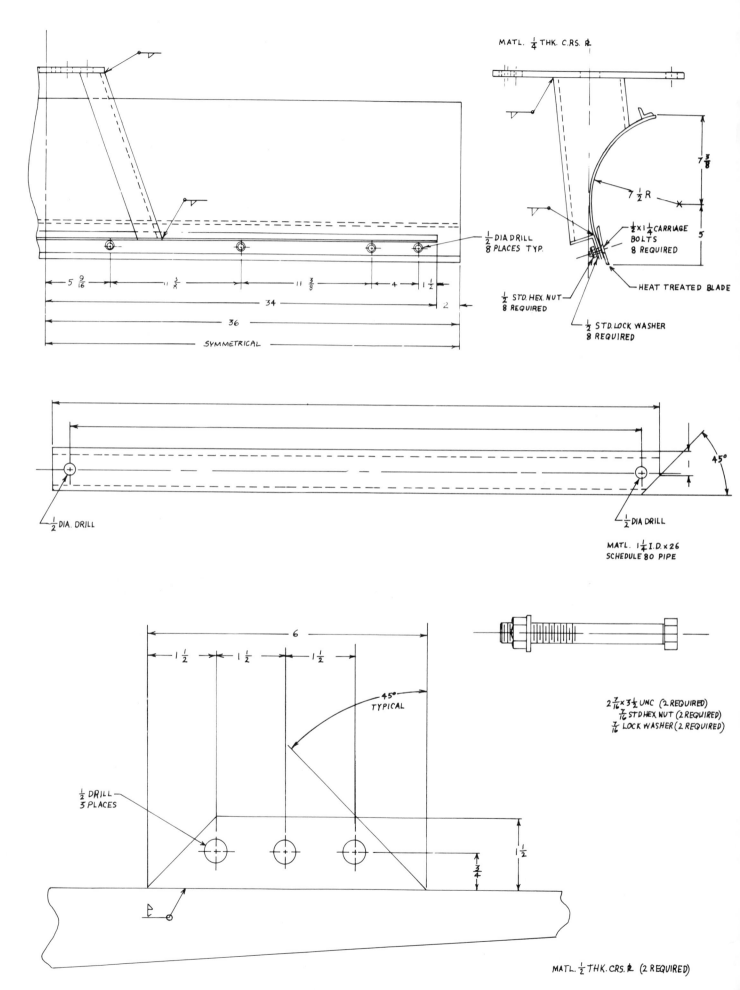

MATL. $\frac{1}{4}$ THK. C.RS. ℞

$\frac{1}{2}$ DIA DRILL
8 PLACES TYP.

$\frac{1}{2} \times 1\frac{1}{4}$ CARRIAGE
BOLTS
8 REQUIRED

HEAT TREATED BLADE

$\frac{1}{2}$ STD. HEX. NUT
8 REQUIRED

$\frac{1}{2}$ STD. LOCK WASHER
8 REQUIRED

$7\frac{3}{8}$

$7\frac{1}{2}$ R

5

$5\frac{9}{16}$ $11\frac{3}{8}$ $11\frac{3}{8}$ 4 $1\frac{1}{2}$

34

2

36

SYMMETRICAL

$\frac{1}{2}$ DIA. DRILL

$\frac{1}{2}$ DIA DRILL

45°

MATL. $1\frac{1}{4}$ I.D. $\times 26$
SCHEDULE 80 PIPE

6

$1\frac{1}{2}$ $1\frac{1}{2}$ $1\frac{1}{2}$

45°
TYPICAL

$\frac{1}{2}$ DRILL
3 PLACES

$1\frac{1}{2}$

$\frac{3}{4}$

B

$2\frac{7}{16} \times 3\frac{1}{2}$ UNC (2 REQUIRED)
$\frac{7}{16}$ STD HEX NUT (2 REQUIRED)
$\frac{7}{16}$ LOCK WASHER (2 REQUIRED)

MATL. $\frac{1}{2}$ THK. CRS. ℞ (2 REQUIRED)

4

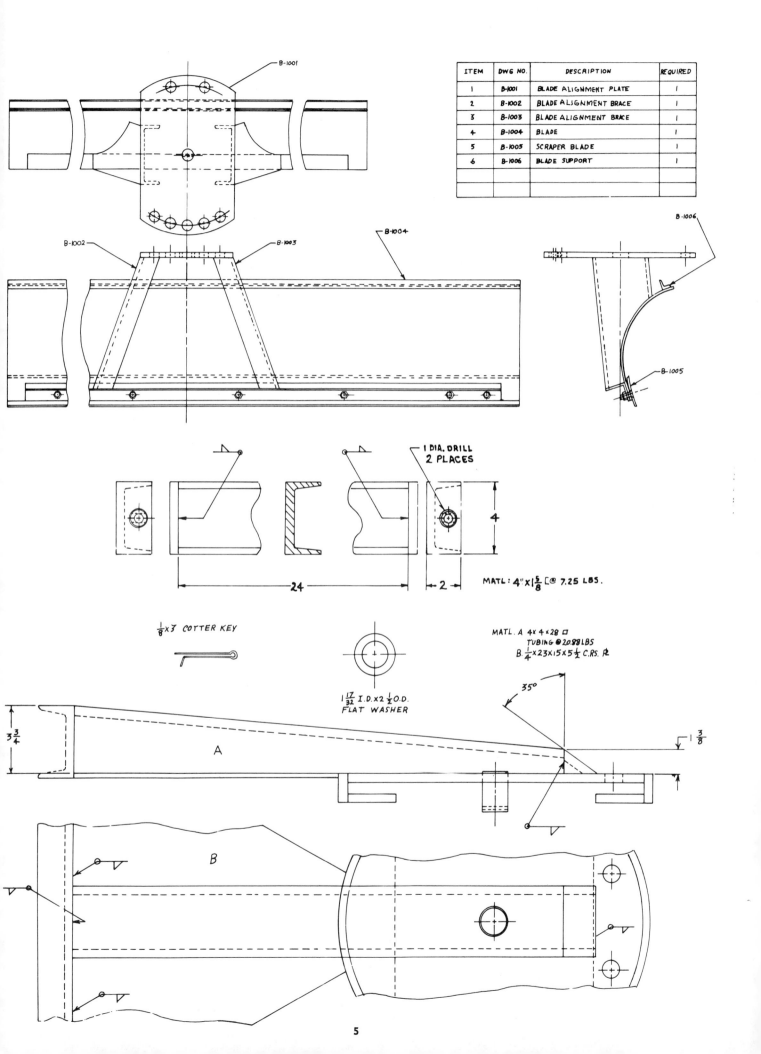

ITEM	DWG NO.	DESCRIPTION	REQUIRED
1	B-1001	BLADE ALIGNMENT PLATE	1
2	B-1002	BLADE ALIGNMENT BRACE	1
3	B-1003	BLADE ALIGNMENT BRACE	1
4	B-1004	BLADE	1
5	B-1005	SCRAPER BLADE	1
6	B-1006	BLADE SUPPORT	1

B-1001

B-1002

B-1003

B-1004

B-1006

B-1005

1 DIA. DRILL
2 PLACES

4

24

2

MATL: 4"×1 5/8 [@ 7.25 LBS.

1/8×3 COTTER KEY

1 17/32 I.D.×2 1/2 O.D.
FLAT WASHER

MATL. A 4×4×28 □
TUBING @ 20.88 LBS
B. 1/4 ×23×15×5 1/2 C.RS. R

35°

3 3/4

A

1 3/8

B

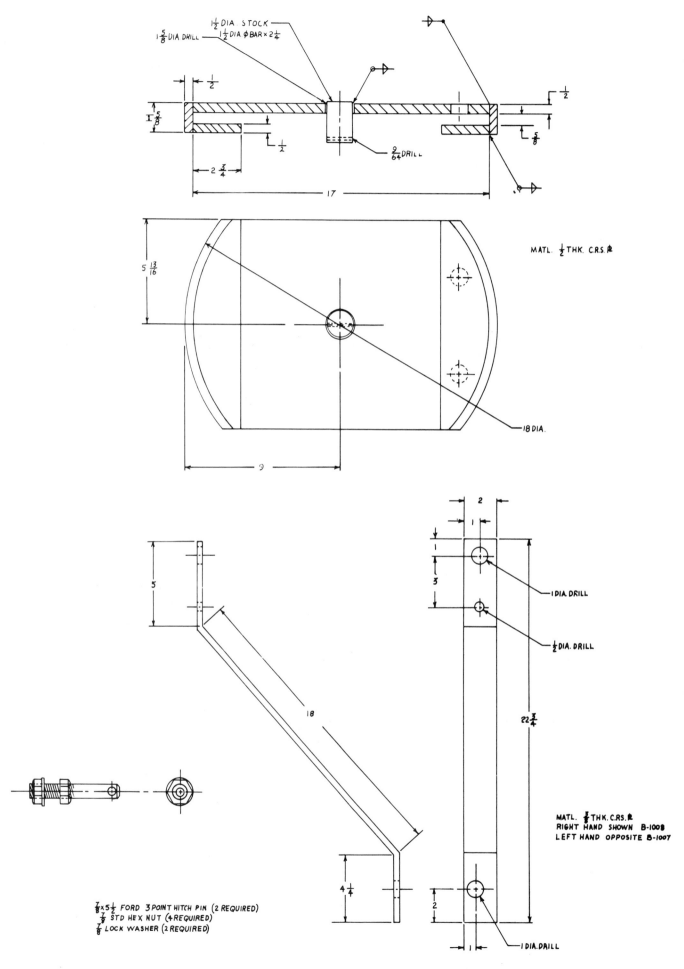

1 5/8 DIA. DRILL

1 1/2 DIA. STOCK
1 1/2 DIA. φ BAR × 2 1/4

1/2

1 5/8

1/2

2 3/4

9/64 DRILL

17

1/2

5/8

5 13/16

MATL. 1/2 THK. C.R.S. ℞

9

18 DIA.

5

18

4 1/4

2

1

1

3

1 DIA. DRILL

1/2 DIA. DRILL

22 3/4

2

MATL. 3/4 THK. C.R.S. ℞
RIGHT HAND SHOWN B-1008
LEFT HAND OPPOSITE B-1007

1 DIA. DRILL

7/8 × 5 1/2 FORD 3 POINT HITCH PIN (2 REQUIRED)
7/8 STD HEX NUT (4 REQUIRED)
7/8 LOCK WASHER (2 REQUIRED)

6

Engine Powered Sorghum Cane Mill

Author: *Clifford Bledsoe*
               Dale Birdseye
               David Grayson
               Ted Moffett
Instructor: *Virgil Stanley*
School: *Tri-Cities Reg. Voc.-Tech School*
City & State: *Blountville, TN*

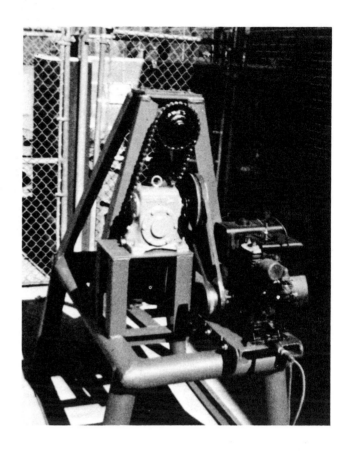

The mill extracts juices from sugar cane to be processed into molasses. This is accomplished by feeding the cane through three rollers which have a clearance of ⅛" and ¹⁄₁₆" between the rollers. The juice is then recovered through a pipe at the bottom of a mill.

The mill was converted from a horse drawn type to a more conventional gasoline engine. This power source eliminates the use of a 15' sweep pole from which the horse or mule was hitched. The engine turns at approximately 900 R.P.M. and is reduced to 8½ R.P.M. at the rollers.

The frame structure being made of pipe is equipped with skid plates to make it more easily moved by tractor.

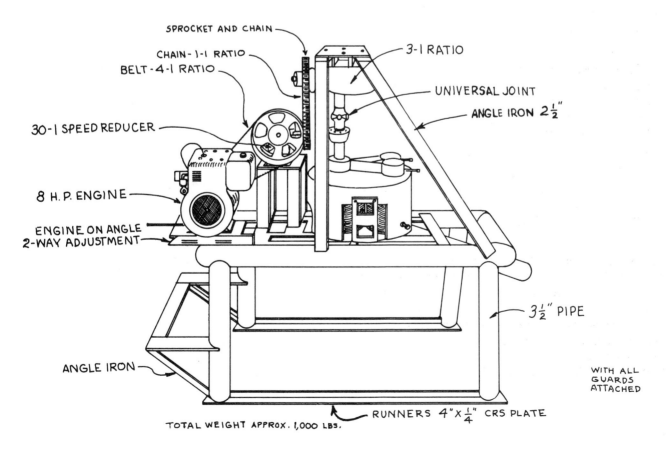

SPROCKET AND CHAIN

CHAIN-1-1 RATIO

BELT-4-1 RATIO

3-1 RATIO

30-1 SPEED REDUCER

UNIVERSAL JOINT

ANGLE IRON 2½"

8 H.P. ENGINE

ENGINE ON ANGLE
2-WAY ADJUSTMENT

3½" PIPE

ANGLE IRON

WITH ALL GUARDS ATTACHED

RUNNERS 4" X ¼" CRS PLATE

TOTAL WEIGHT APPROX. 1,000 LBS.

Box Grader

Author: Craig Sullivan
Instructor: Arthur Campbell
School: Mt. San Antonio College
City & State: Walnut, CA

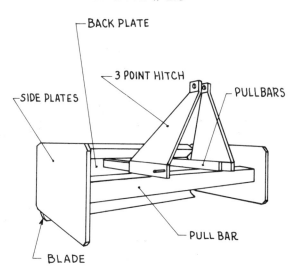

Two side plates: ⅜" x 28" x 18" rectangular steel plates are cut out of a sheet of ⅜" steel with a radiograph. Tack weld them on a metal table parallel to each other and perpendicular to the table 5' 6" apart.

Back plate: ¼" x 15" x 65" plate is placed parallel between the side plates leaving a 2" gap at the bottom.

Blade Angler: ¼" x 2½" x 65", 2 pieces are tacked together at a 30° angle and placed under the back plate to take up the 2" space. The two strips are welded to the bottom of the back up plate, all the way across.

Back filling Hinge: ¼" x 8" x 65": weld on the back plate, running parallel with it. The plate itself has been welded to pipe and the pipe has been cut in sections with every other piece welded to the back plate. The other pieces have been welded to the hinge plate with a piece of ½" rod going through the center of the pipe so it acts like a hinge.

Pull Tube: 2 - 4" x ⅛", angle iron 65" long welded together to form a square tube 65" long, placed between the two side plates to the front opposite the back plate. It is 7" off the table level, across, and 3" from the front of the side plates.

3 Point Hitch: 2 pieces of ⅜" steel in a 30° triangle shape, 25" high, 12¼" wide, one placed on the pull bar 19⅞" from the side plate and the same with the other one. With 2 bars 2" x ½" x 25" just on the inside of each triangular shaped plates - running parallel with the side plate, and table, ending at the back plate and at the pull tube. Weld the pull bars to pull-tube and triangle shape steel. Then heat the triangle shapes just at the pull bar all the way

across, pulling the tops of the triangular shapes together. Then heat the 3" squares, bending it so its straight up and down. Then weld a plate between them 2" apart.

Materials
One piece of ⅜" plate 18" x 82"
One piece 4" x 4" angle iron 12" long
One piece of ¼" plate 35" x 65"
Two cutting blades & bolts
Two pull pins
One ½" rod 65" long

BOX SCRAPER

BACK PLATE

3 POINT HITCH

PULLBARS

SIDE PLATES

PULL BAR

BLADE

Wood Splitter

Author: Ernest Mendes
Instructor: Ed Fisher
School: Hilmar High School
City & State: Hilmar, CA

Construction of Wedge
A T-Iron is cut to 11½'' high. Cut two pieces of ½'' x 9'' x 11½'', butt them to the back of the T-iron and angle them to the front to form a point and weld them solid. Then cut a piece of 1'' x 2'' x 11½'' iron, cut it into a point and grind it smooth. Cut a piece of metal ½'' x 4'' x 15'' and make a skid plate; weld a piece of metal ½'' x 3'' x 8'' on each side of the skid plate and mount two steel wheels on each plate. Then weld the wedge to the skid plate.

Construction of Ram Mounting
Cut two pieces of metal ¾'' x 7½'' x 8½'' and weld them to the I-beam for the rear ram mounting. For the front ram mounting, two pieces of metal ½'' x 3½'' x 4'' with 1½'' hole in them are used, the corners are rounded and welded to the back of the wedge for the front ram mounting.

Construction of Foot Plate
Cut a piece of metal ¾'' x 14½'' x 21'', round the corners, weld to the I-beam. On the back of the foot plate weld two pieces of ¾'' x 2'' x 21'' for brace on foot plate.

Construction of Log Bumper Bars
From a 1½'' shaft, cut two pieces 45½'' long, bend to shape and weld to mounts. Mount them in front on a piece of ¾'' x 6'' x 10'' metal and on a rear piece of ½'' x 4'' x 8'' metal. Weld to I-beam.

Construction of Axle and Tongue
Cut two pieces of heavy wall tubing, one 2'' inside diameter and the other 2¾'' outside diameter both 56'' long. Drill a ½'' hole 3'' deep on each side, center, slip spindle into the tubing, put ½'' bolt through to lock spindle into position, lay a 3'' channel on top of axle and weld to give a flat surface. A 3'' box channel is cut in a half moon on one end to fit axle and weld to axle. Two 4'' channel iron 48'' long is placed on the tongue 30'' from the front of axle to the first channel allowing 6'' spacing for the second one; place and weld. These two pieces of channel iron makes for the engine mounting and it supports both tanks. Two rectangular 6'' x 10'' tubing tanks 7' long are placed on top of axle and front engine mount, spaced 36'' apart overhanging front engine mount 2½'' square and weld.

Construction of Tanks
Rectangular tubing ³⁄₁₆'' x 6'' x 10'' is cut into two pieces 7' long, close the ends with a ⅜'' steel plate. One tank is for gas and the other is for oil. Cut three holes in the oil tank, one for a suction line, one for an oil cap and the third for a return oil filter. Mount a gauge on the inside of both tanks. At the rear of both tanks there is a ¾'' drain plug. For the gas tank cut one hole for the gas cap. Drill and tap one hole for shut-off fuel line. The tanks make part of the frame of the trailer.

Construction of Pivot Point for I-Beam

Two 2″ x 6″ box tubing 16″ long, cut one end round, cap and weld. Cut the other end at a 62° angle. Mount both pieces at rear of tank, flush with the inside; place and weld. Cut two pieces of ⅜″ wall tubing, one, 2¾″ outside diameter 36″ long and the other, 2⅞″ inside diameter 35″ long. Slip one over the other allowing ½″ at each end; place at the rounded end of the box tubing 1½″ down, center and weld. Take one 4″ channel 11″ long, place on center of hinging point and weld giving a flat surface for the I-beam.

Construction of Resting Point and Stopping Point for I-beam

Two 3″ channel are cut to 14½″ long. Weld together for a box channel, then cut a ¾″ x 3″ x 8″ piece of metal, drill two holes 5″ apart, weld to the box channel. Cut a piece of rubber 1½″ x 3½″ x 8½″ and bolt to the top of the box channel. Weld box channel to the center of axle.

Stopping point

Make a 3″ box channel 39″ long, cut a ¾″ x 3″ x 8″ piece of metal, drill two holes 5″ apart weld to the box channel, then cut a piece of rubber 1½″ x 3½″ x 8½″ and bolt to the end of the box channel. Weld the box channel to the back of the tongue and bring it out the rear of the trailer.

Materials

Quantity	
2	⅜″ rectangular tubing 6″ x 10″ x 7″
2	4″ channel 48″
1	3″ channel 48″
1	Heavy duty I-beam 3½″ x 6″ x 97″
2	1½″ shaft 45½″
1	1½″ shaft 6″
2	¾″ x 7½″ x 8½″ metal
2	½″ x 9″ x 11½″
1	T-iron 3½″ x 9″ x 11½″
1	½″ x 4½″ x 15″
2	½″ x 3″ x 8″
4	Steel rollers
1	¾″ x 14″ x 21″
1	¾″ x 2″ x 21″
1	1″ x 2″ x 11½″ metal bar
1	¾″ x 6″ x 10″ metal plate
1	½″ x 4″ x 8″ metal plate
1	2″ x 6″ x 36″ box tubing
1	⅜″ wall tubing 36″ long (2⅞″ I.D. x 3⅝″ O.D.)
1	⅜″ wall tubing 35″ long (2″ I.D. x ¾″ O.D.)
1	4″ channel 11″ long
1	⅜″ wall tubing 56″ long (2″ I.D. x 2¾″ O.D.)
1	3″ box channel 78″ long
1	3″ box channel 39″ long
1	3″ box channel 14″ long
2	¾″ x 3″ x 8″ metal
2	1½″ x 3½″ x 8½″ rubbers
1	VF - 4 Wisconsin
2	7-14/5 tires and wheels
2	Spindles and hubs - 4 bolt pattern
1	12 gallon a minute 3,000 PSI oil pump @2200 RPM
2	32″ long hydraulic hoses
2	44″ long hydraulic hoses
3	24″ long hydraulic hoses
1	13½″ long hydraulic hose
1	9″ long hydraulic hose
1	Oil gauge
1	Fuel gauge
2	Filler caps
1	4½″ x 30″ ram with 2½″ shaft
1	2″ x 8″ single action ram
1	High pressure double action valve
1	Single action valve
1	3,000 lb. pressure guage

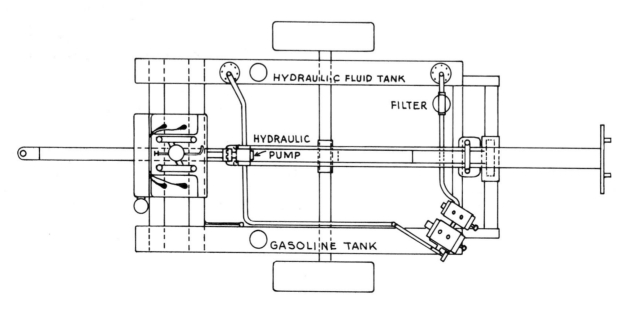

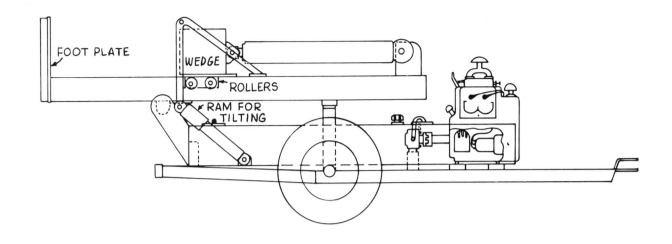

FOOT PLATE

WEDGE

ROLLERS

RAM FOR TILTING

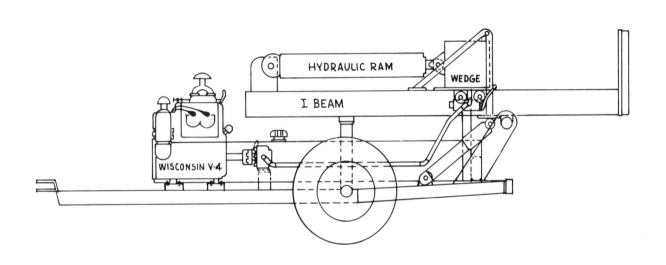

HYDRAULIC RAM

WEDGE

I BEAM

WISCONSIN V-4

Operation and Construction of the Multiple Implement Connector

Author: Fred Stewart
                     Kenneth Helt
Instructor: Fred Goldman
School: Southeastern Community College
City & State: W. Burlington, IA

The multiple implement connector is a device that is used to pull more than one implement at one time. The device is equipped with extension hydraulic hoses and has lighting for the rear implement. The system is designed to save the farmer time, gas, and decrease soil packing.

Material that was chosen for the construction was square tubing because of its light weight and durability.

The amount of material needed to complete fabrication are:

1. ³⁄₁₆'' x 4'' x 4'' x 16'
2. ³⁄₁₆'' x 3½'' x 3½'' x 10'6''
3. ³⁄₁₆'' x 1'' x 1'' x 28''
4. ³⁄₁₆'' x 1½'' x 1½'' x 8''
5. ¼'' plate 3'' x 12½''
6. Spindels, wheels and tires
7. Lights and wiring
8. Hydraulic hoses

The main frame work houses the tongue supports, with the wheels to the lower rear of the main frame. The tongue was fabricated to telescope through the tongue supports, to be fully adjustable both horizontally and vertically to accomodate any size implement desired, to be pulled before or after the multiple implement connector.

Lights were installed to provide adequate lighting for the rear implement. The lights are adjustable to correspond with the height of the rear implement.

In order to operate the hydraulic system on the rear implement, hydraulic hoses had to be installed, with connectors on either end of the multiple implement connector.

The construction was fabricated first by cutting the square tubing to the desired lengths using a power horizontal band saw. For the 90° angles needed for the main frame work the square tubing was cut at a 45° angle at either end of the frame pieces. Cutting 45° angles was chosen over butting the pieces together because the frame would then have higher durability and better appearance.

After all pieces were cut to proper length and angles, the front and rear rectangular main frame work was set on a work bench so that clamps could be used. The pieces were then squared and each joint to be welded was spaced ¹⁄₁₆'' apart to obtain total weld penetration. Then the frame was clamped down to the table and each corner tack welded to minimize warpage during welding. Then putting the frame work on the floor, all other pieces were added using the same procedure.

Holes were drilled in both the tongue and tongue supports, so the tongue could be moved to accomodate different implements.

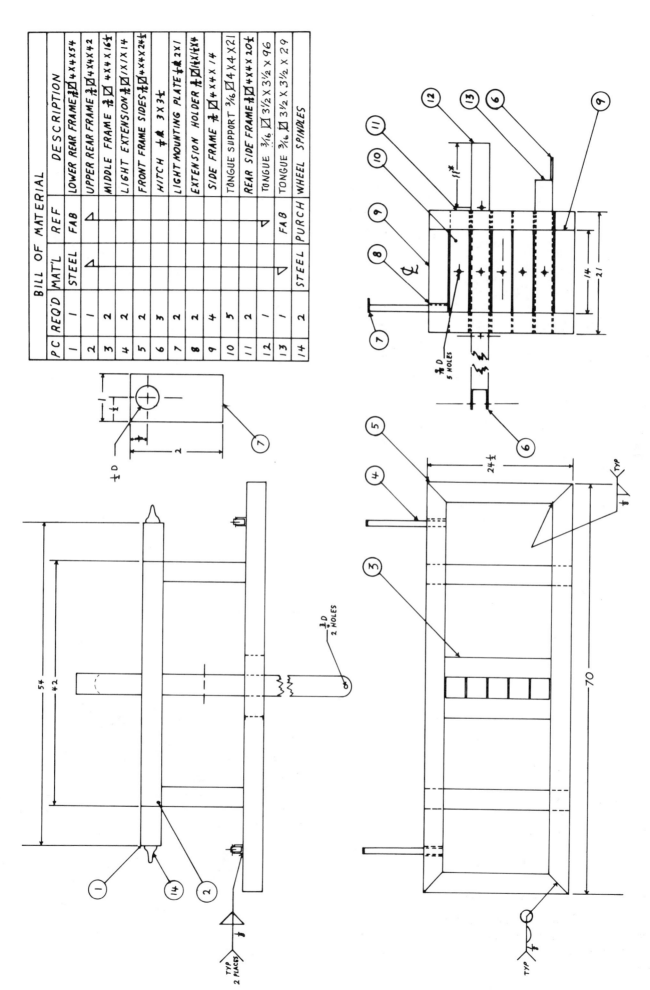

				BILL OF MATERIAL	
PC	REQ'D	MAT'L	REF	DESCRIPTION	
1	1	STEEL	FAB	LOWER REAR FRAME ¾□4×4×54	
2	1			UPPER REAR FRAME ¾□4×4×42	
3	2			MIDDLE FRAME ¾□4×4×16¼	
4	2			LIGHT EXTENSION ¾□1×1×14	
5	2			FRONT FRAME SIDES ¾□4×4×24½	
6	3			HITCH ¾▣ 3×3¼	
7	2			LIGHT MOUNTING PLATE ¼▣ 2×1	
8	2			EXTENSION HOLDER ¾□4¼×¼×4	
9	4			SIDE FRAME ¾□4×4×14	
10	5			TONGUE SUPPORT ³/₁₆□4×4×21	
11	2			REAR SIDE FRAME ¾□4×4×10¼	
12	1			TONGUE ³/₁₆□3½×3½×96	
13	1		FAB	TONGUE ³/₁₆□3½×3½×29	
14	2	STEEL	PURCH	WHEEL SPINDLES	

Squeeze Chute

Author: James G. Smith
Instructor: Ronald E. Squires
School: Univ. of Nevada, Reno
City & State: Reno, Nevada

The purpose of the chute is to restrain cattle while being branded, vaccinated, etc. by clamping down on the neck and squeezing in on the body.

Pre-Fabrication

Construction Procedure

There are five basic parts to the chute:
1. The frame
2. The sides
3. The front gate and head catch
4. The rear gate
5. The ratchet assembly and squeeze mechanism which is on top of the chute.

The first step was to assemble the frame and the sides separately, then put them together. This required pipe bending, welding cross supports on the bottom, and making clamps for the 2" pipe which would eventually hold the door in place and provide the point of attachment for an adjustable brace which slants from front to back on either side. The clamps were made from 2" lengths of 2½" pipe so it would just fit over the frame pipe. A nut and set screw holds the clamp in place. Hinges for the front gate consisted of 2" lengths of 2½" pipe which were allowed to turn around the frame pipe, and held in place by clamps above and below.

The upper half of the squeeze surface consisted of six removable, upright 1" pipes, each 26½" long. They ride in a frame which is clamped to the legs of the side. The whole mechanism is adjustable up and down for dif-

ferent size cattle. The lower half of the squeeze surface was wood with a door allowing access to the lower parts of an animal's body while in the chute.

Two support pipes run the length of the chute on top. The ends are flattened and bolted to the frame via a ¼" x 1½" strap welded to the pipe frame. These pipes held the frame fairly securely while I set the completed sides in place. The pivot holes in the frame and the legs of the sides had been drilled earlier.

The front gate and head catch was salvaged from a scrap iron pile. The only problem was that it was made to be worked from the opposite side from where I wanted it. By changing around a few parts I was able to convert it so it could be used from the correct side.

The rear gate was made in a quarter pie shape so it would swing into and out of the chute alley. 2" channel iron was used for the gate with 3" channel as the track to guide it as it swings. A handle and latch was made from about 18" of ⁷⁄₁₆ rod.

The ratchet assembly consisted of a 1½" pipe shaft, a 12" notched wheel (1½" plate), a 10" belt pulley 4" wide for the rope to wrap on and another 12" diameter plate to hold the rope in place. A chain winds up on the shaft as the rope is pulled, pulling in the sides while the notched wheel prevents it from slipping back until it is released.

Springs pull the sides back into place. By using a 10" pulley on the rope having the chain wrap up around a 2" pipe, 5 to 1 leverage is gained for squeezing the animal.

Materials	**Length**
2″ pipe	79″
½″ x 2½″	20″
¼″ x 1½″ strap	102″
¼″ x 2½″ strap	14″
2½″ pipe·	28″
1″ pipe	36′
⅜″ x 1¼″ strap	24″
1¼″ x 1¼″ x 1¾″ angle	16′
⅛″ x 2″ plate	12″
3⁄16″ x 1″ strap	32″
⅜″ x 2½″ flat	10″
1½″ pipe	33′
3⁄16″ x 1½″ strap	110″
3⁄16″ x 1¼″ x 2″ angle	24″
½″ plate 12″ dia.	
⅛″ plate 12″ dia.	
¼″ x 1¾″ strap	18″
light chain	6″
3⁄16″ x 2″ x 1″ channel	13″
¼″ plate 6″ x 6″ x 8″	
¼″ plate 8″ x 8″ 11″	
3⁄16″ x 1″ strap	42′
3″ x 1¼″ x ¼″ channel	32″
7⁄16″ rod	114″
10″ dia pulley x 4″	
⅜″ x 1¼″ flat iron	10″
2 springs	6″
front gate	
1 gal. paint	
1 gal. thinner	
bolts	
8 - ⅜″ x 2½″	
1 - ½″ x 2½″	
40 - s ½″ x ¼″ carriage bolts	
4 hinges	
2 latches	
boards	
4 - 2″ x 6″	6′
4 - 2″ x 6″	12″
2 - 2″ x 12″	6′
2 - 2″ x 12″	62″
1 - ¾″ nylon rope	14′
1 - ½″ nylon rope	5′
Acetylene and oxygen	
Welding rod	

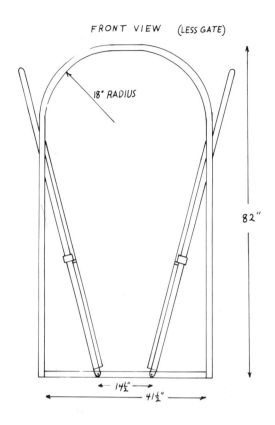

FRONT VIEW (LESS GATE)

18″ RADIUS

82″

14½″

41½″

SIDE VIEW

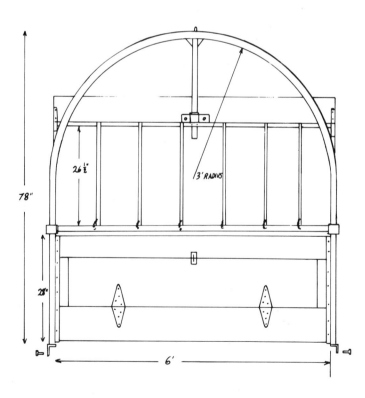

78″

26½″

3′ RADIUS

28″

6′

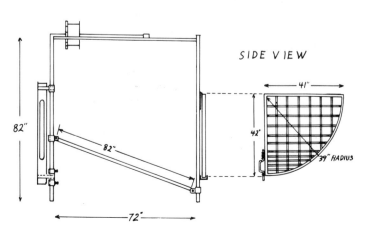

SIDE VIEW

82″

82″

72″

41″

42″

39″ RADIUS

Design and Construction of A Hydraulic Log Splitter

Author: Darwin H. Cook
Instructor: John L. Uebele
School: Waukesha County Technical Institute
City & State: Pewaukee, WI

Most of the materials were obtained at minimal or no cost (Table 1). Tires, wheels and spindles (56) were salvaged from a wrecked 1970 Dodge automobile. Two leaf springs (1) were salvaged from the front axle of a pickup truck. Two I-beams (6) were salvaged cutoffs left over from a construction site. The hydraulic ram (22) was acquired as salvage from a local industry. The used hydraulic control valve (35) and pump (34) also were purchased as salvage. A new filter (38) and hoses (39, 40) were purchases. The small gasoline engine (36) was removed from outdated gardening equipment.

Main I-beam Carriage Construction
Two 6' I-beams (6) were used to construct the combination main oil reservoir and reinforcement beam, upon which the logs are to be split. The use of the two I-beams welded together provided the structural strength and additional oil storage capacity in the unit.

Axle and Spring Construction
The automobile spindles were welded to 2" diameter double strength pipe (2). The wheel rims were aligned by placing them in a 10" structural channel, thus automatically aligning themselves. The spindles then were tack welded to the 2" diameter pipe.

The springs (1) were centrally located and pre-drilled plates (4) were horizontally welded to the 2" diameter pipe (2). This provided a place to mount the leaf springs.

Axle to Main Beam Construction
Mounting the main beam to the axle's springs was accomplished by fabrication of mounting brackets. Plates (7, 8) were welded together and welded to the main beam. The mounting brackets attached to the end of the leaf springs were trimmed with an oxy-acetylene cutting torch and welded to the mounting brackets.

Fender Mounting and Construction
The fenders were constructed of 16 gauge material (23-28). Metal grilled tail light guards were fabricated to prevent accidental breakage of the tail lights.

Ram to Main Beam Mounting
The large hydraulic ram was mounted on top of a fabricated box welded to the top of the main beam. This was done to mount the cylinder higher, thus pushing centrally on an average 12" diameter log.

Engine and Pump Mounting
Additional oil reservoir was achieved by fabricating an adjoining box (9-12) to the main beam reservoir. The height allowed the pump to be mounted over the hydraulic ram, thus keeping the log splitter as short as possible.

The hitch section (48) was fabricated from strip stock (13, 14) to form an angle iron V to which the 1⅞" ball hitch was welded. Safety chains were also added. Special hooks were fabricated from a high grade steel bolt and then welded with E-7018 to the ends of the chain.

Splitting Wedge Fabrication
The splitting wedge was fabricated from ½" plate. The curvature on the frontal surfaces was produced by using a large hydraulic brake, and the additional plates were oxy-acetylene cut to complete the wedge.

The splitting wedge is moveable and removable by removing the bolts that pin it in position. The leading edge of the splitting wedge is built up by overlapping beads of E-308-16 stainless steel to form a point, then ground to the desired shape. A class demonstration then was given on Metal Spraying. In the demonstration, carbide particles were introduced in a molten nickel matrix which was then sprayed on the leading edge. The end product was a splitting wedge with a strong durable cutting edge.

The pushing platten (61) was oxy-acetylene cut from 1" stock and holes drilled and tapped to accept hardened allen cap screws which were ground to a point. This will prevent the wood from shifting off this platten. The idea of having guides for this platten to follow was added after the log splitter was used because excess flexing of the hydraulic ram was noticed. The guides (32) prevented the flexing of the ram, and also provided a cradle for the logs.

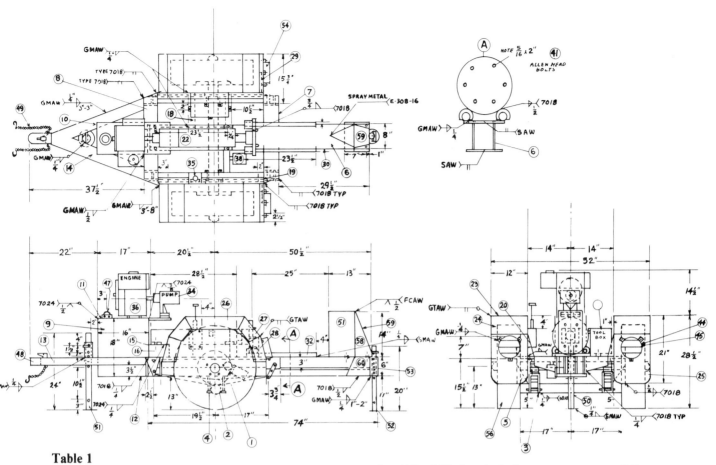

Table 1
Materials

1. 3′ 2″ Leaf Spring	2 Req
2. 2″ x 34″ Standard Pipe	1 Req
3. ⅝″ x 5″ U-Bolts	2 Req
4. ¼″ x 1″ x 4″ Plate	4 Req
5. ¼ x 3″ x 6″ Plate	2 Req
6. 4″ x 6″ x 6′ I-beam	2 Req
7. ¼ x 5½″ x 10″ Plate	4 Req
8. ¼ x 5½″ x 11″ Plate	4 Req
9. ¼ x 16″ x 18″ Plate	2 Req
10. ¼ x 10″ x 18″ Plate	2 Req
11. ½ x 10″ x 24″ Plate	1 Req
12. ¼ x 10″ x 16″ Plate	1 Req
13. ¼ x 2″ x 34″ Plate	2 Req
14. ¼ x 3½″ x 34″ Plate	2 Req
15. ¼ x 9½″ x 29″ Plate	1 Req
16. ¼ x 4″ x 29″ Plate	2 Req
17. ¼ x 6″ x 4″ Plate	1 Req
18. ¼ x 2″ x 10½″ Plate	2 Req
19. ¼″ x 2″ x 3<″ x 34″	2 Req
20. ¼ x 2″ x 6″ Plate	4 Req
21. 7½″ x 9″ x 13″ Tool Box	1 Req
22. Ram 28″ fully extended	1 Req
23. 12″ x 18″ 16 gauge	2 Req
24. 8″ x 12″ 16 gauge	4 Req
25. 12″ x 16″ 16 gauge	4 Req
26. 4″ x 18″ 16 gauge	4 Req
27. 4″ x 8″ 16 gauge	4 Req
28. 4″ x 8½″ 16 gauge	4 Req
29. ½″ x 30″ electrical pipe	1 Req
30. ½″ x 32″ electrical pipe	2 Req

31. ½″ x 36″ electrical pipe	2 Req
32. 1¼″ round stock 23″	2 Req
33. 2½″ x 3½″ slides	2 Req
34. Pump Vickers vane pump #25997	1 Req
35. Control Valve, Husco #5041	1 Req
36. Engine, Wisconsin Heavy Duty 8 hp. model S-8D	1 Req
37. Fluid filled gauge, UCC	1 Req
38. Filter, Lenz	1 Req
39. 67″ ¾″ hydraulic hose	1 Req
40. 48″ 1½″ hydraulic hose	1 Req
41. ⁵⁄₁₆″ x 2″ allen head bolts	6 Req
42. ¼″ x 2″ hex head bolts and nuts	4 Req
43. ½″ x 2″ allen head bolts and nuts	2 Req
44. 2″ x 6″ pipe	2 Req
45. ¼″ x 6″ rod	6 Req
46. ⅝″ x 1¼″ hardened bolts	4 Req
47. Breather Cap 2″	1 Req
48. Hitch 1⅞″	1 Req
49. Chain ¼″ x 20″	2 Req
50. 2″ x 20″ pipe	1 Req
51. 2″ x 24″ pipe	1 Req
52. ³⁄₁₆″ x 4″ Plate	2 Req
53. 2¼″ x 6″ pipe	2 Req
54. Light stop and tail 4″	2 Req
55. 20′ #16 copper wire	1 Req
56. Polyglass Goodyear 14″ tires	2 Req
57. ½″ x 8″ x 14″ Plate	2 Req
58. ½″ x 5″ x 14″ Plate	2 Req
59. ½″ x 5″ x 16″ Plate	1 Req
60. ½″ x 8″ x 6″ Plate	3 Req

Multi-Purpose Field Sprayer

Author: J. Kelsey
Instructor: R. Hulfachor
School: Northern Illinois University
City & State: Dekalb, IL

Construction of the basic frame work for the field sprayer was done with 2" x 4" mild steel tubing having a ¼" wall thickness. The various length pieces that were used in fabricating the carrier unit were hand cut with an oxyacetylene cutting torch.

Two 3" angle iron supports were welded to the stub wheel spindles. The total spindle unit was then welded into the field sprayer carrier unit approximately 1" to the rear of center.

To the tongue and carrier unit were welded two 1" angle irons. The two angle irons aided in combatting tongue side pressure while providing a place to rest a waffle plate platform from which the operator can add and also view the mixing of chemicals.

On the rear of the field sprayer were welded two 4" angle irons that are used to carry the spray boom. The spray boom is U-shaped to two 1" angle irons 20" in length which can be fastened to the 4" angle irons at any height desired. This adjustable feature is quite essential because various chemicals require that their application be at a specific height.

The large 2" angle iron frame at the rear of the field sprayer carries the weight of the spray booms keeping them at the proper spraying height. Also during travel to and from the fields the angle iron frame supports the spray booms in their travel positon.

Protecting the spray booms from collision damage, a breakaway system was used that consists of a modified universal joint. The pair of universal forks were welded to four ¾" round bar stock pieces 4" in length enabling the universal units to be slipped inside the ¾" galvanized pipe spray booms and fastened into position by bolts. The universal unit, acting as a 4-way hinge provided a breakaway system to guard against spray boom damage and also allowed the spray booms to be raised for road travel or storage.

A 300 gallon polyethylene spray tank was supported on the carrier unit by a saddle. The angle iron legs on the saddle were placed on the carrier unit so that part of the legs needed to be cut away. This design enabled the weight of the saddle and tank to be placed directly on the carrier unit and not on the bolts that hold the saddle and tank in position. In positioning the saddle and tank unit it was moved 1" forward of center; this setting plus the offset in the wheel spindles placed a greater amount of weight in front of the wheels than to the rear. On older

field sprayers that have everything centered over the wheels it was not uncommon for the unit to fall over backwards when unhitched.

Located on the 2" angle iron stand just behind the tractor operator was placed the spray boom selector valve. The height of the stand was at a level that required the operator to only make a quarter turn to manipulate the selector valve. Besides being an on-off valve the boom selector valve could designate what section of the spray boom it would operate. This eliminated chemical overlap and reduced total cost in chemically treating a field.

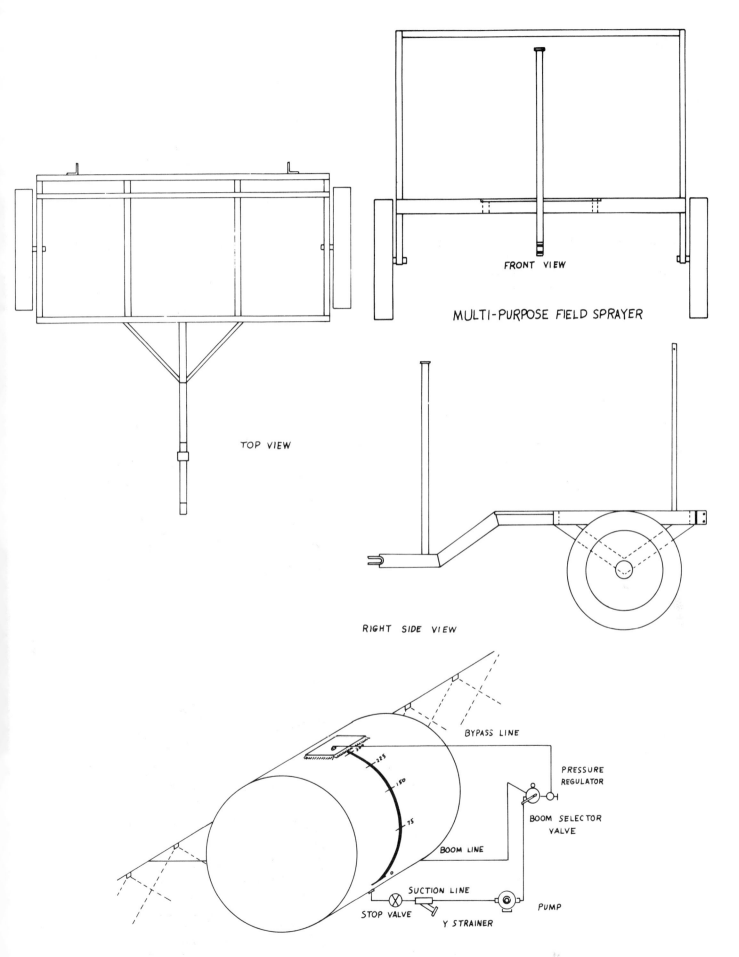

TOP VIEW

FRONT VIEW

MULTI-PURPOSE FIELD SPRAYER

RIGHT SIDE VIEW

BYPASS LINE

PRESSURE
REGULATOR

BOOM SELECTOR
VALVE

BOOM LINE

SUCTION LINE

STOP VALVE

Y STRAINER

PUMP

225

150

75

SCHEMATIC FOR SPRAY SYSTEM

Log Splitter

Author: *James Myers*
                    Dale Attili
                    Michael John Heinsler
Instructor: *Edward Zorn*
School: *Greece Olympia High School*
City & State: *Rochester, NY*

The axle and wheels were from a Volkswagon front end. The steering spindles were welded so the wheels would stay parallel. The end of an eight inch piece of pipe was fishmouthed so it could be welded to the axle. On the top of the pipe a piece of steel was welded and clamped to the frame. It would be welded in place when the assembly was finished. When the logsplitter is complete it could be adjusted so the weight would be equally distributed.

For the frame 5 x ½″ channel iron was purchased at a local scrap yard. A box frame, 24″ x 97″ was made from this, an I beam for the center was made by welding two pieces of channel iron back to back.

A bent ram was salvaged from a John Deere 690 power shovel. This was to be used to push the logs into the wedge. It was straightened at a local machine repair shop so it would be suitable for our use. It was then mounted in the front with a ⅝″ x 5″ x 7″ steel plate on each side. In each of these plates a 2″ hole was bored. A bolt was passed through the ram and the two plates. These plates were perpendicularly welded to the frame with a piece of 4″ x ½″ angle iron for reinforcement. The part of the ram that extends was held down by a slider bracket. These are plates on both sides of the ram that slide along the I beam keeping it from going upward when pressure is applied. They are made of two, ¾″ x 3″ x 7″ pieces of steel. They each have a hole for another 2″ bolt and a ⅝″ slot cut parallel to the bottom, ⅝″ from the edge.

The power for the hydraulic pump for the ram was supplied by a seven horsepower Briggs and Stratton engine. The engine was connected to the pump by snow blower reduction gears. The engine speed was controlled by a lawn mower throttle mounted to the frame.

The hydraulic pump for the ram was salvaged from the body hoist of a ten-ton truck. A four way valve was used to control the forward and return stroke of the ram. For a fluid reservoir we used a beer keg. The fluid, gages and hoses were purchased from a dealer of heavy equipment.

The wedge was made from a piece of 11″ x 2″ x 5″ steel. A sixty degree angle was ground a ¼″ on each side to keep the wedge from bending. Then it was welded to the back of the frame above the I beam.

When the logsplitter was completed, we tried to split the log and the frame bowed. This problem was solved by cross-bracing the frame with two ½″ steel rods. These were threaded at each end. A hole was drilled near the wedge on each side and on each side of the angle iron at the front of the ram for braces. When we tried to split a

log again it split easily without bending the frame. The logsplitter was painted yellow to keep the machine free of rust. When we tried to split a log the second time, the machine worked. The log split easily and the frame remained rigid.

Three Point Hitch Grain and Fertilizer Spreader with Five Bushel Hopper

Author: James Alan Graves
Instructor: R. V. Callahan
School: N. Little Rock Ole Main High School
City & State: N. Little Rock, Ar.

Materials

36" x 96" Black Iron 16 gauge sheet metal
1" x 1" Angle Iron ⅛" Thick   3' 9"
2" x 1" Channel Iron ¼" Thick   8' 7"
5" x 2" Channel Iron ¼" Thick   2' 2"
4" x 2" Channel Iron ¼" Thick   5"
⅛" x 1½" Strap Steel   2' 2"
4" Square Tubing   4½"
3 pieces 8620 Steel 1" dia.   6"
1 piece 8620 Steel 2½" dia.   1¾"
Steel Pipe 1¾" O.D.   7' 8"
2 ⅞" - NC Hex Nuts
6 20-32 Allen Head Cap Screws
2 ⁵⁄₁₆ - 24 Set Screws
6 ⅜" - 16 ½" Set Screws
9 ¼" - 28 Hex Head Bolts
10 ¼" - 28 Self locking Nuts
6 3½" x ⅜" 16 Hex Head Bolts
4 5½" x ⅜" 16 Hex Head Bolts
8 1½" x ⅜" 16 Hex Head Bolts
12 ⅜" - 16 Hex Nuts
LSA 103 YR Boston Spiral Miter Gear
LSA 103 YL Boston Spiral Miter Gear
25" x 25" Gauge Aluminum

Universal
4 pieces ¾" x 1¼" ¼" Plate
4 Grease Fittings
1 8620 Cube 1" x 1" x 1"
2 pieces 1" x 1¾" ¼" Plate
4 Round Head Rivets ½" long
1 1" Tubing   11"
1 ¾" Tubing   11"
1 3 bolt self aligning Precision Bearing
3 Flanged Bearings with O.D. 1⅛" and I.D. ¾"
1 ¼" Cotter Key
1 ⅛" Cotter Key
⅛" Key Stock
3 ¾" True Arch Rings
6 Flange Retainers
2 qts. of paint
1 qt. primer MP 100
1 qt. white paint
4 cone Strainers
5 lbs. of 7018 Rod
5 lbs. of 6011 Rod
3 lbs. of 6013 Rod
5 Grinding Discs

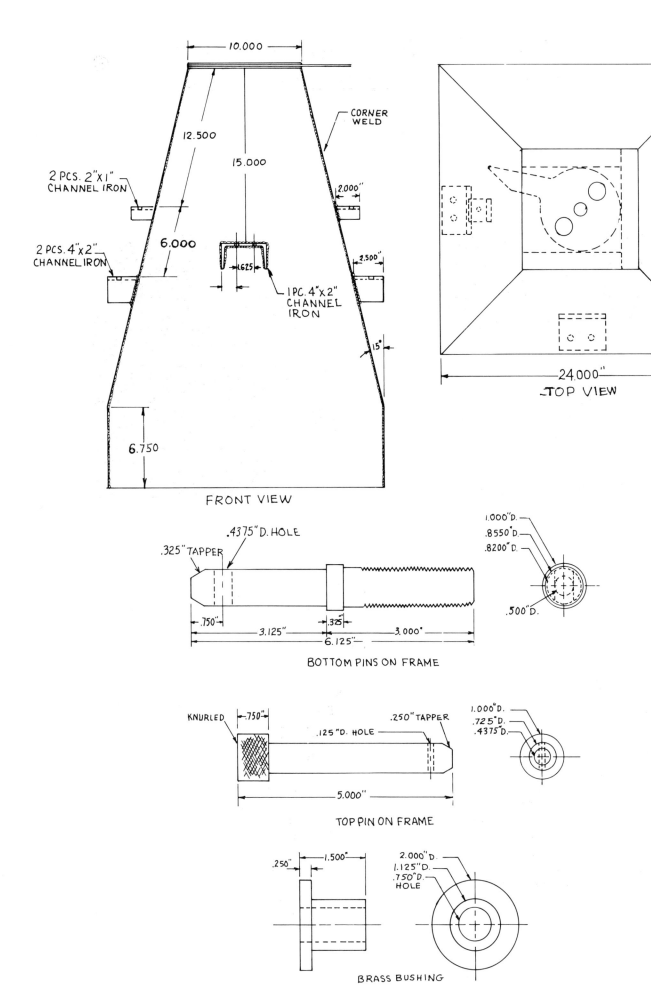

10.000

CORNER
WELD

12.500

15.000

2 PCS. 2"x1"
CHANNEL IRON

2.000"

6.000

2 PCS. 4"x2"
CHANNEL IRON

.625

2.500"

1 PC. 4"x2"
CHANNEL
IRON

15°

6.750

FRONT VIEW

24.000"

TOP VIEW

.4375"D. HOLE

.325" TAPPER

1.000"D.
.8550"D.
.8200"D.

.750"

.325"

.500"D.

3.125"

3.000"

6.125"

BOTTOM PINS ON FRAME

KNURLED

.750"

.250" TAPPER

.125"D. HOLE

1.000"D.
.725"D.
.4375"D.

5.000"

TOP PIN ON FRAME

.250"

1.500"

2.000"D.
1.125"D.
.750"D.
HOLE

BRASS BUSHING

22

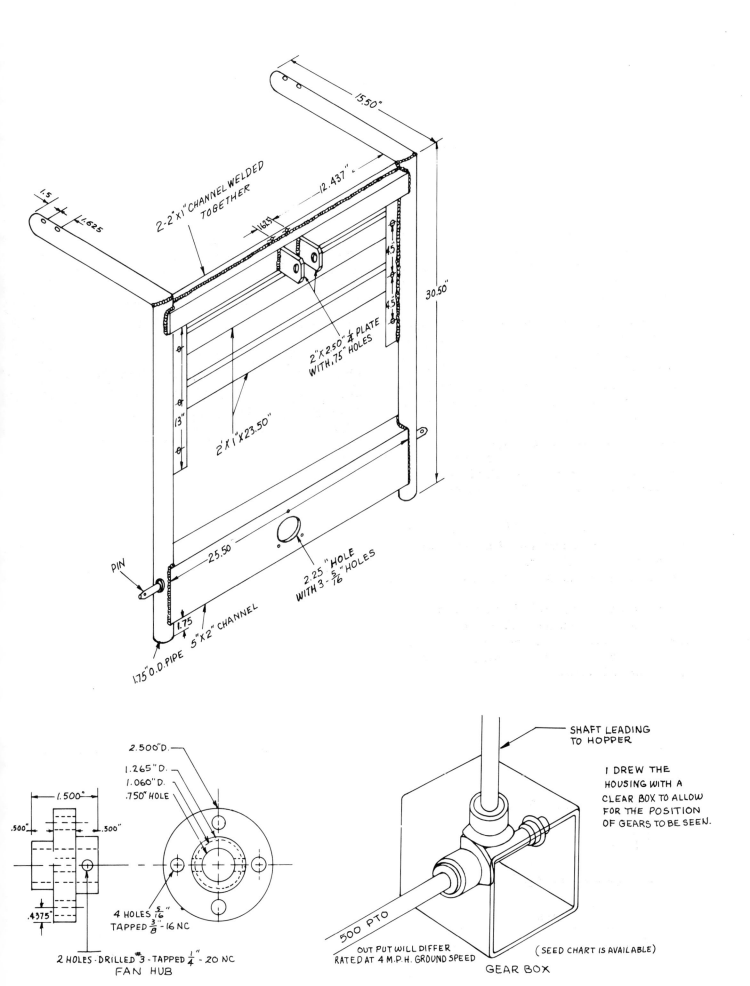

15.50"

2-2"X1" CHANNEL WELDED TOGETHER

12.437"

1.5

1.625

11.625

2"X 2.50" ¼ PLATE WITH .75" HOLES

4.5

4.5

30.50"

2'X1'X23.50"

13"

PIN

25.50

2.25 " HOLE WITH 3 - 5/16" HOLES

1.75"O.D.PIPE   5"X2" CHANNEL

1.75

1.500"

.500"   .500"

.4375"

2.500"D.

1.265"D.

1.060"D.

.750" HOLE

4 HOLES 5/16"
TAPPED 3/8"-16 NC

2 HOLES · DRILLED #3 · TAPPED ¼" - 20 NC

FAN HUB

SHAFT LEADING TO HOPPER

I DREW THE HOUSING WITH A CLEAR BOX TO ALLOW FOR THE POSITION OF GEARS TO BE SEEN.

500 PTO

OUT PUT WILL DIFFER
RATED AT 4 M.P.H. GROUND SPEED

(SEED CHART IS AVAILABLE)

GEAR BOX

23

Hay Feeder

Author: Don Dewerff,
      John Frazier
Instructor: Paul Stevenson
School: Kansas State University
City & State: Manhattan, KS

The feeder is built on skids so it can be easily pulled from place to place in a cow lot. The actual length is 19' 7''. All the pipes were welded in the Tee position for added strength. This required much cutting to form each joint. Identical sides were made.

After forming and welding the side portions together, the braces or center pieces were welded to the sides. Metal clamps were used to help hold the pipes together while tacking. The pipes were positioned so the water does not remain in the pipes when it rains. The best way to keep water out is to cover the ends of the pipes or lay one pipe on top of the next at a 90° angle and weld.

The end section was made to swing open and closed as it was moved in the field. The strap iron was heated and bent around the two-inch pipe. This iron serves as a mounting bracket for the 2 x 10's which fit on each end of the feeder.

Strap iron 2½'' was welded to the center and end braces for a mount to bolt boards to. Rods were diagonally spaced at 14'' intervals to reduce hay loss. A slightly wider space is recommended for dairy cows - perhaps 16''.

Holes were cut in the pipes for inserting the rod instead of just welding the butt end of the rod to the pipe. The feeder was painted with a rust preservative. The 2 x 10's were bolted in place with ⁵⁄₁₆'' carriage bolts and the feeder was ready for use.

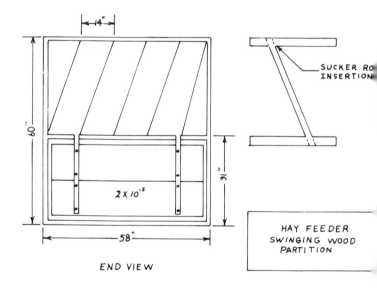

END VIEW

HAY FEEDER
SWINGING WOOD
PARTITION

SUCKER ROD
INSERTION

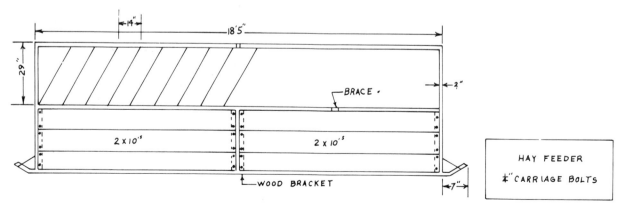

SIDE VIEW

HAY FEEDER
¼'' CARRIAGE BOLTS

Four Horse Hot Walker

Author: Donald Shaw
Instructor: James Tripp
School: Central Florida Community College
City & State: Ocala, FL

The four horse hot walker is a mechanical means of exercising and cooling out horses after vigorous exercise, and provides a means of exercising horses with limited man-power.

Frame Construction

There are two primary sections in this component. Construction is of 2″ pipe 30″ long, screwed into "T" joints and welded. Two vertical 2″ x 59″ members are screwed into the "T" joints on the base members. Four 2″ x 35″ support members are welded into place 6″ from the ends of the horizontal members, angled in to the vertical frame support. The vertical members are joined by a 2′ x 47″ horizontal section on the upper terminal end. Vertical and horizontal members are joined by two 90°, 2″ couplings and welded. 45″ down and parallel to the upper horizontal cross member, a 2″ x 48″ pipe was welded into place.

Drive Train

A differential and axle assembly was welded into place on the upper and lower horizontal cross members, with the axle housing and brake drums assuming vertical positions.

The differential and axle assembly serve as the drive train for the rotating section of the hot walker. By setting the brake at the lower drum head, the upper drum head is caused to rotate. This arrangement also provides a safety factor for balky horses. A proper friction setting will allow the lower drum to rotate, preventing electric drive motor burn out.

The electric motor and drive assembly is attached to a plate welded to the lower horizontal frame assembly. The differential input shaft is chain and sprocket driven from the electric motor.

Upper Unit

The basic part of the rotating upper unit is a 2″ x 34″ long pipe with a 7½″ square plate at the bottom. At the top, is welded a ¼″ x 7½″ round plate. The lower plate is attached to the differential and axle assembly with lug bolts.

The arms for the walker are constructed of 16′ pipe. Twelve feet out, on the bottom of each pipe, is welded a plate to connect the bottom support arm, which is braced to the 7½″ plate on the bottom of the upper unit. A ½″ rod, 14′ long is welded to the top of each arm, and runs from the arm to the 7½″ round plate and is braced with short sections of ½″ rod.

To assemble the arms to the stanchion, the 2″ pipe is slid into the 2½″ pipe in the center. At the top, the ½″ rod is inserted through a hole in the round, top plate. A bolt is placed through the ½″ rod to prevent it from slipping out. The bottom support is a 10′ square tubing attached to the plate on the arm and to the plate at the base of the stanchion with ¼″ bolts. The arms are further supported horizontally by a ½″ cable run through a plate, 7′ out on each arm, and secured by a 10″ turn buckle. In the end of each arm is welded a "U" shaped rod to attach the lead ropes.

Base

The base of the walker is bolted to a 6′ x 6′ concrete slab.

Materials	Quantity
20′ x ½″ rods	4
20′ x 2″ black pipes	5
2″ 90° couplings	2
2″ "T" joints	2
20′ x 1¼″ square tubing	2
34″ x 3½″ black pipe	1
8′ x 2½″ black pipe	1
7½″ square plate	1
7½″ round plate	1
¾″ nylon rope	16′
Heavy snaps	4
Dayton ½ horse motor	1
Ford rear end - used	1
½″ cable	60′
10″ turn buckle	1
1″ "U" clamps	4
¼″ x 2″ x 2½″ plates	8
DeRusto Paint	1 qt.

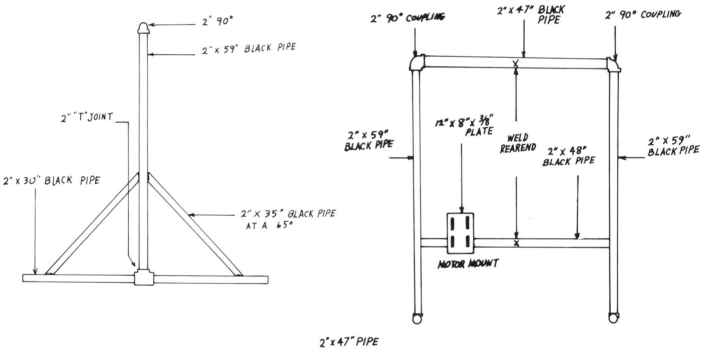

2" 90°

2" x 59" BLACK PIPE

2" "T" JOINT

2" x 30" BLACK PIPE

2" x 35" BLACK PIPE
AT A 65°

2" 90° COUPLING

2" x 47" BLACK PIPE

2" 90° COUPLING

2" x 59" BLACK PIPE

12" x 8" x 3/8" PLATE

WELD REAREND

2" x 48" BLACK PIPE

2" x 59" BLACK PIPE

MOTOR MOUNT

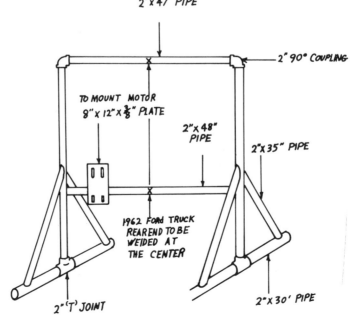

2" x 47" PIPE

2" 90° COUPLING

TO MOUNT MOTOR
8" x 12" x 3/8" PLATE

2" x 48" PIPE

2" x 35" PIPE

1962 FORD TRUCK REAREND TO BE WELDED AT THE CENTER

2" "T" JOINT

2" x 30' PIPE

26

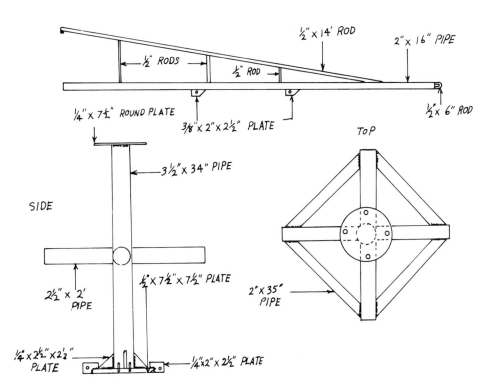

½" x 14' ROD

2" x 16" PIPE

½" RODS

½" ROD

¼" x 7½" ROUND PLATE

3/8" x 2" x 2½" PLATE

½" x 6" ROD

TOP

3½" x 34" PIPE

SIDE

2½" x 2' PIPE

½" x 7½" x 7½" PLATE

2" x 35" PIPE

¼" x 2½" x 2½" PLATE

¼" x 2" x 2½" PLATE

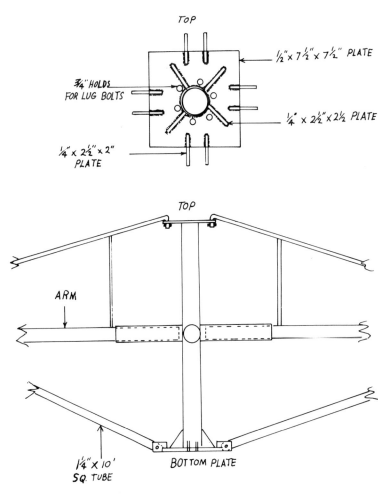

TOP

½" x 7½" x 7½" PLATE

¾" HOLES FOR LUG BOLTS

¼" x 2½" x 2½ PLATE

¼" x 2½" x 2" PLATE

TOP

ARM

¼" x 10' SQ. TUBE

BOTTOM PLATE

Overhead Double Implement Hitch

Author:	*Glen Gibson*
Instructor:	*Jeff Grote*
School:	*Lampasas High School*
City & State:	*Lampasas, TX*

Materials Used:

59¼″ 2″ pipe (some upset)
12″ 2⅜″ pipe
21″ ⅜″ x 4″ angle iron
25″ x 8″ 1″ steel plate
22″ 1¼″ steel rod (includes hitch clevis)
⅜″ steel rod
⁵⁄₁₆″ steel rod
Approx. ¾ of 1 sq. ft. ⅝″ flat steel
Approx. 1½ sq. ft. ³⁄₁₆″ sheet metal

Main Frame

Take two pieces of upset tubing 2″ x 142″ with a curve in one end, lay them parallel touching each other, then arc weld together.

Front Drop Pipe and Rear Hitch Plate

Cut saddles in the front end of the main frame and weld a piece of 2″ tubing 30″ long at a right angle to the frame. Next cut the rear pipes at the bottom of the curves at a level angle with the height of the front hitch, and weld a piece of 1″ x 25″ steel hitch plate to the bottom of the curves.

Front Hitch

The front hitch is made from a broken 1¼″ diameter rod and clevis from a railroad car. Cut the hitch an overall length of 22″ including clevis. Next cut a slightly larger hole in the drop pipe at 28″ from the top. Slip the rod through the holes to the clevis and weld in place.

This leaves 12″ of rod to the rear. Heat this and bend to form a hook which will match the clevis ring on the harrow.

Rear Axle

The rear axle is made from 2″ x 68″ upset tubing. Two front auto hubs are welded to the pipe at the spindles. After the welding is completed the axle is set under the rear hitch plate at 14″ forward from the back hole in the hitch plate. Tack, square with the front hitch hole and weld solid and brace under the hitch plate.

Bracing

Use two pieces of 2″ x 57″ pipe for the rear axle braces. Weld to the axle at the spindles and to the main frame at 42″ toward the front frame and the rear axle at the center. The front brace is made from the same material as the rear ones and is cut 32″ long. Weld to the drop directly above the hitch clevis and to the main frame at 28″ toward the rear.

Hydraulic Lift
Undercarriage

Take a piece of pipe 2⅜″ inside diameter cut 12″ long and weld it to the underside of the main frame 44″ from the front. Brace this to the main frame with ¹⁄₁₂″ steel on the under side, and ³⁄₁₆″ sheet metal from the top of the frame.

Crossbar and Liftarms

Slide a piece of 2″ upset tubing 68″ long, through a 2⅜″

pipe leaving 28″ on both sides. Curve and weld two pieces of steel ½″ in width to the pipe to keep from sliding from one side to the other. Next weld two pieces of tubing 28″ long to the cross pipe at a right angle. Brace these with two pieces of tubing 15″ long welded from the cross pipe to the lift arm. Split a piece of ⅜″ x 4″ angle iron making two pieces of ⅜″ flat iron and cut 21″ long and weld to the end of the lift arms forming a "T" shaped lift arm. Cut two holes in each end of the flat iron. Slot toward the bottom to form catches for ¼″ chain.

Cylinder Arms

Use two pieces of tubing 15″ long as risers to the cylinder. Weld them to the crosspipe at the ends of the 2⅜″ pipe. Weld together at the top to form the shape of a roof of a house. At the top weld a piece of ⅝″ steel between the two risers. Cut a hole in the top for the cylinder pin.

Cylinder Mounts, Holdup Rod and Hose Supports

Cut the bottom cylinder mount from ⅝″ steel 4″ x 4″ and weld to the top pipe at the main frame 17″ from the front and cut a hole in this for the cylinder pin. Next, make a holdup rod from ⅜″ x 12″ rod with a 1″ right angle bend in both ends to hold the lift in position. Weld a piece of ⅜″ steel 2″ x 2″ to the main frame. The same as the bottom cylinder mount a hole was cut in it and one end of the rod was put through it and a washer welded on the end. Next, cut a hole in the top cylinder mount for the rod to go through. Make a ¼″ hole in the end of the rod so when in up position the rod can be placed through the top cylinder mount and pinned with a clickpin. For the hose support on the front weld a piece of ⅜″ rod 18″ long to the main frame just behind the front drop pipe. Then heat it and make a circle and one half to hold the hoses. On the rear make a ring from 5⁄16″ rod and weld to the main frame.

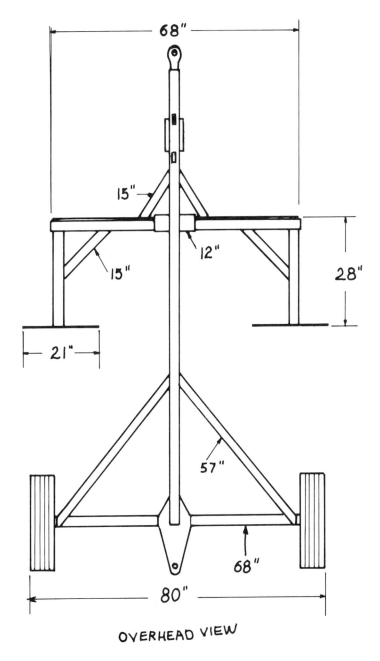

OVERHEAD VIEW

Farrowing Crate

Author: Perry Larson
Instructor: Jerry Ashenbrenner
School: Rosholt High School—District No. 5
City & State: Rosholt, WI

Materials Used:

Name	Quant.	Size	Material
Feed chute slide	1	24″ x 30″	16 gauge sheet metal
Feed chute sides	2	16″ x 30″	16 gauge sheet metal
Feed slide braces (corners)	2	⅛″ x 1¼″ x 1¼″ x 30″	angle iron
Feed chute slide reinforce	2	⅛″ x.1″ x 21½″	flat stock
Feed chute braces	2	⅛″ x 1″ x 30″	flat stock
Main body corner irons	4	⅛″ x 1½″ x 1½″ x 48″	angle iron
Front boards	4	1″ x 5″ x 24″	oak
Angle iron braces	4	⅛″ x 1½″ x 1½″ x 24″	angle iron
Back door	1	¾″ x 23″ x 40″	plywood
Side rails	8	1″ x 1½″ x 84″ by 14 gauge	rectangular tubing
Side braces	10	1″ x 1½″ x 18″ by 14 gauge	rectangular tubing
Top rails	2	¼″ x 1¼″ x 84″	flat stock
Top braces	2	¼″ x 1¼″ x 28″	flat stock
Door track irons	2	⅛″ x 1¼″ x 1¼″ x 48″	angle iron
Door handles	2	5″	light metal
Creep ends	4	½″ x 24″ x 24″	plywood
Creep sides	2	½″ x 24″ x 84″	plywood
Creep corner braces	4	⅛″ x 1¼″ x 1¼″ x 22″	angle iron
Creep side, bottom brace	2	⅛″ x 1¼″ x 1¼″ x 81½″	angle iron
Creep end, bottom brace	4	⅛″ x 1¼″ x 1¼″ x 24″	angle iron
Creep connecting brackets	4	⅛″ x 1″ x 1″ x 24″	angle iron
Stove bolts and nuts	56	¼″ x 1″	metal
Carriage bolts and nuts	16	¼″ x ¼″	metal

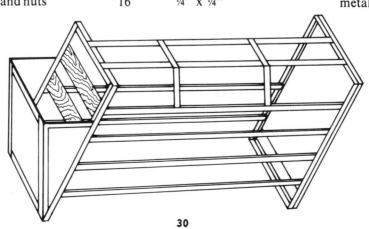

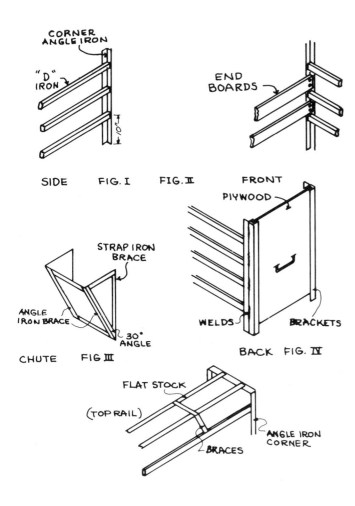

SIDE   FIG. I   FIG. II   FRONT

CHUTE   FIG III   BACK FIG. IV

Sides—To make the sides use 7 foot lengths of rectangular tubing and 4 foot lengths of angle iron. Weld the tubing horizontally to the angle iron. Place the bottom rail 10″ from the floor and space the remaining rails 10″ apart.

Front—For the front use 4 1 x 5 x 24″ oak boards and bolt them to the main body angle iron corners with ¼ x 1¼″ carriage bolts. Weld 2 pieces of ⅛ x 1½ x 1½ x 24″ angle iron on the top and bottom of the front end to stabilize the body of the crate.

Feed Chute—To construct the feed chute use 2 pieces of 30″ angle iron (feed slide braces), reinforced with 1″ flat stock. For the front use a 24 x 30″ piece of 16 gauge sheet metal, bolted to the angle iron supports with flat head stove bolts. For the sides use 16 gauge sheet metal cut at 30 degree angles, and bolt to the support irons. After assembling the chute, clamp it to the main body and tack weld. Remove the clamps, flip crate on its side and make many intermittent butt welds.

The Back—The back consists of a 23 x 40 x ¾″ plywood sliding door and two 1¼ x 1¼ x 24″ angle iron end braces. Weld the 2 pieces of angle iron on the top and bottom of the main body of the crate. Butt weld intermittently the track for the sliding door, which is 2 pieces of 1¼ x 1¼ x 48″ angle iron. Place the sliding door (23 x 40″ ¾″ plywood) in the track.

Piglet Creeps—Weld the bottom brace, creep side (1¼ x 1¼ x 81½″ angle iron) to the bottom brace creep side (1¼ x 1¼ x 22″). At the welded corner, place a piece of 1¼ x 1¼ x 24″ angle iron vertically and weld to bottom frame. Weld 1 x 1 x 24″ connecting brackets to each end so there is a way of fastening plywood to the main gate so it can be disassembled. Using 8 carriage bolts per side, bolt ½ x 24 x 84″ plywood to long side and ½ x 24 x 24″ plywood to short side.

Top—Weld 2 evenly placed top rails (¼ x 1¼ x 84″ flat stock) to the main body top ends. Then weld 2 top braces (evenly spaced) to the top rail and side rail to prevent the sow from jumping up.

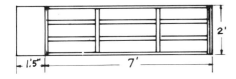

TOP VIEW

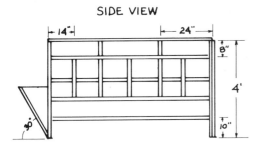

SIDE VIEW

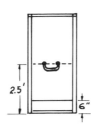

END VIEW

Evaporator and Boiling Pan For Making Maple Syrup

Author: Karl Parsells
Instructor: Richard F. Bienvenue
School: Rutland Area Voc. Tech. Center
City & State: Rutland, VT

Materials used:

Evaporator

1 each 4' x 10' x 16 GA. H.R.S.
60' 1¼ x 1¼ x ¼" Angle Iron
60" 1¼ x ¼" Flat Stock HRS
12" ½" Round Stock HRS
60 x 1 x ¼" Flat Stock HRS
18 each ¾ x ¼" 20 Round Head Stove Bolts & Nuts
24 x 1¼ x ⅛" Flat Stock
10½ x 3 x ⅛" Sheet Metal

Boiling Pan

1 pc. 37¼ x 44⅛" bottom 2 sides type 304SS—22 GA.
2 pcs. 25 x 6⅞" ends
3 pcs. 3¾ x 45⅞" baffles
2 ¾" pipe copper nipples

Pan Frame

This is made from 1½ x 1½ x ¼" angle iron. Cut two pieces 23⅜" and two pieces 52" and miter at a 45 degree angle. Tack the four pieces together, then run a bead all the way around the joints on both sides. When that is done, take an inside dimension of the width, and cut another piece of angle iron so that the flat sides will all meet. Tack this piece in place, then weld both ends on both sides. When this is all welded, clamp the sides tight to the frame and tack it. Then run a bead all the way around.

Grate Frame

Cut two pieces 15¾" and two pieces 25½" long from 1½ x 1½ x ¼" angle iron. Miter all the ends to a 45 degree angle. Put the four pieces together and tack weld them, then weld the joints up on both sides. When cutting the legs for this frame, allow enough room for the firebricks.

Door Frame

Cut two pieces 11½", one piece 17½" and one piece 12½". Put these pieces together, tack them and check for fit in the door hole. After it is in and to the shape, weld. Put from the door hole again and clamp it tight to the

front, and tack weld it. When the top door frame is done, cut two pieces 6½", and one piece 14¾" for the bottom door frame. Put this one together the same as the top one.

To put the angle iron on the outside of the evaporator, cut two pieces 17", four pieces 12¾", two pieces 6¼", one piece 24", and one piece 19". These pieces are cut and angled so that they will fit where they belong. Once these pieces are cut and angled place them on the sheet metal and tack weld them. Once tack welded, drill ¼" holes in the angle iron about every 5" and bolt the angle iron to the sides using ¼-20 machine screws and nuts. After this has been finished weld all joints and grind flush.

To make the legs, cut two pieces of angle iron in length and cut two pieces of flat stock 1¼ x 1¼ x ¼" and weld to the end of each piece of angle iron. Tack weld these legs to the angle iron frame on the evaporator. Then cut a piece of angle iron to fit in between the legs, and weld all the joints.

Top Doors

Take the pieces that were cut out of the front. Scribe a line down the middle and then take a center punch and punch marks in this piece about every ⅜ to ½" apart. Cut down the center, then weld the pieces right to the door. Cut two pieces 12" x 1¼" x ⅛" for the stops for the door. Put one on the inside and one on the outside. Tack weld these pieces on the doors.

Bottom Door

Take the piece that was cut out of the front. Cut some 1" x ¼" steel for the top of the door and the sides. When these pieces are cut weld them on. Round the corners with the grinder.

Hinges for Top Doors

Cut two pieces of steel 1½ x ¼ x 6". Scribe a line on these pieces for 1½" x ¾". Cut the pieces and drill a ²⁵⁄₆₄" hole in each piece on the 1½" end.

Cut four pieces ½" round stock about 2" long. Bend ends 90° ¾" long. Place 1 piece of ¼" material previously cut on the door, position the round stock. Cut the round stocks to length if needed, when this has been done, tack weld the ¼" piece to the door, and the round stocks to the front of evaporator. Do this to the top one. Before welding everything solid, place shims under the frame of the doors, about ¹⁄₁₆" on the top and bottom. This is to allow for clearance for opening and closing the doors.

The Boiling Pan
The Boiling pan is made from 22 gauge type 304 SS.

Take the 3 pieces 3¾ x 45⅞", lay out for bends and cut as per drawing. The top is marked ¼" down the full length and folded at the ¼" marks all the way down. This not only stiffens the pieces, but provides a rounded edge that can prevent cuts when cleaning the pan.

The bottom is marked ½" down the full length. This is bent 90° for spot welding and soldering. The ends are marked at ¾" and bent for spot welding and soldering.

Take the 37¼ x 44⅛" x 22 gauge SS. Find the center. This is critical, because by starting from the center you have a way of double checking yourself for mistakes.

Measure for the bottom, in this case the width is 23½", then 6" up for the sides, then ½" and ¼" for the top edge. After this is done, layout for two holes in the six sides and punch out for drains. The hole size depends on the type fittings used.

Starting with the center, lay out four equal spaces, place the 3 strips on the marks, starting with the center one. Spot weld it in place, then the two other side pieces. If this is done after the sides are bent up, you won't be able to spot weld it all the way down.

Now make the bends. The first ones though shallow, are made longitudinal on the sides, this stiffens the sides. The next bends are the ¼" and then the ½" ones. Be careful to make sure these edges face the outside of the pan, not the inside. Next bend the 6" sides up. Now you have the bottom and sides completed.

The end pieces have four bends to make the ¼" and ½" ones across the top, and ¾" ones on the sides. After this is done, place ends on pan and clamp. Check to make sure everything fits and tack weld.

After this is done, heli-weld the bottom seam closed, grind weld and lead solder all joints seams, wash pan to remove flux from soldering.

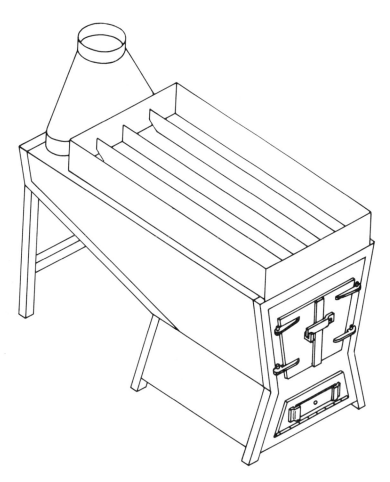

33

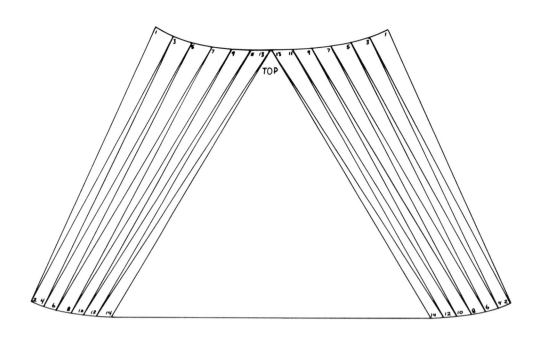

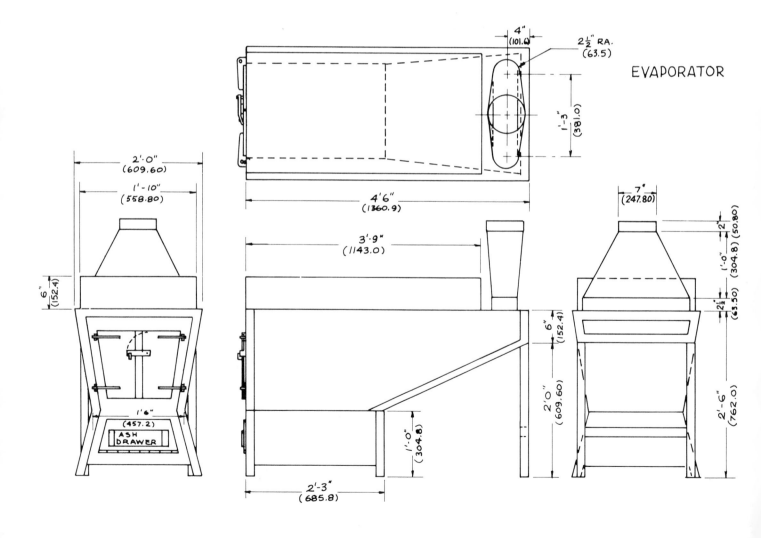

EVAPORATOR

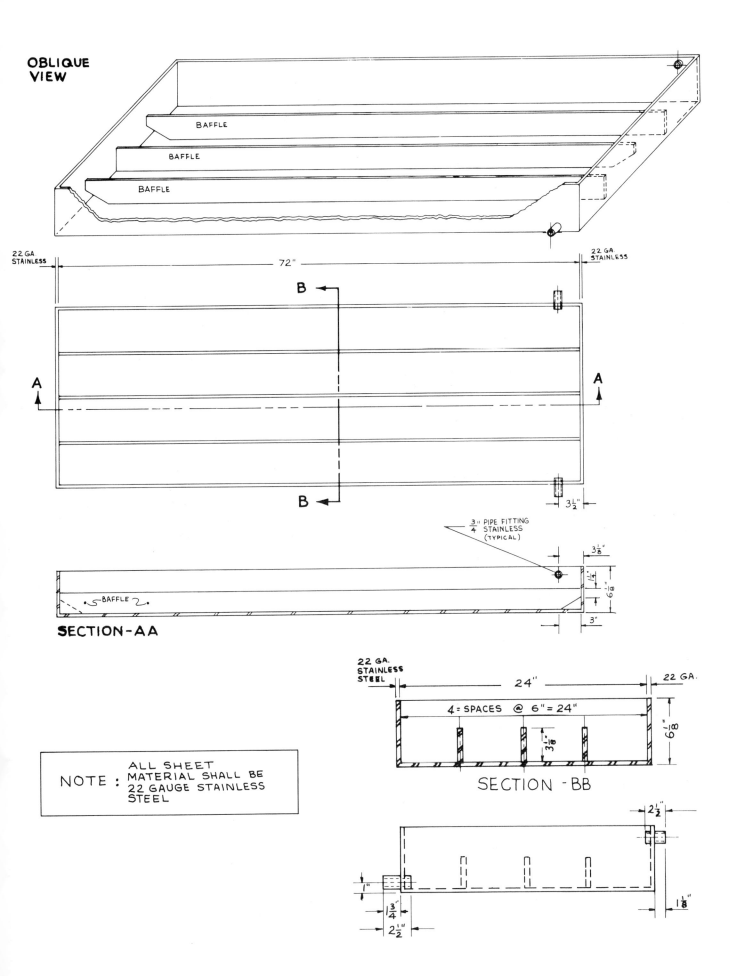

OBLIQUE
VIEW

BAFFLE

BAFFLE

BAFFLE

22 GA
STAINLESS

22 GA.
STAINLESS

72"

B

A   A

B

3½"

¾" PIPE FITTING
STAINLESS
(TYPICAL)

3⅛"

¼"

6⅛"

3"

BAFFLE

SECTION-AA

22 GA.
STAINLESS
STEEL

22 GA.

24"

4 = SPACES @ 6" = 24"

6⅛"

3⅛"

SECTION-BB

NOTE : ALL SHEET
MATERIAL SHALL BE
22 GAUGE STAINLESS
STEEL

2½"

1"

1⅛"

1¾"

2½"

35

Fence Post Peeler

Author: Barry Sanders
Instructor: Dan Nelson
School: Haleyville Area Vocational Center
City & State: Haleyville, AL

Frame

Cut 4 pieces of channel iron for the two long sides and 4 pieces of 1½'' angle iron for the upright supports. Weld these together to form two rectangles. Cut 2 short pieces of channel and 2 short pieces of angle to connect the two rectangles. Weld these to form a box-type rectangle. For the peeler head supports cut two pieces of 4'' angle, measured 30'' up from the bottom of the frame and weld one on each side. These pieces of angle will support the pillar blocks on each side of the peeler head. To help stabilize this angle cut two pieces of 1½'' angle and weld them from the center to the bottom on each side.

For the post supports use 3 conveyor rollers to help hold and support the post when peeling them.

Enclose the peeler head part of the frame for safety. Cut a piece of 13 gauge metal to fit the top of the frame and bolt on. For the sides use heavy gauge expanded metal and cut out holes for the peeler shaft to fit through. Fasten sides by drilling holes in the frame and bolting them on with ⅜'' bolts. To make the peeler portable rig up a 3-point hitch on one end. Weld the side pins 12'' from the bottom of the frame and bolt a piece of angle across the middle with some top link ears welded to it.

Peeler Head

Cut two 12'' discs out of ⁵⁄₁₆'' plate. Take this plate and drill a series of holes around the outside edge and another series along the inside edge. There are ten holes around each edge for U bolts to fit in, so the holes should be drilled in groups of two. Next take two 2'' steel collars with keyways in them and weld them to the plate.

Take a 24'' piece of 2'' diameter stock to make the peeler shaft. Turn down one end to fit the PTO universal joint and cut keyway slots in the shaft 12'' apart. To assemble the peeler head slide one plate on one end of the shaft, and then slip a piece of 2⅛'' diameter steel tubing down against it. Then slide down the other plate. The piece of steel tubing is 12'' long so it acts as a spacer when the peeler chains are tightened up. Center the disc and tighten down the allen screws in the collars on the keys in the shaft keyways.

Hook up the peeler chains. Cut these up in the lengths needed with bolt cutters. There are a total of 5 sets or ten chains used on the peeler head. Hook a U bolt through each end of the lengths and stick them through each plate with one U bolt fitted through the outer edge of one plate and the inner edge of the other. Then take the next chain and fit it up just the opposite. Even though the chains are pulled up tight they need a way to give a little for safety and to prevent damage to the head. Take some heavy duty hydraulic hose and cut up some ½'' sections with a hand hack saw. Slip these over each side of the U bolts and then pull the chains up tight with flat washers and nuts. These sections of hose act as sort of a clutch to enable the chains to give a little if necessary. Take two 2'' pillar blocks and put one on each side of the shaft. Put the peeler head in the frame and mark off where to cut the holes to bolt the pillar blocks on. After cutting the holes bolt the pillar blocks down. With the head in place bolt the expanded metal back on the sides and paint the frame with a rust resistant paint.

Frame: Materials Used

Channel (3'') 16'
Angle (1½'') 10'
Angle (4'') 5'
Expanded metal or mesh
Sheet metal (13 gauge)
Conveyor rollers 3
Bolts (⅜'') 12

Peeler Head: Materials Used

Shaft (2'') 2'
Disc (12'' dia. ⁵⁄₁₆'' thick) 2
Steel collars (2'') 2
U bolts and nuts 20
Tubing for spacer
Pillar blocks 2
Twist link chain 10'
Bolts to bolt down pillar blocks (⅝'') 4
Length of used hydraulic hose
3-point hitch hook up material
Paint

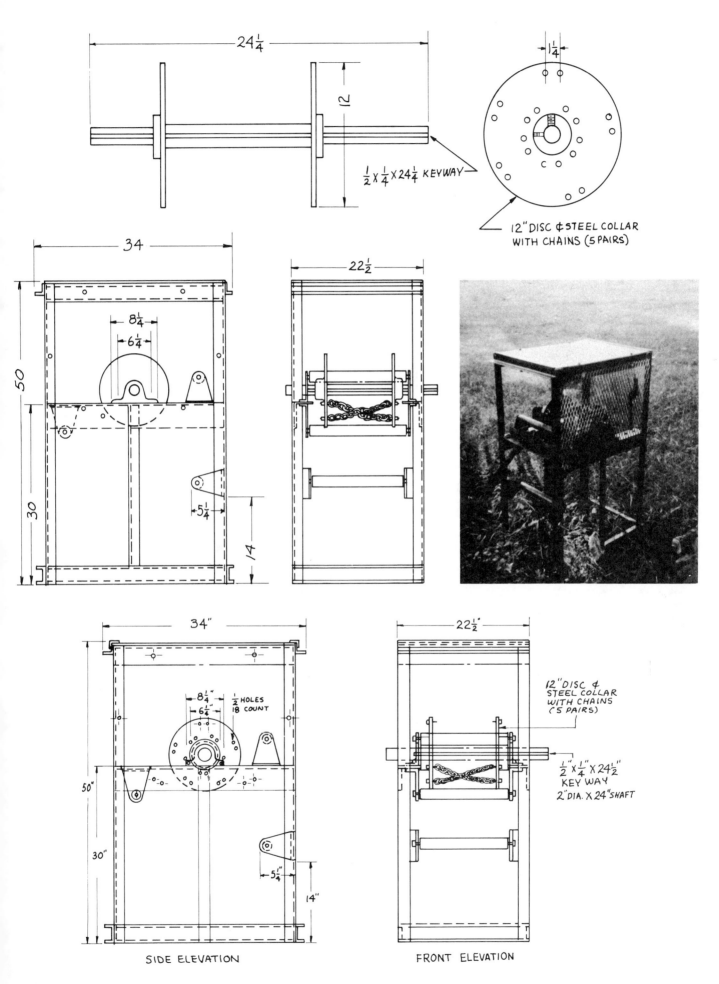

$24\frac{1}{4}$

12

$\frac{1}{2} \times \frac{1}{4} \times 24\frac{1}{4}$ KEYWAY

$1\frac{1}{4}$

12" DISC ¢ STEEL COLLAR WITH CHAINS (5 PAIRS)

34

$8\frac{1}{4}$

$6\frac{1}{4}$

50

30

14

$5\frac{1}{4}$

$22\frac{1}{2}$

34"

$8\frac{1}{4}"$

$6\frac{1}{4}"$

$\frac{1}{2}$ HOLES 18 COUNT

50"

30"

14"

$5\frac{1}{4}"$

SIDE ELEVATION

$22\frac{1}{2}"$

12" DISC ¢ STEEL COLLAR WITH CHAINS (5 PAIRS)

$\frac{1}{2}" \times \frac{1}{4}" \times 24\frac{1}{2}"$ KEY WAY
2" DIA. X 24" SHAFT

FRONT ELEVATION

37

Split The Energy

Author: Michael Nielsen
Instructor: John Phelps
School: Anoka Vo-Tech
City & State: Anoka, MN

Planning and construction:

All of the hydraulic components are matched to each other. The hydraulic pump has to be matched to the engine to get the proper cylinder speed and P.S.I. desired. The cylinder has to be carefully chosen in respect to the length and the load it is going to handle. With the engine and pump I purchased these are approximately 2500 PSI.

The construction started with a piece of rectangular tubing ⅜" thick and 4" x 8" x 80".

Main Body & Reservoir

The tubing acts as the main body and reservoir. The amount of reservoir required for the hydraulic on the splitter is five gallons. The area within the tube will hold over eight gallons, so it works out very well. There is enough space for the oil, with space above the fluid for fluid expansion and separation of the air from the fluid.

Wedge

The wedge is made of mild steel 1" x 7" x 12" with a 20° milled edge. The wedge extends 8" above and 4" below the surface of the tube. The reason for this is added strength in making sure the wedge will not be allowed to break off. The wedge is welded to the front end of the tube, on top, and underneath the tube.

The front ¼" of the wedge was ground back, arc welded with hard facing applied, and ground back to its original shape. All welding on this project was ⅛" and 5/32" 7018 rod.

Push Plate & Slide

The push plate and slide was made to slide on top of the main body and hold the log in place while it is being pushed through the wedge. The push plate was welded to the ram with a ½" x 1" spike welded to the front of the

plate to keep the log from jumping out.

Engine & Hydraulic Components

The engine is a vertical shaft, eight horsepower four cycle. The engine was direct coupled to a five gallon per minute hydraulic pump. This combination is rated at about 2500 PSI. The cylinder I used was a 3½" piston diameter with a rod diameter of 2". The five gallons per minute pump will push a cylinder of this size 120" a minute. The cylinder on the splitter is 30" in length. Most of the wood split is between 18-24" in length. The cycle time on the splitter is about 35 seconds. There is a four way valve on this system which will reverse the direction of the ram.

Wheels & Axles

The wheels were taken from a 1960 Buick, using the spindles and bearings of the same. These were welded to a 2" square tube. The axle was then welded to the body with even weight at both ends. Gussets were welded from the body to the axle for added strength. This unit is completely portable and easy to handle.

Large Round Hay Bale Carrier-Unroller

Author: John C. Bienhoff
Instructor: P. Stevenson
School: Kansas State University
City & State: Manhattan, KS

Lift Arm and Bale Center Construction:

The lift arms were made by welding two automotive spindles to two 6″ supports of rectangular tubing. The hubs were removed from the spindles to keep from burning the grease seals within each hub. Secondly, the two spindles and supports were welded with vee butt and fillet welds to the two rectangular tubing lift arms to form the left and right lift arms. Each lift arm was then fitted to the two pipes which compose the outer components of the arm hinges and welded with fillet and flush vee butt welds. Thirdly, a lift arm brace of flat strap was cut, bent, and fillet welded to each lift arm and outer hinge pipe. In the fourth step, the lift arm tie rod mounts were cut from flat strap and the tie rod adjustment holes were drilled. The lift arm tie rod mounts were then fillet welded to the lift arms, keeping in mind that there are left and right arms. Following this, holes were drilled and threaded in the outer hinge pipes to accept two grease fittings in each of the two outer hinge pipes.

After the two lift arms were constructed, the two identical bale centers were made as depicted in drawing two. One end of each bale center pipe was sharply orange-peeled. The orange-peeled end of each bale center pipe was then bent together and welded to form a point. In the second step, two disks were cut from sheet metal for each bale face disk and welded together with a fillet weld. Next, a hole was cut in the center of each of the two bale face disks to allow the hub and bale center pipe to protrude through each disk. The holes of the five hub lugs were then drilled in each disk. To complete this segment of construction, the two center pipes were welded to the bale face disks with a fillet weld on the bale side of the disk and a flush circular vee butt weld on the hub side of the disk.

Construction of the main frame began by cutting the upper and lower frame supports from rectangular tubing. Holes were then cut in the ends to allow the interior pipes of the lift arm hinges to protrude through the two rectangular supports. Secondly, the two interior pipes of the lift arm hinges were cut and were welded to the lower rectangular frame support with circular fillet and flush vee butt welds. The third step in construction was to cut the four pipe wear washers. Two of these washers were placed over the interior lift arm hinge pipes and fillet welded to the lower rectangular frame support. The fourth step involved slipping the two lift arms over their respective interior hinge pipes and attaching the upper rectangular frame support with circular fillet and flush vee butt welds. Lastly, the two remaining pipe wear

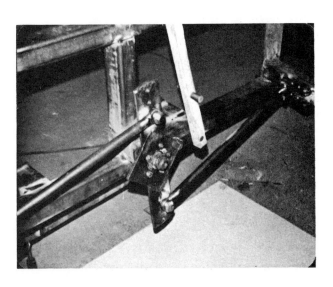

washers were each cut in half perpendicular to their diameters. These half-washers were placed around the interior hinge pipes and between the upper rectangular frame support and the lift arm exterior hinge pipes to be welded to the frame support with fillet welds.

The next segment of the main frame construction was to attach an automotive spindle to a rectangular tubing support. The arm turnstyle was attached to this hub later in construction. Secondly, the spindle and support were welded to the lower rectangular frame support with fillet and vee butt welds. Thirdly, a length of rectangular tubing was fillet and vee butt welded to the upper frame and turnstyle supports. The upper hydraulic cylinder mounting was then constructed.

Arm Turnstyle and Tie Rod Construction
Construction of the arm turnstyle began with cutting a hole in the center of an 8″ square piece of ½″ thick metal plate to allow the automotive hub to protrude through the center of the arm turnstyle. The second step involved locating and drilling the five hub lug holes. This was followed by cutting two lengths of flat strap metal and welding them to the center piece of turnstyle using vee butt welds.

Two lengths of extra heavy inch pipe were cut to serve as tie rods. The ends of the pipes were flattened to make sure that each flattened pipe end was perpendicular to its opposite end. Secondly, a category 1 top-link ball and socket was welded to each end of each pipe with the ball and socket on one end of the pipe on a horizontal axis while the ball and socket on the opposite end of the pipe was on a vertical axis. The balls and sockets were welded to the pipes with fillet welds using nickel welding electrodes.

Three Point Hitch Hookup Construction
Construction of the three-point hitch hookup began by cutting two lengths of angle iron to serve as the two lower three-point linkage attachments. Four adjustment holes were drilled in one leg of each angle iron to accept the three-point pull pins. Each angle iron was

welded at right angles to a 6″ length of rectangular tubing. Two support braces were welded between the lower hitch attachments and the main frame lower rectangular support. The lower hitch attachment was completed after cutting and welding a length of ¼″ thick flat strap metal to serve as a lower hitch attachment stiffener.

To make the hitch mast two lengths of ½″ thick flat strap metal was cut and drilled with 8 top-link adjustment holes. Two 6″ lengths of rectangular tubing were used as mast extensions. Lengths of ¼″ thick flat strap metal were cut and welded just inside the ends of each piece of rectangular tubing. This added strength to the machine and approved the appearance.

Materials	length
Rectangular tubing:	
4″ x 3″ x ¼″	28′ 6″
Flats	
¼″ x 2½″	2′ 5½″
½″ x 3″	11′ 2¾″
½″ x 2″	4′ 10¼″
½″ x 4″	4′ 2½″
½″ x 8″	8″
1″ x 8″	3½″
Angle	
4″ x 4″ x ½″	2′ 4″
Standard black pipe	
3″	2′ 11½″
2½″	3′
Extra strong black pipe	
2½″	4′
1″	5′ 2″
Sheet metal	
1 - ¼″ x 1′ 6″ x 4′	

Hardware
3 - five bolt automotive hubs with spindles, lugs and nuts
2 - ¾″ x 3″ bolts with lock washers and nuts
2 - ¾″ x 4″ bolts with lock washers and nuts
2 - category II pull pins
4 - category I top - link balls and sockets
4 - grease fittings

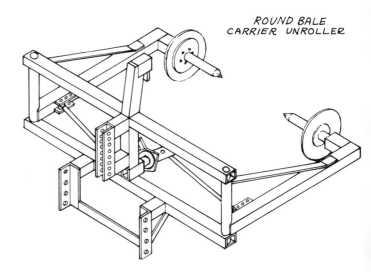

ROUND BALE
CARRIER UNROLLER

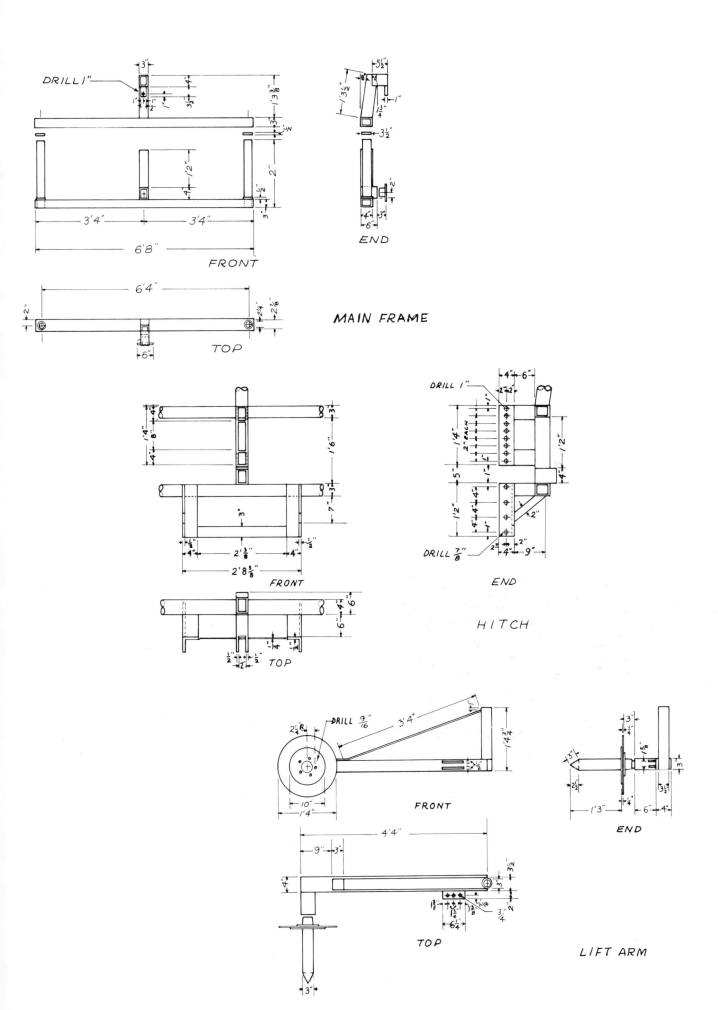

MAIN FRAME

HITCH

LIFT ARM

41

Design and Fabrication of Diesel Engine Stand and Drive Unit for Irrigation Pump

Author: Vincent A. Young
Instructor: W. K. Davidson
School: San Joaquin Delta College
City & State: Stockton, CA

This project was started with a bare block 4 cyl. diesel engine without motor mounts. A basic sketch was done utilizing angles for support and torque specifications. 3″ square tube was used for legs and rectangular boxed frame. Legs were set at 60° angles to the boxed frame for maximum support. Mounting pads were welded and ¾″ holes were drilled. Motor mounts were hand cut at 90° angles and welded. 3″ square tube was used to lift and adjust height from frame to motor. 3″ x ¾″ class 6 bolts were welded into ½″ plates 3″ square and welded to motor mount legs. 1″ rubber was used between motor mounts and mount legs to relieve torque.

A radiator mount was added to the frame. 1¼″ square tube was boxed into bottom mounts of the radiator and welded. The top of the radiator was solid mounted to the frame with channel iron welded with 6011 rod. An air cleaner was mounted with 3″ square tube cut at a 30° angle and welded to the frame for easy access and service. A battery box was made from 1″ angle iron and welded to frame, angle iron hold down was used to hold any size battery.

A control box and gauge panel were mounted on 1″ square tube at the correct height for easy access. Ignition and all gauges were mounted in a 16 gauge steel box.

A 13″ extension was added to the basic frame to hold 2 carrier bearings and main drive shaft to pump. After adjustments were made to be sure of correct angle to fly wheel, bearings blocks and frame were welded.

A guard to cover the flywheel and drive shaft assembly was made from ¼″ plate steel to conform to flywheel dimensions and then covered with ⅛″ plate steel rolled to shape to cover carrier bearings and drive shaft. Holes were cut in the guard for bearing lubrication. This complete assembly was welded together and then bolted to the frame assembly for easy removal for maintenance.

The fuel tank assembly was mounted 44″ off the ground and was built from a 1¼″ square tube. This tank will be nursed by a 500 gallon underground tank. The other head gravity feed tank is a 50 gallon rectangular tank mounted on rubber to avoid static electricity.

This Engine Assembly is currently being used to pump irrigation water on the school farm, and was made to run unchecked in 48 hour intervals.

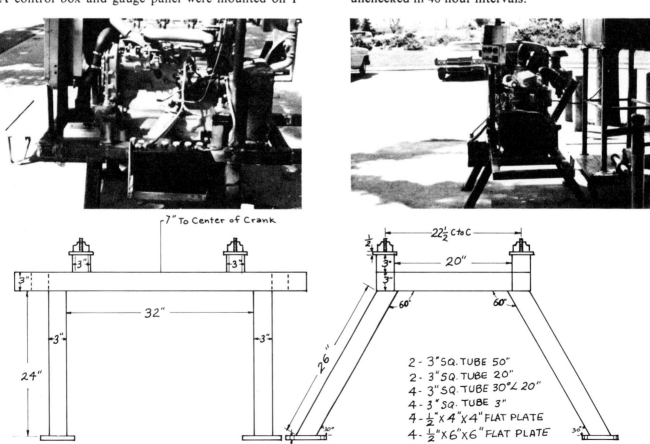

2 - 3″ SQ. TUBE 50″
2 - 3″ SQ. TUBE 20″
4 - 3″ SQ. TUBE 30° ∠ 20″
4 - 3″ SQ. TUBE 3″
4 - ½″ x 4″ x 4″ FLAT PLATE
4 - ½″ x 6″ x 6″ FLAT PLATE

Tractor Operator Shield

Author: John Swanbom
Instructor: Jerry Ditty
School: St. Petersburg Vo-Tech Inst.
City & State: St. Petersburg, FL

The tractor operator shield was designed to meet the specific needs of citrus grove maintenance. Orange and grapefruit trees are hemispherical in shape and extend from ground level to thirty feet in height. When a grove is young a tractor has no trouble maneuvering through. But as the grove matures trees planted twenty-five feet apart begin to fill in row centers until lack of clearance becomes a hazard to the operator. When he disks, circling each tree individually, he has no warning of projecting branches which may brush off glasses, injure eyes or even cause the operator to lose control of the tractor. Compounding this problem is the dangerous tendency of branches to ride over the cowling and come down on the hand throttle forcing it to the wide open position just prior to the branches hitting the operator in the face.

The tractor-operator shield design had to meet five criteria:

1. protect the driver from branches
2. protect the hand throttle
3. be designed as small and smooth as possible to minimize damage to fruit and foliage
4. meet the above criteria without restricting the operator's vision
5. be easily removable

The most difficult problem to deal with was the close tolerances required. The holes in the tractor transmission housing were factory drilled and tapped thus requiring that plates fitting up to this housing be precisely drilled. Since the holes were blind it was impossible to mark the plates using the holes directly. The problem was solved by placing a piece of aluminum foil over the holes and gently pushing down on them leaving marks on the foil. The centers of these marks were then found and the template used to center punch the half inch plates. The holes matched exactly.

The pipe framework could now be done separately assuming the two halves were kept in correct relationship with each other and exact spacing was maintained where the pipes were to be welded to the half inch plates. This was accomplished by clamping an angle iron across the pipes that fasten directly to the plates, butting up to the long verticle pipes. This allowed a roll movement for adjustment while maintaining the required space. The pipe framework was welded using the uphill mode and 1/16" root opening to assure complete penetration. The plumbing union was welded into place, again requiring very careful alignment. Once the union was welded the pipe framework could be welded to the half inch plates. Since any distortion from welding would change the relationship of the holes of one plate to the other it was necessary to tack the pipes with the plates bolted securely to the tractor. It was important that the tacks be sound to minimize distortion. There remained one more piece of the basic frame to be welded on, the machined solid round stock. This could only be put on after the union was welded in place, the pipes welded to the plates and the plates fastened to the tractor. The unit was now a rigid extension of the tractor. Anything that was to fit between the two halves of the unit must be in precise alignment with both of them as they were when permanently mounted. It is for this reason that the machined round stock could not be welded earlier. It very likely would have thrown the union threads of the bolt holes out of alignment. To weld on the round stock the right side had to be removed from the tractor, the piece inserted into pipe on the left hand side, the right side put back on the tractor and the round stock welded. The basic framework was then complete. What remained was to make a framework for the expanded metal. This was done with 1" angle iron that was welded to the pipe and then bent to conform to its shape. The removable frame was welded together and the expanded metal welded to it. The 1/2" pipes were heated and bent and welded on. The expanded metal was welded onto the sides. Holes were drilled to hold the removable frame in place. Again since both sides were rigid these holes had to be drilled while the unit was bolted to the tractor.

It was subsequently found that all five of the previously stated criteria were effectively met. The unit has shown no sign of cracks from the heavy fatigue forces imposed by diesel tractor vibration. In short, it has fulfilled the design requirements.

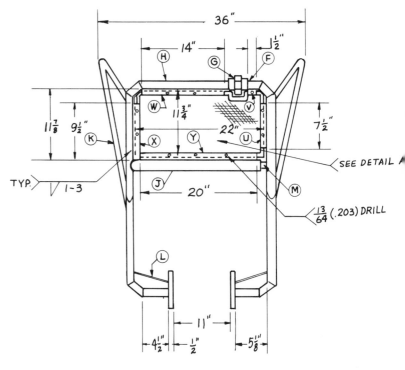

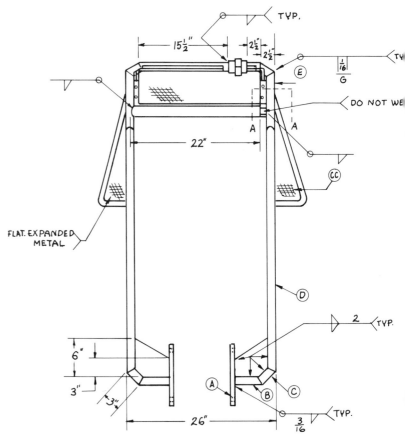

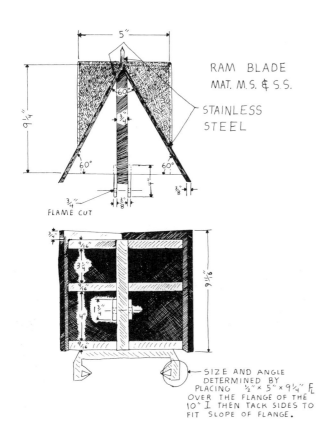

RAM BLADE
MAT. M.S. & S.S.

STAINLESS STEEL

5"

9¼"

60°

60°   60°

¾"   4"   ⅜"

¾"   ⅜"

FLAME CUT

9¼"

⁹⁄₁₆"

3¾"

⁹⁄₁₆"

4"

⁹⁄₁₆"

¾"

SIZE AND ANGLE DETERMINED BY PLACING ½" × 5" × 9¼" PL OVER THE FLANGE OF THE 10" I THEN TACK SIDES TO FIT SLOPE OF FLANGE.

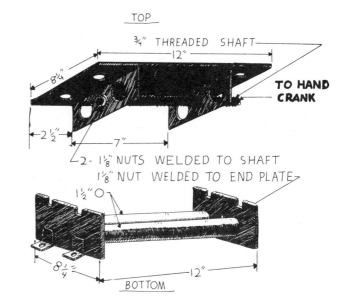

ADJUSTABLE MOTOR MOUNT TO ENGAGE OR DISENGAGE BELTS THAT DRIVE THE PUMP MAT. M.S.

TOP

¾" THREADED SHAFT

12"

8¼"

2½"   7"

TO HAND CRANK

2 - 1⅛" NUTS WELDED TO SHAFT
1⅛" NUT WELDED TO END PLATE

1½" O

8¼"   12"

BOTTOM

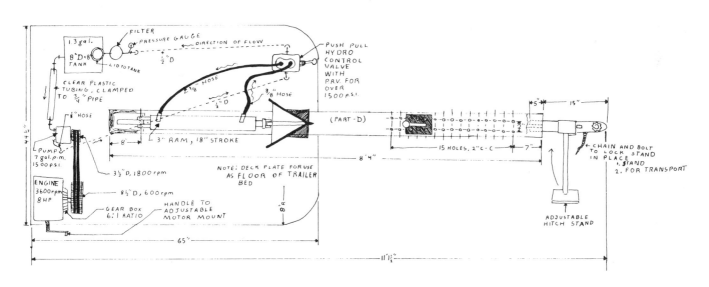

13 gal.

8"D × 8" TANK

FILTER

PRESSURE GAUGE

DIRECTION OF FLOW

½" D

CLEAR PLASTIC TUBING, CLAMPED TO ¾" PIPE

LID TO TANK

⅜" HOSE

½" D

⅜" HOSE

⅜" HOSE

PUSH PULL HYDRO CONTROL VALVE WITH P.R.V. FOR OVER 1500 P.S.I.

½" HOSE

PUMP 7 gal. p.m. 1500 p.s.i.

ENGINE 3600 rpm 8 HP

GEAR BOX 6:1 RATIO

3½" D, 1800 rpm

8½" D, 600 rpm

HANDLE TO ADJUSTABLE MOTOR MOUNT

8"

3" RAM, 18" STROKE

(PART-D)

NOTE: DECK PLATE FOR USE AS FLOOR OF TRAILER BED

8' 4"

8" R

15 HOLES, 2" C-C

7"

5"   15"

CHAIN AND BOLT TO LOCK STAND IN PLACE
1. STAND
1. FOR TRANSPORT

ADJUSTABLE HITCH STAND

65"

11' 1½"

NOTE: FOR DETAIL OF ADJUSTABLE MOTOR MOUNT AND RAM BLADE SEE ACCOMPANYING DRAWINGS AXIS IS LOCATED SO WEIGHT BIAS IS TO THE FRONT PART-D = 10" STD I BEAM.
5 TON THRUS TO RAM BLADE

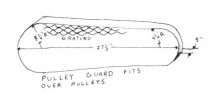

GRATING

27½"

5"   4" R   5"

PULLEY GUARD FITS OVER PULLEYS

Straddle Type Implement Carryall

Author: Joe Cotta
Instructor: Richard Regalo
School: Merced Union High School
City & State: Merced, CA

Materials Used:

3" x 4" x .250" rectangular tubing	200 feet
3" x 5" x .250" rectangular tubing	5 feet
2" x 3" x .250" rectangular tubing	12 feet
2" x 2" x .250" square tubing	18 feet
3" x 5/8" flat	2 feet
3" x 1/2" flat	1 foot
3" channel	3 feet
2 7/8" upset oil well pipe	45 feet
2' x 4' x 1/2" plate	60 lbs.
1/2" round	5 feet
5/16 chain	3 feet
Boston Gear Boxes 15:1	2
12" Diameter steering wheels	2
74 tooth #60 sprocket	2
12 tooth #60 sprocket	2
#60 chain	12 feet
grease zerts	15
Bud Hub and Spindles	4
20" wheels	4
7.50 x 20" tires	4

Specifications

Width Overall	8' 10"
Length Overall	34'
Height Overall	7' 8"
Height of useable space	6'
Length of useable space	19'

Wheel size	20"
Tire size	7.50 x 20"
Turntable size	20" x 1/2" circle
Wheel base	25' 7"
Frame width	6' 6"
Spindles	5200 pound capacity
Gear boxes	15:1 gear ratio

For the axle use a 5' piece of 3" x 5" x .250 rectangular tubing. Weld the spindles on and get them at the proper toe-in, cut a 1½" hole through the center of the axle. Insert a 3" piece of 1¼" black pipe to be used as a bushing. Weld and grind the bushing smooth. For the turntable cut two pieces of ½" flat to a diameter of 20".

Next cut a 1½" hole in the center of each of the flat circles. Insert a 1½" x 5" piece of cold roll shaft into the hole and weld two passes. On the top plate, drill holes for the two grease zerts and tape them with an ⅛" pipe tape. Set the top plate over the bottom plate. Cut a 4" piece of 1½" black pipe, slip over the shaft and weld to keep the two plates together. The turn table must be allowed to rock 1" to each side to compensate for any rough fields or roads which one may travel with the carryall. Cut two triangular pieces of ½" plate the base being 12" long. Drill a 1¼" hole in the center of them and set on the under side of the bottom turn table plate so the axle can be placed between them and still be centered on the plate, then weld. Cut a 1¼" shaft 4" long, slip through the axle and weld on both sides of the plates. To construct a hitch assembly use 2" x 2" x .250" square tubing. Cut two lengths 60" and notched 4" from one end at a 20° angle. Then cut top end at a 25° angle. Heat and bend the bottom of the hitch sides. Construct the tongue out of a 8" piece of 4" x ½" flat. Drill a 1" hole 1¼" from the end and round the tip for safety. Notch the front of the hitch ½" in the center at a depth of 4" so the tongue will slide inside. Cut two lengths of 2" x 2" x .250" tubing 40" long for braces. Cut a 60° angle at the top end and a 15° angle at the bottom end. Then place inside the hitch and weld them.

To mount the hitch to the front axle, use four pieces of 4" x ½" flat rounded on one end. Drill 2" from the end to a bit diameter of ⅞". Place these in the center of the axle at the proper points so the hitch can be mounted between them. Drill the hitch on both points where it is to be mounted 2" from the ends to insure strength.

Construct the frame of the carryall out of 3" x 4" x .250" rectangular tubing. Cut two lengths of the tubing 22' long and six lengths 6' long. Divide the 22' lengths into 41" spacings, place the 6' pieces in the spacings and weld them.

Carryall Frame Bridge Truss
Construct a bridge type truss from two lengths of 3" x 4" x .250" square tubing. Cut these pieces 22' long with a 20° angle at each end. Notch a 37° angle 38" from each end, bend and tack. Cut six pieces of tubing 1' long to brace the bridge, then square it and weld.

Lifting Pipes and Bearings
Cut twelve pieces 3" long of 3" standard pipe. Drill ¹¹⁄₃₂" holes in the center for grease zerts. Cut 12 pieces of 3" channel 3" long. Place 3" pipes inside the channel and weld so the grease zerts are straight up. Place each of the bearings in the correct location.

Attaching Front Running Gear to Frame
Lift the frame 6' off the floor. Center the turntable with the frame. Make 4 braces coming down from the frame to the turntable. Cut the back braces 83" long at a compound angle of 47° downward and 38° inward where it is mounted to the frame. Cut a 38° compound angle at the bottom where it is mounted to the turntable. Then tack the rear braces to the frame and the turntable. For the front two braces cut two pieces of tubing 6' long at a compound angle of 58° and 30° inward.

Cut a 47° compound angle at the bottom where it is mounted to the turntable, tack and weld.

Rear Straddle
Cut 2 lengths of 3" x 4" x .250" rectangular tubing 4' 11" long at a compound angle of 75° downward and 5° outward where it mounts to the frame. Tack these. Cut the forward braces for the rear axle mounts at a compound angle of 55° downward and 5° outward where it is mounted to the frame. They are 70" long with the bottom end at a 20° angle to meet the rear brace.

To mount the rear spindles use a 3" piece of 3" x 5" x .250" rectangular tubing and mount by welding them.

Then mount the tubing and spindle to the axle mounts by squaring and leveling them with the frame. Then brace these using a wedge of the 3" x 5" x .250" tubing. To cap off the bottom of the axle mounts and also brace the tubing used in the spindle assembly use a piece of ¼" flat. This flat is cut to fit the under side of the mounts and then welded. The final brace used in the rear axle mounts should be cut 4' long at a compound angle of 30° downward and 5° outward on the top side and 50° downward and 5° outward on the bottom side. Place them from the center of the rear frame cross beam down 30" on the rear axle mounts.

Gussetts and Braces
Fit and mold eight ¼" flat gussetts on the front end. Cut and fit to form a boxed type brace. Gussett the rear of the carryall in the same fashion, using ¼" flat cut to fit the 14" gussetts. To discourage any twisting action, brace from one top corner of the bridge to the other with 2" x 3" x .250" rectangular tubing thus tying in the top of the carryall. Additional bracing should be put between each of the spaces between the bridge pillars. Cut these from 3" x 4" x .250" rectangular tubing 2' long at a 45° angle on each end.

Safety Locking Device
Cut out a 10" circle from ¼" flat in a skip tooth ratchet arrangement for a locking device.

Lifting Mechanism
Slide the locking device over the 2⅞" pipe which was to be used for the lifting pipe. Cap the pipe so it can not slide back and also weld a sleeve on the inside of the rear bearing so it will not slide forward. Cut holes in the pipe for the chain pegs 16" from each bearing so there will be 2 pegs per spacing. Use ½" rod for the pegs at a length of 3½". Slip inside the pipe and weld. Use two 74 tooth size No. 60 chain sprockets. Next mount the gear boxes. Mount a No. 12 sprocket on the gear box going to a No. 74 sprocket on the lifting pipes. To mount the gear boxes use a 14" piece of ⅝ flat. Fit this plate to be welded between the two downward turntable braces. After welding these mounts 17" from the top frame, gussett the plates to insure strength. Then mount the gear boxes in the proper positions. Drill four ⅜" holes for each box, bolt the boxes down and chain the sprockets with heavy duty size 60 chain. Mount a 12" diameter steering wheel on each gear box.

All that is needed now is to paint and the project is done.

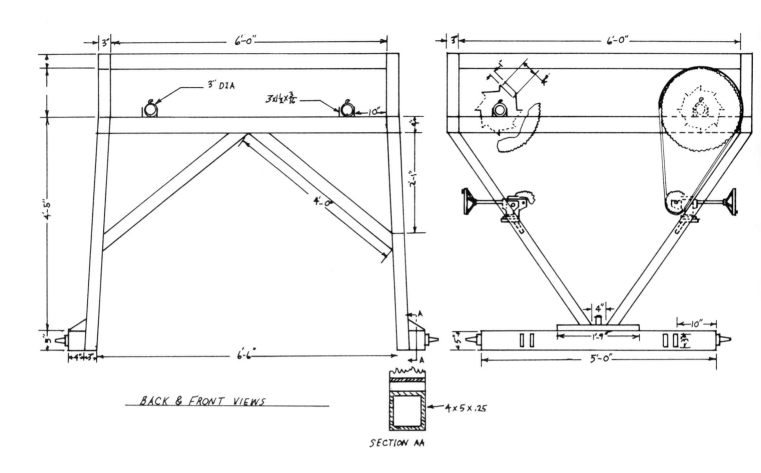

3" DIA

3x1½x3/16

3" DIA ... 10"

6'-0"

3"

4'-5"

2'-1"

4'-0"

5"

4" 3"

6'-6"

BACK & FRONT VIEWS

3"

6'-0"

4"

1'-9"

4"

10"

5'-0"

4½"

SECTION AA

4x5x.25

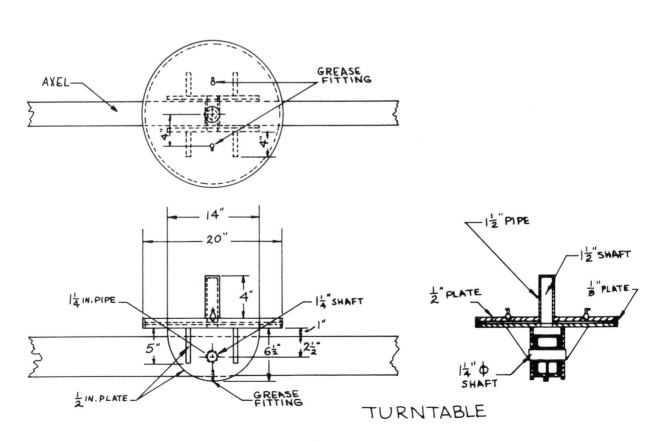

AXEL

GREASE FITTING

8

4"

4"

14"

20"

1¼ IN. PIPE

1¼" SHAFT

4"

5"

6½"

2½"

1"

½ IN. PLATE

GREASE FITTING

1½" PIPE

1½" SHAFT

½" PLATE

⅛" PLATE

1¼" Φ SHAFT

TURNTABLE

50

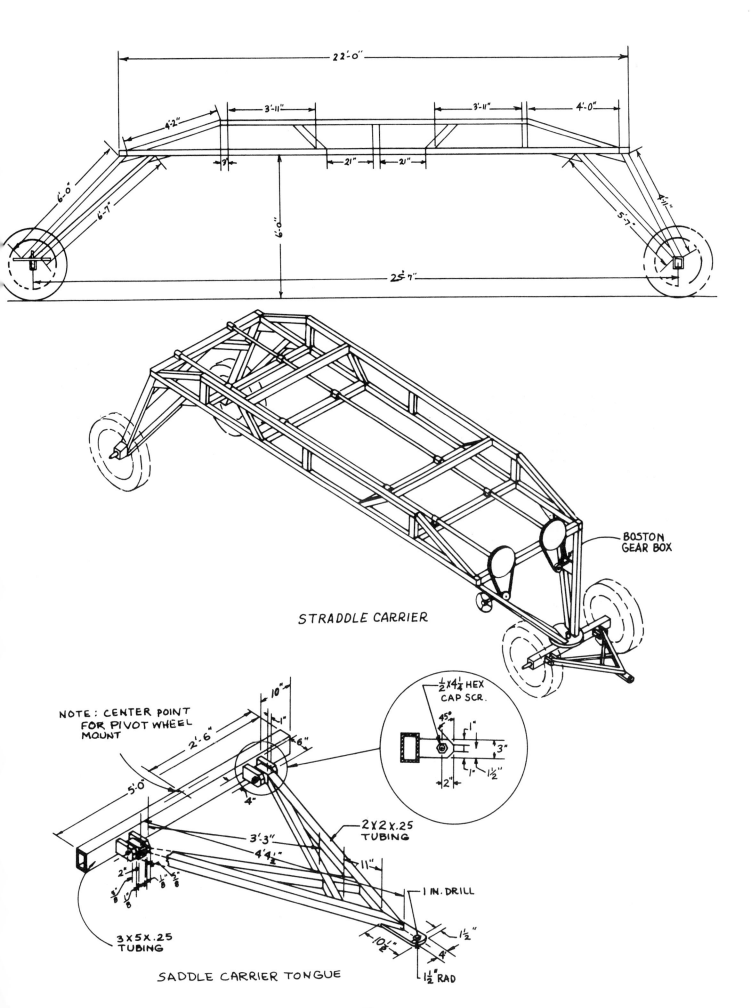

22'-0"

4'-2" 3'-11" 3'-11" 4'-0"

6'-0" 6'-7"

3" 21" 21"

6'-0"

5'-7" 4'-1"

25'-7"

BOSTON
GEAR BOX

STRADDLE CARRIER

$\frac{1}{2} \times 4\frac{1}{4}$ HEX
CAP SCR.

45°

1"
1" 3"
1" 1½"
2"

NOTE: CENTER POINT
FOR PIVOT WHEEL
MOUNT

10"
1"
6"

2'-6"

5'-0"

4"

2X2X.25
TUBING

3'-3"
4'-4½"

11"

I IN. DRILL

2"

3X5X.25
TUBING

10½" 1½"

4"

1½" RAD

SADDLE CARRIER TONGUE

51

Center Drop Gravity Wagon

Author:	Steven M. Zeller
	James M. Maguin
Instructor:	Paul N. Stevenson
School:	Kansas State University
City & State:	Manhattan, KS

BILL OF MATERIALS

1	14 ga.	72″ x 144″	Sheet
1	12 ga.	48″ x 144″	Sheet
1	12 ga.	48″ x 96″	Sheet
2	14 ga.	60″ x 144″	Sheet
2	20 ft.	3″ x 3″ x ¼″	Angle
1	20 ft.	3″ x 5″ x ¼″	Angle
5	20 ft.	2″ x 2″ x ⅛″	Angle
1½	20 ft.	2½″ x 2½″ x 3/16″	Angle
1	10 ft.	2½″ x 2½″ x ¼″	Angle
4	20 ft.	⅛″ x 4″	Strip
1	8 ft.	2½″ x 3/16″	Strip
2	20 ft.	¾″ I.D.	Pipe
1	9 ft.	1″ I.D.	Pipe
1	3 ft.	⅝″	Re-bar
76	⅛″ Welding Rods		
3996	Mig Counts		
Sandblasting			
2	gal.	Metal Primer	
3	gal.	Red Implement Paint	
Sprockets, chain, and hub			Salvage

The gravity box design, was desired as it allows rapid unloading of grain without the expense and design problems inherent with hydraulic type systems. This gravity box was designed with a center dump to allow easy unloading at the local elevator or by a power take off (PTO) driven auger into a bin for on farm storage; this also provided a more balanced distribution of weight. The narrow under carriage design allows tremendous versatility in that it can be mounted on a fifth wheel frame, truck frame, or on a (4-wheel wagon) running gear.

The 8 ft. x 12 ft. dimensions were decided upon to allow a grain capacity of approximately 350 bu. and to provide a minimum of a 30° slope for the ease of unloading high moisture grain. Two other important factors were the 8 ft. maximum width for highway use and the 12 ft. length to fit our truck chassis and wagon gears.

We started the project by cutting the 2 ft. wide sides from 12 gauge sheet using an abrasive disk mounted on a circular saw. The sheets were Metal Inert Gas (MIG) welded together at the corners to form a 8 ft. x 12 ft. box. Then 2½″ x 2½″ x 3/16″ angle iron was welded to the outside of each corner to add additional strength. The angle iron was cut 13½″ longer than the side to allow the mounting of wood extensions above the sides. A piece of 2″ x 2″ x ⅛″ angle iron was then welded along the top edge of the sides to add rigidity.

A box formed from the sides was then inverted (topside down) to allow easier construction of the hopper sides. The hopper sides were cut from 14 gauge sheet metal using a metal shear. The two 12 ft. hopper sides were fastened to a portable crane and lifted into position and the top edges welded to the bottom sides. The frame for the center drop was made from 2″ x 2″ x ⅛″ angle iron and welded into position, to provide support to the two sides. This allowed for the exact placement of the two remaining hopper sides. The two 8 ft. wide hopper sides were then lowered into position and welded along the seams. To provide additional strength to the hopper, seams 4″ x ⅛″ strip was bent into a V-shape using a hydraulic break and then welded on the outside of the hopper seams.

The strips that covered the two 12 ft. seams and the seams that extended to the center drop were bent to a

135° included angle. The strips that covered the two 8 ft. seams were bent to form a 120° included angle.

With the actual bin completed, work began to form a durable and rigid undercarriage. Two pieces of 3″ x 3″ x ¼″ angle iron was welded to the 12 ft. hopper sides 12″ below the bottom of the vertical sides. Then, because of the different slopes of the 8 ft. and 12 ft. hopper sides, two pieces of 3″ x 5″ x ¼″ angle iron was welded on the hopper (8 ft.) sides to form a square frame around the hopper 12″ below the bottom of the vertical sides. Four legs to support the frame was cut from 3″ x 3″ x ¼″ angle iron. The legs were extended down to the main beams and welded. The beams were formed by butting two pieces of 6″ x 2″ channel iron together to form a box section. Then two pieces of 3″ x 5″ x ¼″ angle iron was welded on each end between the main beams to tie them together.

To add lateral stability to the legs, four pieces of 2½″ x 2½″ x ³⁄₁₆″ angle iron were used to brace the legs to the corners of the bin frame. The legs were braced longitudinally by using 2½″ x 2½″ x ¼″ angle iron running from the legs to the main beams. To provide additional support to the bin frame along the 12 ft. sides, four pieces of 2″ x 2″ x ⅛″ angle iron were spaced evenly apart along the two sides and welded to the bin frame and main beams.

To provide additional support to the middle at the hopper sides four pieces of 2″ x 2″ x ⅛″ angle iron were welded to the bin frame and extended down to the frame around the center drop.

The bottom door was cut from ³⁄₁₆″ plate steel and smoothed up for easy sliding in its track. The door slides were made by putting two pieces of 2″ x 2″ x ⅛″ angle iron to the angle iron frame surrounding the bin opening to form a track. The angle iron was spaced ¹⁄₁₆″ to allow clearance for easy door operation, but to prevent grain or fertilizer from jamming the door.

The door opening mechanism consists of a rack welded to the bottom of the door, which engages to a pinion gear on a shaft mounted to the main beams. On one side of the shaft, the support is welded solid to the main beam and on the other side the shaft support is bolted to the beam to allow for easy removal of the shaft for lubrication and inspection.

To drive the pinion gears shaft a small sprocket was welded to the shaft. The chain from this sprocket runs down to an arbor shaft made from a short piece of 1″ I.D. pipe and ⅞″ shaft. On one end of the shaft a sprocket is mounted and on the other end a removeable steering wheel is mounted. The arbor shaft housing is supported by pieces of 2″ x 2″ x ⅛″ angle iron welded to one of the bin legs and the main beam. The steering wheel was formed by bending a piece of ⅝″ re-bar into a circle and mounting it to a hub using four short pieces of steel rod.

To provide additional support for the wood extensions,

six pieces 2½″ x ³⁄₁₆″ strips were cut and welded to the 2″ x 2″ x ⅛″ angle iron running around the top of the vertical sides.

The frame for the tarp canopy was formed from five pieces of ¾″ I.D. pipe. The first piece was mounted lengthwise over the center of the bin and welded to the 2½″ x ³⁄₁₆″ strips (wood extension supports). This piece of pipe was bent so that there was four feet in the center twelve inches above the top of the wood extension supports. This was done to provide rapid water shed from the tarp. The other four pieces of pipe were cut and bent to join the center pipe for added rigidity and complete the tarp canopy frame.

The wagon bolsters and clamps which went on the wagon gear to hold the box secure to the rear axles were made by the author. In the front the bolsters were made so that the box would float when going over uneven ground.

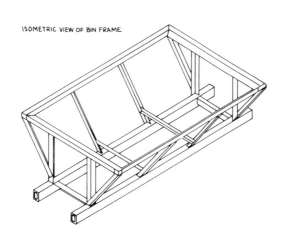

ISOMETRIC VIEW OF BIN FRAME.

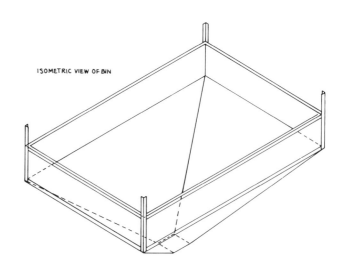

ISOMETRIC VIEW OF BIN

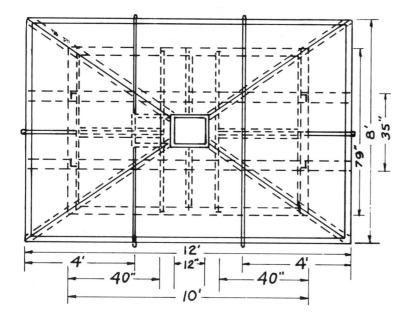

CENTER DROP GRAVITY WAGON

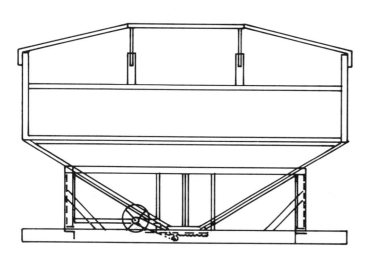

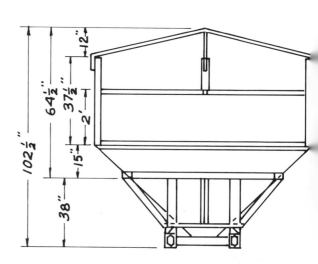

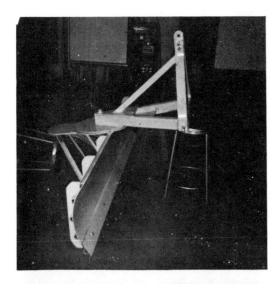

All Purpose Plow

Author: Ted Rewasiewich
Instructor: Paul Goral
School: Milwaukee Technical High School
City & State: Milwaukee, WI

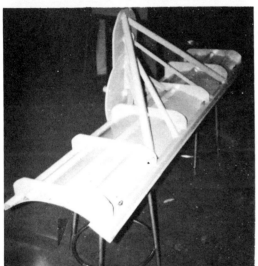

The Blade

Roll 2 pieces of ³⁄₁₆″ cold rolled steel 43″ x 21″ lengthwise to a curve, 18½″ high and 3½″ deep. Weld the two pieces of the blade lengthwise together producing a blade 86″ long.

Now make supports for the blade for strength. Take 6 pieces of ³⁄₁₆″ cold roll steel 16½ x 4¼″ and scribe the outside curve of the blade on the metal lengthwise from corner to corner. This leaves six pieces of metal with an arc cut on one side and the other side still having two square corners. These corners are to be rounded to a radius of 1″ before welding them to the blade. Place one support 2″ away from each edge of the outside of the blade and space the other four supports 15¾″ apart. Place the supports on the outside arc or curve of the blade with the curve you cut in the plate downward on the blade and centered on the blade so as not to touch the edges of the blade. Intermittent welds are used to keep warpage at a minimum. These supports are to be called C supports later on in the instructions.

For linial support five pieces of ³⁄₁₆″ x 15¾″ x 2″ angle iron are placed between and at the very edge of the C supports. These pieces are welded between the five equally spaced C supports in the very center of the blade.

Two pieces of angle iron ³⁄₁₆″ x 86″ x 2″ are welded lengthwise to the top and bottom edges of the blade. The angle iron must be notched out where the C supports hit it. This is done by grinding a groove in the angle iron to the distance necessary for the angle iron to rest on the edge of the blade with no interference from the C supports.

Cut ten pieces of angle iron ³⁄₁₆″ x 15¾″ x 2″ and center them between the angle iron at the edges of the blade and the angle iron in the center of the blade for support and secure with intermittent welds.

For the final bracing of the blade, cut six pieces of 2¹⁄₁₆″ x 2″ x ³⁄₁₆″ angle iron and place them equally spaced between the C braces and the very side edges of the blade.

After all the supports have been put into place make the edge of the blade stronger so it won't erode. Take bar stock 87″ x 4″ long and connect it to the very bottom of the blade so that an inch extends beyond the edge of the blade. Space the stock so that bolts will hold it to the blade without interfering with the supports. Using a ⁹⁄₁₆ drill, drill six holes in the place marked so that it penetrates both the stock and the blade. Tightly connect the blade with half inch bolts.

To make the pieces which connect the blade with the mounting bracket, take two disks 18″ in diameter and clamp them together one directly over the other. From the center of the disks take a compass and scribe a circle with a diameter of 18″. Divide this scribe circle into 24 equally spaced parts. Center punch the 24 equally spaced markings on the scribed circle. Using a ¾″ drill drill a hole every place you center punch on a scribe circle making sure the drill goes through both plates.

Before unclamping the two disks drill a ¹⁄₁₆″ hole through the center point. Unclamp the two disks. Take a scribe and set it for a radius of ¾″. From a center of a disk scribe the circle. With an oxy-acetylene torch cut the scribed hole out of the plate. The other plate will be used in making the mounting bracket. Take a pin 1½″ x 5″ x 1½″ and a pipe 1½″ x 3″ x 1½″ which slides freely over the pin. Put the pipe aside with the other disk for later use. Using the disk with the cut hole in the center place the pin in it, making sure it is flush to the surface of the disk on one end.

Make sure the pin is perpendicular to the surface of the disk. Reverse weld the pin to the disk.

Take a piece of cold rolled steel ⅜″ x 6″ x 8″ and cut a 6″ radius on one of the ends.

Now take a scribe and draw an arc with the same radius as the disk on the opposite side of the previous arc cut on that piece. Weld the plate just made to the disk with the pin in it. Place the blade of the plow so that it is perpendicular to the floor. Take the disk and place it on the top edge of the blade so that the center of the blade is directly beneath the center of the disk. Make sure the plate is facing the back of the plow where the bracing is. Have the disk parallel to the floor so it is 90° to the blade. Now weld the disk to the blade.

Put angle iron braces from the plate attached to the disk to the braces on the back of the blade.

CONSTRUCTION OF MOUNTING BRACKET

Take one piece of ⅛″ tubing 3″ x 3″ x 27″ and two pieces of ⅛″ tubing 3″ x 3″ x 31″, on the longer pieces cut two ends with 25 degree angles and two ends with 65 degree angles. Weld the two pieces so that the two 25 degree faces are welded facing each other. The two ends with 65° cuts get welded to the smaller piece of tubing.

On the two pieces of cold rolled steel ⅜″ x 23″ x 2½″ mark off from one end three lines each two inches apart. In the center of these lines drill three ¾″ holes in each piece of stock. After the holes have been drilled bend the

stock. From the edge of the bar where the measurements for the holes were taken, mark off a line 8½″ on both bars and bend a 45° angle on both bars. On the 8½″ line make a 45° bend on both bars. Now they are ready to be welded to the triangle.

Measure and cut out a tapered piece.

Weld the side opposite the holes to the outside face of the smaller piece of square tubing in the triangle. Refer to blueprint for more detail.

Take a piece of ³⁄₁₆″ cold rolled steel 14½″ x 14½″. After the plate is constructed weld it over the connection of the two 77° faces of the triangle.

For extra strength a piece of square tubing 2¼″ x 2″ x 23¼″ is welded between the cold roll bars and the surface of the plate just constructed. The tubing is fit between the bars as close to the 45° bend as possible and 2″ away from the edge of the plate. The angle on the tubing is 45° to the plate and 45° between the bars. The tubing is welded securely to both the bar and the plate.

Bring out the pipe and disk set aside before while constructing the blade. Using a scribe, scratch the diameter of the pipe from the center point that was drilled out in the middle of the disk. Cut this hole out. Weld the pipe to the disk so one end is flush to the disk on one side. Make sure it is perpendicular to the surface of the disk. This must fit over the pin on the other disk.

On the center line of the plate mark a line from the tip of the triangle 9″ in. Using a scribe scratch a circle the same diameter of the pipe which slid over the pin on the blade. With an oxyacetylene torch cut the hole through the plate and the tubing so the pipe will fit through it. Weld the pipe in the hole securely to the triangle. Also weld the disk to the bottom pieces of the triangle. Make sure you check the blueprint before welding so everything is properly fitted.

On the two sides of the square tubing, where the bar stock is welded, there must be holes drilled. The holes are ¾″ in diameter. On the bar stock draw a 4″ square, find the center of the square and center punch it. Using a ¾″ drill, drill one hole on each side of the tubing. Mark the face of the smallest square pieces of tubing that is opposite the disk. This is shown on the blueprint with two holes in it. The holes are 2″ x 2″ and are 1″ from all three sides. Cut out by a torch. This is so the alloy pins which go through the holes in the side can be tightened down to the mounting bracket.

Connect the mounting bracket and the blade together by slipping the pin on the blade into the pipe on the mounting bracket. To secure them together slip the bolts through the holes in the disks and tighten the nuts. To change the blade to a desired angle remove the bolts and rotate the blade until the angle desired, then replace the bolts and nuts.

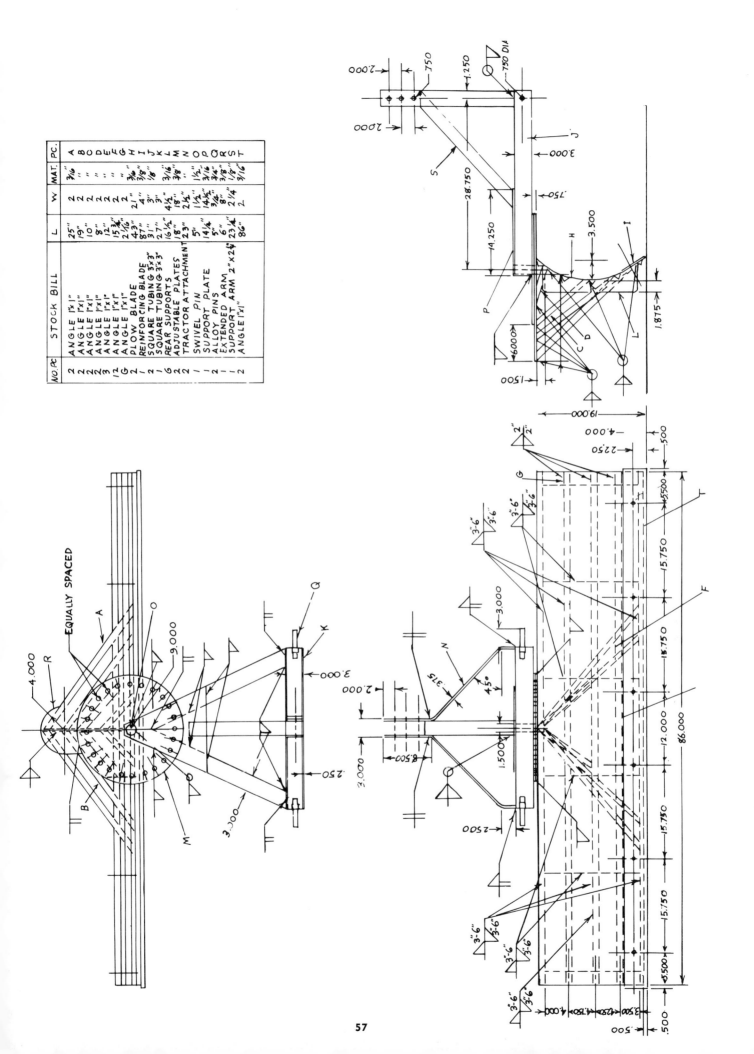

NO.PC	STOCK BILL	L	W	MAT.	PC.
2	ANGLE 1"x1"	25"	2	3/16	A
2	ANGLE 1"x1"	19"	2	"	B
2	ANGLE 1"x1"	10"	2	"	C
2	ANGLE 1"x1"	8"	2	"	D
3	ANGLE 1"x1"	12"	2	"	E
12	ANGLE 1"x1"	15 3/4"	2	"	F
G	ANGLE 1"x1"	2 1/16"	21"	3/16	H
2	PLOW BLADE	4.3"	4"	3/8	I
1	REINFORCING BLADE	87"	3"	1/8	J
1	SQUARE TUBING 3"x3"	31"	3"	"	K
6	SQUARE TUBING 3"x3"	27"	4 1/2"	3/16	L
2	REAR SUPPORTS	16 1/2"	18"	3/8	M
2	ADJUSTABLE PLATES	18"	2 1/2"	"	N
2	TRACTOR ATTACHMENT	23"			O
1	SWIVEL PIN	5"	1 1/2"	1 1/2	P
1	SUPPORT PLATE	14 1/4"	14 1/2"	1/2	Q
2	ALLOY PINS	5"	3/4"	3/4	R
2	EXTENDED ARM	6"	8"	3/8	S
1	SUPPORT ARM 2"x24"	23 3/4"	2 1/4"	1/8	T
2	ANGLE 1"x1"	86"	2	3/16	

57

SECTION B
TABLE OF CONTENTS
HOME AND RECREATIONAL

The Incinerator

Author: Stephen W. Savoie
       Jerry A. Joiner
Instructor: William Foster
School: Hammond Area Voc. School
City & State: Hammond, LA

1. The **bonnet** is a cover made from a half section of 10″ x 12″ pipe with a strap 1″ x 2″ welded on each side to the stack pipe. The purpose of the bonnet is to keep water out of the incinerator.
2. The **damper rod** is a ⅜″ hot roll rod 16″ long. The rod is bent at a 90° angle so that one side is 8″ long and the other 8″ long. Purpose is to open and close the damper.
3. The **damper** is a circle made from a ¼″ plate 6⅜″ in diameter. Opposite sides ground at a 45° angle. Purpose is to regulate fire in incinerator.
4. The **mesh screen** is a circle made from a ³⁄₁₆″ mesh 6½″ in diameter. The mesh screen fits on the inside of the stack pipe to keep burning ashes from escaping.
5. The **stack pipe** is a 7″ standard pipe 2′ long. The stack is to draw smoke from the incinerator.
6. The **hinges** (2), 1³⁄₁₆″ x 5″ x ¼″, (2) 1″ x 3″ x ¼″, are cone shaped for opening and closing lid.
7. **Top back half** of lid is made of ⅜″ plate with five sides. Two sides 8″ at a 78° angle and two sides 12″ at a 51° angle and one side 2′2″ at a 180°. Also this plate has a 6½″ diameter circle cut out for the stack.
8. **Sleeves** (2), 2″ x 2″ x 1″ with ¾″ hole, cut to a 51° angle. Purpose is to hold grate shaker rod in place.
9. **Grate handle**, rod of ¾″ hot roll 7½″ x 30″. The grate handle is bent 90° angle at 7½″. Purpose is to shake the grate so that ashes will fall into drawer.
10. **Lid** made of ³⁄₁₆″ plate with 6 sides. Two sides 4″ at a 13½° angle, three sides 12″ at a 51° angle, and one side 2′2″ at a 180° angle. Purpose for this lid is to open and close the incinerator.
11. **Lid weather stripping**, 1″ x 45″ x ³⁄₁₆″. Strip bent to fit around lid. Purpose is to keep water from getting into incinerator.
12. **Gutter**, 1¼″ x 2′2″ x ³⁄₁₆″. A piece of angle iron is cut to fit at the base of the lid to catch any water entering the incinerator from the lid.
13. **Lid handle**, ½″ hot roll 9″ long. Lid handle bent 1½″ on each side leaving 6″ for handle.
14. **Shell**, six of the seven sides are of ¼″ plate 1′ x 3′. Two of the six sides are grooved out so water will drain out from the gutter. The seventh side is made of ¼″ plate 1′ x 2′ (front).
15. **Back Baffle** was designed by using balsa wood to scribe a template. Back baffle are 7″ x 7″ x 5¾″ x 7″ x 5¾″ x ¼″. The plate is placed at a 45° angle so that the ashes will fall down the baffle into the ash collection drawer.
16. **Side baffle,** was designed by using balsa wood, to scribe a template. Side baffle are 2 pieces measured 2½″ x 9″ x 12″ x 14″ x 4″ x 24″ x ¼″ placed at a 45° angle, so that the ashes will fall into the collection drawer.
17. **Grate,** 1¼″ x 19″ x ³⁄₁₆″ strips with 1″ spacing. Front half of the grate is 7″ wide and back half of grate is 6″, so that grate will pivot and ashes will fall into drawer.
18. **Weather stripping,** two pieces of ¼″ strips 1¼″ x 2¼″ x 2⅝″ x 1½″. One piece of ¼″ strip 1½″ x 12″ x 1½″ x 13″ strips were cut on a 45° angle. Purpose to keep water out of the drawer.
19. **Guide bars** (2), ¾″ x 22″ x ½″. Guides drawer in and out of the incinerator.
20. **Lighter hole cover,** 2′ x 2½″ cut at a 45° angle to keep water out of the lighter hole.
21. **Lighter hole,** 1¾″ in diameter. Used for lighting trash.
22. **Legs,** 3″ pipe 6″ long. Each end cut at a 45° angle in the same direction for support of the incinerator.
23. **Grate Handle nut,** 1″ nut used for a stop to keep grate handle from sliding out.
24. **Ventilation holes,** 1″ x 8″ strip cut out of the bottom of the incinerator. Purpose to allow air to get to flame.
25. **Bottom plate,** hexagon shape plate. Each side has 12″ measurements.
26. **Leg pads,** 3 pads of ¼″ plate cut to 6″ diameter for balance of the incinerator.
27. **Back handle,** 1″ x 4″ x ¼″ used to lift drawer for disposing of ashes.
28. **Back plate,** 8″ x 11¾″ x ⅛″ used for bottom of drawer.
29. **Bottom plate,** 11¾″ x 22″ x ⅛″ used for bottom of drawer.
30. **Side Plate,** 2 pieces 8″ x 22″ x ⅛″ used for sides of drawer.
31. **Grate rest,** 5½″ x ¼″ used as a rest for the grate, when in the down position.
32. **Front plate,** 12″ x 13″ x ³⁄₁₆″ used as the front of the drawer.
33. **Drawer Weather Strip,** 1½″ x 12″ x ³⁄₁₆″ used to keep water from getting into the incinerator. The two side strips are cut on the contour of the incinerator.
34. **Drawer Handle,** ½″ hot roll rod 9″ long. The rod was bent at each end 1½″ leaving 6″ for the handle for opening and closing the drawer.

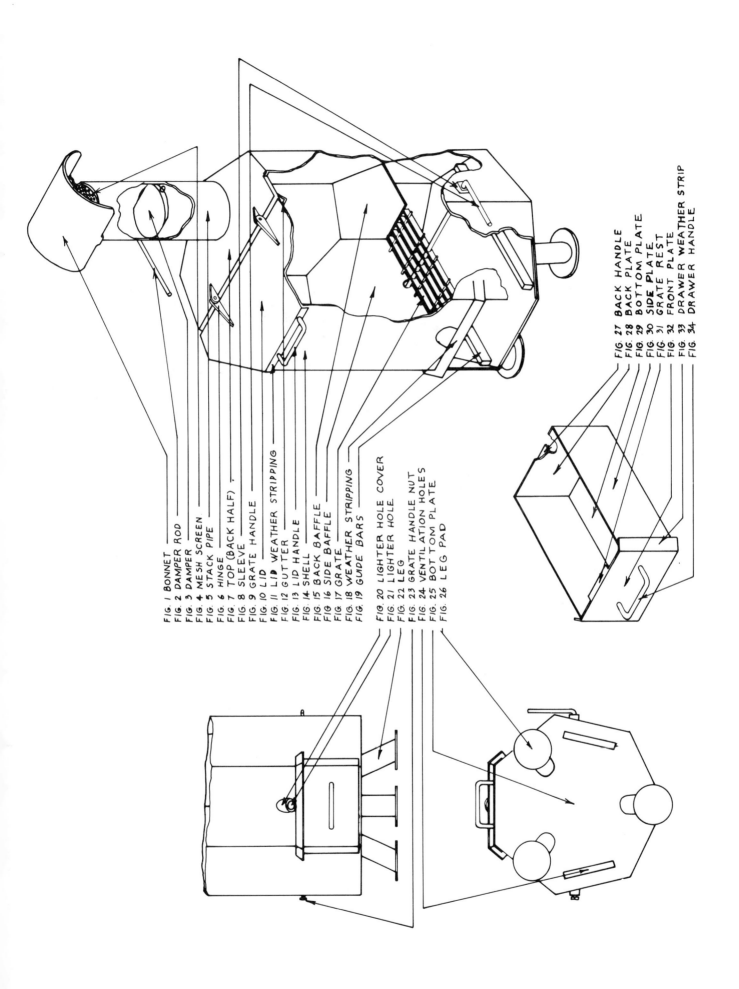

FIG. 1 BONNET
FIG. 2 DAMPER ROD
FIG. 3 DAMPER
FIG. 4 MESH SCREEN
FIG. 5 STACK PIPE
FIG. 6 HINGE
FIG. 7 TOP (BACK HALF)
FIG. 8 SLEEVE
FIG. 9 GRATE HANDLE
FIG. 10 LID
FIG. 11 LID WEATHER STRIPPING
FIG. 12 GUTTER
FIG. 13 LID HANDLE
FIG. 14 SHELL
FIG. 15 BACK BAFFLE
FIG. 16 SIDE BAFFLE
FIG. 17 GRATE
FIG. 18 WEATHER STRIPPING
FIG. 19 GUIDE BARS

FIG. 20 LIGHTER HOLE COVER
FIG. 21 LIGHTER HOLE
FIG. 22 LEG
FIG. 23 GRATE HANDLE NUT
FIG. 24 VENTILATION HOLES
FIG. 25 BOTTOM PLATE
FIG. 26 LEG PAD

FIG. 27 BACK HANDLE
FIG. 28 BACK PLATE
FIG. 29 BOTTOM PLATE
FIG. 30 SIDE PLATE
FIG. 31 GRATE REST
FIG. 32 FRONT PLATE
FIG. 33 DRAWER WEATHER STRIP
FIG. 34 DRAWER HANDLE

Fabrication of Spiral Staircase

Authors:	*Mark G. Cornick*
	Keith B. Spanhut
Instructor:	*F. Goldman*
School:	*Southeastern Community College*
City & State:	*S. Burlington, IA*

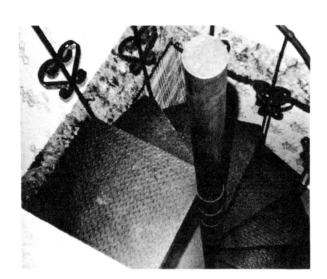

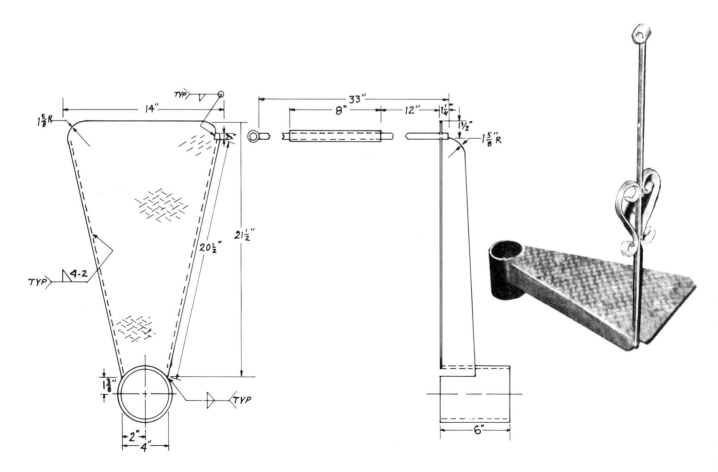

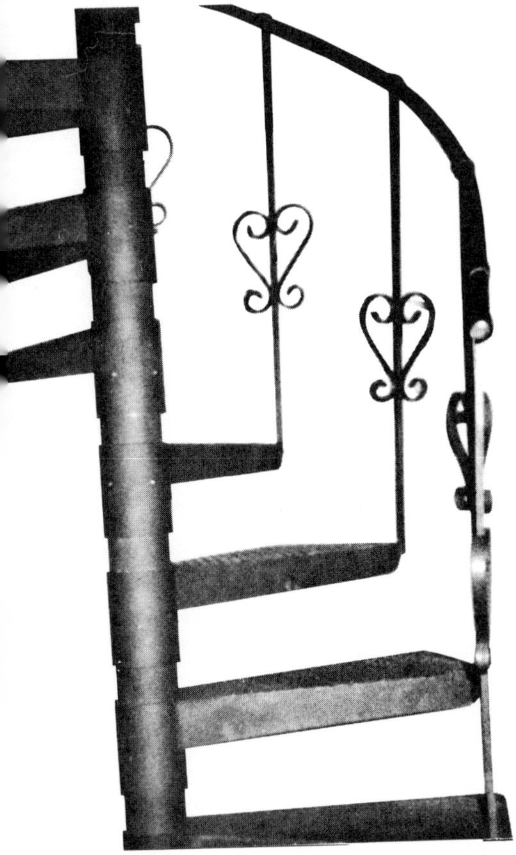

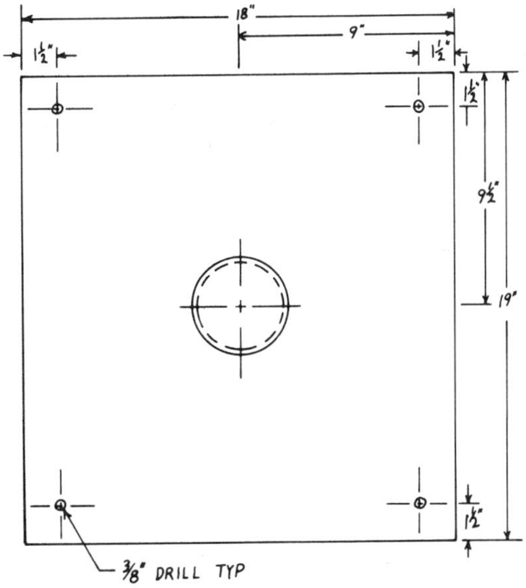
18"
9"
1½"
1½"
1½"
9½"
19"
1½"
3/8" DRILL TYP

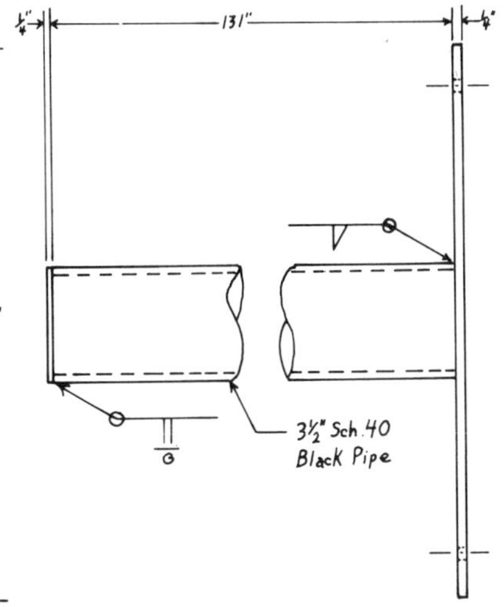
¼"
131"
¼"
3½" Sch. 40
Black Pipe

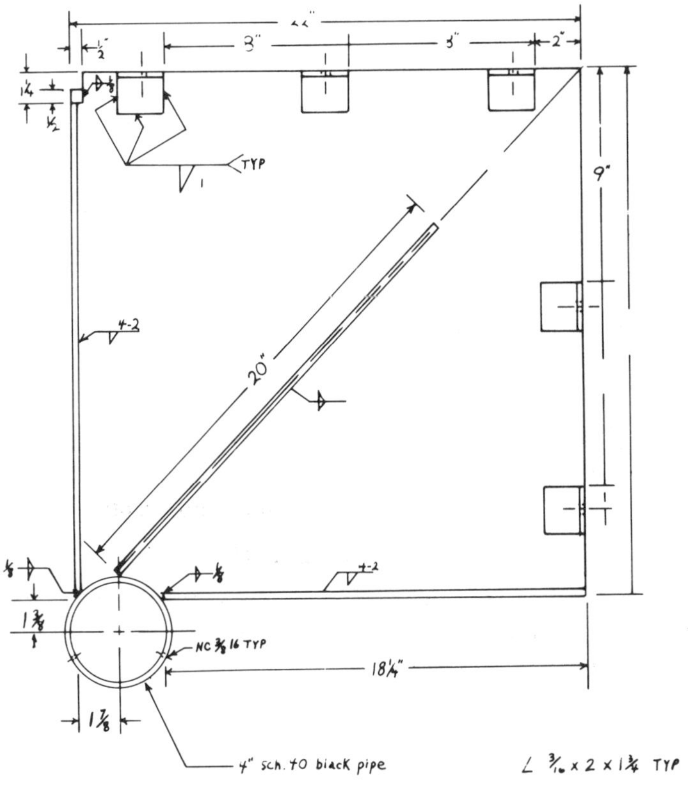
3"
3"
2"
½
1¼
½
TYP
9"
4-2
20"
4-2
1⅜
NC ⅜ 16 TYP
18¼"
1⅞
4" sch. 40 black pipe
∠ 3/16 x 2 x 1¾ TYP

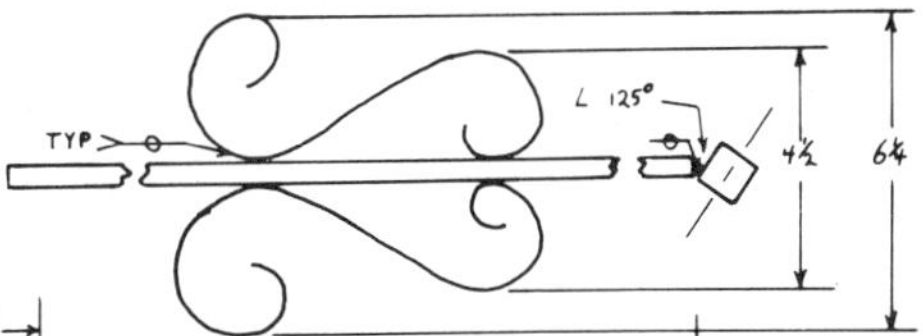
TYP
∠ 125°
4½
6¼

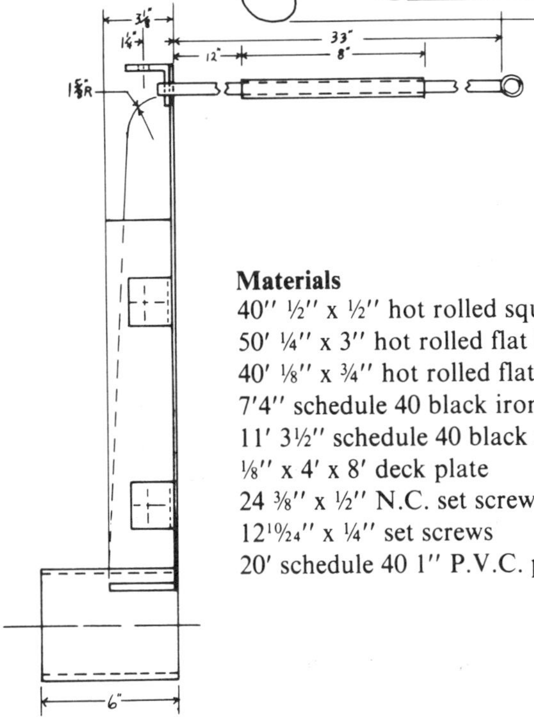
3⅛
1¼"
33"
12"
8"
1⅝R
6"

Materials

40′′ ½′′ x ½′′ hot rolled square stock
50′ ¼′′ x 3′′ hot rolled flat bar
40′ ⅛′′ x ¾′′ hot rolled flat bar
7′4′′ schedule 40 black iron pipe
11′ 3½′′ schedule 40 black iron pipe
⅛′′ x 4′ x 8′ deck plate
24 ⅜′′ x ½′′ N.C. set screws
12 10/24′′ x ¼′′ set screws
20′ schedule 40 1′′ P.V.C. pipe

A Crane or Small Boat Davit

Author: B. Scott
Instructor: C. Furtek
School: Middle Bucks Voc-Tech
City & State: Samison, PA

This unit is a Portable Crane consisting of the Fabricated Boom with Winch Mounting Pad, a Column of Schedule 40-2½″ steel pipe and two Fabricated Brackets permanently mounted on the wood bulkhead.

The fabricated boom consists of top and bottom stringers of ¼″ steel plate, cheek pieces or webs of ⅛″ and winch seat and tip plates (for the sheave mount) of ¼″ plate. Formed into the boom at an angle of 120° is a section of 3″ steel pipe which telescopes over the pipe column. This arrangement allows full circle rotation.

All material was flame cut by hand, tack welded into place and finish welded. All exterior welds were ground and the unit primed and painted to resist salt atmosphere corrosion.

The winch is a single-reduction (5:1 ratio) commercial unit fitted with an extra long fabricated crank to give an average overall mechanical advantage of about 40:1.

The hoist cable is ³⁄₁₆″ diameter galvanized aircraft cable with a safety hook.

The brackets were fabricated from ¼″ plate and 3″ pipe sections.

Statistics:

Capacity: Estimated at 1 ton

Reach: 44″ center line of column to hook centerline

Weight of Boom: Approximately 60 pounds.

To launch and recover a thirteen foot "Boston Whaler" using a three-leg cable bridle. (Weight: approximately 500 pounds).

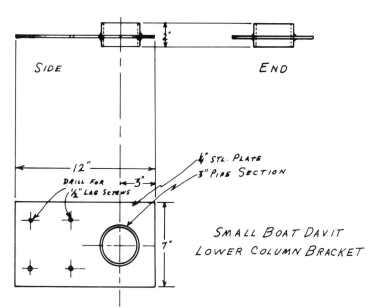

SIDE   END

12"

DRILL FOR
½" LAG SCREWS

3"

7"

¼" STL. PLATE
3" PIPE SECTION

SMALL BOAT DAVIT
LOWER COLUMN BRACKET

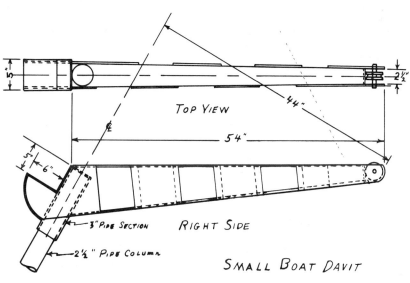

5"

TOP VIEW

44"

2½"

£

54"

5"

6"

3" PIPE SECTION

RIGHT SIDE

2½" PIPE COLUMN

SMALL BOAT DAVIT

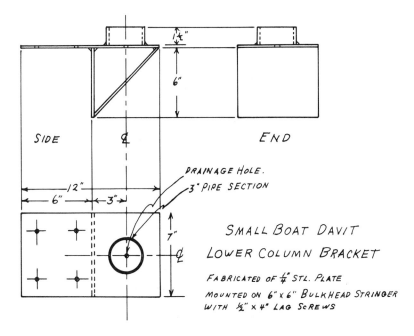

SIDE   £   END

1¼"

6"

12"

6"   3"

DRAINAGE HOLE.
3" PIPE SECTION

7"

£

£

SMALL BOAT DAVIT
LOWER COLUMN BRACKET

FABRICATED OF ¼" STL. PLATE
MOUNTED ON 6" x 6" BULKHEAD STRINGER
WITH ½" x 4" LAG SCREWS

Fireplace Log Holder

Author: Thomas David Kuma
Instructor: John Pilszak
School: South High Vocational School
City & State: Pittsburgh, PA

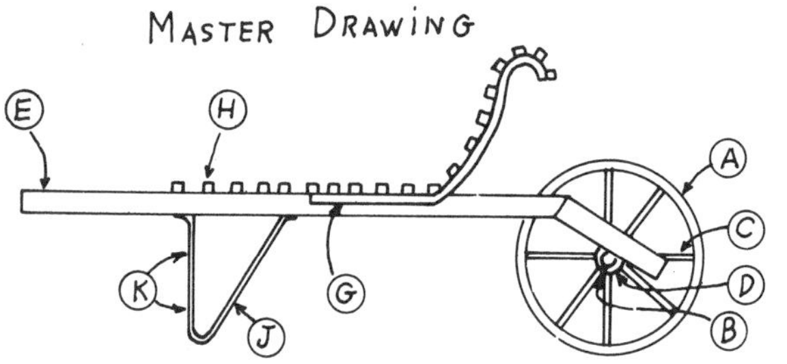

MASTER DRAWING

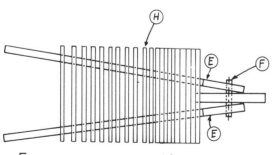

FIREPLACE LOG HOLDER
ASSEMBLY

The handles on this wheel barrow log holder are made from discarded square tubing. They can be made from other material such as small diameter pipe, conduit, bar stock or whatever you may find in your garage or elsewhere.

Detail (G) can be bent any shape to suit the individual taste.

This log holder is painted with flat lamp black paint.

Material Needed

1 piece scrap steel pipe	8″ dia. x 1″ wide
1 piece scrap steel pipe	1″ dia. x 1¼″ long
8 pieces scrap steel bar stock	⅜″ dia. x 3⅞″ long
2 pieces scrap steel band iron	⅛″ x 1″ x 1¾″
1 piece scrap steel bar stock	¾″ dia. x 4½″ long
2 pieces scrap steel square tubing	0.35 wall. x 1″ square 33″ long
2 pieces scrap steel bar stock	⅜″ x ⅜″ x 18″ long
19 pieces scrap steel bar stock	⅜″ x ⅜″ x 14″ long
2 pieces scrap steel band iron	⅛″ x 1″ x 15″
2 pieces scrap steel band iron	⅛″ x ¾″ x 10″

Instructions for assemblying fireplace log holder

1. Cut all details as shown on page 2.
2. Assemble detail (B) in center of (A) space detail's (C) equally to form spokes for a wheel, tack weld where necessary.
3. Cut and form detail (D) and (E), assemble and tack weld (D) to (E) to hold the axle as shown on master drawing.
4. Cut and form (J) assemble (J) to (E) as shown on main drawing 12″ from rear of wheel barrow, weld where necessary.
5. Cut and form detail (G) and assemble to (E) as shown on master drawing, and tack weld.
6. Place (A-B-C) assembly between two (E) details, install detail (F) through (C).
7. Cut details (H) and assemble (H) on details (E) with 1″. spacing as shown on master drawing, weld wherever necessary.
8. Detail (K) is optional, depending on the individual taste.
9. Clean and paint log holder with flat lamp black paint, or any other color scheme to suit the surroundings.

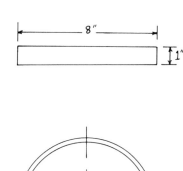

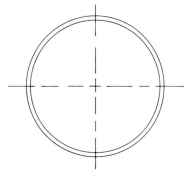

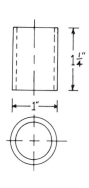

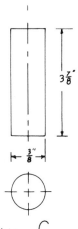

DETAIL A
WHEEL RIM
8" Ø STEEL PIPE X 1"
AMOUNT REQUIRED 1

DETAIL B
WHEEL HUB
1" x 1¼" STEEL PIPE
AMOUNT REQUIRED 1

DETAIL C
WHEEL SPOKES
⅜" x 3⅞" STEEL BAR STOCK
AMOUNT REQUIRED 8

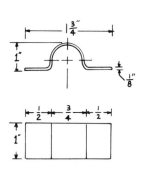

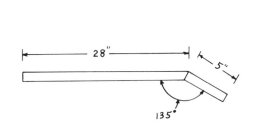

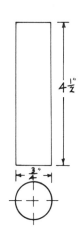

DETAIL D
AXLE BRACKET'S
⅛" x 1" x 1¾" STEEL BAND IRON
AMOUNT REQUIRED 2

DETAIL E
HANDLE BARS
0.35 x 1 x 33 STEEL TUBING
AMOUNT REQUIRED 2

DETAIL F
WHEEL AXLE
¾" x 4½" STEEL BAR STOCK
AMOUNT REQUIRED 1

The Steer

Author:	R. Mattson
Instructor	B. Keffeler
School:	Canada Junior College
City & State:	Redwood City, CA

Forehead and Jaws

Materials
2 pieces steel plate, ⅛″ x 3½″ x 7″ (forehead)
2 pieces steel plate ⅛″ x 6″ x 7″ (jaws)

Step 1 Arc Weld the pieces of 3½″ x 7″ steel plates together at 100-110 amps. Cut outside edges to form the angles of the eyes on the beverly shear. Sketch all lines on steel plate with a metal scriber or chalk.

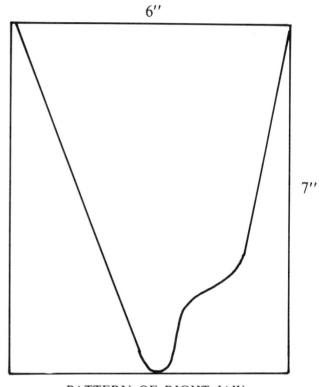

6″

7″

PATTERN OF RIGHT JAW

Step 2 Follow in the same manner, by sketching the outline pattern of the jaw. Use the two pieces of ⅛″ x 6″ x 7″ steel plate for the jaws.

Note: Reverse the paper pattern for the left jaw.

Step 3 After cutting both jaws, arc weld them to the forehead. Weld at 100 amps, set aside for later use.

7″

7″

FOREHEAD PATTERN

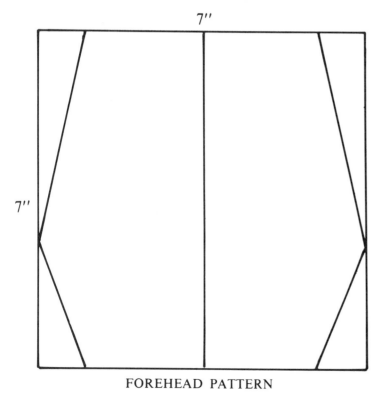

Horns

Materials:

2 pieces steel plate, ⅛″ x 5″ x 8″

Step 4 Cut outside edge to form the angle of the horn.

Note: Reverse paper pattern for the right horn.

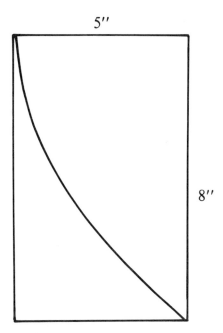

5″

8″

LEFT HORN PATTERN

Forging

Step 5 Heat the jaws in the forge until a cherry red color is obtained. Grasp the forehead with metal tongs. Form the jaws on the horn of the anvil with ball peen hammer. Repeat until jaws form a smooth blending circle. A gap underneath of 3″ is left between the jaw pieces. It will be added later with steel plate.

Step 6 Heat forehead, wait until metal is cherry red. Form a ridge down the middle of the forehead. Add lumps for each eye socket top. Cool and set aside.

Step 7 Heat both horns in the forge next. Wait until horn metal is cherry red. Form the metal over the horn of the anvil at first. For a sharper point construction, pound the two edges together on the face of the anvil. Forge until it is a slender cone with a bottom diameter of 1½″.

Step 8 Repeat for other horn, cool and set aside for later use.

Construction of head

Materials:

2 pieces steel plate, ⅛″ x 3″ x 5″ (side plates)
2 pieces strap, ⅛″ x 2⅜″ x 6″ (eyes)
1 piece steel plate, ⅛″ x 5″ x 6″ (back)
1 piece steel plate, ⅛″ x 4″ x 5″ (inner plate)
1 piece steel plate, ⅛″ x 3″ x 7″ (under jaw)
1 piece steel plate, ⅛″ x 6″ x 7″ (under head)
4 pieces angle iron, ⅜″ x 3″ (teeth, supports)

Step 9 First work is on the forehead. A ⅛″ x 3″ x 5″ piece of steel plate is cut at the angle shown below. Place side plate behind the future place of the eye hole. Tack weld the side place at 110 amps in this position below.

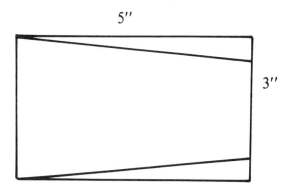

5″

3″

69

Step 10 Repeat for other side

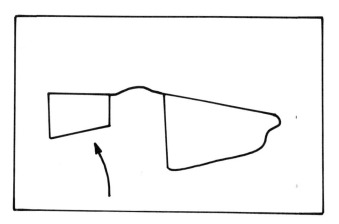

SIDE PLATE POSITION

Step 11 The eyes are next. The natural eye hole is oval-shaped and at an angle. The use of ⅜″ metal strap is needed. Bend strap to pattern below.

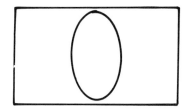

STRAP PATTERN

Step 12 Fit the oval strap into the lump on the forehead forged earlier. Tack weld into position at 120 amps. Fill in gaps around the eye with small pieces of ⅛″ steel plate.

Step 13 Repeat for other side.

Step 14 The back of the head should be cut out as follows on the beverly shear.

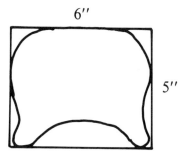

HEAD PATTERN

Step 15 Arc weld the back onto the rear of the forehead and side plates at 100 amps. This adds strength to the head.

Step 16 To prevent warpage during future arc welding, add an inner plate behind the jaws. Cut the ⅛″ x 4″ x 5″ steel plate on the beverly shear to fit the cirlce right behind the jaws. It will look like this below.

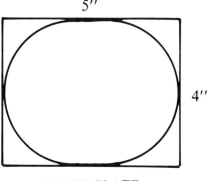

INNER PLATE

Step 17 Cut ⅛″ x 3″ x 7″ steel plate to fit gap underneath the jaws. Follow this pattern.

Note: Cut V into the end to conform with jaw tips.

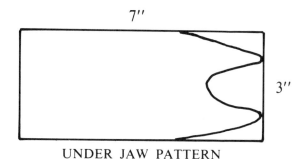

UNDER JAW PATTERN

Step 18 Weld entire jaw section together to form one unit. Fill in any gaps with one-eighth inch steel plate when holes exist.

Step 19 Fill in remaining hole that is between the eyes and the back of the head underneath the head. Use single piece of one-eighth inch steel plate that measures 6″ x 7″. Weld at 100 amps, fill any holes that are present.

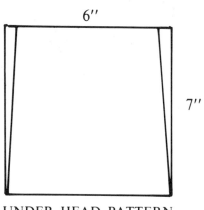

UNDER HEAD PATTERN

Step 20 Arc weld at 100 amps the ¾″ angle iron. Four pieces of three inches each are used for rear supports and teeth. The teeth are left straight, the rear supports are bent as shown in the picture on the following page.

Step 21 Weld horns to upper corner of the side plates near the back of the head.
Future welding will blend these into the head.

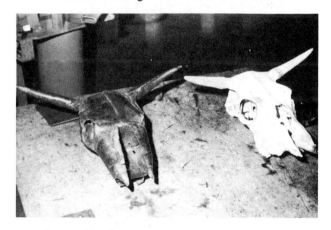

Applying the Beads

The use of ⅛″ steel plate to give a good foundation for the arc welding beads. At 130 amps, the beads put side by side has a beautiful effect on the finished product.

Step 22 Use E7014 Rod at 130 amps. Start on the top of the forehead near the horns.
Starting the beads.

Step 23 Continue the beads down straight towards the jaw. During the process of covering the surface with welding beads, stop to cool off head, and chip slag off the welds.

Step 24 Wire buff occasionally so the job will not be big when finished.

Step 25 Follow the curve of the horn with welding beads at a right angle to the forehead beads. This gives the steer head a contrast of different flowing bead directions.

Step 26 Weld the teeth and rear supports into the general welding scheme.

Step 27 Chip slag off final welds, then wire buff to highest luster.

Step 28 Lacquer to preserve luster.

Step 29 Drill holes through the rear supports, attach wire between the two holes. The finished project is ready for hanging on a stable wall.

MATERIALS NEEDED

forehead (2)	⅛″ steel plate	3½″ x 7″
Jaw (2)	⅛″ steel plate	6″ x 7″
Side Plate (2)	⅛″ steel plate	3″ x 5″
Eye (2)	⅜″ x ⅛″ metal strap	4″ long
Inner plate (1)	⅛″ steel plate	4″ x 5″
Under jaw (1)	⅛″ steel plate	3″ x 7″
Under head (1)	⅛″ steel plate	6″ x 7″
Horns (2)	⅛″ steel plate	5″ x 8″
Hanging wire (1)	⅛″ round	8″ long

The Universal Goal

Author:	*W. Abrams*
Instructor:	*D. Crosby*
School:	*Western State College of Colorado*
City & State	*Gunniston, CO*

The Universal Goal was designed and fabricated for the Physical Education Department. The main reason for having it built was because of the extremely high price of athletic equipment. Having a Universal goal that can perform several practical uses seemed to be well worth the time and cost of the materials for its development.

The Universal goal is manufactured with 1¼″ and 1″ black pipe. Black pipe was used instead of galvanized pipe or angle iron because it was felt that by bending the pipe it would add to the esthetic beauty and overall strength. The pipe was bent with a tube bender and all joints were swedged and ground to a close fit to aid in the welding process, because when joints aren't tightly fitted the pipe has gaps that are hard to fill.

The sides and front bridging were cut, fit and welded first. This aids the construction because most of the welds can be adequately performed "in position". The crossrails and support V's are added, then the handrails and the hook in the back for transportation: being pulled by a tractor. Add the wheels, and the main structure is completed. After putting on hurricane wire and paint your Universal Goal is completed.

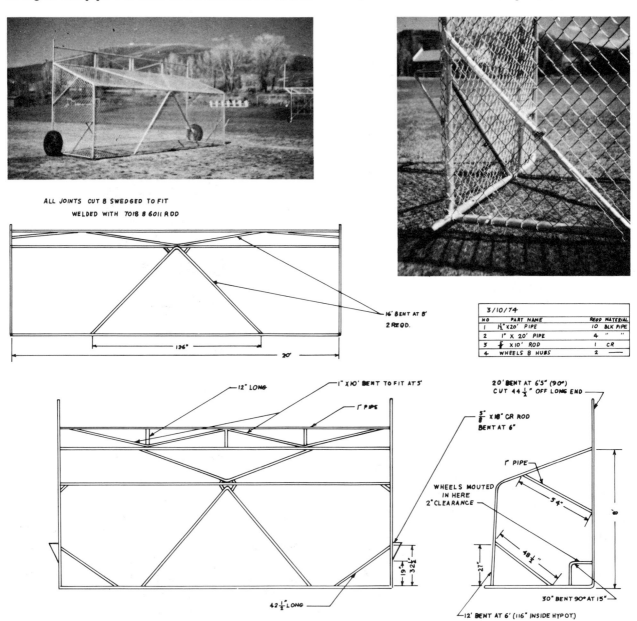

3/10/74			
NO	PART NAME	REQD	MATERIAL
1	1¼" X20' PIPE	10	BLK PIPE
2	1" X 20' PIPE	4	"
3	⅝ X10' ROD	1	CR
4	WHEELS B HUBS	2	

Octagonal Fireplace

Author: Danny E. Waddell
Instructor: R. R. McWhorter
School: S.E.K. Vocational-Technical School
City & State: Coffeyville, KS

The first step was to calculate dimensions and angles for each piece and to lay it out on the metal. All pieces were then cut with a hand cutting torch and ground with a hand grinder for smoothness.

Each part; the base, stem, body, cone, and damper was seperately fit together and welded. All assembled parts were then fit together and welded to form the structure. All welds were then ground for smoothness.

The opening was then cut and design of a log grate and doors were made.

The log grate was made of ⅜'' square steel bar. Each of the nine pieces were cut and ground. Seven of the pieces were heated and bent with a 1'' rise for the support legs and the log holders. All pieces were then fit together and welded.

The doors were made of wire mesh and 10 guage steel. The framework was made to fit the angles of the main structure. Wire mesh was then oxy-acetylene welded to the framework. Handles were then welded on and the doors were attached with hinges for easy access and opening.

The final step was painting. A primer coat was put on the entire fireplace, doors, and accessories. Then two coats of black hi-heat paint were added. The wire mesh was painted with gold hi-heat paint for accent.

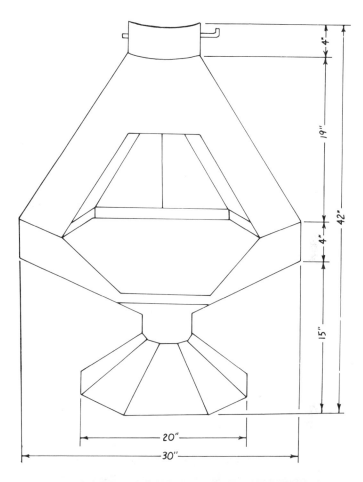

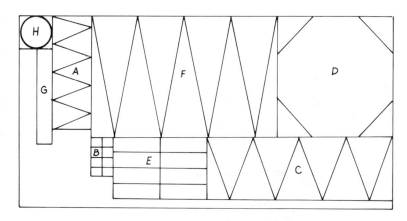

LAYOUT SKETCH   4'×8' SHEET 10 GA. METAL

PART A - BASE - 8 PIECES - 8'' X 10''
PART B - STEM - 8 PIECES - 2.5'' X 3''
PART C - BODY - 8 PIECES - 12'' X 16''
PART D - BODY - 1 PIECE - 30'' OCTAGON
PART E - BODY - 8 PIECES - 12'' X 4''
PART F - CONE - 8 PIECES - 12'' X 30''
PART G - DAMPER - 1 PIECE - 4'' X 24''
PART H - DAMPER - 1 PIECE - 8'' CIRCLE

Tri-Beds

Author: R. Myers
Instructor: K. Hillery
School: Central Arizona College
City & State: Coolidge, AZ

The beds were made out of square tubing, the corner posts are 2″ x 2″ x .065 and the rails are 1″ x 1″ x .065. The scrolls were made out of ¾″ x ⅛″ flat strap. The bottom bunk is welded together solid while the rails of the top bunk are bolted using ⁵⁄₁₆″ cap screws. Two inch ball bearings are used for the bed knobs.

The square tubing was cut to correct lengths and the ¾″ x ⅛″ flat strap cut and bent into scrolls before welding. All lay-out work was done before any welding or tacks were made. The rails were then squared and tacked together. The scrolls were added and tacked into place. The head and foot pieces were then squared and tacked. All welds were then completed and then ground or filed off flush.

The four pieces of 1″ x 1″ x ⅛″ angle iron were clamped to four pieces of ¾″ x ⅛″ flat strap, then drilled on five inch centers with a ²¹⁄₆₄″ bit. Two ⁵⁄₁₆″ nuts were then tacked to the strap and each strap numbered to correspond with the angle iron. The angle iron was then welded to the rails of the top bunk, and then marked and drilled on the corner posts. The plates with nuts were inserted inside the posts in alignment with the holes and then tacked.

The ball bearings were tacked to the 1½″ pipe on the inside, then welded to the 2″ x 2″ x⅛″ plates. The completed bed knob was then welded to the corner posts of the top bunk. The bed knobs for the bottom bunk were also welded in this manner except a guide was added so they could be inserted into the 2″ square tubing when the beds were used as twin beds.

Four guides were made by using a 6″ long piece of 2″ square tubing and cutting it lenthwise with an angle grinder using a ⅛″ disc. The guides were then welded back together to form a 1⅞″ square tube that would fit inside of the 2″ square tubing. One inch of the guide was sawed off and welded to the bed knobs of the bottom bunk. A ⅜″ hole was drilled into the upper part of the corner posts and a piece of ⅜″ cold rolled steel inserted and welded 1″ from the top so as to prevent the guides from falling all the way down inside the 2″ square tubing.

Materials

24 feet of 2″ x 2″ x .065 square tubing
   4 pieces 48″ long for corner posts of top bunk
   4 pieces 18″ long for corner posts of bottom bunk
   4 pieces 6″ long for the guides.
125 feet of 1″ x 1″ x .065 square tubing
   8 pieces 76″ long for rails
  12 pieces 36″ long for rails on head and foot of beds
   6 pieces 38″ long for slats to hold mattresses
  26 pieces 5″ long for spacers in rails
114 feet ¾″ x ⅛″ flat strap
  56 pieces 24″ long for scrolls
   4 pieces 6″ long for plates to hold top bunk
   8 2″ ball bearings
   8 pieces 1½″ pipe 1″ long
  12 pieces 2″ x 2″ x ⅛″ squares for bed knobs
   4 pieces 2″ x ⅜″ cold roll
   8 ⁵⁄₁₆ cap screws with nuts
   4 casters (any style)
Paint and Primer

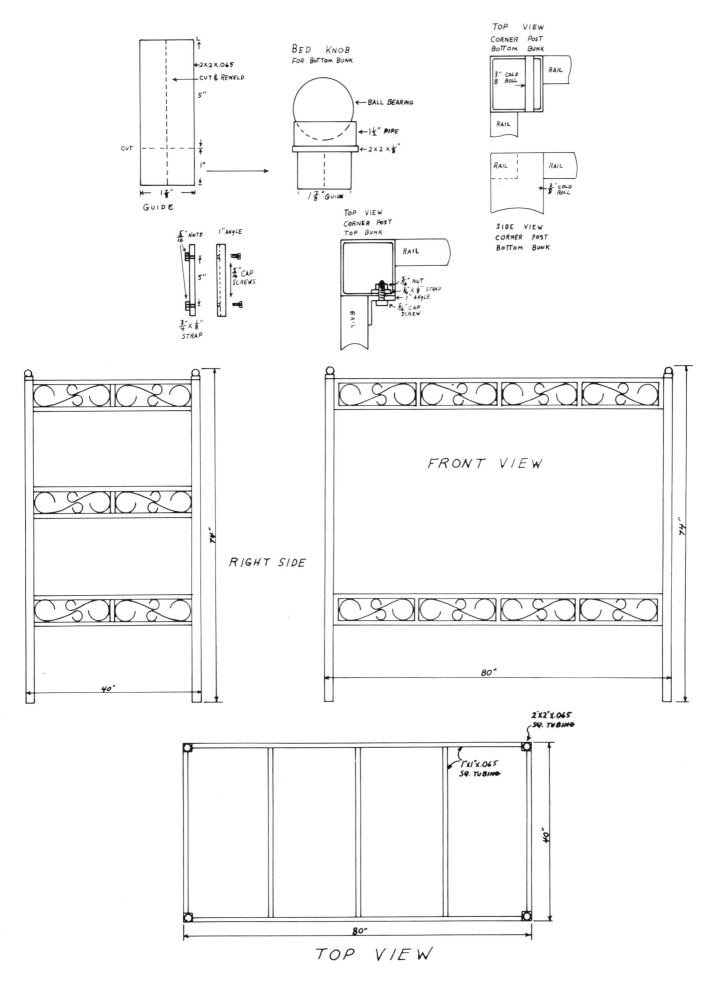

GUIDE

L
←2×2×.065
←CUT & REWELD
5"
CUT
1"
1 ¼"

BED KNOB
FOR BOTTOM BUNK

←BALL BEARING
←1½" PIPE
←2×2×⅛"
1 ⅞" GUIDE

TOP VIEW
CORNER POST
BOTTOM BUNK

⅜" COLD
8 ROLL
RAIL
RAIL

RAIL
RAIL
⅜" COLD
8 ROLL

SIDE VIEW
CORNER POST
BOTTOM BUNK

5/16" NUTS
1" ANGLE
5/16" CAP
SCREWS
5"
¾" × ⅛"
STRAP

TOP VIEW
CORNER POST
TOP BUNK

RAIL
5/16" NUT
¾" × ⅛" STRAP
1" ANGLE
5/16" CAP
SCREW
RAIL

RIGHT SIDE

74"
40"

FRONT VIEW

74"
80"

2"×2"×.065
SQ. TUBING
1"×1"×.065
SQ. TUBING

40"
80"

TOP VIEW

75

All Aluminum Multi-Purpose Pontoon

Authors: Noah Hall, Jr.
              Larry Gross
              John W. Tapio
              Ronald H. Caudill
              Rickey Caudill
Instructor: J. Calitri
School: Hazard State Vocational-Technical
              School
City & State: Hazard, KY

The portable pontoon boat is so constructed that it may be taken down and put together again in approximately 24 hours. It was built in this manner so it can be moved without special equipment or permits from one lake to another or from one region to another. This gives it a great economic advantage over other boats of this type.

General Specifications

In order to give the afore mentioned multi-purpose pontoon added dimension and capabilities, additional items will be added in complementing the excellent work done by the welding students.

In order to mobilize the unit, motor and steering units will be added to suit the owner's specifications. In order to make the multi-purpose pontoon more adaptable to all weather conditions, and for safety purposes, the cabin will be fully insulated and carpet added to the interior and exterior surfaces. Electrical outlets and power units will be made available so that the unit will be almost self-contained.

These added attractions should make for an elaborate flotation device with the addition of styrofoam in each of the pontoon units. Of course these attractions will not require the use of welding skill and technique but are merely listed to give the viewer a complete and thorough idea of what welding skills have made possible in the construction of such an elaborate recreational vehicle.

Approximate cost of pontoon construction, using surplus material, is $2500.

Quantity	Material	Description	Quantity	Material	Description
12	Aluminum Sheets ³⁄₁₆″ x 48″ x 144″	10-Pontoons 2′ x 2′ x 6′	15	Aluminum Pipe	Uprights Top Railing ⅛″ x 2″ x 34½″
8	Aluminum Sheets ³⁄₁₆″ x 48″ x 144″	Bottom Deck 12′ x 30′	2	Aluminum Pipe	Railings ⅛″ x 2″ x 16′
4	Aluminum Sheets ³⁄₁₆″ x 48″ x 144″	Top Deck 12′ x 16′	1	Aluminum Pipe	Railing ⅛″ x 2″ x 9′
			1	Aluminum Pipe	Railing ⅛″ x 2″ x 12′
3	Aluminum Sheets ³⁄₁₆″ x 48″ x 144″	Cover Cabin Sides 6½′ x 14′	39	Aluminum Plate	Floor Plates for Uprights ³⁄₁₆″ x 4½″ x 5″ to bolt railings to decks.
72′	Aluminum Skirting	Bottom Deck ³⁄₁₆″ x 4¼″ x 72′			
32′	Aluminum Skirting	Top Deck ³⁄₁₆″ x 6″ x 32′			

Note: All Bolts Stainless Steel

Quantity	Material	Description	Quantity	Material	Description
17	Aluminum H-Beams ¼″ x 3½″ x 4″ x 12′	Bottom Deck Foundation	272	Machine Bolts	Bolt Deck to Pontoons ⅜″ x 1¼″
9	Aluminum H-Beams ¼″ x 3½″ x 4″ x 12′	Top Deck Foundation	100	Flat Head Bolts	Bolts Deck Sections ⅜″ x 1¼″
14	Aluminum H-Beams ¼″ x 3½″ x 4″ x 12′	Cabin Frame Work	96	Machine Bolts	Bolts Railing to Bottom Deck ⅜″ x 1¼″
68	Aluminum Angle	Side Anchors ⅜″ x 3½″ x 4″ x 5″	60	Machine Bolts	Bolts Railing to Top Deck
4	Aluminum Plates	Tie-Ups ¾″ x 6″ x 2′, each with 3 - 1¼″ drilled holes	96	Machine Bolts	Blots Top to Sides and Sides to Deck ⅜″ x 1¼″
16	Aluminum Angle	Angle ¼″ x 1½″ x 1″ x 2′	28	Flat Head Bolts	Joins Front and Rear to Top Deck ⅜″ x 1¼″
32	Aluminum Angle	Angle ¼″ x 1½″ x 1″ x 13″	16	Machine Bolts	Joins Front and Rear to Bottom Deck ⅜″ x 1¼″
28	Aluminum Plate	Braces ³⁄₁₆″ x 3⅝″ x 6″	4	¼″ Plexiglass	Front Glass on each side of door 25 ⅜″ x 34 ⅜″ built in
12	Aluminum Plate	Gussets ³⁄₁₆″ x 12″ x 12″			
4	Aluminum Plate	Gussets ³⁄₁₆″ x 6″ x 6″	4	¼″ Plexiglass	Rear Glass on each side of door 25 ⅜″ x 34 ⅜″ built in
24	Aluminum Pipe	Uprights Bottom Railing ⅛″ x 2″ x 34½″	2	Aluminum Doors	¼″ x 32½″ x 46″ Plexiglas 3′ x 6′4″
4	Aluminum Pipe	Railings ⅛″ x 2″ x 15′	4	Windows	Aluminum Slide Windows 5′ x 2′
4	Aluminum Pipe	Railings ⅛″ x 2″ x 36′			

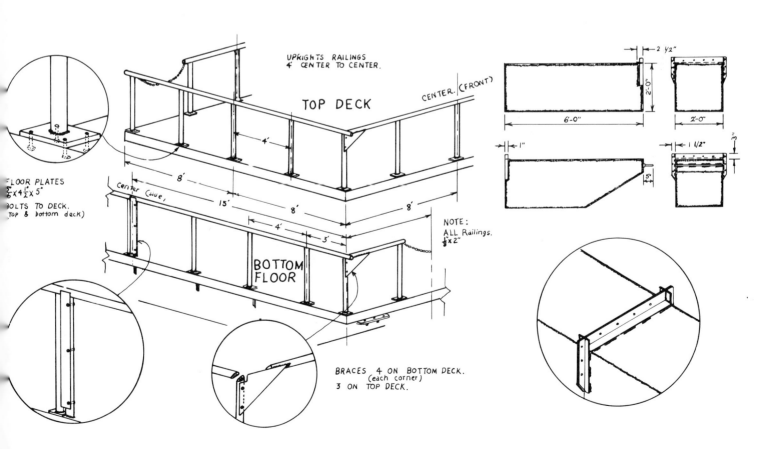

UPRIGHTS RAILINGS 4′ CENTER TO CENTER.

TOP DECK

CENTER (FRONT)

FLOOR PLATES ³⁄₁₆ x 4½ x 5″ BOLTS TO DECK. (TOP & bottom deck)

Center (side)

4′

8′

15′   8′   8′

4′   3′

BOTTOM FLOOR

NOTE: ALL Railings ⅛ x 2″

BRACES 4 ON BOTTOM DECK. (each corner) 3 ON TOP DECK.

2 ½″

6′-0″   2′-0″   2′-0″

1″   5″   1½″   3″

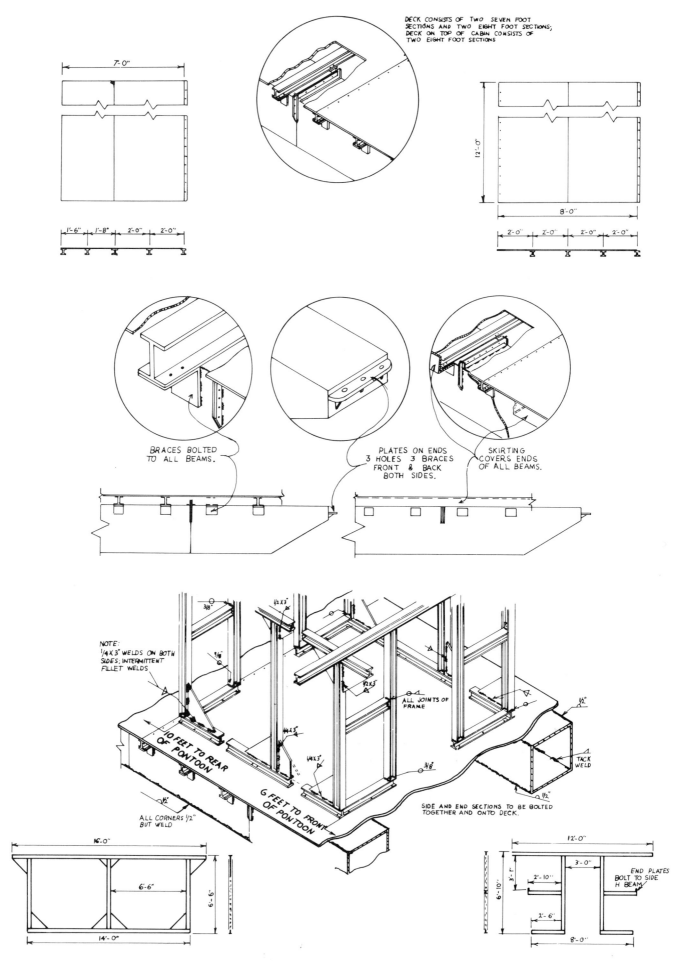

DECK CONSISTS OF TWO SEVEN FOOT SECTIONS AND TWO EIGHT FOOT SECTIONS; DECK ON TOP OF CABIN CONSISTS OF TWO EIGHT FOOT SECTIONS

7'-0"

12'-0"

8'-0"

1'-6" 1'-8" 2'-0" 2'-0"

2'-0" 2'-0" 2'-0" 2'-0"

BRACES BOLTED TO ALL BEAMS.

PLATES ON ENDS 3 HOLES 3 BRACES FRONT & BACK BOTH SIDES.

SKIRTING COVERS ENDS OF ALL BEAMS.

NOTE:
1/4 X 3" WELDS ON BOTH SIDES; INTERMITTENT FILLET WELDS

1/2 X 3"

3/8"

1/8"

1/2 X 3"

ALL JOINTS OF FRAME

1/2"

10 FEET TO REAR OF PONTOON

1/4 X 3"

1/4 X 3"

6 FEET TO FRONT OF PONTOON

3/8"

1/2"

TACK WELD

SIDE AND END SECTIONS TO BE BOLTED TOGETHER AND ONTO DECK.

1/2"

ALL CORNERS 1/2" BUT WELD

16'-0"

6'-6"

6'-6"

14'-0"

12'-0"

3'-0"

3'-1"

6'-10"

2'-10"

2'-6"

8'-0"

END PLATES BOLT TO SIDE H BEAM

78

The Phoenix

Authors: *Michael Kempf*
                                Don Giminarro
Instructor   *W. Branton*
School: *Mesa College*
City & State: *Grand Junction, CO*

The Phoenix became a stylized composite of the features of many birds. It has a swan's neck and body, a pheasant's ring, an eagle's claws and beak, a peacock's feather and a bird-of-paradise's tail and crown feathers. The wing spread we studied mostly from pelicans.

Construction and Mounting:

Structural strength was achieved quite easily by following the example of natural form, line and contour. Necessary considerations for supporting the bird's weight on the building all seemed to fall into place. The weight per size ratio was kept quite low by the structural openness—two men of average strength can lift the piece in spite of its 9½ x 11 foot dimensions.

The tail and leg joints act as the principle support structures, and the wings stabilize the piece and eliminate the need for cables and turn-buckles. The openness of the bird is also an advantage here in that it catches very little wind. There are eight points of attachment to the building in all. Only the very top ones extend through the wall as they are above the roof level. The remaining holds are five inch lags because the inside of the building is not accessible at their locations.

The ¾ inch bar forming the main lines of the body and neck were bent between tow trees after intermittent heating with oxy-acetylene torch. The lines to the sides of the neck are of ½ inch rod and were bent over, under and inside a heavy chunk of 8 inch pipe. The ¼ inch rods comprising the remainder of the lines other than the plate were bent by hand and by the use of home-made jigs with which we "mass-produced" the five principal feather patterns. Support feathers of the tail were cut from ⅛ inch plate and welded at approximate 20 degree angles to each other. Around and over them are the heart-shaped bird-of-paradise feathers. To the front of these is the single peacock feather which is kinetic and moves in the wind causing the chimes on the back of it to ring. As this feather is also of mild steel rod, there could be some danger of eventual metal fatigue, so the base of the feather is securely welded at its perimeter also.

The body is geodesic-like in its modular feather construction. The wings are ³⁄₁₆ inch plate at the back and ¼ inch rod at the front so that, as with most other parts of the bird, front and back are seen simultaneously. The beak and nose bone are made of plate also. A fantasy horn which sits behind the nose bone is a hand-screw from an old vise. Above it extend two plumes also cut from plate and perforated with the torch for delineation. Between the plumes is a "third-eye" of marble held in place by a ring that was heat-swelled around it. The other crown feathers are of ¼ inch rod and #9 wire for modular detail.

The legs are made from two-inch thin-wall tubing along the top to represent bone mass, and one inch check-pattern rebar to represent tendons. Stick electrode was used to carry out the check pattern over the tubing. Talons are of ¾ inch rebar with arc welded knuckles. The "thumbs" are held in place and adjustable by ½ inch bolts welded to the insides of the feet. They were constructed to allow firm clamping of the talons into the sign board as these are the only sign mounts.

The tongue is held in place by two spring steel wires that extend into the throat and allow the tongue to bob in the wind. **The Phoenix** has an egg. It is a white onyx egg appropriately placed and visible within the body. A hole was drilled into one end of the egg to fit snugly over the ¼ inch rod by which it is attached to the inner framework.

Accent colors throughout, and an effect of extended age, were achieved by the use of bronze, brass, copper, stainless steel and silver brazing rods, and by the fluxes and discoloration which resulted from the use of these. The final coloration over the entire bird was achieved by use of copper sulphate solution to cause accelerated rusting. A coat of spar varnish was applied to tone down the rust color and as a preservative.

The sign boards were hand-carved with raised gilt lettering — gold-leaf application. The wood that we chose has a close natural resemblance in color to black walnut, but is actually aged redwood planking that was taken up from the floor of a railway water-tower. The sign in the birds feet appears quite heavy but a man can lift it with one arm. Redwood was used also for blocks to hold the piece out from the building to avoid rust stains. A more durable wood for our climatic conditions cannot be found.

The Fabrication of a Spiral Staircase

Author:	M. Cornick
	K. Spanhut
Instructor:	F. Goldman
School:	Southeastern Community College
City & State:	W. Burlington, IA

The following staircase was fabricated for a two story house. The spiral staircase is fastened and supported at two points, the bottom and the top of the staircase. There are no supports under the stairs. This gives it the look of being free-standing and defying the law of gravity and is a very effective staircase.

The strength of the staircase, lies in the part of the 1″ lip above the treads and the 3″ lip below the bottom of the treads. The drawing and illustration of the lip shows the pressure points applied to the staircase. (Plate 2C)

The drawing on Plate 2 was transfered onto the 10 ga. mild steel. They were then cut accordingly. The curvature of the treads had to be very accurate because they form the shape of the outer side piece as to mating the pieces together for a sound weld. The treads were placed on their points on the outer side and tacked together. By rolling the tacked portion it inables the other treads to be tacked together also. The staircase started to become heavier as treads were added to it. This created the problem of rolling the metal. At this point a few strong men were needed to roll and hold the staircase for tack-ing the rest of the 13 treads. Plate 3B

The inner side however, could not be formed in the same manner as the outer side had been. The inner side had to be rolled through an 8′ rolling machine, capable of turning a piece into a 30″ diameter. The spiral was formed by rolling the strip of metal at an angle so that the horizontal part of the treads were running perpendicular to the roll. The strip was run through the machine until the diameter of the spiral was 30″, give or take an inch. Bolting the staircase to a beam in the shop at the correct height of 8′ 10½″, it will stretch to that dimension by its own weight. The piece is then placed and clamped into position according to the points layed out. It is then tacked into place. After the innner side is secure, the staircase can be lowered from the beam to put the finishing welds on.

After the tacking of the staircase was completed, the finishing weld was applied. Here the big problem of the heat from the weld might cause warping and change dimension of the spiral staircase, because of that, a short 3″ weld at 5″ intervals method was mandatory.

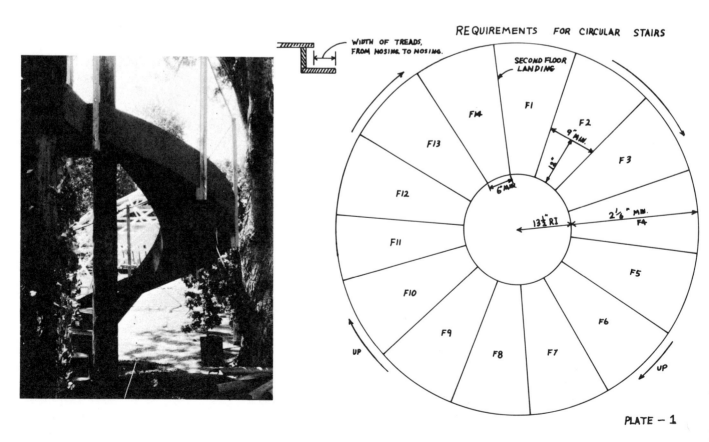

REQUIREMENTS FOR CIRCULAR STAIRS

PLATE – 1

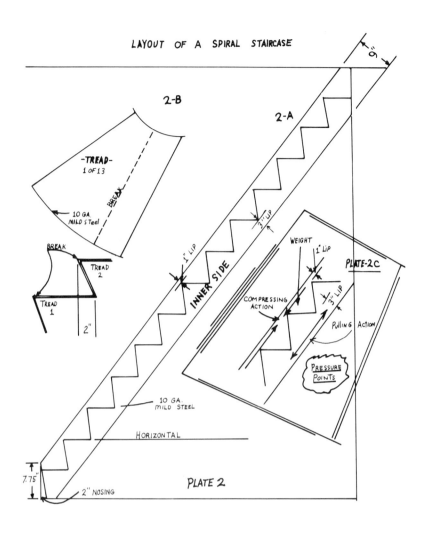

9"

2-B

2-A

-TREAD-
1 OF 13

BREAK

10 GA.
MILD STEEL

BREAK

TREAD
2

TREAD
1

2"

1" LIP

INNER SIDE

3" LIP

WEIGHT

1" LIP

PLATE-2C

COMPRESSING
ACTION

3" LIP

Pulling Action

PRESSURE
POINTS

10 GA.
MILD STEEL

HORIZONTAL

7.75"

2" NOSING

PLATE 2

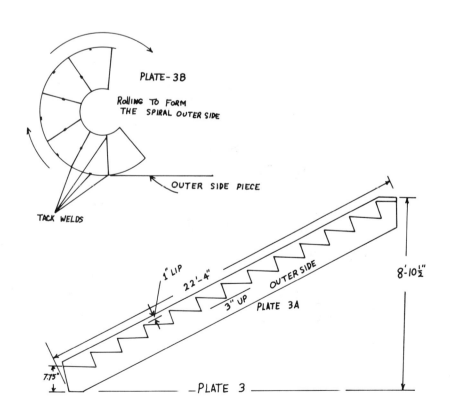

PLATE- 3B

ROLLING TO FORM
THE SPIRAL OUTER SIDE

OUTER SIDE PIECE

TACK WELDS

1" LIP

22'-4"

3" UP

OUTER SIDE

PLATE 3A

8'-10½"

7.75"

— PLATE 3 —

Brass and Glass Fireplace Enclosure

Author: Michael D. Gullihur
Instructor: Wendell Ohlson
School: Western Nevada Community
                   College
City & State: Reno, Nevada

Fabrication began by rolling a piece of 1½″ x ⅛″ steel strap into a 36″ diameter half circle. The rolled strap was then spot welded to a heavy guage steel table and a length of 1½″ x 1½″ x ⅛″ angle iron was hot drawn around it, flange out. 11″ beyond the horizontal center-line of the half circle, the angle iron was left straight to later form vertical hinging surfaces. Next a section of 3″ x 1½″ x ⅛″ channel iron was arc welded to the ends of the angle iron half circle. This provided a suitable base for the main framework and also completed the basic frame assembly.

For the construction of the doors, the next step in my project, I chose angle iron. Using a universal bender the 1″ x 1″ x ⅛″ angle iron was formed flange in, to match the inside diameter of the main framework. Cutting this half circle directly in the center, horizontal and vertical angle iron members were welded to each side, thus completing the basic door assemblies.

Due to the strength required, and the relatively short vertical surface of the frame and doors, the next step was to fabricate suitable hinges. Sections of ½″ diameter round stock were drilled .007 over the selected hinge pin size. This would compensate for any expansion or contraction when eventually placed into service. The drilled hinge sections were arc welded to 8″ pieces of ¼″ x ¾″ strap steel. These pieces were then arc welded to the main frame and door assemblies, and with hinge pins installed completed still another aspect of construction.

A series of vent holes approximately ¾″ x 2½″ were flame cut vertically in the channel iron portion of the main assembly. Two small doors were made out of ⅛″ steel sheet. Hinge sections were fabricated and arc welded to both the doors and the main frame assembly. When closed, these doors completely cover the vent openings, preventing warm room air from escaping when the fireplace is not in use.

The last operation was to braze the entire visible surface of the framework and doors. This included all hinges and the back side of the vent area covers. To provide the final finish the excess flux was removed and the surfaces were lightly buffed. Due to the irregular brazed layers, varying degrees of luster are present, thus producing a completely original antique gold finish.

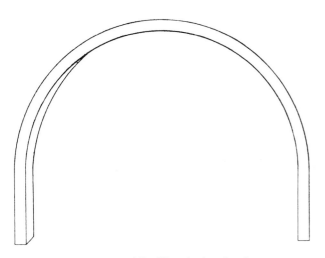

Figure 1: 1 1/2" x 1 1/2" x 1/8" angle iron hot drawn, flange out, to form a half circle 36" in diameter. 11" ends left straight to later form hinging surfaces.

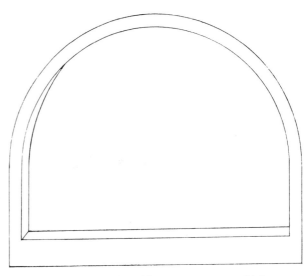

Figure 2: 3" x 1 1/2" x 1/8" channel iron arc welded to ends of angle iron half circle.

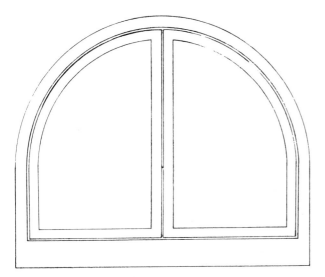

Figure 3: 1" x 1" x 1/8" angle iron formed, flange in, to fit 36" inside diameter of main framework. Cut directly in half, horizontal and vertical members were then arc welded to each section, thus completing the basic door assemblies.

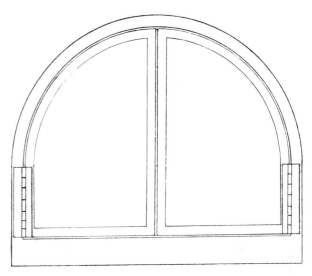

Figure 4: Fabricated hinges arc welded to main arch support and doors.

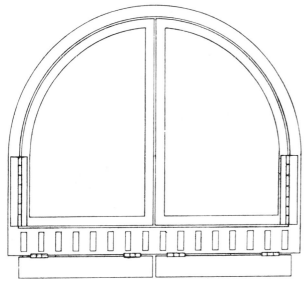

Figure 5: Vertical openings approximately 2 1/2" x 3/4" flame cut on 2 1/2" centers. Vent covers and hinges arc welded to frame assembly.

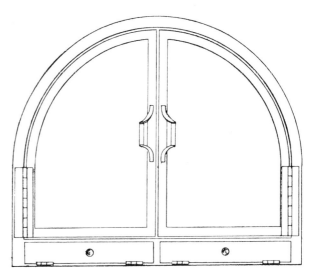

Figure 6: Handle supports arc welded to door assemblies. Phenolic handles and knobs manufactured.

83

The Hollywood Spiral Staircase

Authors: Duane Agrimson
                  Gary Eisen
                  Gary Stampka
Instructor: Bruce Lyngklip
School: Winona Area Technical Institute
City & State: Winona, MN

The center pole was constructed from one 3″ (inside diameter) standard pipe 9′ long. The vertical rails were constructed from twenty 1″ x 1″ x 40″ square tubing. The scrolls were designed from thirty-six ⅛″ x 1″ x 51″ steel strips. The steps were built from twelve ⅛″ thick steel, pie-shaped with the end dimensions of 15″ and 3″ with a 1″ lip bent on three sides. Under each step is a brace to support the step. The brace is shaped like a right triangle and is centrally attached under the steps with fillet welds. The hand rail located between vertical tubing rails is made from twenty-five ⅛″ x 1″ x 16″ steel strips. The inside hand railing is built from one ⅛″ x 1″ x 6′ steel strip. It is attached to and curves with the center pole.

The procedure for construction is as follows:

1. First secure the center pole to the balcony making sure it is perpendicular to the floor. Then fasten the pole to the floor.
2. Tack on the steps one at a time starting at the top. Make sure each step is level by using two levels lengthwise and widthwise. There is a rise of 8″ between the steps.
3. Start at the bottom and weld each step solid with fillet welds. At the same time, weld on the vertical square tubing for support so as to minimize the possibility of warpage.
4. Attach the ⅛″ x 1″ x 16″ steel strip to the vertical square tubing for the hand rail, which is located 32″ above the step.
5. Weld on the scrolls, 2 per step, centrally between the vertical square tubing by using close butt welds.
6. Repeat the whole process of putting up the hand railing to the balcony.
7. Mount the inside hand railing to the center pole, which is located 3″ away from the pole, with ½″ wrought iron.
8. Round the projecting corner of the bottom step. This is done to ensure safe passage without a possible injury. The step was cut with stick electrode and a hacksaw.
9. File the sharp edges, clean the slag, and wire-brush the spatter.

The Design of an Exterior Spiral Stair

Author: Gary William Grimes
Instructor: R. Zaiden
School: Technician Training School
City & State: McKees Rocks, PA

The riser and tread are the foremost factors in stair design. The overall floor-to-floor height was taken and divided by 7.50″ (17′ 6″ ÷ 7.5 = 28 risers). This allowed for 9 risers from the slab to the first floor, and 19 risers to the second floor. An additional 3 steps following the contour of the stairs will be placed in the concrete slab which will be discussed later in this report. The design called for these stairs to be made with an inside and outside hand rail. An 84.50″ outside diameter was obtained by using a 4″ Schedule 40 pipe for step hubs and a 32″ step set 8″ away from the hubs.

There are 18 treads from the first floor to the second floor forming a 360 degree circle. To obtain a tread size, I took the outside diameter, found the circumference and divided by 18 (84.5 x 3.1416 = 265. 46− 18 = 14.75). The same procedure was used to find the 3.5″ inside dimension. The step was to be made of ³⁄₁₆″ checkerboard plate 4 x 15 x 32 with a 2.25″ bent edge. The bending operation was done at a local metal shop. To give rigid support to each step a double ⅜ x 2 x 30 inch bar would be welded to the tread and hub. Since these stairs were of such a large diameter, it was imperative that each step be welded perfectly square to the hubs. I designed two jigs that counteracted the forces of welding, but also make the alignment of 26 step assemblies quite simple. All the material used to make the jigs was purchased inexpensively at a local scrap yard. Jig No. 1 was used to align the bars to the hub. With the 2 C-clamps and the ⁹⁄₁₆″ bolt there would be no chance for movement or bending. With the assembly secured in place the jig was rotated so all other welds could be made flat with a ⅛″ 7018 electrode. The bar and hub assembly was allowed to remain in the jig until the majority of the heat was gone after welding. Jig No. 2 was used to weld the tread to the hub assembly. Again, the use of clamps minimized distortion and made welding easy.

After setting up scaffolding, dimensions were carefully taken as to where to locate the second floor platform and supports. All holes were drilled in the masonry and the second floor supports were anchored with lag screws and shields. The platform itself was raised and fastened with clamps. Before the center column base plate could be located, a plumb bob and line were dropped through the hub of the platform down to the slab where the base would rest. I decided on locating the base in this manner to avoid any dimension difference between the second floor and foundation of the building. The center column base was purchased in a scrap yard, then cleaned, drilled and counterbored. After the ⅞″ holes were drilled in the concrete and the double expanding lead shields were tapped in place, a latex adhesive was applied for a moisture tight seal. The base was fastened with 3 set screw machine bolts for a flush surface. Any size or shape base plate could have been used, but the 8 inch round pad made for a neater job. Centers were marked for the base plates used to support the first floor platform. These base plates were ⅜″ x 7″ with 2 pieces of No 4 rebar welded to the bottom. Slightly undersized holes were drilled in the concrete for these bases. Again, an adhesive was applied and the plates were tapped into position.

With the second floor platform resting on its side on the supports the 3.50 Schedule 40 center column pipe was raised in place. Using a 2 x 6″ plank with 2 x 4″ scabs wedged between the two adjacent buildings, the center column was able to be tied off until it could be welded to the base plate. When the weld was complete, the first 8 step assemblies and 1 — 7.50 pipe hub (FUTURE FIRST FLOOR PLATFORM) were lowered by rope to the slab. The remaining 18 step assemblies were placed and the second floor platform was lowered into its final position. The platform was welded to the supports and center column, then all clamps were removed. After checking the position of the steps, they were then welded in place. The lower steps made an excellent 360 degree scaffold to use while welding. The top step had to be notched to have a right angle fit at the support bracket of the second floor platform. The first floor platform and support poles were all anchored and welded in place. The handrail balusters were cut to length and were made plumb to the steps with a level. The outer handrail had to start and stop 4.5″ from the brick face of the building. I wanted all the railing connections to be similar in appearance. To obtain this I decided to place a steel anchor shield in the masonry and bolt a 3″ backing washer to the face of the brick. This allowed me to set my railing connection flush and weld it vertically down, fastening it securely to the brick surface. The small amount of heat generated by welding these 4 connections neither damaged the brick nor loosened the steel anchor shield.

With all the steel secured the three steps in the concrete slab were marked and located. Following the spiral contour of the stairs, the concrete was scored 3 inches deep using a carborundum wheel on a chain saw. The concrete was removed, forms were placed and the new steps were poured.

With all the major construction out of the way the 1.25 inch braided steel cable was ready to be formed down the stairs. I used this steel cable for several reasons, the first being its strong structural aspect, and the ease with which it could be fastened to the balusters.

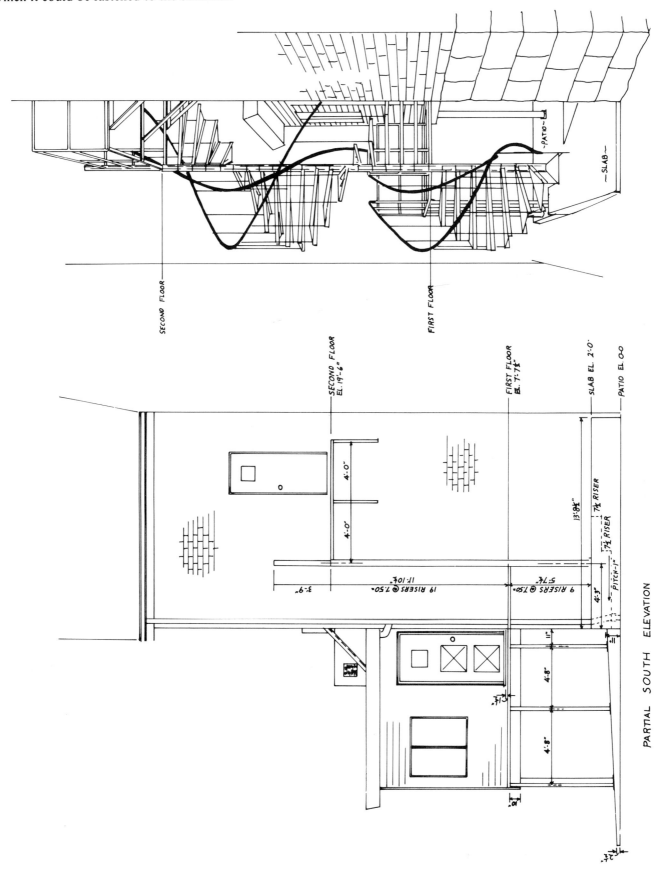

PARTIAL SOUTH ELEVATION

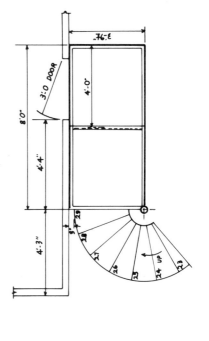

2ND FLOOR FRAMING & PARTIAL
STAIR PLAN - 1ST TO 2ND FLOOR

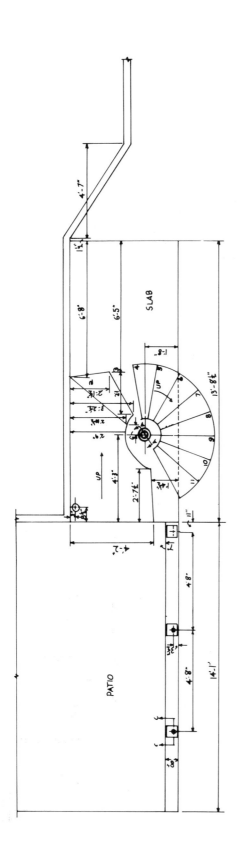

STAIR PLAN - PATIO TO FIRST FLOOR

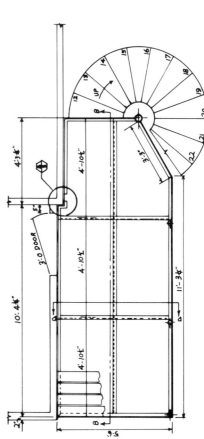

1ST FLOOR FRAMING & PARTIAL
STAIR PLAN - 1ST TO 2ND FLOOR

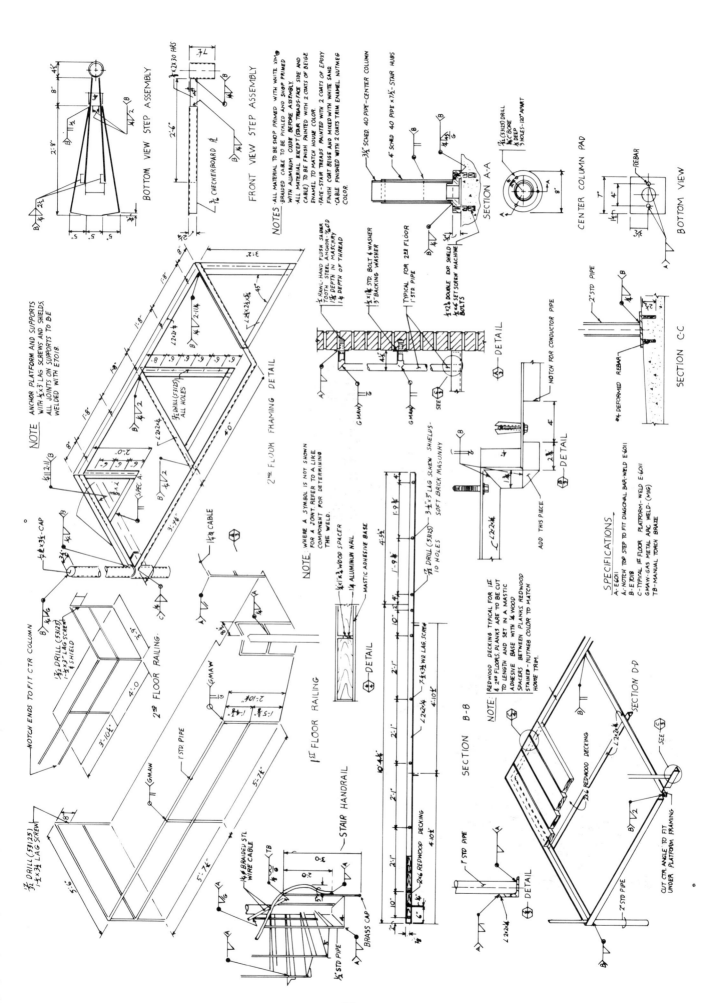

Bike (Motorcycle) Lift

Author: *Dennis R. Smith*
                     Craig A. Upton
Instructor: *Fred Goldman*
School: *Southeastern Community College*
City & State: *W. Burlington, IA*

The top deck and end with roller become a ramp after latch release. After pushing a bike up the ramp, the ramp comes down and deck latches. If the bike needs to be off of its wheels, the center lift is used. The center lift lifts directly under the engine of the bike.

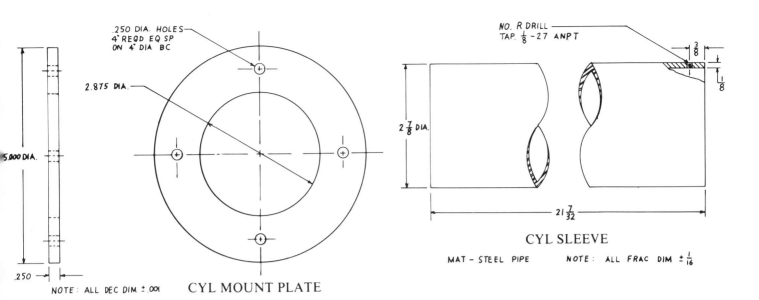

.250 DIA. HOLES
4" REQD EQ SP
ON 4" DIA BC

2.875 DIA.

5.000 DIA.

.250

NOTE: ALL DEC DIM ±.001

CYL MOUNT PLATE

NO. R DRILL
TAP. 1/8 -27 ANPT

3/8

1/8

2 7/8 DIA.

21 7/32

CYL SLEEVE

MAT – STEEL PIPE   NOTE: ALL FRAC DIM ± 1/16

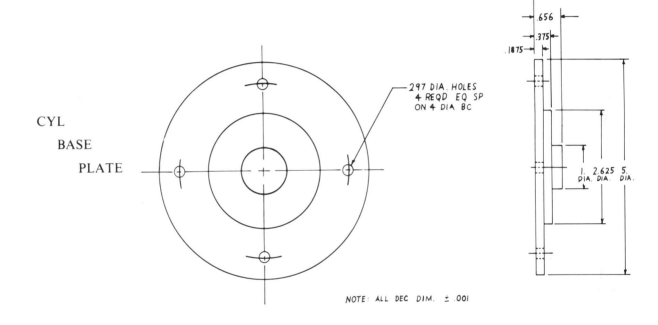

CYL

BASE

PLATE

.297 DIA. HOLES
4 REQD EQ SP
ON 4 DIA BC

.656

.375

.1875

1. 2.625 5.
DIA. DIA. DIA.

NOTE: ALL DEC DIM. ± .001

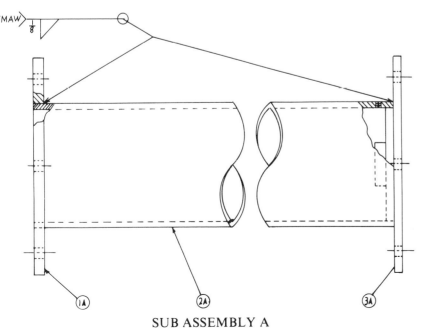

SMAW
1/8

SUB ASSEMBLY A

BILL		OF	MATERIALS	
PC	REQD.	MAT.	REF	DESCRIPTION
1A	1	STEEL	FAB	CYL CAP MTG
				PL 1/4 X 5 DIA
2A	1		STOCK	CYL SLEEVE
				22 LG PIPE
				2 7/8 OD x 2 5/8 ID
3A	1		FAB	CYL BASE PL
				11/16 X 5 DIA

91

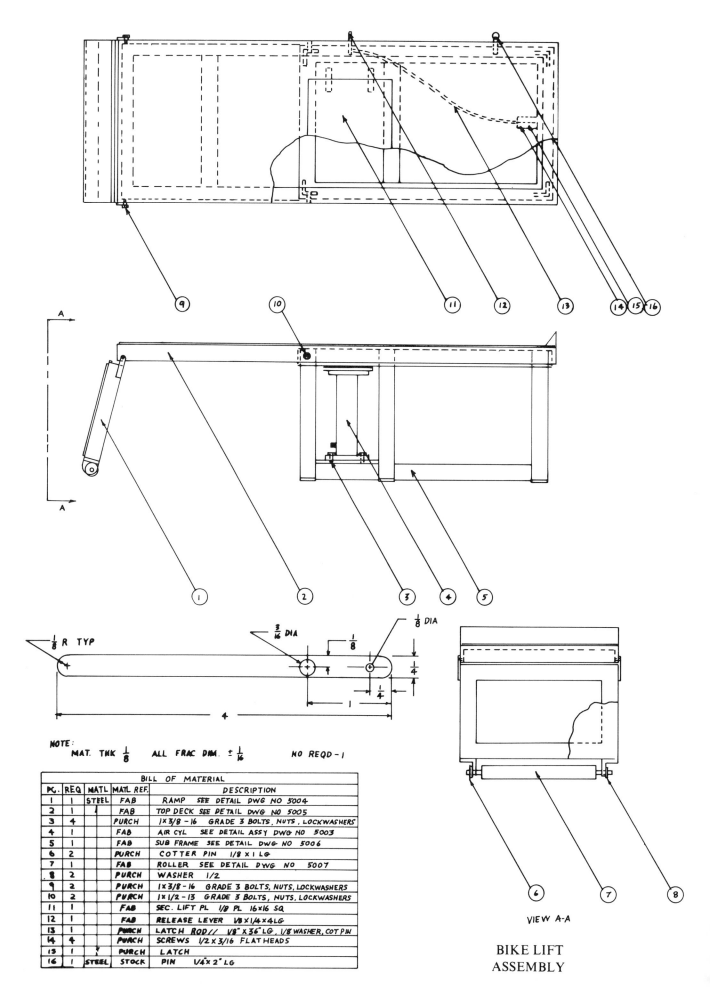

$\frac{1}{8}$ R TYP

$\frac{3}{16}$ DIA

$\frac{1}{8}$ DIA

$\frac{1}{8}$

$\frac{1}{4}$

$\frac{1}{4}$

1

4

NOTE: MAT. THK $\frac{1}{8}$ ALL FRAC DIM. $\pm\frac{1}{16}$ NO REQD-1

BILL OF MATERIAL				
PC.	REQ	MATL	MATL REF.	DESCRIPTION
1	1	STEEL	FAB	RAMP SEE DETAIL DWG NO 5004
2	1		FAB	TOP DECK SEE DETAIL DWG NO 5005
3	4		PURCH	1×3/8-16 GRADE 3 BOLTS, NUTS, LOCKWASHERS
4	1		FAB	AIR CYL SEE DETAIL ASSY DWG NO 5003
5	1		FAB	SUB FRAME SEE DETAIL DWG NO 5006
6	2		PURCH	COTTER PIN 1/8 × 1 LG
7	1		FAB	ROLLER SEE DETAIL DWG NO 5007
8	2		PURCH	WASHER 1/2
9	2		PURCH	1×3/8-16 GRADE 3 BOLTS, NUTS, LOCKWASHERS
10	2		PURCH	1×1/2-13 GRADE 3 BOLTS, NUTS, LOCKWASHERS
11	1		FAB	SEC. LIFT PL 1/8 PL 16×16 SQ
12	1		FAB	RELEASE LEVER 1/8×1/4×4LG
13	1		PURCH	LATCH ROD// 1/8" × 36" LG, 1/8 WASHER, COT PIN
14	4		PURCH	SCREWS 1/2×3/16 FLATHEADS
15	1		PURCH	LATCH
16	1	STEEL	STOCK	PIN 1/4"×2" LG

VIEW A-A

BIKE LIFT
ASSEMBLY

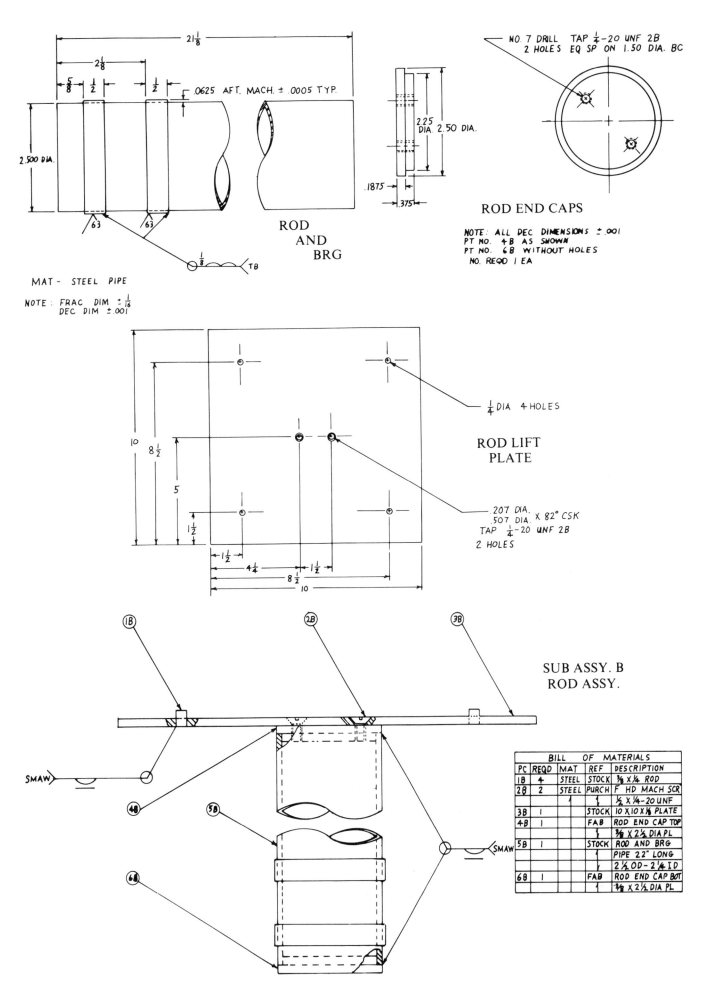

NO. 7 DRILL TAP ¼-20 UNF 2B
2 HOLES EQ SP ON 1.50 DIA. BC

ROD END CAPS

NOTE: ALL DEC DIMENSIONS ±.001
PT NO. 4B AS SHOWN
PT NO. 6B WITHOUT HOLES
NO. REQD 1 EA

21⅛

2⅛

⅝   ½   ½

.0625 AFT. MACH. ±.0005 TYP.

2.500 DIA.

63   63

**ROD
AND
BRG**

2.25
DIA. 2.50 DIA.

.1875

.375

MAT - STEEL PIPE

NOTE: FRAC DIM ±1/16
DEC DIM ±.001

⅛   TB

**ROD LIFT
PLATE**

10

8½

5

1½

1½

4¼

1½

8½

10

¼ DIA 4 HOLES

.207 DIA.
.507 DIA. X 82° CSK
TAP ¼-20 UNF 2B
2 HOLES

1B   2B   3B

**SUB ASSY. B
ROD ASSY.**

SMAW

4B

5B

6B

SMAW

BILL	OF	MATERIALS		
PC	REQD	MAT	REF	DESCRIPTION
1B	4	STEEL	STOCK	⅜ X ¼ ROD
2B	2	STEEL	PURCH	F HD MACH SCR
				½ X ¼-20 UNF
3B	1		STOCK	10 X 10 X ⅛ PLATE
4B	1		FAB	ROD END CAP TOP
				⅜ X 2½ DIA PL
5B	1		STOCK	ROD AND BRG
				PIPE 22" LONG
				2½ OD - 2¼ ID
6B	1		FAB	ROD END CAP BOT
				⅜ X 2½ DIA PL

93

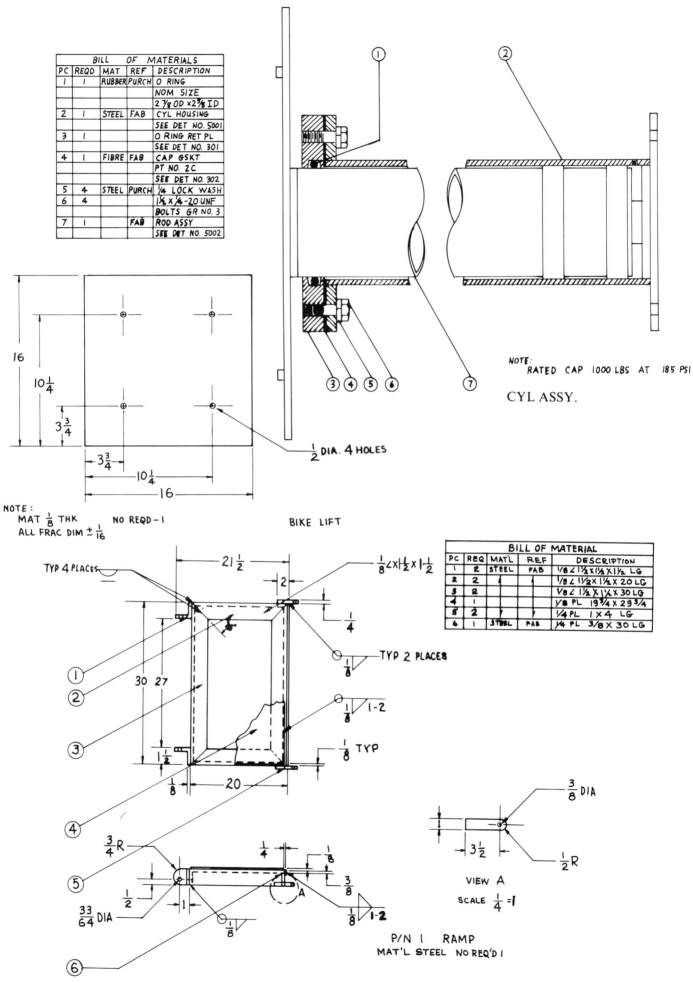

BILL OF MATERIALS				
PC	REQD	MAT	REF	DESCRIPTION
1	1	RUBBER	PURCH	O RING
				NOM SIZE
				2 7/8 OD × 2 5/8 ID
2	1	STEEL	FAB	CYL HOUSING
				SEE DET NO. 5001
3	1			O RING RET PL
				SEE DET NO. 301
4	1	FIBRE	FAB	CAP GSKT
				PT NO. 2C
				SEE DET NO. 302
5	4	STEEL	PURCH	1/4 LOCK WASH
6	4			1 1/4 × 1/4-20 UNF
				BOLTS GR NO. 3
7	1		FAB	ROD ASSY
				SEE DET NO. 5002

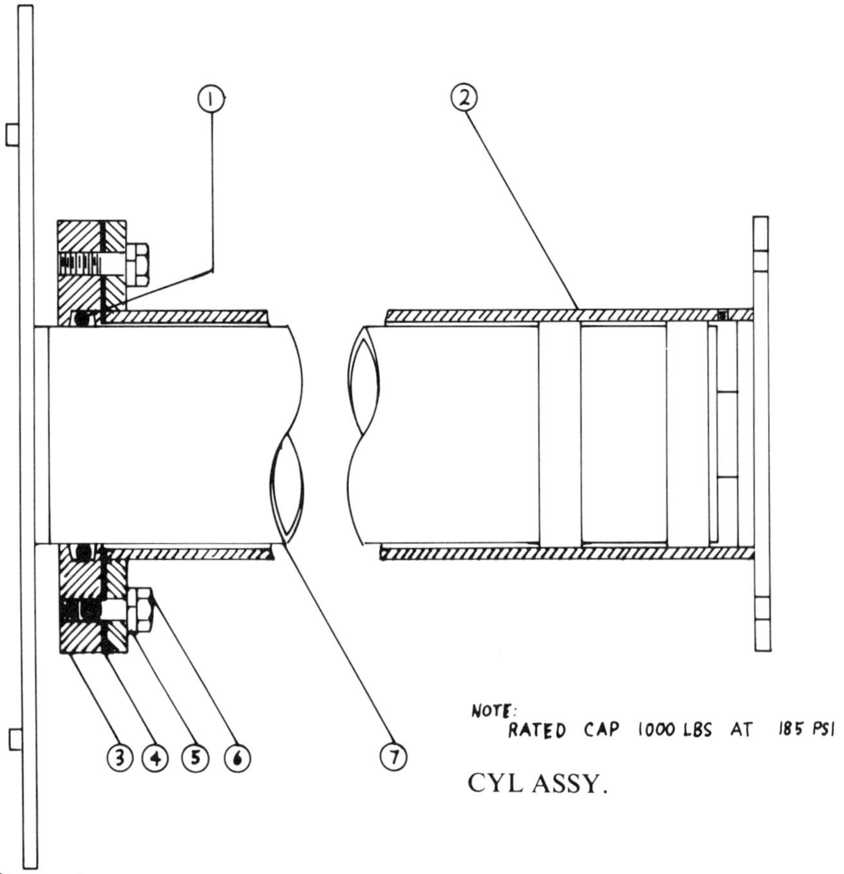

1
2
3
4
5
6
7

NOTE:
RATED CAP 1000 LBS AT 185 PSI

CYL ASSY.

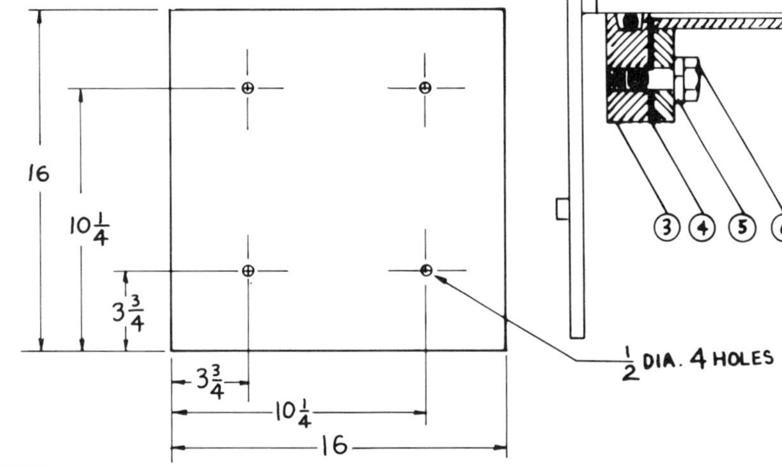

16
10 1/4
3 3/4
3 3/4
10 1/4
16
1/2 DIA. 4 HOLES

NOTE:
MAT 1/8 THK NO REQD-1
ALL FRAC DIM ± 1/16

BIKE LIFT

BILL OF MATERIAL				
PC	REQ	MAT'L	REF	DESCRIPTION
1	2	STEEL	FAB	1/8∠1½×1½×1½ LG
2	2			1/8∠1½×1½×20 LG
3	2			1/8∠1½×1½×30 LG
4	1			1/8 PL 19¾×29¾
5	2			1/4 PL 1×4 LG
6	1	STEEL	FAB	1/4 PL 3/8×30 LG

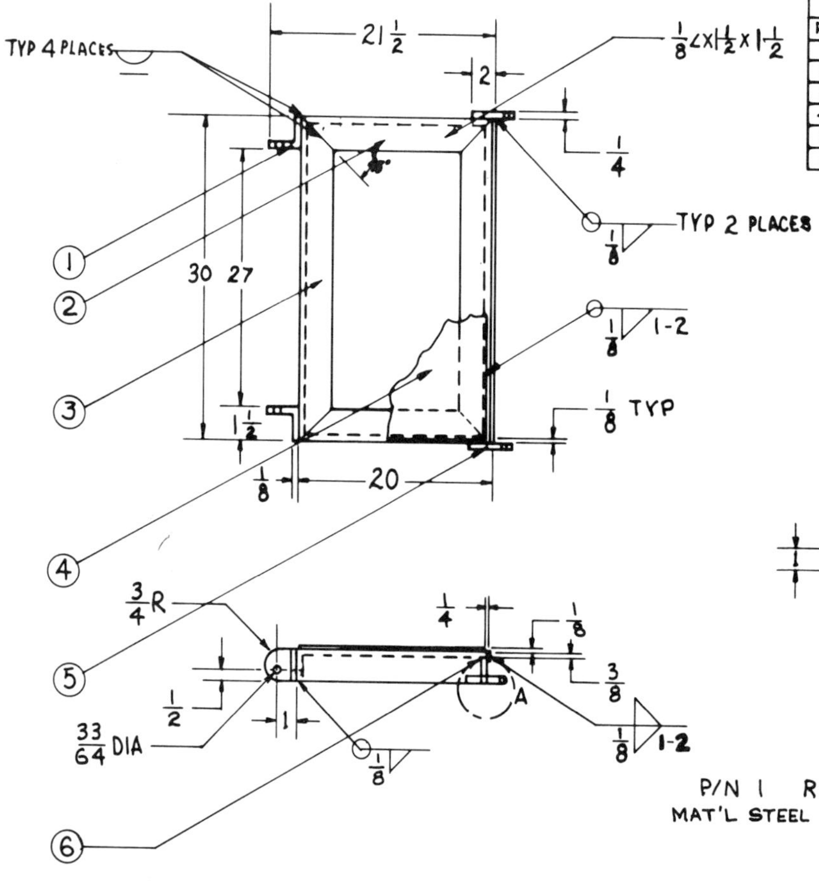

TYP 4 PLACES
21 1/2
2
1/8∠×1 1/2×1 1/2
1/4
TYP 2 PLACES
1/8
30
27
1/8 1-2
1 1/2
1/8 TYP
1/8
20
1
2
3
4
5
6
3/4 R
1/4
1/8
3/8
1/2
1
33/64 DIA
1/8
A
1/8 1-2

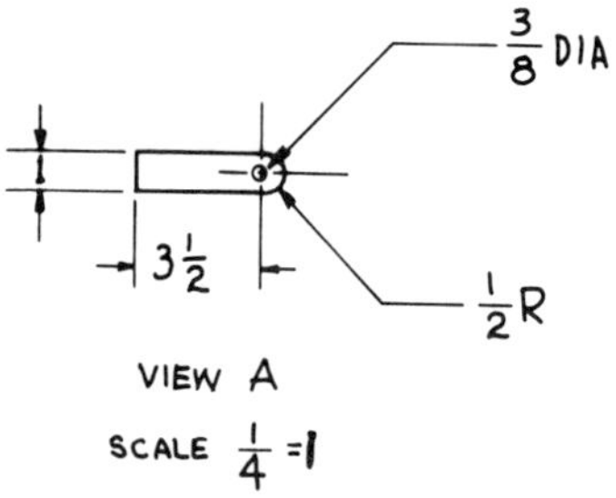

3/8 DIA
1
3 1/2
1/2 R

VIEW A
SCALE 1/4 = 1

P/N 1 RAMP
MAT'L STEEL NO REQ'D 1

BILL OF MATERIAL				
PC	REQ	MAT	REF	DESCRIPTION
1	2	STL	FAB	1/8 ∠ 1 1/2 X 1 1/2 X 30 LG
2	2			1/8 ∠ 1 1/2 X 1 1/2 X 7'0" LG
3	2			1/8 ∠ 1 1/2 X 1 1/2 X 27 LG
4	1			1/8 PL 1/4 X 1 LG
5	4			1/8 PL 1 X 3 LG
6	1	STL	FAB	1/8 PL 8 X 30 LG

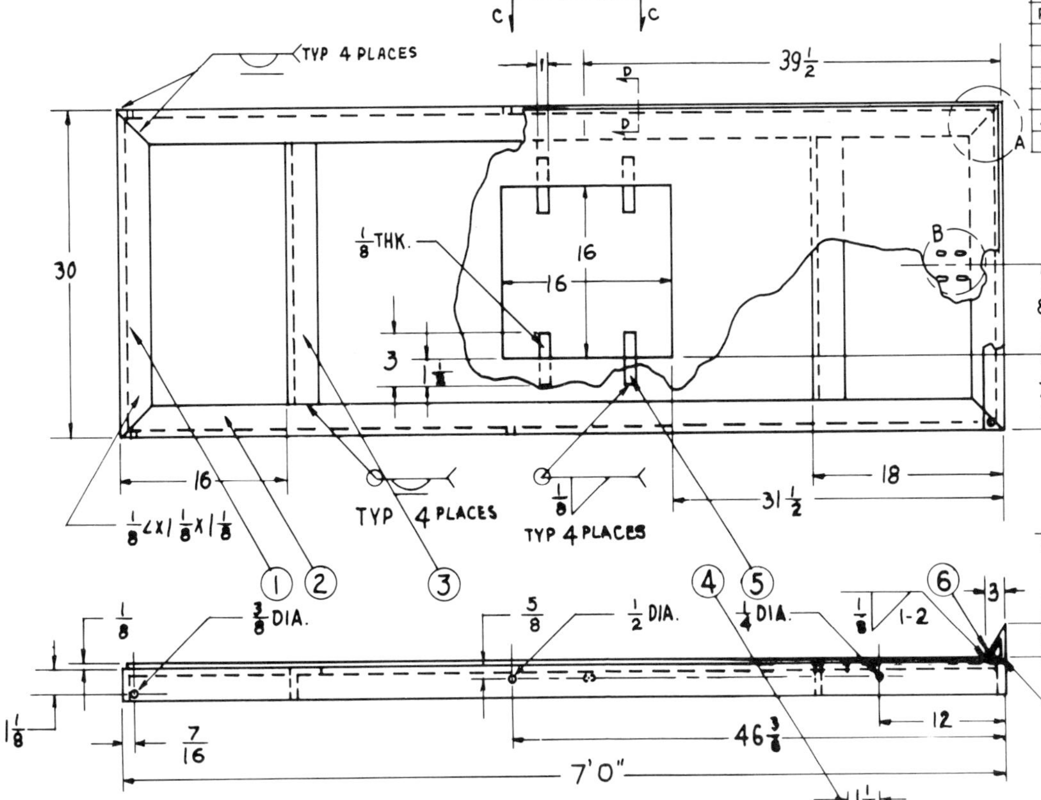

C C
D D
TYP 4 PLACES
39 1/2
30
1/8 THK.
16
16
3
8
7
16
18
31 1/2
1/8 ∠ X 1 1/8 X 1 1/8
TYP 4 PLACES
TYP 4 PLACES
1 2 3 4 5 6
1/8
3/8 DIA.
5/8
1/2 DIA.
1/4 DIA.
1-2
3
5
1 1/8
7/16
46 3/8
12
7'0"
A
B

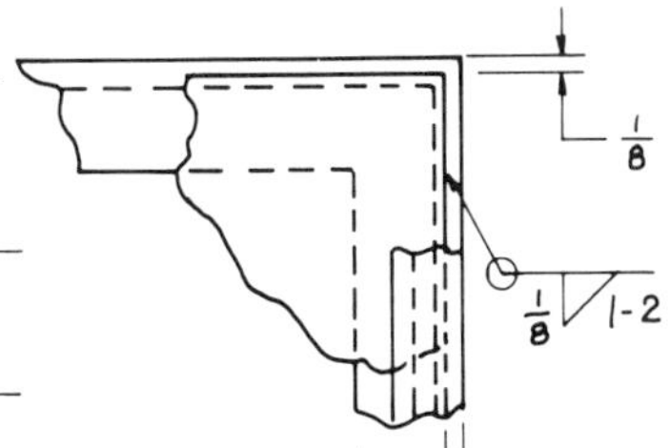

1/8
1-2

VIEW A

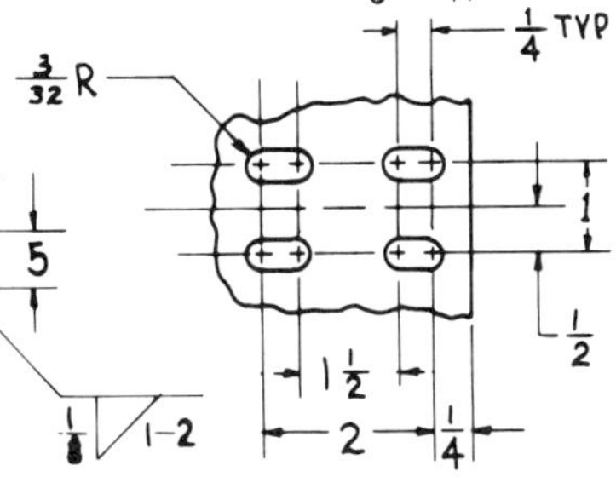

3/32 R
1/4 TYP
1
1/2
1 1/2
2
1/4

VIEW B

P/N 2 TOP DECK
MAT'L STEEL NO REQ'D 1
SCALE 1/8 = 1

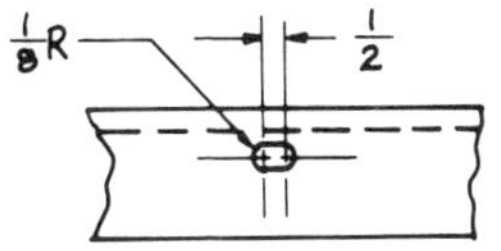

1/8 R
1/2

VIEW C-C

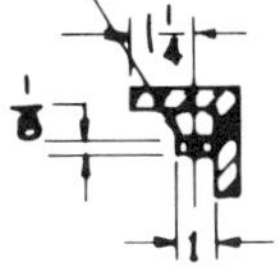

1 1/4
1/8
1

VIEW D-D

BILL OF MATERIAL				
PC	REQ.	MAT	REF	DESCRIPTION
1	1	STEEL	FAB	1/8 PL 1 X 10 1/2 LG
2	1			1/8 PL 1 X 8 LG
3	2			1/8 PL 1 X 16 LG
4	3			1/8 L 1 1/2 X 1 1/2 X 29 1/2 LG
5	2			1/8 ∠ 1 1/2 X 1 1/2 X 48 LG
6	1			1/8 PL 12 3/8 X 29 1/2
7	2			1/8 ∠ 1 1/2 X 1 1/2 X 12 7/8 LG
8	6			1/8 ∠ 1 1/2 X 1 1/2 X 24 3/4 LG
9	2			1/8 ∠ 1 1/2 X 1 1/2 X 28 7/8 LG
10	6	STEEL	FAB	1/8 PL 1 1/2 X 1 1/2

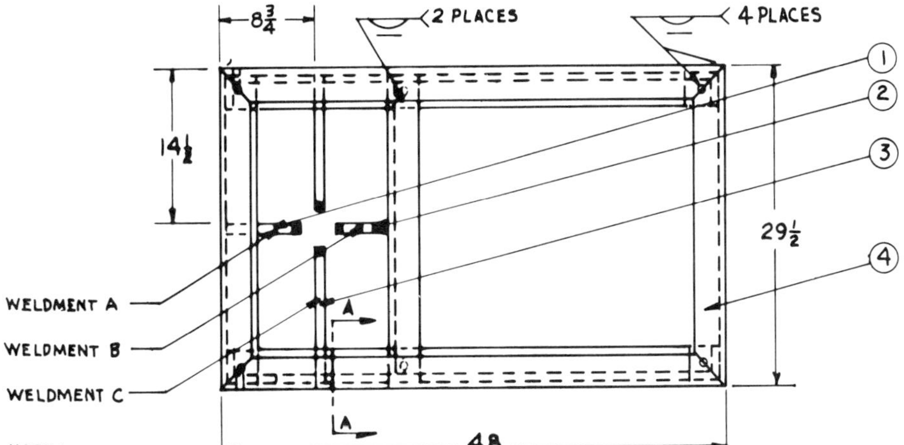

8 3/4
2 PLACES
4 PLACES
14 1/2
29 1/2
1 2 3 4
WELDMENT A
WELDMENT B
WELDMENT C
A
A
48

NOTE:
DETAIL OF WELDMENTS
A, B & C ON DRAWING
NO. 5007

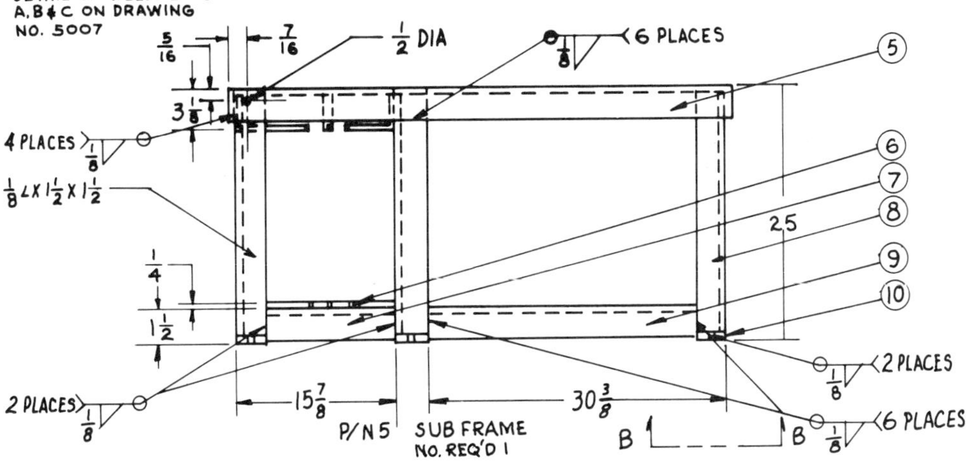

5/16
7/16
1/2 DIA
1/8
6 PLACES
3 1/8
4 PLACES
1/8 ∠ X 1 1/2 X 1 1/2
5 6 7 8 9 10
25
1/4
1 1/2
2 PLACES
2 PLACES
6 PLACES
15 7/8
30 3/8
B B

P/N 5 SUB FRAME
NO. REQ'D 1

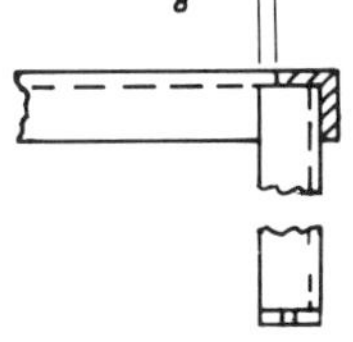

1/8

DETAIL SEC A-A

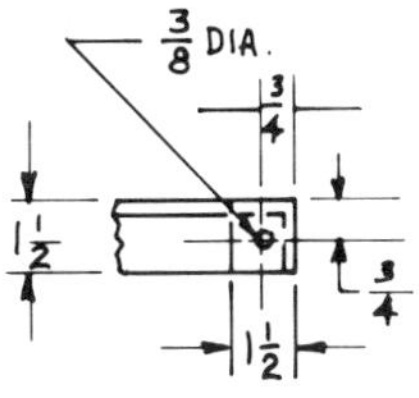

3/8 DIA.
3/4
1 1/2
3/4
1 1/2

DETAIL SEC B-B

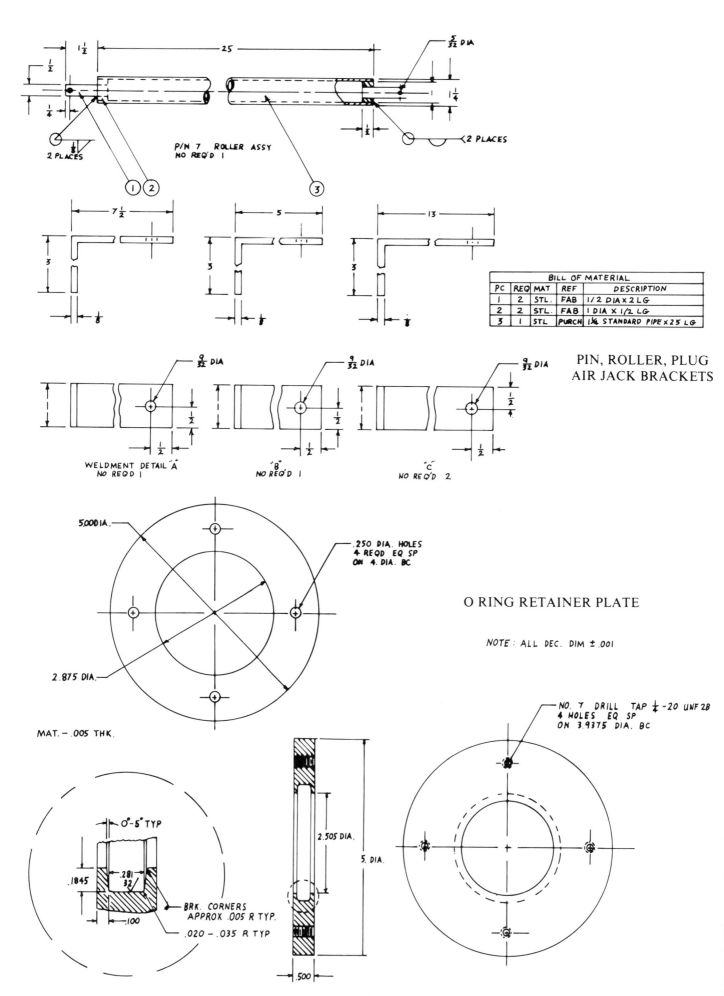

BILL OF MATERIAL

PC	REQ	MAT	REF	DESCRIPTION
1	2	STL.	FAB	1/2 DIA x 2 LG
2	2	STL.	FAB	1 DIA X 1/2 LG
3	1	STL	PURCH	1¼ STANDARD PIPE x 25 LG

P/N 7 ROLLER ASSY
NO REQ'D 1

WELDMENT DETAIL "A"
NO REQ'D 1

"B"
NO REQ'D 1

"C"
NO REQ'D 2

PIN, ROLLER, PLUG
AIR JACK BRACKETS

O RING RETAINER PLATE

NOTE: ALL DEC. DIM ±.001

5.000 DIA.

.250 DIA. HOLES
4 REQD EQ SP
ON 4. DIA. BC

2.875 DIA.

MAT. – .005 THK.

NO. 7 DRILL TAP ¼ -20 UNF 2B
4 HOLES EQ SP
ON 3.9375 DIA. BC

0°-5° TYP

.1845

.281
.32

.100

BRK. CORNERS
APPROX .005 R TYP.

.020 – .035 R TYP

2.505 DIA.

5. DIA.

.500

Horse Shoe Dance

Author: *Claudia Widdiss Fludd*
Instructor: *J. C. Manee, Jr.*
School: *Atlanta Area*
       Technical School
City & State: *Atlanta, GA*

The first step in fabrication is to cut out the exact shape of the bottom and top forms in thin cardboard. Trace the shapes on to ⅛″ plate. After the shapes are cut, clamp the cardboard and metal plates together of matching size and use an electric grinder to make the parallel forms exact.

Next step in fabrication is to cut out some metal pieces that curve properly to the basic design. Use the cardboard and curve it on the metal shapes already cut. Next cut and grind the metal plates in the same fashion as before.

In order to get the metal to curve properly, tack each pair of shapes together at the point where they would naturally meet. Then with a C-Clamp slowly tack and clamp the metal until the curve is completed (sometimes heating the metal and hammering is necessary). On the middle curve use three separate pieces of plate. After the metal is in place run a bead down each seam. The edges are in right angle fashion to keep a clean, uniform line for grinding.

The third step is fabrication again with the cardboard, cut each shape in three sections at the point of the most curve. After these sections are cut and ground, starting from the bottom of each curve shape tack the metal sections onto the curved form at the point where they would naturally meet. Tack a C-clamp onto the curved form and tighten the clamp until the inside section curves correctly, tacking it again. Slowly move up the form welding each section together until all the triangular shapes are completed. On the inside of each shape run passes with a ³⁄₁₆″ E-6013 AC, to cover up the appearance of the welded sections and add texture to the design.

The four remaining shapes are cut starting with the cardboard and executed the same as the curved shapes only clamps aren't necessary for welding the pieces together. Also pieces are cut and welded to seal the end of each form.

The last step is to weld all the sections together starting from the bottom. A wash of muratic acid and water over the entire piece will give it a uniform coat of rust.

The entire piece is made from ⅛″ plate steel. "Horse-Shoe Dance" stands approximately 5′ 10″ -H x 3′ -L x 3½′ -W.

Home Flight

Author:	R. Mattson
Instructor:	R. Craig
School:	San Francisco State University
City & State:	San Francisco, CA

Body:

Materials:

1 Piece Steel Plate, ⅛'' x 6'' x 10'' (Body)
1 Piece Steel Plate, ⅛'' x 2½'' x 8'' (Neck)
1 Piece Steel Plate, ⅛'' x 3'' x 3'' (Head)
1 Piece Steel Plate, ⅛'' x 4'' x 8'' (Tail)
2 Pieces Steel Plate, ⅛'' x 3'' x 4'' (Legs)

Step I   Cut with Beverly Shears outside edge and triangles to form body. Follow the drawing below.

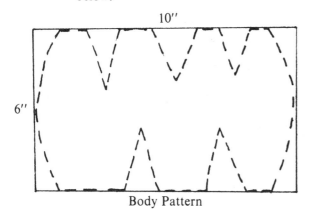

Body Pattern

Forging:

Step I   Heat the cut metal in the forge until a cherry red color is obtained. Grasp the body with the metal tongs. Form the body by folding all edges together.

> *Safety:* Wear eye and clothing protection while working with hot metal on the forge.

Step II   Cool formed metal. Arc weld all seams with E 6013 electrodes together at 100 amps. Reheat circular body to cherry red in forge. Round out square or rough edges with ball peen hammer as pictured below.

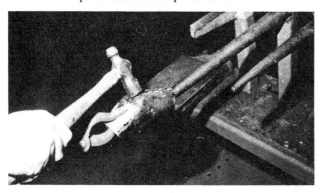

Step III   Cut tail piece out as patterned below.

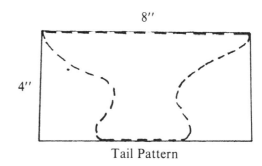

Tail Pattern

Step IV   Using the same process as before, heat tail until cherry red. Form the eight inch section to match rear part of body. Cool tail section. Weld the circular tail piece together, then weld tail to rear section of body.

Step V   Put body and tail in forge. Again, smooth out rough edges and form tail by using a screwdriver pictured below.

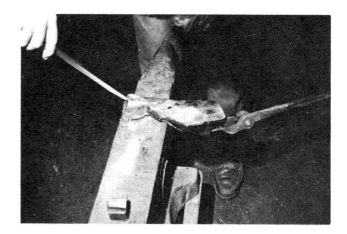

Step VI   The neck can be formed after cutting the pattern below.

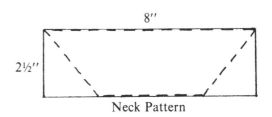

Neck Pattern

Step VII   After cutting metal, place in forge until cherry red. Bend until the two angled edges meet. Cool the neck and weld seam together at 100 amps.

Step VIII   Weld neck's widest section to the front part of the body.

Step IX   Cut out a three inch diameter piece of eighth inch steel plate.

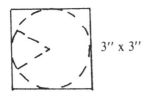

3″ x 3″

Head Pattern

Step X   Heat head piece in the forge. Form until the metal is thimble-shaped. Cool head, weld the cone together, then weld head to neck section as pictured below.

Step XI   With all four sections of the body welded together, surfacing of the entire body with welding beads can begin. Eighth inch steel plate is used so the welding beads won't burn through the material. Weld beads at 100 amps along the length of the body. Continue until entire surface is covered with beads.

Safety: Wear eye protection when chipping slag from welded body.

Step XII   Place body in forge. Heat up the body to a cherry red condition. Mold body to final desired shape. The body should appear like the picture below.

Step XIII   Cut out the two leg patterns as drawn below.

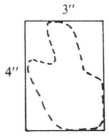

3″

4″

Note: Reverse Paper Pattern for Right Leg

Left Leg Pattern

Step XIV   Heat both leg parts in the forge until cherry red. Shape left leg (pattern above) first by folding the widest section together until circular. Repeat for right leg. Cool both legs, then weld each leg together at the seam.

Step XV   Weld, at 100 amps, legs to body in this position as pictured below.

Step XVI   Weld all surfaces of the two legs to match with the body. On the bottom of each leg, cut a round piece of steel plate to seal the opening. Drill a ¼″ hole in the middle of the round piece of metal. This provides an opening for the legs later on.

Wings:

Materials:

4 Pieces Steel Plate, ⅛″ x 4″ x 10″ (Wings)

Step XVII   The wings were cut eight inches long in the beginning. The wings were found to be too short. A two inch tip was added so the wings would be in proportion.

Step XVIII Cut pattern below in duplicate for each wing. Each wing consists of two pieces.

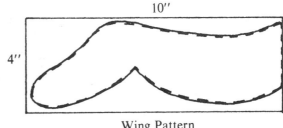

10″

4″

Wing Pattern

Step XIX   Weld the two pieces of each wing together in a "V" arrangement. Shown on next page.

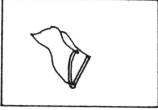
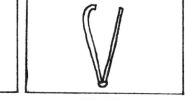

"V" Arrangement   Side View

Step XX   Place wing in the forge.

Step XXI   Shape unwelded side thicker than welded side as shown in the drawing and the picture.

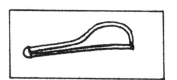

Side View

Step XXII   After the thick section is formed, weld (at 100 Amps) together the wing edges. Cover wing with welding beads in a pattern to simulate rows of feathers as diagrammed below.

Welding Pattern

Step XXIII   Repeat for right wing.

Step XXIV   After both wings are shaped and welded, heat in forge until metal is cherry red. Shape each wing to desired thickness (about ¼" thick on the back of the wing, ½" thick on the front of the wing).

Step XXV   In the picture above, the left wing is being bent outward to simulate flight on the finished project.

Step XXVI While the project is being built, wire brushing helps keep the pieces clean during construction.

> *Safety:* Wear eye protection because little bits of slag come off the project during wire brushing.

Step XXVII Weld, at 120 amps, finished wings to the body in the position show on next page.

Construction of Tree:

Materials: 1½″ Pipe.....23″ (Trunk and Limb)
⁵⁄₁₆″ Steel Plate....6″ x 20″ (Base)
⅛″ Steel Plate.....2″ x 2″ (Claws)
¼″ Round Steel.....8 Inches (Legs)

Step I Cut one ½″ pipe twenty-three inches long. Insert one end of pipe in the Hossfeld Bender.

Step II Bend first 13 inches of pipe into a gentle curve. After bending the curve, cut 10 inches off the straight end (this will be the tree limb).

Step III Use cutting torch to make irregular edge on top of the trunk and end of limb. Cut base of trunk with the power hacksaw to even up edge for base contact.

Step IV Chalk ⁵⁄₁₆″ steel plate as a guide for the cutting torch.

Step V Weld, at 100 amps, beads parallel with the pipe. Cover entire surface of trunk and limb with beads to simulate bark.

Step VI Weld, at 130 amps, the trunk to the base as drawn below.

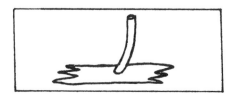

Trunk Position

Step VII   Weld, at 100 amps, limb to trunk nine inches above the base. Weld in a manner to blend the trunk and limb together.

Step VIII   Weld, at 120 amps, welding beads to act as exposed roots. Weld on top of old welds to build roots higher. Run roots to all edges of the base.

Step IX   Cut out claws and legs as drawn below.

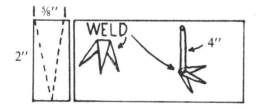

Claws and Legs

Step X   Weld, at 80 amps, each claw together in two groups of three. Weld ¼″ legs at junction of claws. Insert the two legs into the two holes provided in the leg stumps of the body. Place bird, with legs inserted, on tree branch. Lean bird in desired position so it won't fall. Weld claws to the limb. With a hammer, bend claws to conform with the limb. Lift bird off tree for final wire brushing. The claws stay on the tree so that the bird may be removed for future cleaning or moving.

Step XI   With the bird removed, use a portable drill (¼″) to drill the eyes in the head. Cut two small triangles out of ⅛″ steel plate, about ¾″ long, for the beak. Form and place the beak below the eyes. Cool the bird completely with cold water. Dry and wire brush finished bird and tree to a bright luster. Spray with clear lacquer.

Materials:
1 Piece Steel Plate, ⅛″ x 6″ x 10″ (Body)
1 Piece Steel Plate, ⅛″ x 2½″ x 8″ (Neck)
1 Piece Steel Plate, ⅛″ x 3″ x 3″ (Head)
1 Piece Steel Plate, ⅛″ x 4″ x 8″ (Tail)
2 Pieces Steel Plate, ⅛″ x 3″ x 4″ (Legs)
4 Pieces Steel Plate, ⅛″ x 4″ x 10″ (Wings)
1 Piece Steel Plate, ⅛″ x 2″ x 2″ (Claws)
1 Piece Steel Plate, ⅛″ x 1″ x 1″ (Beak)
1 Piece Steel Rod, ¼″ x 8″ (Lower Legs)
1 Piece 1½″ Pipe, 23 inches long (Trunk and Limb)
1 Piece Steel Plate, ⁵⁄₁₆″ x 6″ x 20″ (Base)

A Working Skiff

Author: *Grant Stephens*
Instructor: *David Thiedeman*
School: *Kodiak Regional Vocational High School*
City & State: *Kodiak, Alaska*

Materials Used:

quant.	dimension	wt.
1 each	.190 x 6' x 16' 5086 Aluminum	253
1 each	.125 x 5' x 20' 5086 aluminum	173
1 each	.125 x 4' x 12' 5086 aluminum	84
5 each	2½" IPS Sch 40 pipe 20' 6061 aluminum	
1 each	½" pipe 4' 6061 aluminum	
20 each	1 lb. spools 5356 welding wire	20

Bottom Layout

The bottom was laid out on a sheet of ³⁄₁₆ x 72 x 192", 5086 aluminum. A center line was established the length of this sheet. At one end of this sheet a five inch distance was laid off perpendicular to the centerline. This point is called "A". 42" from this same end on centerline a point "B" is established.

The inside curve which determines the lift of the bow is formed by bending a piece of ¼ x ¾" strap iron which was held at the points "B" and "A" and having the middle of this piece offset 1" toward the center line.

The outside curve is determined by establishing three points. One 72" back from the same end as point "A" on one edge (this is point "C") and one 84" from the same end on the same edge (this is point "D"). The third point "E", is established at 36" from point "A" on the line between "A" and "C". Using a piece of strap iron in the same manner as in making the inside curve, it was supported at points "A", "C", and "D" and offset at point "E" 5". This same procedure is followed on the opposite side.

Cutting the inside curves was the next step. The inside curves were cut from point "A" to point "B" along the curve and the same was done on the opposed side. In order to lessen the sweep of the bow and to spread the stress formed over a larger area, a cut was required along the center line 30" beyond point "B" to point "F".

The bow was pulled together by placing a come-along in notches cut in the waste stock (see diagram). The center V was then skip welded as a tight fit was established.

The outside cut was made from point "A" to point "C" along the curve to make the flare of the bow. All cuts were made with a circular saw with carbide tipped blades.

Side Layout

The sides were laid out on a sheet of ⅛ x 60 x 240", 5086

aluminum. This sheet was then split into two ⅛ x 30 x 240" sheets. A point was established 7¾" from the stern end, this was called point "G", and forms the angle of the transom. From this point a line was drawn to the opposite corner which is called "H", forming a fifteen degree angle. This is done to both sides.

The sheet was placed along the curve of the bottom. Point "G" was held at the stern edge of the bottom and the sheet was pulled around the bottom edge until point "I" was established where it touched the tip of the bow. A perpendicular line is drawn to the point "I". This was called point "J". From a point 20" forward of point "J" a line is drawn to point "I". This establishes the shape of the bow.

Since the bottom formed a curve along the adjoining edge of the side, that curve had to be drawn along the sheet while the side was still held in place along the edge of the bottom. Side one was cut and laid on side two and used as a template to assure that both sides turn out the same. The bow of sheet 2 was not cut until both sides had been skip welded in place. This allows exact fitting at the bow.

Transom Layout

The transom pieces were laid out on a sheet of ⅛'' 5086 aluminum. Because the width of the piece needed was considerably wider than the stock width, two additional pieces "N" and "O" were needed. These pieces were tacked on each end of a sheet ⅛ x 20 x 60''.

In order to strengthen the seams, one-half section of 2½'' IPS schedule 40 pipe 13'' long was skip welded to each side of the joint. On the inside of the transom a half section of pipe was welded horizontally across the top of the 13'' piece.

Rails

All rails and stiffeners were made from 2½'' IPS schedule 40 pipe which was split. Using one pipe on each side, and not mixing up the half section assured a tight fit. This sandwich arrangement adds strength.

The inside sections were bent to the curve along the bow first. In making the curve a large vice was used. Starting 24'' back on the bow-end of the section, the curve was started. The 24'' measurement was used because the side curve started about that distance back from where the sides met at the bow.

Every 6'' a slight bend was made, assuring a gradual curve. This curve was compared to the skiff until it was the same. All of the rails were bent to the same shape as the first to assure uniformity in the shape of the skiff sides.

The half pipes were fitted at the bow.

The tacking procedure was started at the bow by using "C" clamps to pull the pieces together. Top and underside tacks were made as the fit was established. When the transom was reached, the pipe was cut off to the correct length. The same procedure was used for all rails.

After the outside pipe was tacked into place, the bow-end was cut off flat so that a plate could be welded across the pipes making the bow stem flat.

The solid welded rails have a floatation factor of about 100 pounds.

Back Tank

Two floatation tanks were constructed so that the sum of their floatation capabilities was about 900 pounds.

The motor requirements call for a 20'' height on the transom 10'' below the sides. The height of the near vertical piece was 30'' and formed a false transom. This was to prevent swamping if a wave was taken over the stern. Measurements were taken and piece "K" was laid out on a sheet of ⅛'' 5086 aluminum. Piece "K" was then cut out and tacked into place.

At this point two 1'' holes were made: one in the transom and one in piece "K". A piece of ¾'' aluminum pipe was welded to the bottom of the skiff to serve as a drain through the tank.

Piece "L" was made in a similar manner. Measurements were taken between piece "K" and the transom, and "L" was laid out on a piece of ⅛'' 5086 aluminum. Five pieces of ⅛ x 1 x 1'' angle aluminum were skip-welded to the underside to make it more rigid. Piece "L" was then tacked into place.

Bow Floatation Tank

The bow tank was fit to the shape of the boat. Calculations determined the tank should float three hundred pounds and the size the tank should be 36 x 62 x 15'' high.

Care was taken to make all fits within ⅛'' or closer. All seams under the tank were welded solid. The tanks were then skip welded into place.

Inside Bottom Stiffeners

The stiffeners were made from 2½'' schedule 40 IPS pipe which was split. They were cut 70'' long and then bent to fit the curve of the bottom. Five were made and spaced 18'' apart starting 18'' forward from the back tank. The ends were cut off at 45° angles and caps were welded on. These caps were welded both inside and outside. The outside weld was then ground smooth so there were no sharp corners. After all the stiffeners were tacked into place, they were skip-welded four or five inches long, on four or five inch centers.

Bottom Skegs

The skegs were made from 2½'' schedule 40 IPS pipe which was split. 3 skegs were welded to the bottom of the skiff 20'' from the center skeg. The back end of the center skeg was kept 8'' from the stern of the skiff so as not to interfere with the water flow to the outboard motors. The two side skegs were placed about 4'' from the stern. It was important that all the skegs were parallel to the direction of travel so that the skiff would not pull to one side. The skegs were skip-welded to the bottom on 12'' centers with 4'' beads.

Final Welding

Before the tanks were put in, the sides and transom were welded solid to the bottom under the tanks. After the tanks and bottom stiffeners were in, the rest of the skiff was welded solid. The sides were welded to the bottom. The top of the rails were welded solid and ground off flush. After all the inside welding was completed, the skiff was turned over and the outside joints were welded solid. The bottom was then welded to the sides, the transom was welded to the bottom and sides, and both the inside and the outside of the rails were welded to the skiff. The rail on the back tank was welded solid. Also the outside joints were cleaned with a saw to remove the oxide that could not be reached with a wire brush.

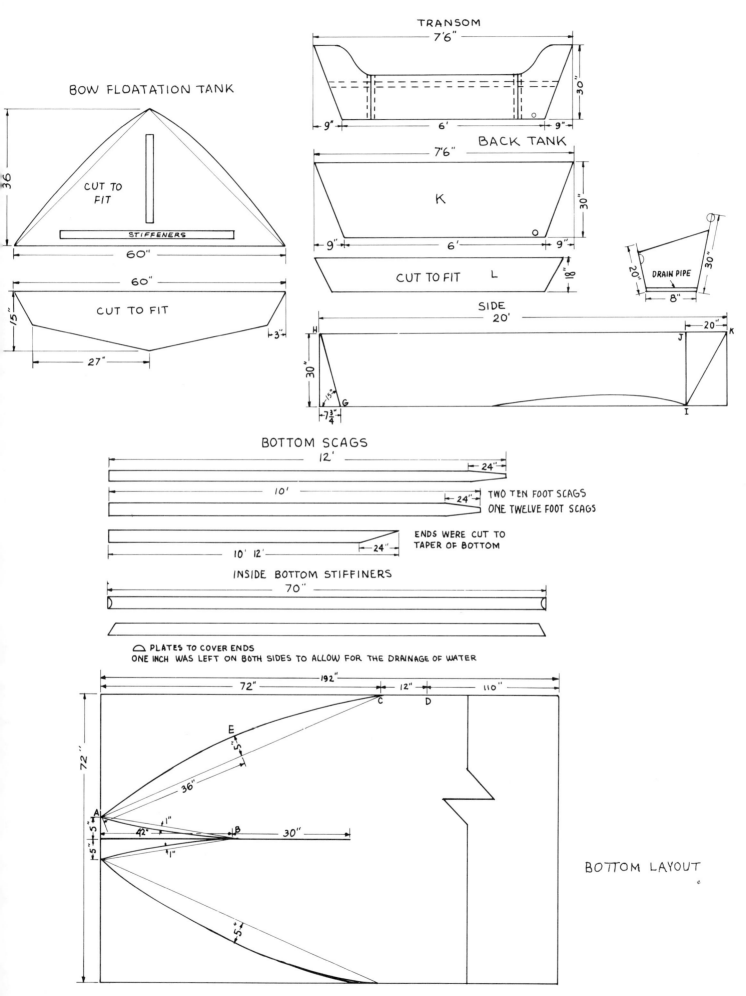

BOW FLOATATION TANK

CUT TO FIT

STIFFENERS

36

60"

60"

15"

CUT TO FIT

27"

3"

TRANSOM

7'6"

30"

9"   6'   9"

BACK TANK

7'6"

K

30"

9"   6'   9"

CUT TO FIT   L

18"

DRAIN PIPE

20"   30"

8"

SIDE

20'

20"

H   J   K

30"

15°

G

7¾"   I

BOTTOM SCAGS

12'

24"

10'

24"

TWO TEN FOOT SCAGS

ONE TWELVE FOOT SCAGS

10' 12'

24"

ENDS WERE CUT TO
TAPER OF BOTTOM

INSIDE BOTTOM STIFFINERS

70"

◠ PLATES TO COVER ENDS
ONE INCH WAS LEFT ON BOTH SIDES TO ALLOW FOR THE DRAINAGE OF WATER

192"

72"   12"   110"

C   D

E

5"

36"

72"

A

5"

5"

1"

42"   B   30"

5"

1"

5"

BOTTOM LAYOUT

Natural Gas Barbeque

Author: Francis R. Price
Instructor: C. C. Howard
School: Aurora Technical Center
City & State: Aurora, CO

Eleven-guage mild steel was selected as the construction material for the barbeque.

First: Check the materials list provided and collect the required materials and components.

Second: Layout the lid, bottom, and sides of the barbeque using the plans provided.

After the layout has been completed, X-bend the top of the lid to provide maximum support to this component. This type of bending will also enhance the appearance of the lid.

Once the lid has been bent, cut air slots in the bottom of the barbeque. Use a corner-to-corner tack when assembling the bottom of the barbeque. When tacking the bottom, do not let the bead exceed more than ³⁄₁₆". If the tacking bead exceeds more than ³⁄₁₆", you may encounter some difficulty in grinding the bottom.

Lid assembly is the next step. First check the squareness of the bottom of the barbeque. The lid will be assembled and tacked to the bottom to assure a perfect fit. Place the component parts needed for the lid upon the newly constructed base and tack the components together. Use one inch tacks, and stagger the tack weld to prevent distortion of the lid.

Hinges were constructed from ¾" pipe stock, see figure 1, for hinge construction and dimensions. Weld the hinges into place on the lid and bottom of the barbeque. Do not tack the hinges. Grind the tacks, which are holding the lid to the bottom of the barbeque and weld both the lid and the bottom of the barbeque. See figures 2 & 3 for dimensions, leg angles, and construction of lower shelf. One inch square tubing was utilized in the leg construction. Barbeque leg angle is important, as the legs will keep the barbeque upright when the lid is opened abruptly.

The lower shelf is also constructed of one inch square tubing and is butt-welded to the legs. This shelf's sole function is to hold the gas line for the burner, see figure 2.

Mount the 6" wheels to the legs, and then weld the 8" handle to the legs. See figure 2 for handle placement. Remember this barbeque is extremely heavy and the greatest mechanical advantage is needed to move the unit. Heat conduction to the handle is at a minimum.

See figure 1 for vent construction. Weld the vent to the lid using the short arc method. Vent dimensions are both functional and add to the appearance of the barbeque. These dimensions should not be altered.

Construction of the heating element is the next step: Keep in mind the pattern if the barbeque is to function properly. See figure 4 for burner layout and dimensions. Burner construction utilized 1" x 1½" rectangular tubing and a wall thickness of ⅛". Drill pilot holes with a ³⁄₃₂" orfice drill and ¼" spacing. An orfice drill bit should be used; however, satisfactory results can be obtained by

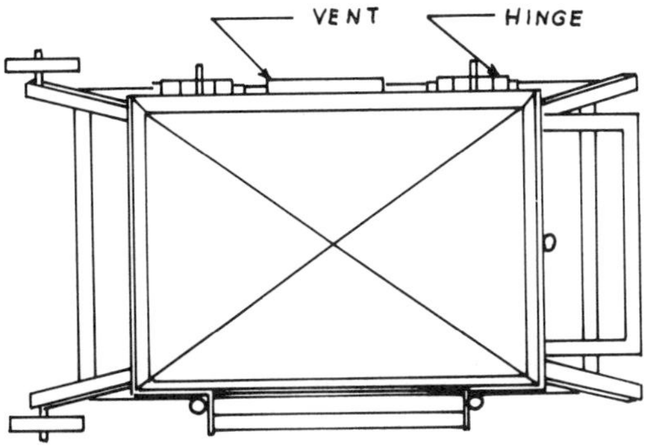
VENT
HINGE

Fig 1

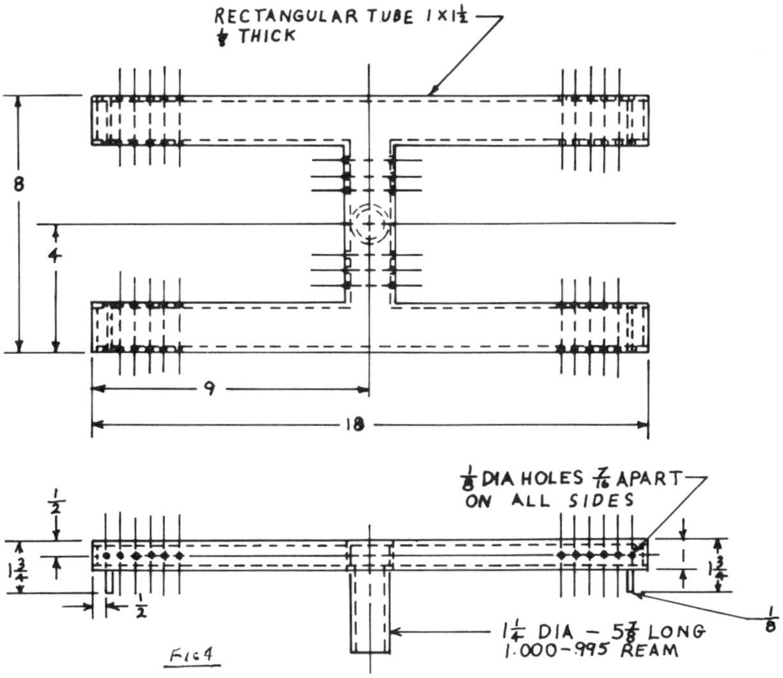
RECTANGULAR TUBE 1x1½
⅛ THICK
8
4
9
18
⅛ DIA HOLES 7/16 APART ON ALL SIDES
½
1¾
½
1¾
1¼ DIA – 5⅞ LONG
1.000-.995 REAM
⅛

Fig 4

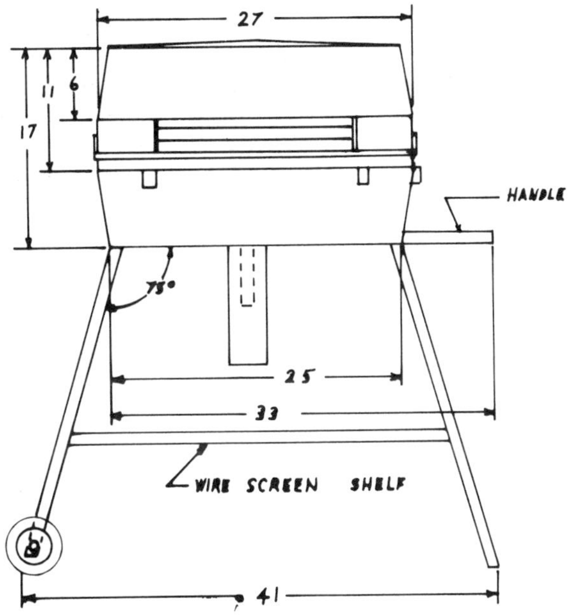
27
17
11
6
HANDLE
75°
25
33
WIRE SCREEN SHELF
41

Fig 2

using a standard metal drill. When welding the burner you must avoid any weld which could leak. A weld which leaks is dangerous.

Construction of the charcoal shelves incorporates ¼″ round stock. The cooking grates are two separate pieces and are made from 3/16″ round stock, see figure 3 for location of grates. Construct the bread rack from the same material. See figure 3 for location and dimensions.

The wooden shelf is placed as indicated in photo. Weld a ½″ flat stock bar around the bottom of the barbeque; this will cover the space between the lid and the bottom of the barbeque. Grind all welds and use a disc sander to remove any weld splattered on the exterior of the barbeque.

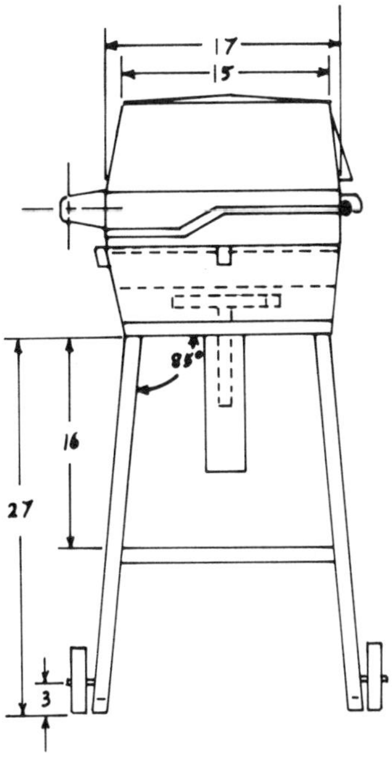
17
15
85°
16
27
3

Fig 3

Materials Needed

Lid	15″ x 24″ x 11 ga
Vent	5″ x 7″ x 4″ x 11 ga
Hinges	¾″ pipe x 1½″ x 4″
Lid Front	9″ x 27″ x 11 ga
Lid Rear	7″ x 27″ x 11 ga
Lid Sides (2)	9″ x 7½″ x 17″ x 11 ga
Bottom Front	8″ x 27″ 11 ga
Bottom Rear	9″ x 27″ x 11 ga
Bottom Sides (2)	8″ x 9½″ x 17″ x 11
Legs (4)	1″ sq. tubing x 27″
Burner	1½″ x 1″ rec. tubing x 18″
Screen shelf	17″ x 33″
Cooking grate (2)	13½″ x 16½″ x 3/16″ rd
Charcoal grate	15″ x 25″ x ¼″ rd
Bread grate	5½″ x 25″ x 3/16″ rd
Wheels (2)	6″ ball bearing
Wooden Shelf	6″ x ¾″ x 27″
Wooden handle lid	16″

Spare Tire Carrier

Author: Jim Pfadenhauer
Instructor: R. J. Madsen
School: Burlington Community High School
City & State: Burlington, IA

This spare tire carrier for a camp trailer is inexpensive and relatively easy to make. The necessary materials and steps are listed below.

Materials:

34″	⅜″ steel rod
21″	2¼ x 2¼″ steel tubing
1 pc.	6 x 7 x ¼″ flat plate steel
22″	2¼ x ¼″ flat band iron
18″	1½ x 3/16″ flat band iron
1 pc.	6 x 4 x ¼″ steel strip
1 pc.	6 x 1½ x ¼″ band iron
18″	¼″ round steel rod
1	3/16 x 3″ bolt
1	3/16″ wing nut
2	5/16″ bolts and nuts
2 sets	5/16″ lugs and lug nuts
1	spring
1 can	primer
1 can	paint

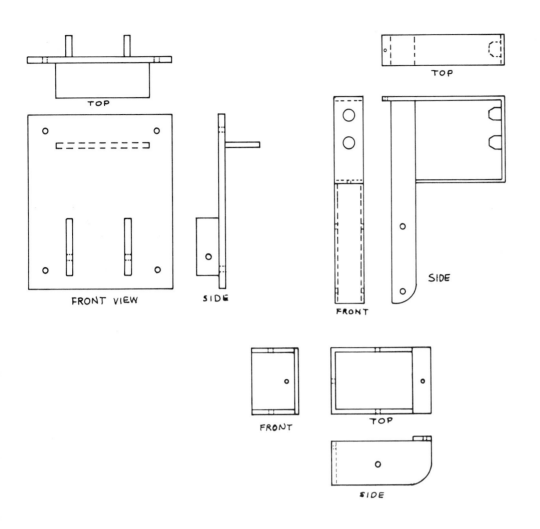

TOP

FRONT VIEW

SIDE

TOP

FRONT

SIDE

FRONT

TOP

SIDE

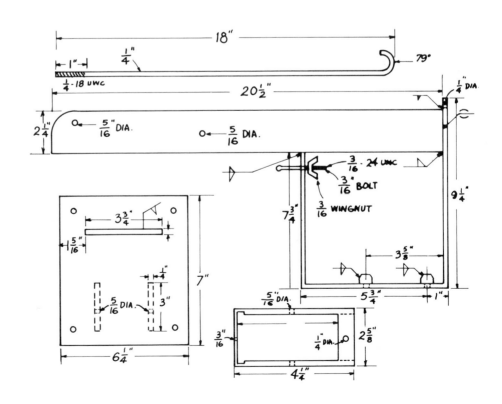

18"

$\frac{1}{4}$"

1"

79°

$\frac{1}{4}$-18 UWC

$20\frac{1}{2}$"

$\frac{1}{4}$" DIA.

$2\frac{1}{4}$"

$\frac{5}{16}$" DIA.

$\frac{5}{16}$ DIA.

$\frac{3}{16}$- 24 UWC

$\frac{3}{16}$" BOLT

$\frac{3}{16}$ WINGNUT

$9\frac{1}{4}$"

$7\frac{3}{4}$"

$3\frac{3}{4}$"

$\frac{5}{16}$"

$\frac{1}{4}$"

7"

$\frac{5}{16}$ DIA.

3"

$3\frac{5}{8}$"

$5\frac{3}{4}$"

1"

$6\frac{1}{4}$"

$\frac{5}{16}$" DIA.

$\frac{3}{16}$"

$\frac{1}{4}$" DIA.

$2\frac{5}{8}$"

$4\frac{1}{4}$"

Motorcycle Trailer

Author: Dan Rudy
Instructor: R. J. Madsen
School: Burlington Community High School
City & State: Burlington, IA

1. Cut 24' of 2½ x 2½ x ¼" angle iron into two 8' strips and two 4' strips.
2. Take three pieces of 3¼" x ⅝" x 4' 7" long steel strips and drill nineteen holes down the center of them using a ⅜" drill bit and spacing them 3" apart.
3. To form the trailer frame lay two pieces of 8' angle iron parallel 4' 7" apart.
4. Place one 3¼" x ⅝" x 4' 7" steel strip on each end of the angle iron and the third strip through the middle.
5. Weld the trailer frame together in flat position.
6. Take 4½' of 2½" diameter pipe and measure 3¼" off from the back of the pipe, and ½" up from the floor.
7. Then cut the pipe so it will sit flush to the end of the trailer.
8. Take the two pieces of 4' angle iron and cut the ends.
9. Put them on each side of the trailer sitting inward toward the pipe to the tongue of the trailer.
10. Weld angle iron and pipe to the trailer and to each other in the flat position.
11. For supports cut a piece of 20' 1" x 1" x ¼" angle iron into four 4' 7" strips.
12. Space evenly between the steel strips and weld.
13. Buy an axle to fit the trailer.
14. Measure 3½' from the back of the trailer and clamp the axle and weld to the trailer in horizontal and flat position.
15. Get lumber for the bed of the trailer. Seven pieces of 1" x 5½" #3 lumber, 8' long, and six pieces of 1" x 2½" #3 lumber, 8' long.
16. Clamp the lumber to the trailer so they are evenly spaced apart.

17. Using a ⅜" drill bit drill the holes through the lumber by drilling through the bottom of the support braces which can be used for guides.
18. Get three pieces of 6" channel 7' long. These will be bolted to bed and help hold the cycles stable.
19. Mark the places where holes are to be drilled in the channel iron and using a ⅜" bit, drill holes.
20. To make the front rail take 16' of 1" square tubing and cut into two pieces 2½' long, one piece 5' 2" long, and one piece 5' long.
21. Measure 7' up from the back of the trailer on each side and clamp the two pieces of 2½' square tubing to it.
22. Weld the square tubing vertically to the side of the trailer.
23. Place the piece of 5' 2" square tubing on top of the two pieces of 2½' tubing and clamp it on and weld.
24. Take this 5' piece of tubing, space it properly between the two 2½' uprights and weld it.
25. Bend a 1" round pipe to form the handle.
26. Clamp the handle to the trailer and weld.
27. Buy trailer hitch, tail lights, nuts and bolts, paint, thinner, and paint brushes.
28. Clamp the trailer hitch to the 2½" diameter pipe and weld in flat position.
29. Make a bracket to bolt tail lights so they are able to fit on the trailer and weld the bracket to the trailer.
30. Bolt the tail lights to the bracket.
31. Bolt the wood to the frame and channel iron to the wood.
32. Clean the metal paint.

Material Used:
21 ft. of 6" channel iron
26 ft. of 2½ x 2½ x ¼" angle iron
20 ft. of 1 x 1 x ¼" angle iron
16 ft. of 1" square tubing
7 pieces of 1" x 5½" #3 lumber
6 pieces of 1" x 2½" #3 lumber
paint and thinner
trailer hitch
tie downs
tail lights
nuts and bolts
trailer wheels
axle

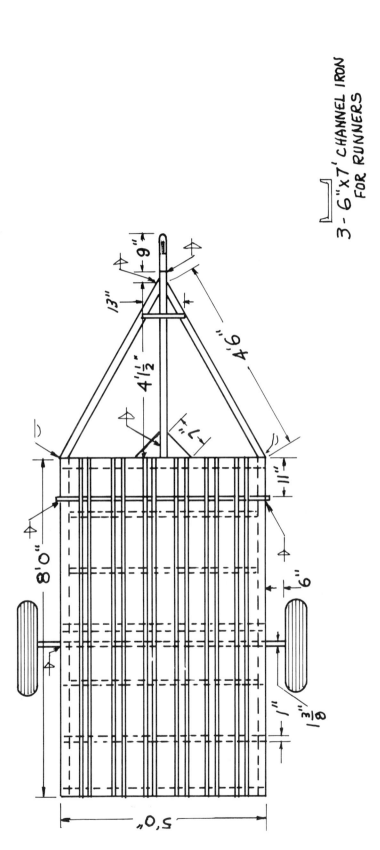

3 - 6"x7' CHANNEL IRON FOR RUNNERS

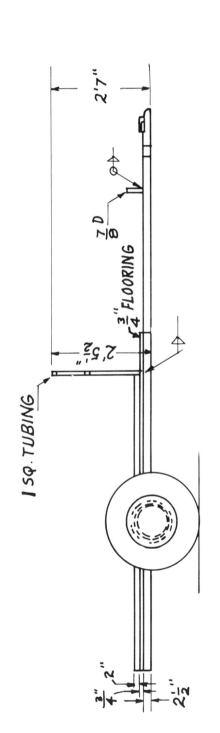

MOTORCYCLE TRAILER

Wheel Barrow

Author: Tom Eschbacher
Instructor: Mr. Herbert Ward
School: North County Tech.
City & State Florissant, MO

Constructing the Bottom
Draw a half circle 7¾'' radius and extending lines 19⅞''
on a five degree angle on both ends of the half circle.
After you have done this draw the connecting line. (It
should come out to be 17¾''). Cut out pattern.

Constructing the Sides
Take a large piece of metal and draw two squares 2' long
and 7½'' wide. Then cut off a 45° angle on one of the corners. Final measurements should now be 24'' x 19⅞'' x
7½'' x 11''.

Constructing the Back
To make the back, shear a piece of metal 25¾'' x 7½''.
Then, take a combination square, set on 45° and cut it on
both sides of the piece of metal at the corners. Final size
should be 25¾'' x 11'' x 17¾''.

Constructing the Front
To make the front of the bed, draw a semi circle 13⅞''
radius and 7½'' wide, cut it out and roll it to fit the bottom and the sides of the wheelbarrow.

Constructing the Frame
To make the frame take two 54¾'' pipe ½'' in diameter
and cut one end off each pipe end at 45°. After you have

done this take a 13¾'' pipe and cut off both ends at a 34°
angle. Fit the three pieces of pipe together. The open
ends should measure 22¼''. To make it stronger make a
base 1'' wide 14½'' long and set it 15¼'' from the front.
When parts are positioned, tack all pieces.

Constructing the Wheel Supports
Draw 2 squares 4 x 2'' on a ⅜'' plate (mild steel). Using
the shear cut them out. Using a combination square, cut
a 70° angle on the edge of both pieces of metal. After it is
cut, drill a ¾'' hole for the axle. To find the approximate
plate to drill the hole measure 1 x 1'' on the opposite side
of the 70° cut side.

Constructing Legs and Leg Supports
Shear out two strips of metal 17⅞'' long and 1'' wide.
Then cut two strips 16¾'' long and 1'' wide on ³⁄₁₆'' metal.
Join the two strips of metal by a piece of metal 3'' long
and 1'' wide to form the legs. (The two 17⅞'' strips are set
at a 65° angle).

Constructing the Cross Brace
Shear out two strips 18'' long and 1'' wide. Place one side
5'' from bottom of legs and place other end 4⅞'' from the
top of legs. Then cross other strip to the same measurements.

112

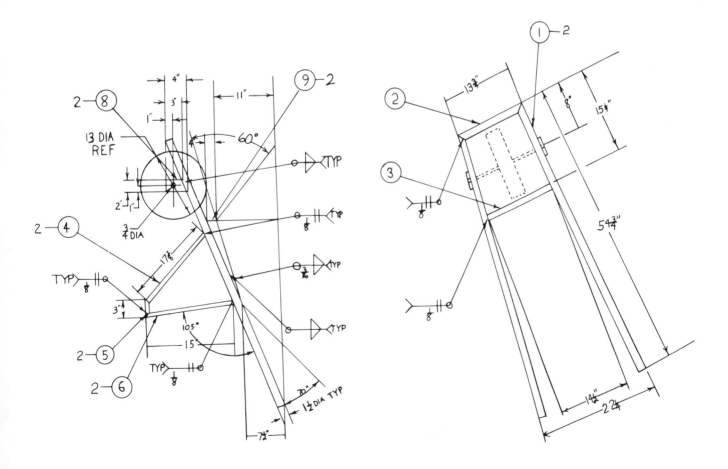

Design and Fabrication of Interior Spiral Staircase

Author: William Herrington,
                   Timothy McNeil
Instructor: Danny Looney
School: Pinellas Voc-Tech Inst.
City & State: Clearwater, FL

When we received our materials, we went ahead and laid out our 13 steps on the plate using the dimensions given on our plans. We first marked out a center line 27″ long, on one end we centered a 3½″ perpendicular line, on the other end we centered a 13¾″ perpendicular line. We connected the ends of the large and small lines on each side of the center line to give us the outside shape of the step. Using a compass, we struck a 1¾″ radius from the center point of the small line. This section of the step will connect to our 3½″ O.D. pipe. Once again, using the same center point, we struck a 27″ radius, giving us the outside curve of our step. All steps were laid out this way, laying them out side by side rotating the large end of the step and the small end of the step in order to conserve materials and time.

On one step you want to use the full diameter of the pipe on the small end of the step. This one will be used as your top step and will cap off the top of the pipe at the same time, making for a neat, finished appearance.

After the steps were laid out, we decided to use a shear to cut the straight edges of the steps in order to conserve time and materials. We then used an oxygen-acetylene cutting rig to cut out both radii.

Our next step was to cut the angle iron, back straps, and gussets used to finish and support the step.

We used angle iron on the bottom of both sides of the step. While giving the appearance of a thick step, it also aids in supporting the step and will keep it from twisting later when weight is applied to the step. The angle was cut using an ironworker to the dimensions given on the plans.

From the remaining plate, the end straps for the step and the gussets to support it were cut. The gussets were rotated large end to small end on the layout to conserve material and once again, a shear was used in order to save time.

We now have all the parts ready to assemble for our steps. They are set aside and we move on to getting our pipe laid out.

The pipe is first cut to exact dimensions using a band saw. The *first step* in laying out the pipe is to mark out the spacing of the steps according to the plans. Here, we made use of a "wrap-a-round" and, starting at the bottom working our way up, our step spacings were laid out. Next, using a punch and hammer we punch marked these spacings for easier identification later on.

The second step is to determine where exactly the step is to be placed on these previously marked spacings. Here we had to keep in mind that we wanted to mount and get off this staircase at exactly the same place. To determine the step placings, we divided the number of steps we had into the circumference of our pipe.

$$\frac{3.14 \times 3.5}{13} = .8458 \text{ or } \tfrac{7}{8}''$$

This answer gives you how much to jog each step around the pipe from the one before it, starting at the bottom and working your way up. First, lay out a center line down the entire length of your pipe. Then, using your answer and punch and hammer, mark out these placings starting at the bottom and going around the pipe in the direction you want the stairs to go.

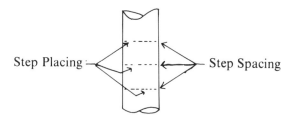

Step Placing   Step Spacing

Now that the pipe is laid out, we set it aside and go back and get our steps assembled.

We first tack welded the angle irons to the outside edge of the step leaving a ¼″ space at the large end of the step to accommodate the end strap. Next, we cut the remaining angle iron out of the small radius so we would have a good fit to our pipe.

Secondly, we shaped the end straps in a roller and fitted and tacked them to the step.

Before placing our steps and support gussets in place on the pipe, we had to calculate how much overlap we would have between steps. We did this by subtracting the circumference of the actual staircase, 169.56 (3.14×54), from the circumference of all 13 steps, 178.75 (13.75 ×13), and dividing this answer by the number of steps we had.

$$178.76 - 169.56 = \frac{9.19}{13} = .7069 \text{ or } ^{11}/_{16}″$$

After determining this answer, we placed the steps and support gussets on the previously marked spots on the pipe. Then, using a level and a framing square, we tack welded each step in place, overlapping each one ¹¹/₁₆ of an inch.

Our next step was to lay out our base plate.

Final welding was our next step. All steps were intermittently welded using the GMAW process using .045 E-60S3 wire. The step connection to the pipe was welded all around with ⅛″ E-7018 electrode using the SMAW process.

After finishing this portion of the staircase, we started work on the hand railing. First, railing supports were cut to the dimensions given on the drawing and tacked to the front edge of each step. Next, we took the remaining square bar and, using a set of rolls, rolled the railing to match the diameter of our staircase. This was then fitted and tacked in place.

Final welding on the railing was done using the GTAW process with Hi-10 wire for strength and appearance.

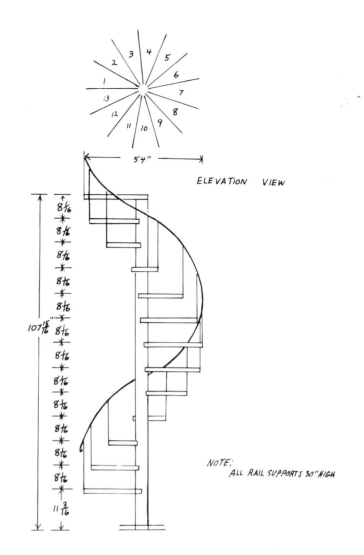

ELEVATION VIEW

NOTE:
ALL RAIL SUPPORTS 30″ HIGH

BOTTOM VIEW OF STEPS

ENLARGED DETAIL (A)

RED/BLACK APPEARANCE OF TOP PLATE ONLY

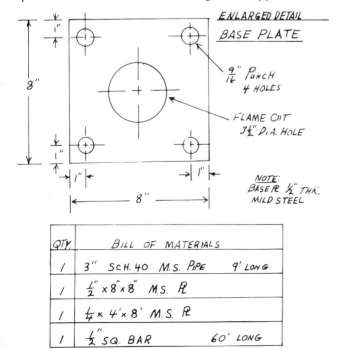

ENLARGED DETAIL
BASE PLATE

⁹⁄₁₆″ PUNCH 4 HOLES

FLAME CUT 3½″ DIA. HOLE

NOTE:
BASE ℞ ½″ THK.
MILD STEEL

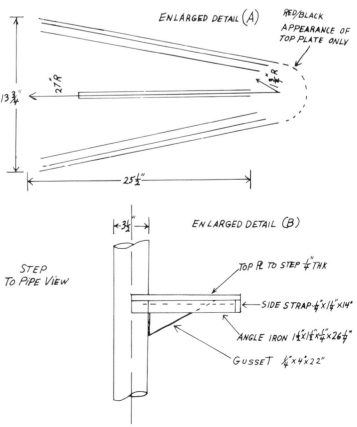

STEP TO PIPE VIEW

ENLARGED DETAIL (B)

TOP ℞ TO STEP ¼″ THK
SIDE STRAP ¼″×1¼″×14″
ANGLE IRON 1½″×1½″×¼″×26¼″
GUSSET ¼″×4″×22″

QTY.	BILL OF MATERIALS	
1	3″ SCH. 40 M.S. PIPE	9′ LONG
1	½″ × 8″ × 8″ M.S. ℞	
1	¼″ × 4′ × 8′ M.S. ℞	
1	½″ SQ. BAR	60′ LONG

Pipe Vined Spiral Staircase

Author:	*Anthony J. Dominski*
Instructor:	*Robert C. Craig*
School:	*San Francisco State University*
City & State:	*San Francisco, CA*

This design is an all metal spiral staircase using formed ten-gauge diamond plate for treads that curve around a central shaft. The handrailing is comprised of ¾'' and ½'' pipes that twist and curve inside each other in asymetric fashion assimilating the random growth of vines. The handrailing serves as an aesthetic element while also functioning as the key structural device for stability.

The intention was to design and build a safe, efficient, lightweight stairway that conformed to the local building code and yet, carried an aesthetic appeal that related directly with its environment, which happens to be the city's flower terminal. Another objective was to eliminate the common problem of torque, twist, and clatter that metal stairways often incur.

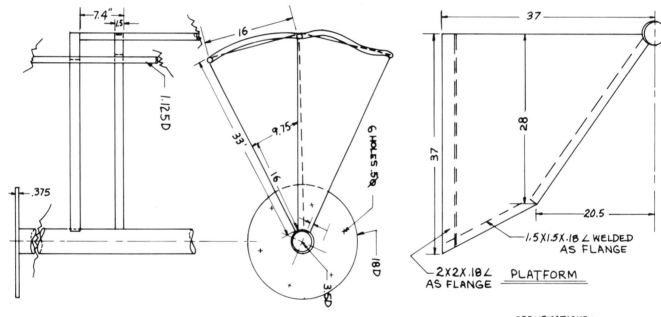

PLATFORM

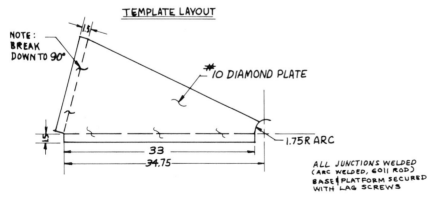

TEMPLATE LAYOUT

NOTE:
BREAK
DOWN TO 90°

10 DIAMOND PLATE

1.75R ARC

33

34.75

ALL JUNCTIONS WELDED
(ARC WELDED, 6011 ROD)
BASE PLATFORM SECURED
WITH LAG SCREWS

SPECIFICATIONS:

FLOOR HEIGHT	– –	125.75''
STAIR TREAD WIDTH	– –	33
RISE	– – –	7.4
RANAT 16'' OUT FROM	–	9.5
CENTER SHAFT		
BANNISTER HEIGHT		30-34
DEGREE OF TURN	– –	445
MINIMUM OVERHEAD	– –	7'4''
CLEARANCE		
OVERALL WEIGHT	– –	560 LB.

MATERIALS:
10# DIAMOND PLATE FOR TREADS
3/4'' ST. BLACK PIPE #40 FOR HANDRAILS
AND 1/2 '' BLACK PIPE FOR SOME OF THE
BANNISTERS.
3'' ST. BL. PIPE #40 FOR CENTER SHAFT
3/8'' MILD STEEL BASE PLATE.
2X2X3/16, 1½ X1½ X3/16 ANGLES USES FOR
PLATFORM FLANGE REINFORCEMENT

Wood Heater and Stove

Author: Robert Hanks
Instructor   Robert V. Wright
School: Lane Community College
City & State: Eugene, Oregon

The stove is designed around a piece of 23", 10 ga., 36" long pipe. A ³⁄₁₆" plate is welded into each end of this pipe. A 13" x 13" square hole is cut into the end and this hole is framed with a ⅛" x 1" flat stock to form a flange for the door. The door itself is made from 1" angle iron and ¼" plate. It fits over the hole much as a lid on a box. The door handle is made from an 18" length of ½" round and cold rolled steel. A 2" length of ½" pipe is inserted through the door and welded in place. The round rod is put 6" into the pipe with a ½" washer welded to the rod on each side of the pipe. The 6 inches protruding inside is bent over to mate with a tapered piece welded to the flange thus forming a latch. A pair of hinges are made from ½" x 2" steel with a ⅜" clevis pin used for a pivot. These hinges are then welded to the door and the end of the stove.

A base is made from ³⁄₁₆" plate. The draft system is made from two 18" lengths of 3" channel iron box welded together to form a tube. One end of this tube is capped and a hole is cut in the side. This tube is then put through a cut hole in the back of the stove in such a way that when it is welded in place it is inside the stove and just below the bottom edge of the door frame. The open end remaining outside the stove is fitted with a sliding door to control the air flow.

Two 3" long pieces of 6" pipe are welded into the top and left protruding 1". These pipes are closed off on top with a ¼" plate. These surfaces are used for cooking in the event of a power failure or they are an excellent place to keep a coffee pot. The center pipe for the chimney is rolled from a piece of ⅛" x 3" cold rolled strip.

The front of the stove is cut out to accept a ⅛" steel box which measures 12" x 24". This box has no bottom or top. The front of the box is made in such a way that a piece of 12" x 24" fire resistant glass will fit it by sliding it in from the top. Behind the glass is a 12" x 24" ⅛" steel plate. This plate is hinged in the center so it may be folded down to view the fire. The plate must be up or closed when the fire is started to prevent the sudden heat from breaking the glass. A 2" x 24" door is at the top of the glass and this is opened to let cool room air flow over the glass.

Iron Fireplace

Author: *Stephanie Williams*
Instructor: *R. H. Texeira*
School: *Maui Community College*
City & State   *Kahului, Hawaii*

The stove is made from a lube oil dispensing tank. The first step is to steam clean and purge the tank. Cut off the tank's angle iron legs with the oxy-acetylene torch and grind welds flush. Invert the tank and flame cut around the cone section to remove it. Shorten the main tank section by eighteen inches and weld the cone back on. All existing pipe fittings are removed and patched. The opening is cut out and bent sections of ½'' pipe are welded around the edge to give it a pleasant appearance.

The base is an old truck rim with one flange cut off. The half rim is inverted and welded to the bottom of the fireplace. The other half of the rim becomes the base for the log grate. The circular grate is fabricated from scrapped #7 re-bar, using low-hydrogen electrodes.

Two swinging arm brackets are installed on both sides of opening from which pots or kettles can be hung to facilitate using the fireplace as a stove.

The fireplace, in its entirety, is then sandblasted, primed and painted with heat resistant, flat, black paint. To add a decorative touch, a steel band can be formed and stainless steel figures welded to it. The band shown was immersed in the ocean to speed up the oxidation process and to give it a golden red texture. However, the stainless steel figures remain unaffected. The band is bolted on the mantelpiece making it a functional and artistic endeavor.

After final installation the inside should be lined with fire brick. The fireplace also has provisions for installing copper coils on the inside for heating water; therby, making it not only a fireplace but also a stove and water heater all in one.

Portable Bar-B-Que Oven With Rotisserie

Author: *Earl B. McGlaughlin*
Instructor: *William L. Findlen*
School: *Northern Maine Vocational Technical Institute*
City & State: *Presque Isle, Maine*

The Bar-B-Que has an 18'' x 30'' grill fashioned from two discarded refrigerator shelves cut down to size and welded together. The removable rotisserie is made with ⅜'' steel rod and ⅛'' copper coated welding rod sharpened for holders, mounted on two 1'' hex nuts with butterfly setscrews for adjustment.

A 12'' x 25'' grate is made with angle iron and 1'' steel strapping for burning solid fuel in suspension for maximum efficiency. A cleanout door is provided at the wheeled end for easy dumping of ashes.

The stand is made of surplus angle iron arranged to facilitate the drum. A piece of marine plywood is used for shelving and two wheels are mounted to provide portability. The drum is removable to allow for replacement when worn out.

Stainless steel plate is used to fashion a working counter and serving area. This is for handling of foodstuff and for easy cleaning.

Gas, Wood, and Smoker Barbecue

Author: Ronnie D. Doyle
Instructor: Kenneth Hillary
School: Central Arizona College
City & State: Casa Grande, AZ

Materials

4' x 6' x 10 Gauge MS Plate	
3'' x 3'' x ⅛'' Angle Iron	5'' long
3'' Sch. 40 pipe	30'' long
20'' Plow Disc	
½'' x 1'' Rectangular Tubing	30'' long
Piano Hinge	30'' long
3'' Channel Iron	1'' wide
⅛'' X ½'' Hex Bolts (24)	1'' wide
⅛'' Nuts (24)	
¼'' x 20'' Allen Cap Screw	
¼'' Round Stock	20'
¼'' Square Bar	10'
Wooden Handle	8'' lg. x 2'' Dia.
Wood Screws (2)	¼'' x 1½''
½'' Square Bar	9'
Broiler attachment from old stove	
Flat strap	2'' x ⅛'' x 8'' long
Flat strap (4)	½'' x ⅛'' x 20'' long
Flat strap (4)	½'' x ⅛'' x 30'' long
Wood strips (16)	½'' x 1'' x 22'' long
Square tubing (4)	1'' x 4' long

Assy 1: Part L is welded to Part M. Tack the two together, check for plumbness and weld.

Assy 2: Parts P, F, Q, and J are fabricated as one sub-assembly. Tack parts together, check for squareness and weld throughout. Weld inside and the outside. These surfaces are to be ground down smooth with a slight roundness on the corners. Locate the center of part Q and tack weld to part L. Be sure to use a framing square to align plate to the pipe. Weld solid.

Assy 3: Weld in parts R, S, & T to the given dimensions.

Assy 4: Tack parts I to J, align these parts, now tack on parts N & H. When this is completed, check for squareness and weld throughout, weld with 6'' spacing between welds. The outside was welded flat, horizontal and downhand, then ground down for a smooth surface.

Assy 5: Tack weld on half side of the piano hinge (part A) to Part H. Hinge can be tacked to the inside or outside of the grill. After bending part B, (or fabricating Part B from two pieces) weld the other half of the hinge to the lid Part B. When all of the first five steps are completed your grill is 90% completed.

Assy 6: Locate lines on Part N and burn out, clean notch and weld Part O into place. There is no need to weld on the inside. Weld part G into place. Be sure to align center of Part G to the center of the grill, and thus aligning Part O with Part G.

Assy 7: The lid handle was 8'' long and 2'' in diameter. Locate the center of the lid, measure up 3'' and spacing of 8'' ID, tack the brackets (Part D) on. Weld brackets on only after insuring the handle is aligned properly. The handle is Part E. Parts D are the bracket.

Assy 8: Part C is welded in so the lid has a resting edge when closed. Weld Part C on the sides and bottom. The barbecue is completed except for locating the holes for the broiler unit and the roastee unit.

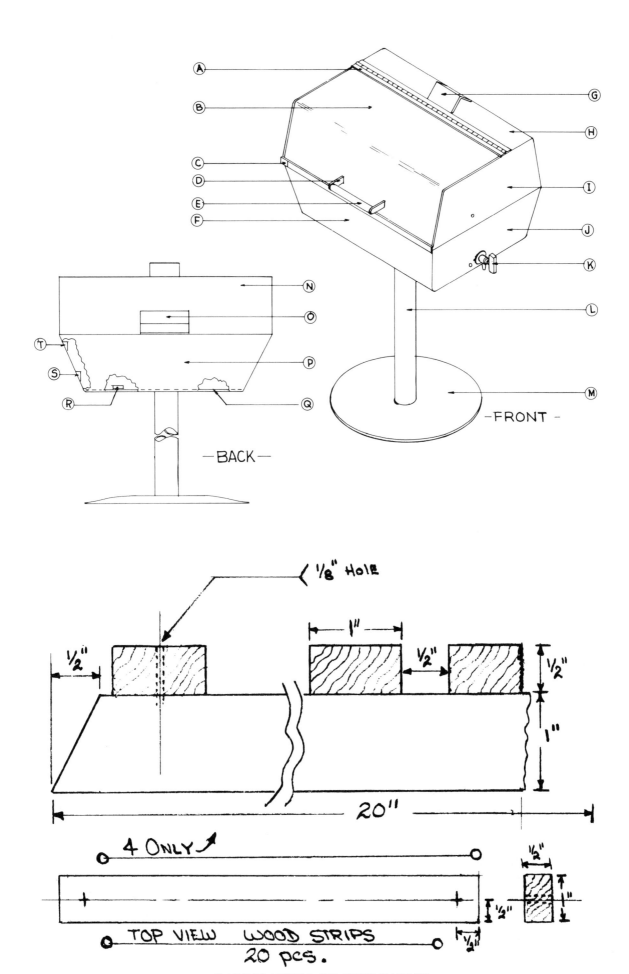

1/8" HOLE

1/2"

1"

1/2"

1/2"

1"

20"

4 ONLY

1/2"

1/2"

1/4"

1/2"

1"

TOP VIEW   WOOD STRIPS
20 pcs.

FABRICATION OF SIDE TABLES

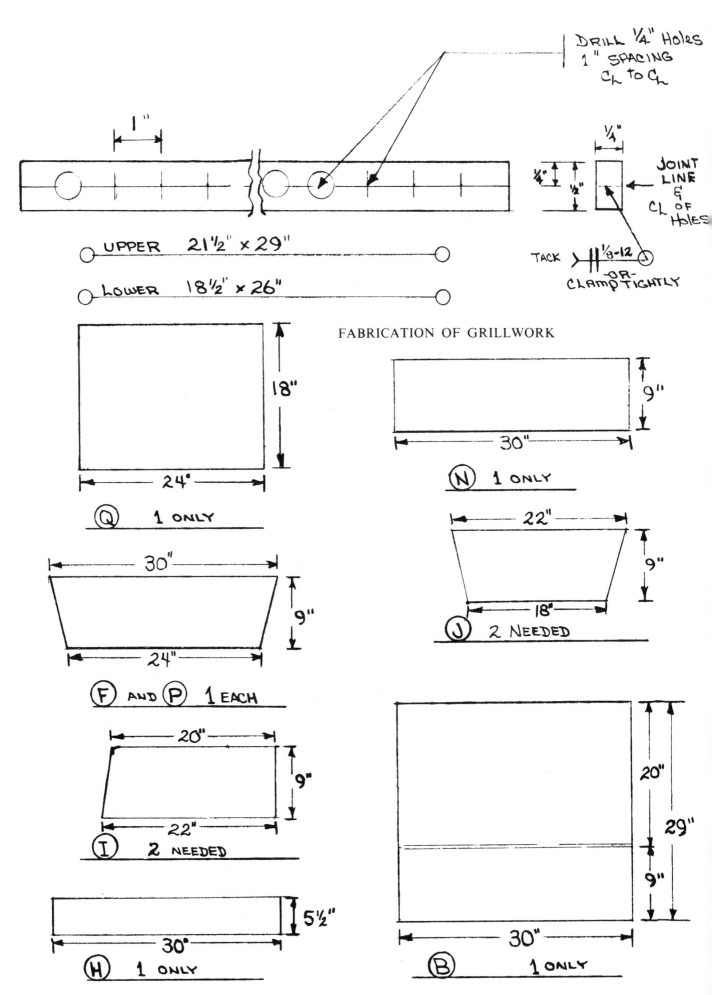

DRILL ¼" HOLES
1" SPACING
C_h to C_h

1"

JOINT
LINE
&
C_h OF
HOLES

¼"

¼"   ½"

UPPER 21½" × 29"

LOWER 18½" × 26"

TACK ⅛-12
-OR-
CLAMP TIGHTLY

FABRICATION OF GRILLWORK

18"

24"

Q   1 ONLY

9"

30"

N   1 ONLY

22"

9"

18"

J   2 NEEDED

30"

9"

24"

F AND P   1 EACH

20"

9"

22"

I   2 NEEDED

5½"

30"

H   1 ONLY

20"

29"

9"

30"

B   1 ONLY

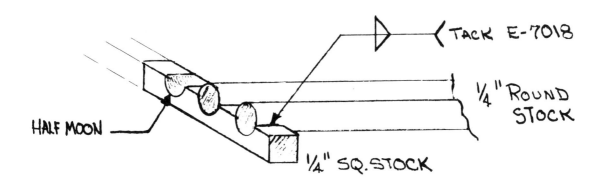

TACK E-7018

1/4" ROUND STOCK

HALF MOON

1/4" SQ.STOCK

FABRICATION OF GRILLWORK

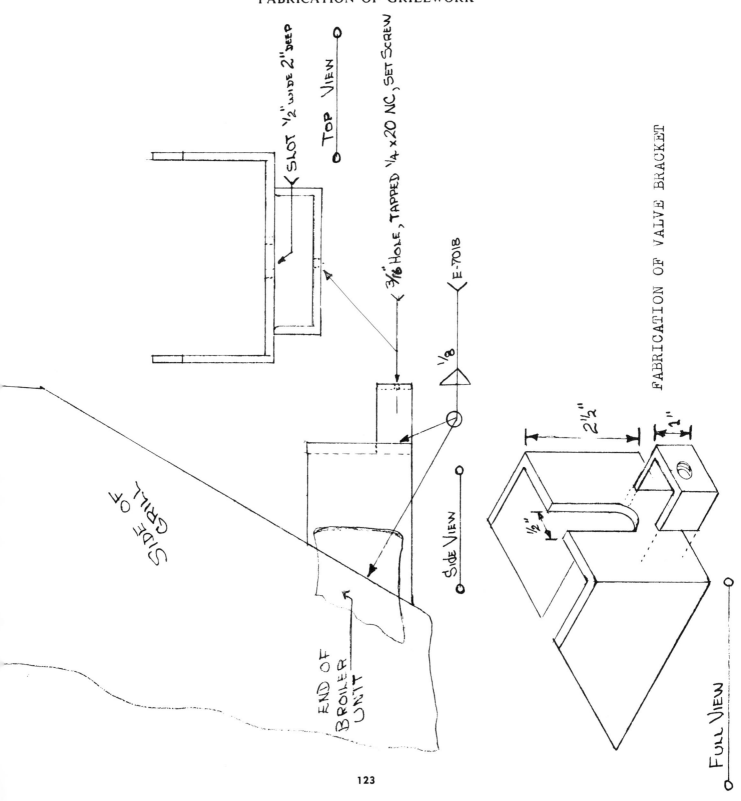

SLOT 1/2" WIDE 2" DEEP

TOP VIEW

3/16" HOLE, TAPPED 1/4 x 20 NC, SET SCREW

1/8 E-7018

SIDE VIEW

SIDE OF GRILL

END OF BROILER UNIT

FABRICATION OF VALVE BRACKET

2 1/2"

1"

1/2"

FULL VIEW

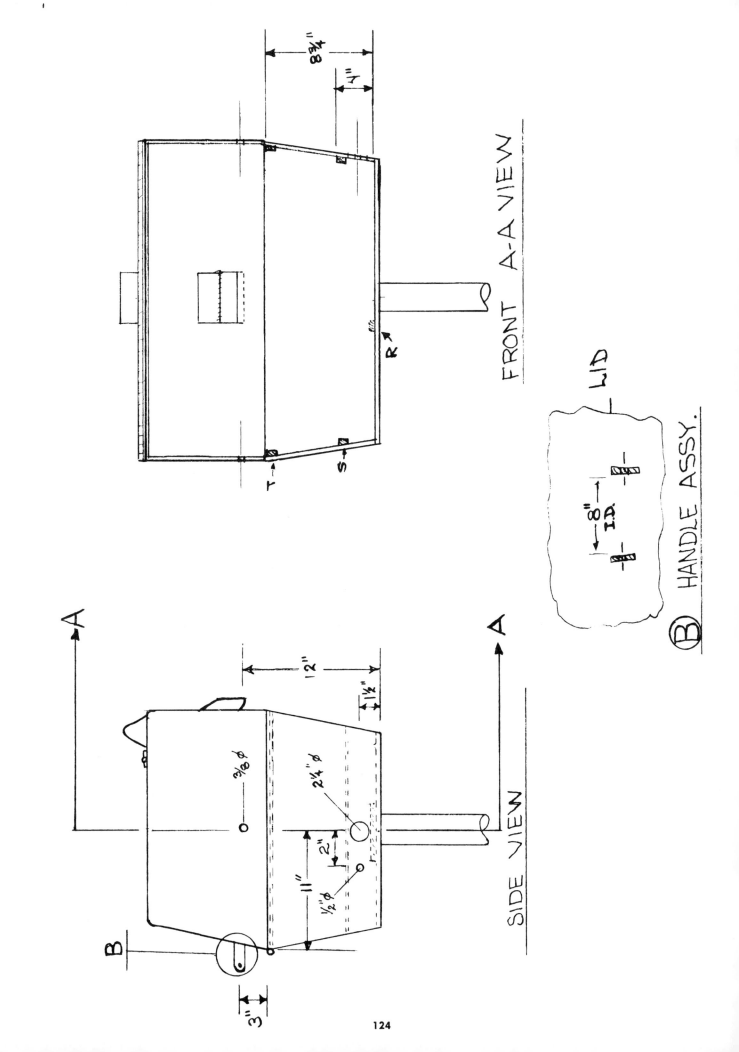

FRONT A-A VIEW

8¾"

1"

R

T

S

LID

8" I.D.

Ⓑ HANDLE ASSY.

A

A

12"

1½"

3/8" ⌀

2¼" ⌀

2"

½" ⌀

11"

B

3"

SIDE VIEW

124

SECTION C
TABLE OF CONTENTS
SHOP TOOLS AND EQUIPMENT

Pickup Truck Versicrane

Author: Mark R. Haynes
Instructor: Hayden M. Soule, Jr.
School: University of Maine
City & State: Orono, Me

The Versicrane features welded construction, versitility and portability. With its 1000 lb capacity, 180° swiveling capability, and low cost, it is designed for farm use, small business deliveries, and home handyman projects.

Power Unit Assembly

The electric motor is a 6 volt starter motor from a 1938-1949 Oldsmobile. This motor is powered on the unit from the 12 volt alternator system of the truck. A voltage of 12 volts is used to provide greater RPM, and thus higher pump flow rates. When run at short intervals, the motor should last for years.

The hydraulic pump is from a 1957 Oldsmobile power steering unit. A 9" galvanized steel cylinder is brazed on top of the existing reservoir for the capacity needed to accommodate the 3" hydraulic cylinder.

The framework uses three ½" x 1" x 6" steel bars welded in a "U" shape, the motor being bolted to the closed end, the pump to the open end. A ⅜" steel plate, 8" x 10" is welded to the bottom of the framework to serve as a skid plate.

Transmission of power from motor to pump is achieved through a 41 pitch chain drive. A 1:2 motor to pump sprocket drive ratio gives the pump added power. To convert the system to chain drive, the pulley was removed from the power steering pump and replaced with a #41, 24 tooth flywheel type sprocket. A #41, 12 tooth sprocket was welded to the unextended pinion gear of the motor. The inside of the pinion housing required some turning on a lathe to gain the clearance needed for the chain and sprocket together.

Electrical connections are made on the standard terminal from the motor and a ground which is welded on the skid plate. Both connections are large enough to accommodate standard auto jumper cable clamps and/or a permanent plug type connection to the truck's electrical system.

The hydraulic system uses ⅝" I.D. hydraulic hose with ¾" coupling. Two couplings were brazed to the old output and reservoir fittings on the pump to facilitate the use of one size of hose. The valve is a standard two way valve, which allows fluid to be either recycled to the pump, (neutral position) pumped to the cylinder (pump

position) or to be released gradually from the cylinder for an easy let-down for the crane (return position).

Once built, this power unit serves as the backbone of the Versicrane. It will develop approx. 1000 PSI. With its standard ¾" female fittings, and the two way permanent-portable electrical system, the power unit not only eliminates the need for a hand operated hydraulic pump on the Versicrane but lends itself to other hydraulic uses such as jacks, splitters, rams, etc.

Crane Assembly

First the crane support rack is constructed. Using 2" x 2" square tubing with ⅛" walls, weld a box type framework, 70¾" wide by 29" high, triangularly braced with 1½" x 1½" square tubing.

These measurements were derived by measuring the stakehole widths (using stakehole centers) of Ford, Chevy, GMC and Dodge trucks, both ½ and ¾ ton with eight foot bodies. Results showed 68¼" to be the average width, with 68" the minimum, and 68½" the maximum. Therefore a framework width of 70¾" will allow the crane to be mounted on all of the major brands of pickup trucks. The 29" height was determined by the height of the pickup cab, desired crane boom clearance and cylinder throw. Bevel all of the framework corners to 45° for strength, ease of welding, and appearance.

Next the support legs are attached. Use two sections of 1½" x 1½" x ⅛" wall square tubing, cut in 56" lengths. These run along the top of the pickup body to distribute

the load of the crane over a larger area. The 56″ length exceeds the maximum center to center stake hole distance of all major brands of trucks by 2″ again allowing the crane framework to be easily adapted to all ½ and ¾ ton American trucks with 8′ bodies. The legs use 9/16″ bolts to secure them into sections of 2″ x 2″ tubing 2″ long that are welded to the base of the crane framework, open end out. The tubing was used instead of mounting tabs because the welding of four sides on the mounts strengthens the lower framework. Braces for these legs bolt onto both the framework and legs using bolt clevices made from pairs of ⅜″ plate, cut 2″ x 2″ for the framework mounts, and 1½″ x 2″ on the leg mounts. These are drilled with a ½″ hole to accept a bolt of the same size.

The crane boom assembly bolts on to the aforementioned rack, legs, and braces. It consists of a boom mounting clevice, a boom swivel rod, cylinder mount, a hydraulic cylinder, two swivel bearings, and the boom. From the top down, the boom mounting clevice is constructed of three ½″ x 4″ x 4″ steel plates welded in a "U" shape, with appropriate holes in either side to accept a ⅝″ pin.

Weld this clevice to the top of the boom swivel rod, a 1″ steel rod 30″ long which is mounted on two 1″ bearings. At the bottom of the rod just above the lower bearing is the lower cylinder mount—a 1″ x 2″ x 3″ steel section which is welded to the boom swivel rod. It also has a 1″

hole for the cylinder mounting pin. The whole unit is bolted to the framework with four 9/16″ x 4″ bolts and two ⅛″ x 2″ x 8″ backup plates.

The boom is a 7′ length of 2″ x 2″ — ⅛″ wall steel tubing, two inches from one end. Weld in a thick wall pipe with ⅝ ID that serves as a bushing. The upper cylinder clevice is constructed of two ⅜″ x 2″ x 4″ pieces of steel plate which are welded to the boom. A ⅝″ hole accepts the cylinder mounting pin. The distance from the boom mounting pin to the cylinder mounting pin is 2′. Atop the boom is a truss to increase the strength of the boom. Directly above the upper cylinder mounting pin, weld a piece of ⅜″ x 2″ steel stock 6″ high and perpendicular to the boom. (7.) Using this as a fulcrum, weld a ½″ steel rod to the fulcrum and to both ends of the boom. The top cylinder mount is constructed of three pieces of ⅜″ x 2″ x 2″ steel plate welded in a "U" and drilled for a ⅝″ pin.

The hydraulic cylinder is a 3″ single acting type, 26″ in overall length, with a 16″ throw. As it is situated on the boom and swivel rod it will give the boom a total lift range of 67″. A moveable front boom clamp allows chains or cables to be attached at different places on the boom for greater leverage.

The whole crane is attached to the truck using stakehole cleats that fit over the legs and rack using 3″ "U" bolts for the rack, and dual ½″ bolts for the legs.

When reversed and mounted in the tailgate stakeholes the rack and legs may also be used alone for carrying boats and pipe, as well as other items too long for 8' pickup bodies.

Power Unit and Crane = Versicrane

Together, the hydraulic power unit and crane equal the pickup truck Versicrane. With its 7 foot boom and 67" lift capability the crane can lift and swivel into the truck such hard to handle items as engines, barrels, logs, cement blocks, large truck tires, castings, machine parts, etc. The power unit will develop 1000 PSI, which goes into the 3" cylinder with a piston cross section of about 7½", thus developing about 7500 lbs. lift. With a 2' cylinder mount—moment arm on the boom, and a 7' boom length, the crain lifts about 1000 lbs. Lifting more than this is not recommended due to possible damage of the truck body and/or tipping of the truck.

With its four mounting points, the Versicrane, unlike bolted in or welded in models, may be easily moved from truck to truck, or be totally removed to make room for the weekend camper. Dismounting and mounting the crane requires about 10 minutes and two people.

In addition, the whole crane framework may be unbolted to break it down into flat components that are easily carried in a truck, van, station wagon or on auto roof racks.

Materials

Item	Quantity
2" x 2" x ⅛" Wall tubing	290"
1½" x 1½" x ⅛" Wall tubing	185"
1" x 1" x ⅛" Wall tubing	65"
1" Steel Rod	30"
⅝" Steel Rod	18"
½" Steel Rod	84"
³⁄₁₆" Steel Rod	26
½" x 2" Bolts and Nuts	4
½" x 4" Bolts and Nuts	3
⁹⁄₁₆" x 3" Bolts and Nuts	4
⁹⁄₁₆" x 4" Bolts and Nuts	2
⁹⁄₁₆" x 5" Bolts and Nuts	4
⅝" I.D. Thickwall Pipe	2¾"
½" Pipe	6"
4" x 4" x ½" Plate	3
6" x 1½" x ½" Plate	2
6" x 1" x ½" Plate	3
2" x 3" x ⅜" Plate	3
2" x 2" x ⅜" Plate	8
2" x 4" x ⅜" Plate	2
2" x 6" x ⅜" Plate	1
8" x 10" x ⅜" Plate	1
2" x 8" x ⅛" Plate	2
3" Hydraulic Cylinder	1
⅝" I.D. Hydraulic Hose	180"
Single Acting Valve	1
6 Volt Starter	1
Power Steering Pump	1
9" x 19" Galvanized sheet metal (18 ga.)	1
¾" Hydraulic Fittings, Female	3

Car Ramps

Author: Fred Brenner
Instructor: Raymond G. Johnson
School: South County Technical
               High School
City & State: Sunset Hills, MO

Step 1 Take 24 pieces of angle iron ³⁄₃₂″ x 1½″ x 12″. On one piece, measure in 1½″ from each end and draw a line from the fillet to the outer edge of one leg of angle iron. Place angle iron flat in vise on bandsaw table line blade up with mark and cut up to fillet. Reposition angle iron in vise to line up fillet with blade and cut down fillet to edge of first cut. Cut opposite end of leg in same manner. Repeat above procedure on remaining 23 pieces of angle iron.

Step 2 Take two pieces of angle iron ³⁄₃₂″ x 1½″ x 24″. Place these two pieces on welding table vertically, fillets facing. Take one 12″ cut out angle iron, place it on welding table horizontally with cut out leg against table. Fit 24″ angle irons into the cut outs. Tack and weld.

Step 3 Take two pieces of angle iron ³⁄₃₂″ x 1½″ x 12″ without cut out. Place them vertically, fillets facing, in the corners that have been formed by the cut out angle iron. Tack and weld.

Step 4 Preparing back plates. The procedures in Step 4 must be done to two pieces of plate ³⁄₃₂″ x 12″ x 15″. Measure down 4″ on the 15″ side and scribe a line parallel to the 12″ side. On this 12″ side, scribe a mark 3″ from both ends. Using ruler, scribe a line from 4″ side mark to 3″ top mark. Place plate in shear and cut marked corners. On uncut 12″ end of plate smear dykem on area 5″ x 12″. Measure in 6″ along edge, mark with center punch. With compass set at ⁴⁄₅, place one end in punch mark and scribe 180° arc.

Step 5 For placement of back plate to frame in preparation for welding. Tack and weld.

Step 6 On back plate along scribed line, place a piece of angle iron without cut out ³⁄₃₂″ x 1½″ x 12″ so that angle is facing out. Tack and weld.

Step 7 Take a piece of cut out angle iron ³⁄₃₂″ x 1½″ x 12″. Place this piece between the two vertical pieces of angle iron—flat side on top—cut out side facing out. Tack and weld.

Step 8 Take two pieces of angle iron ³⁄₃₂″ x 1½″ x 24″. Place the pieces—with fillets facing—on top of 12″ angle iron at either end of workpiece. Using tape measure and measuring from fillet to fillet, check to see 24″ pieces are 12″ apart at both ends. Tack and weld the four ends. The pieces just welded should be tilted toward back plate.

Step 9 Measure and scribe a mark 8½″ from the four ends of the 24″ angle irons just welded in Step 8. Take two pieces of angle iron with cut out ³⁄₃₂″ x 1½″ x 12″. On undersides of 24″ pieces, plate fillets of 12″ pieces on marks—fillets facing. Tack and weld.

Step 10 Take four strips mild steel ³⁄₁₆″ x 1″ x 13½″. On one end of each strip, shear 55° angle. On other end of each strip, shear 35° angle. Take one sheared strip, butt 55° angle against 24″ bottom angle iron and flush 35° angle against 12″ angle iron just welded. Tack and weld. Repeat with remaining three strips.

Step 11 Take mild steel plate ³⁄₃₂″ x 12″ x 24″. Place on top of 12″ x 24″ angle iron frame. Tack the four top side corners. On under side, tack at midpoint at 12″ angle iron supports. In order to prevent distortion, the six tacks will not be welded, but plenty of build up is needed. Butt weld front edge of plate to 12″ angle iron.

Step 12 Take two pieces ½ I.D. x 3″ pipe. Place one end of the pipe at a mark you make 5″ from the bottom and on the outside of both 12″ vertical angle irons. Tack and weld.

Step 13 Take two pieces of mild steel plate ³⁄₁₆″ x 5″ x 8½″. Shear each in half from corner to corner in order to make four triangles 5″ x 8½″ x 9¾″. At bottom of back plate, make a mark 1″ from each corner. At a right angle, butt 8½″ side of triangle against marks on back plate making sure 5½″ side is even with bottom edge of back plate. Tack and weld.

Step 14 Repeat instructions in Steps 1-13 that are necessary to construct another part 1.

Step 15 Take two pieces angle iron ⅛″ x 1½″ x 42″. Round off one leg of each piece. Place these two pieces on welding table vertically, fillets facing. Take one 12″ angle iron with cut out, place it on welding table horizontally with cut out leg against table. Fit 42″ angle irons into the cut outs. Tack and weld.

Step 16 Take two pieces of angle iron ³⁄₃₂″ x 1½″ x 12″ without cut out. Place them vertically, fillets facing, in the corners that have been formed by the cut out angle iron. Using level, check to be sure pieces are squared up. Tack and weld.

Step 17 Take a piece of cut out angle iron ³⁄₃₂″ x 1½″ x 12″. Place this piece between the two vertical pieces of angle iron—flat side on top—cut out side facing out. Tack and weld.

Step 18 Take two pieces of angle iron ⅛″ x 1½″ x 43½″. Round off one leg of each piece. Place the pieces—fillets facing—on top of 12″ angle iron just welded so that rounded ends of 43½″ pieces are even with rounded ends of 42″ angle irons. Tack and weld.

Step 19 On inside leg of 43½″ angle iron just welded, starting from elevated end, use tape to measure and scribe eight marks 5″ apart. Repeat on opposite 43½″ angle iron. Take eight pieces cut out angle iron ³⁄₃₂″ x 1½″ x 12″. From undersides of 43½″ pieces, place fillets of 12″ pieces on marks—fillets facing down the ramp.

Step 20 Take mild steel strip ³⁄₃₂″ x 1 x 11¾″. At bottom of ramp, lay ends of strip flat on 42″ angle irons and snug into wedge at 43½″ angle iron. Tack and weld.

Step 21 Take two pieces angle iron ⅛″ x 1½″ x 6″. Position angle iron in vise on band saw table so cut will start at fillet. Set blade at 40° and cut. Do this to other 6″ piece so cut is made at same end but on other leg. Place

these pieces, fillets facing 40° cut against 43½″ angle iron, uncut end against 42″ angle iron and as far forward as possible.

Step 22 Take two pieces ½″ I.D. x 3″ pipe. Place one end of pipe at a mark you make 5″ from the bottom— and on the outside of—both 12″ vertical angle irons. Tack and weld.

Step 23 Take mild steel plate ³⁄₃₂″ x 12″ x 44″. Fit between legs of 43½″ angle irons so top end is even with fillet of 12″ cut out angle iron. Tack and weld.

Step 24 Take two pieces ⅜″ round steel 10″ long. Make a mark on each piece at 5″ and at 7″. Place end in vise. Using acetylene torch, heat areas at marks while bending to form piece into a 5″ x 2″ x 3″ hook. Do the same to other 10″ piece. These hooks fit into ½″ I.D. pipe to secure the two parts of the ramp.

Step 25 Repeat instructions in Steps 15-24 necessary to construct another part 2.

Materials Used

6 Angle iron with cut out ³⁄₃₂″ x 1½″ x 12″
24 Angle iron with cut out ³⁄₃₂″ x 1½″ x 12″
8 Angle iron ³⁄₃₂″ x 1½″ x 24″
2 Mild steel plates ³⁄₃₂″ x 12″ x 23¾″
2 Mild steel plates ³⁄₃₂″ x 12″ x 44″
2 Mild steel plates ³⁄₁₆″ x 12″ x 15″
4 Angle iron ⅛″ x 1½″ x 42″
4 Angle iron ⅛″ x 1½″ x 43½″
8 Mild steel strips ³⁄₁₆″ x 1″ x 13½″
4 Mild steel plates ³⁄₁₆″ x 5″ x 8½″
4 ½″ I.D. pipe 3″ long
4 ⅜″ round steel 10″ long
4 Angle iron ⅛″ x 1½″ x 6″
2 Mild steel strips ³⁄₃₂″ x 1″ x 11¾″

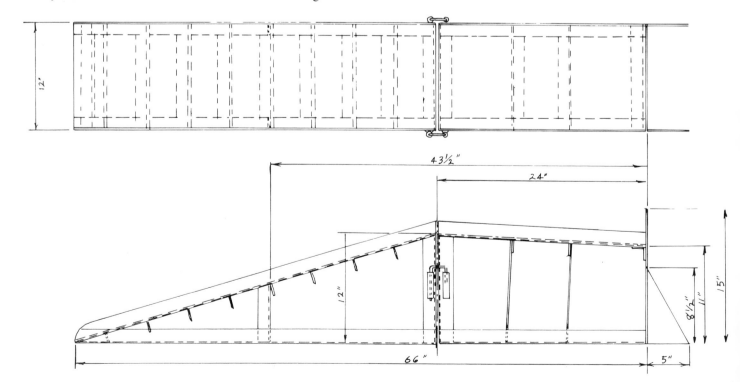

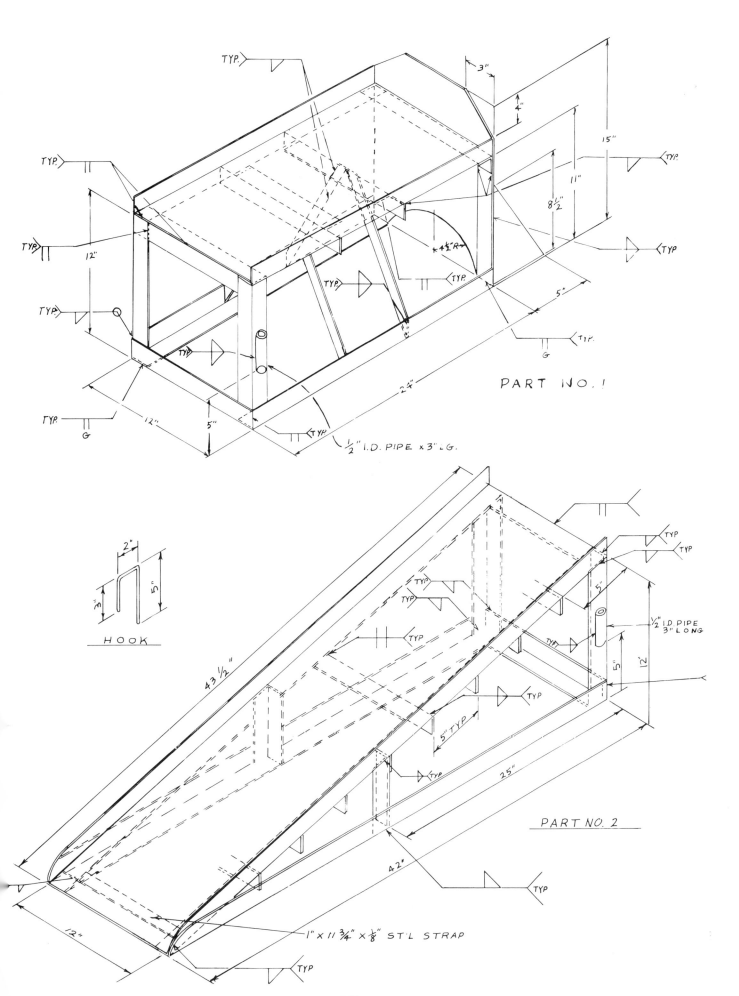

TYP.

3"

4"

15"

TYP.

11"

8½"

TYP.

4½"R

TYP.

TYP.

12"

5"

TYP.

G

24"

PART NO. 1

TYP.

12"

5"

TYP.

½" I.D. PIPE x 3" LG.

2"

5"

3"

HOOK

TYP

TYP

43½"

TYP.

TYP.

TYP.

5"

½" I.D. PIPE
3" LONG

5"

12"

TYP

5" TYP

25"

TYP

PART NO. 2

42"

12"

1" x 11¾" x ⅛" ST'L STRAP

TYP

Plate Dog

Author:	*Clyde F. Coovelt*
Instructor:	*Arthur Campbell*
School:	*Mount San Antonio College*
City & State:	*Walnut, CA*

Using an aluminum template, cut three pieces of ⅝″ steel flat stock, 6½″ wide by 10⅝″ long; one piece 2″ wide by 10″ long by ¼″ thick, for a clevis bracket; one piece of ¾″ by 12″ round stock for a pivot pin; and a shivil hook one ⅝″ piece cut into a 4″ circle. Drill a ½″ hole off center, to serve as a cam to lock in any size sheet or plate,

while moving it from place to place.

Cut out the center plate to allow the cam to turn freely on the axle and weld the three parts together. A chain from the cam to the clevis hook will turn the cam, tighten down on any size plate up to 1¼″ thick.

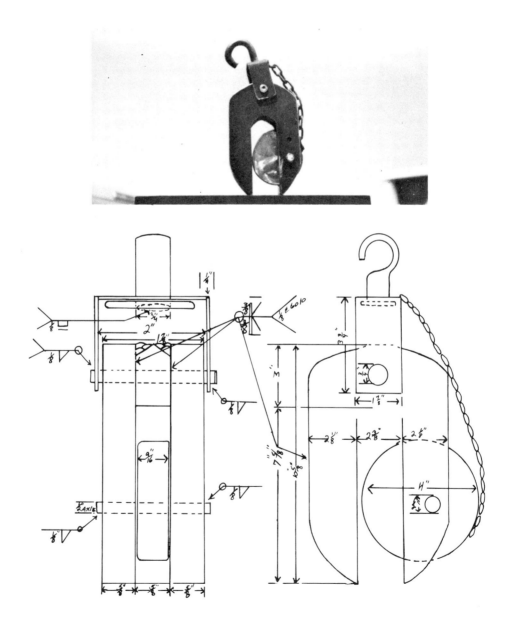

132

Hydraulically Operated Bearing Press

Author: Robert J. Skerl
Instructor: Robert Lee Weisend
School: Portland Community College
City & State: Portland, OR

This bearing press is a device used mainly for removing and installing press fitted parts. Typical parts of this sort are: automobile rear axle bearings, transmission parts and bushings. The press does this by applying several thousands pounds of pressure to a small area of usually a few square inches or less.

The hydraulically operated bearing consists of three main parts: these are , A. Main frame assembly; B. The supports to hold the main frame upright, and C. The pressing mechanism which houses the Hydraulic Jack and Pressing Ram. The third part is attached to the top of the main frame assembly.

The main frame assembly is the support for the entire mechanism. This consists of two upright columns, an upper main frame and an adjustable lower main frame table. The columns consist of two 3½" x 3½" x 57¼" thick parallel steel tubes. The tubes are fastened at the bottom, 27" apart measured from the outside by a ⅜" x 1½" x 1½" angle, 27" long welded in place. The top is fastened together by the upper table. This consists of two 5" x 6.7 lb. Channel 27" long placed ½" below the top of the tubes. A ½" fillet weld is used on the upper and lower joints made up of the channel and tubes. The ends are filled in flush and a two inch long fillet is applied to the inside joints. Ten holes are drilled completely through both upright tubes. These holes 1" in diameter, space 4" apart, measured center to center with the first hole starting 16" from the top of the tubes.

Between these two tubes is the moveable main frame table. This is made up of two 5" x 6.7lb. channels 29" long. These are fastened together 3⅞" apart with the flanges facing away from each other by two 1" x 3⅞" round steel bars placed in the center and 5½ in from each end. These bars are fastened to the channel with a fillet weld completely around the bar. This bar can then slide up and down between the upright tubes and is held at the desired height by inserting pins through the holes in the tubes and allowing the table to rest on these pins. The pins are made of round steel bars, 1" in diameter and 12" long.

The supports which hold the main frame assembly upright are made of two 4" channels 24" long. These are fastened to the main frame, one on each side, by two ½" x 2" bolts, nuts and washers. These bolts are threaded into the main frame uprights from the inside pointing out. The holes for these bolts are centered 2" from the bottom and 2" apart in the upright. The supports have ⁹⁄₁₆ holes, centered on the support and in line with those in the main frame upright.

The pressing mechanism consists of two parallel upright round steel bars spaced 8" apart center to center. The bars are held at the bottom by a steel plate which is attached to the underside of the upper main frame table. The top of the bars are held by a rectangular steel bar. A sliding table moves up and down between these two uprights and is supported by springs. The pressing ram is fitted to the underside of this table and the hydraulic jack set on top of it.

The steel uprights are 1″ round steel bars 27″ long and threaded 5″ from each end with a 14 thread. This allows them to be held in place with three 1″ 14 thread Hex nuts on each end. This allows easy assembly and alignment of the pressing mechanism.

The plate holding the bottom of the uprights is made of ¾″ steel 7″ x 12″ with holes for the uprights in the center of the plate and spaced 8″ apart center to center. In the center of the plate is a 1⅞″ hole fitted with a 1⅞″ O.D. 1⅜″ I.D. sleeve made of seamless tubing 3″ long. This is the lower guide for the ram and is welded in place with a fillet weld completely around the sleeve on both sides of the plate.

The bar holding the top of the uprights is a piece of steel 1¼″ thick measuring 3″ x 12″ with 1″ holes for the uprights centered and spaced 8″ apart center to center.

The sliding table between the uprights consists of a ⅜″ steel plate measuring 6″ x 12″. The plate has two 1½″ holes centered and spaced 8″ apart center to center. Sleeves 1½″ O.D. 1″ I.D. 3″ in length made of seamless tubing are centered and welded into these holes. These act as bushings for the upright guides. In the center of the 6″ x 12″ plate is welded a 2″ round seamless tube 1⅞″ O.D. 1⅜″ I.D. around the circumference, and equally spaced are three 3/16″ threaded holes. Screws are inserted in these holes and holds the pressing ram in place. Two 1¼″ I.D. 12″ long return springs are installed under the table around the uprights.

In conclusion, some methods for correct assembly are as follows. To be sure the main frame assembly is welded together square use a cross checking method. Do this by laying the main frame uprights on a flat surface. Place one upper table channel and the lower brace angle on the tubes, being sure the holes in the tubes are face up. Measure the diagonal corner to corner distance from the outer channel flange to the upper flange on the angle. When the channel and angle are in their proper place and the two diagonal distances are the same, the frame is square.

In assembling the pressing mechanism first cut out all the pieces, cut or drill all the holes and thread the uprights. Then assemble everything in its proper place without welding. Carefully tack each welded piece in its proper position. Check for mobility of the moveable table then weld completely keeping distortion to a minimum. The assembly may need disassembly and honing of the sleeves and possible slight straighting of the table, because the ⅜″ plate may warp a bit. The lower ¾″ plate is then welded to the underside of the upper table of the main frame and the unit reassembled.

This press is designed for use with up to a ten ton hydraulic jack.

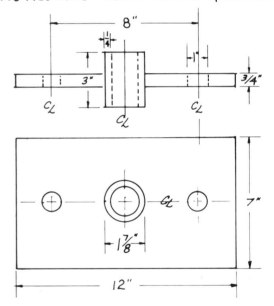

PRESSING MECHANISM LOWER SUPPORT & RAM GUIDE

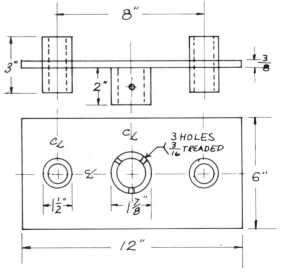

PRESSING MECHANISM SLIDING TABLE

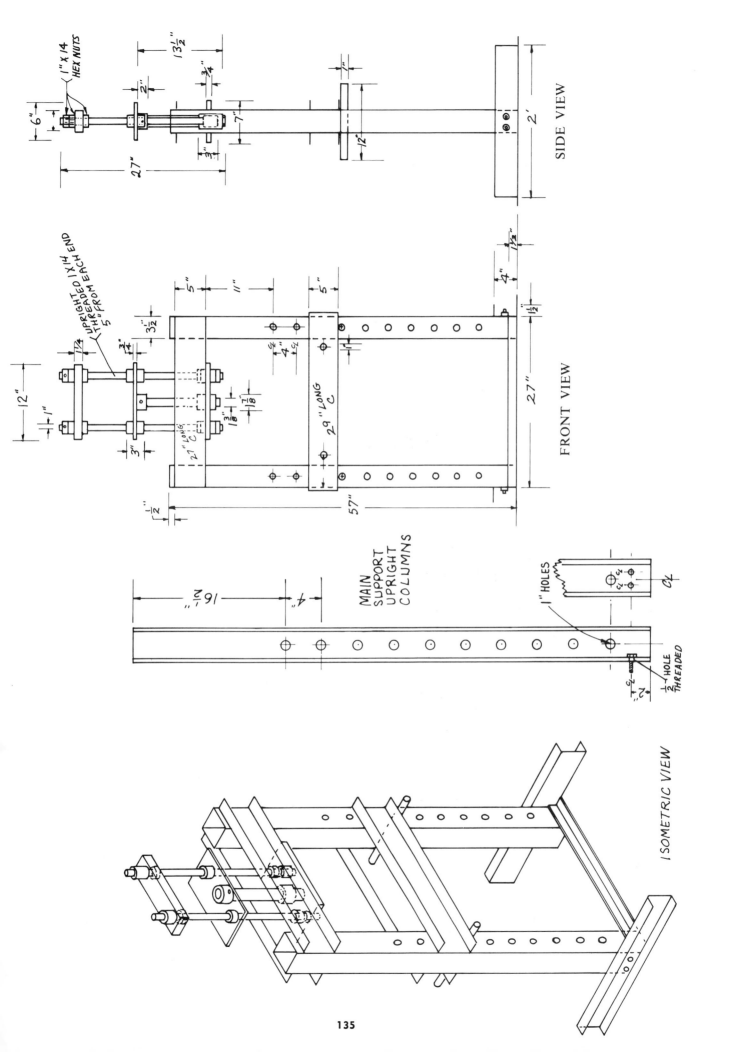

SIDE VIEW

FRONT VIEW

MAIN
SUPPORT
UPRIGHT
COLUMNS

ISOMETRIC VIEW

135

The Construction of a Truck Bed For My Welding Truck

Author: Kevin Dee Felix
Instructor: Dean Sipe
School: Liberal Area Vo. Tech
City & State: Liberal, KS

The first step was making cross-members to the bed frame from seven inch channel iron welded perpendicular to two inch angle iron. The bed of ten gauge sheet metal was at a 90° angle at the edge for a cleaner side. The other piece of sheet metal was bent to create a base for the welder with a two inch lip on both sides of the welder, thus preventing anything from rolling into it. The bed was placed on the cross-members and welded to it.

Two cross-members of heavy wall 1½ square tubing were welded perpendicular to the truck frame, making the truck bed level. The bed was welded to these. Bottle racks were made at the end of the welder on the driver's side as shown in the drawing.

Two top tool boxes were made of sheet metal bent and welded with an inside frame of 1″ channel iron. Overlapping doors were cut for both boxes. Hinges and lock latches were welded on, with pieces of ¾″ x ¼″ strap iron welded to the upper side of the overlapping doors to keep moisture out of the boxes weatherproofed. The boxes were further weatherproofed by placing weather stripping on the inside of the tool box doors.

¼″ sheet metal was used for the bumper to give more strength for the trailer hitch. With the bumper in place, two rectangular and three circular tail light holes were cut out, spaced evenly on the bumper. A hole was cut for the license plate with drilled holes for screws to hold the plate. The cross sills were cut into so that a 3″ pipe would saddle into the cross sills. The 3″ pipe was welded to the top of the bed and also into the cross sills; another 3″ pipe was welded to the bottom of the bumper, giving more strength to the hitch. A 2″ x ½″ strap was welded perpendicular to the hitch giving still more strength to the hitch.

The bottom tool boxes were made by bending sides and bottom for the boxes, cutting the backs and welding in place to complete the boxes. Doors were cut through the bed. With the boxes finished the doors were completed in the same manner as the top tool boxes.

Fender wells were cut to permit changing tires.

A single headache rack was made of 2½″ pipe. A hoosher pole was welded on top of the headache rack for wrapping leads around. The hoosher pole consists of 1″ pipe welded to the top of the headache rack with ¾″ pipe slipped on the inside of 1″ pipe enabling the hoosher pole to move back and forth. Hose rack was added beside the oxygen-acetylene bottles.

A water can holder in front of the tool box, a frame on the left side on the top tool box to hold an ice chest, and a barbequer built from a 8″ pipe, welded it into a bonnet shape completed the truck.

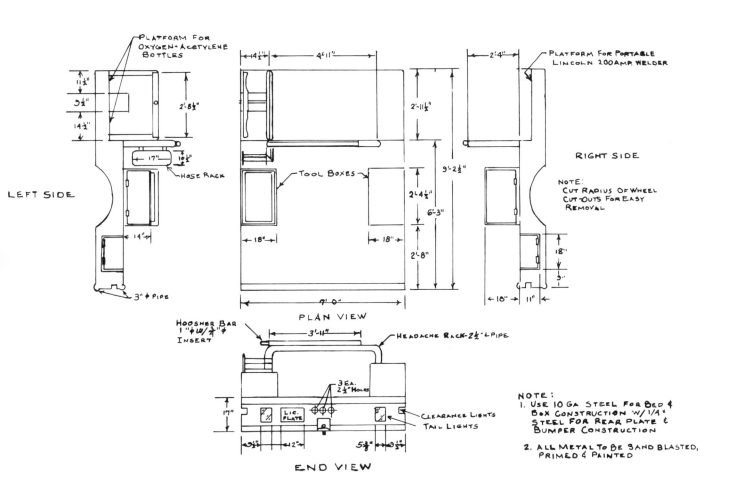

PLATFORM FOR
OXYGEN-ACETYLENE
BOTTLES

PLATFORM FOR PORTABLE
LINCOLN 200 AMP. WELDER

LEFT SIDE

HOSE RACK

3" ⌀ PIPE

PLAN VIEW

TOOL BOXES

RIGHT SIDE

NOTE:
CUT RADIUS OF WHEEL
CUT-OUTS FOR EASY
REMOVAL

HOOSHER BAR
1"⌀ W/ ¾"⌀
INSERT

HEADACHE RACK-2½" L. PIPE

3 EA.
2½" HOLES

LIC.
PLATE

CLEARANCE LIGHTS
TAIL LIGHTS

END VIEW

NOTE:
1. USE 10 GA STEEL FOR BED &
   BOX CONSTRUCTION W/ 1/4"
   STEEL FOR REAR PLATE &
   BUMPER CONSTRUCTION

2. ALL METAL TO BE SAND BLASTED,
   PRIMED & PAINTED

Oxy-Propane Bottle Cart

Author: Timothy C. Gack
Instructor: Steve Vinter
School: American River College
City & State: Sacramento, CA

This cart is made of mild steel tubing and mild steel plate. The wheels and axle were taken from a wrecked toy wagon.

The wheels being mounted in back would allow plenty of room for the bottles while staying within 25 inches in width. This left 3 inches of clearance between the sides of the shop door and the outside edges of the cart frame.

Mounting the wheels in the back gave the added advantage of acting as a more efficient fulcrum when tilting the cart back on the wheels. This in combination with the handle being brought back even with the back edge of the wheels and 4 ft. off the ground acts to give excellent leverage and balance.

In making the cart several problems presented themselves which were not foreseen during the design stage. Not having a tube bender, a problem existed in obtaining the desired bend between the front main support and the handle without flattening out the tubing. A pipe bender with a three-quarter inch pipe die, which was slightly larger than one inch in outside diameter, was used to obtain the proper bend. This was accomplished by sliding the tube an inch at a time through the center of the die and only bending it a fraction of the total degrees of the specified bend. This method produced the desired bend with only a slight amount of distortion. Once the first tube was bent to 40 degrees, the second tube, which was to be the front main support for the opposite side of the frame, was bent exactly like the first.

The second problem encountered was more critical. The center of the tube which was to be the rear main support had to be exactly 12½″ behind a point two inches up from the foot of the front main support.

It also had to be cut so that the axle support when placed as indicated by the drawing would sit 5″ from the ground at the end which the wheels were to be attached. The wheels have a 5″ radius. The rear main support had to be vertical to the ground for balance of the cart when loaded since there was no pattern to work from to determine the proper angles and lengths. The problem was solved by laying the parts, cut slightly longer than the guess-timated length, on a work table and squaring the foot of the front main support and the axis of the rear main support with two adjoining edges of the table. It was then a simple matter to measure and adjust and

grind the ends of the tubes until they fit to agree with how the completed structure was supposed to look when finished.

The axle support was then cut and fitted as shown in the illustration on the previous page. This completed one half of the cart frame when tack welded together. The first half was then used as a pattern for the second. The cross supports were cut and fitted by the same method of measuring, grinding and adjusting until they fit properly and could be tacked.

The final problem encountered consisted of working out an adequate securing device for the bottles. The propane bottle is 12″ in diameter and the oxygen bottle is 7½″ in diameter. Because there might be a change in the bottles, as to acetylene, and considering the difference in the diameters of bottles which can be rented, I decided on a wooden cradle with a chain to secure the bottles.

By fastening the cradle to the frame by means of three eye bolts it would be possible to change to a different cradle if required in order to accomodate different sized bottles. The eye bolts afforded the added advantage of acting as anchors for chain.

The tool box shown in the drawing but not the photos was made of light gauge metal and pop-riveted together and to the frame. The entire box was cut from one sheet of metal and folded to shape before being attached.

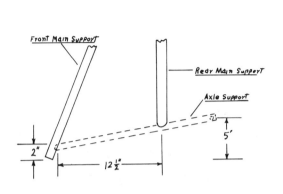

Front Main Support

Redr Main Support

Axle Support

2"

12 1/2"

5'

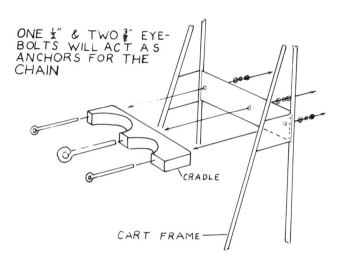

ONE 1/2" & TWO 3/8" EYE-BOLTS WILL ACT AS ANCHORS FOR THE CHAIN

CRADLE

CART FRAME

Exploded view of the Bottle cradle and cart Frame

NOTES:
- Ⓐ 38 1/2" LONG
- Ⓑ 18 3/4" LONG
- Ⓒ 10 DIAMETER WHEELS
- Ⓓ (SEE BLOW-UP)
- Ⓔ AXLE 1/2" ROUNDBAR
- Ⓕ AXLE SLEEVE 3/4" PIPE
- Ⓖ WELD ALL JOINTS WITH E-7018 LH
- Ⓗ ALL NON MOVABLE JOINTS ARE TO BE WELDED SAME AS "G" UNLESS OTHERWISE INDICATED

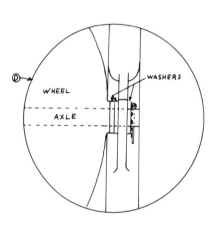

WASHERS

WHEEL

AXLE

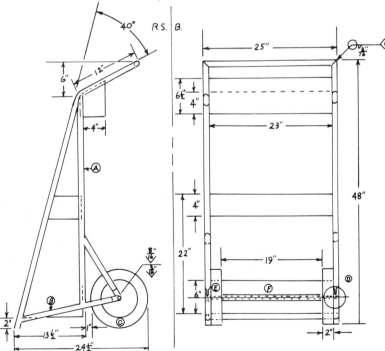

40°   R.S. B.

12"

6"

4"

25"

6 1/2"
4"

23"

4"

22"

19"

48"

2"

13 1/2"

24 1/2"

1"

6"

2"

2"

LIST OF MATERIALS		
ITEM NO.	PART OR MATERIAL	AMOUNT REQ.
1	1" STEEL TUBE : A 500	25'
2	1/8" R	556 SQ."
3	1/16" SHEET METAL	202 SQ"
4	10" DIAMETER WHEELS	2
5	1/2" WASHERS	8
6	COTTER PINS	2
7	3/4" STEEL PIPE	19"

FINISH RUST OLEUM
FED. SAFETY GREEN

OXY-PROPANE CART-PORTABLE

004   SHEET # 1

139

Rust Proof Forge

Author: *Donald Jerry Rhymer*
Instructor: *W. A. Newton*
School: *H. B. Swofford Vocational School*
City & State: *Inman, SC*

Materials

Scrap Stainless Steel Sheet
Scrap Stainless 2" strips
Five-inch stainless pipe
Two-inch Stainless pipe
Old vacuum cleaner
Stainless beer barrel

Weld the flat sheets together to make the top and then turn a one inch flange up on all four sides. Cut the beer barrel in half for the ducks nest, mark a hole in the sheet, cut the hole and weld the top of the forge to the half of the stainless steel beer barrel to make the top and the ducks nest. Weld ¼" pieces of flat stainless into the bottom of the duck nest to serve as the grate. Weld scrap pieces of stainless steel rods into the ducks nest to hold the refractory in place as it is formed in the ducks nest. Then to the bottom of the ducks nest under the grate weld piece of 5" pipe to serve as the ash pit. Break flat strips to make 1" angle out of them to serve as the legs which were about 4 feet long. Weld strips together to make braces for the legs. Scrap pieces of angle iron made out of the flat strips are used to make the mount for the vacuum cleaner blower. Weld the 2" pipe to the end of it, and use a scrap piece of the flat stainless to make a damper to cut the flow of air or to increase it. Cut a hole in the 2" pipe about 3" from the blower and weld another piece of 2" pipe about 4" long into the hole. Weld another piece of 2" pipe into ash pit pipe and join the two with radiator hose. Mount a toggle switch in one of the legs to cut the motor off and on. This forge being all stainless steel except the toggle switch, the pieces of radiator hose and refractory will not rust.

Design and Construction of Engine Crane

Authors: Craig S. Patzwald
Robert D. Canterberry
Instructor: James Tripp
School: Central Florida Community College
City & State: Ocala, FL

Design features
  A. Telescoping legs
  B. Hinged jack base
  C. Casters permitting mobility

Step 1—Base—Refer to Isometric Drawing
  A. Cutting and shaping
    1. Pieces 1 and 2 cut to 46″ in length
    2. Pieces 1 and 2 fishmouth type joint at Piece 3
    3. Piece 3 cut to 30″
    4. Piece 4 cut to 17¾″; angled to fit.
    5. Telescope A-B cut to 40″
    6. Telescope C-D cut to 20″
    7. Caster pads 13, 14, 15, 16 each 5½″ x 7″ x ¼″
    8. Drill holes 4-⅜″—2″ from ends of Pieces 1, 2, and 3, for lock bolts 19, 20, 22, and 23.
  B. Base layout—Angle 1A and 2A-80°
  C. Joining pipes
    1. Electrode—⅛″ dia Lincoln E 6013
    2. Flat position
    3. Fillet—multiple pass all around
  D. Gussets
    1. I and II—³⁄₁₆″ plate
    2. Corner fitted
    3. Mig welded

Step 2—Main Vertical Support
  A. Cutting and Shaping
    1. Piece 5 cut to 5′
    2. Pieces 6 and 7 cut to 10″
    3. Drill ⅜″ holes 3″ from end of Pieces 6 and 7.
    4. Piece 8 is 6″ pipe 3 inches long split in half.
  B. Support Layout
    1. Piece 5—75° angle.
    2. Tack pieces 6 and 7—parallel to piece 5.
    3. Tack piece 8 from piece 6 to piece 7
    4. Tack pieces 11 and 12 from pieces 6 and 7 to piece 3.
  C. Joining Pieces
    1. Electrode—⅛″ dia Lincoln E 6013.
    2. Flat position
    3. Fillet—multiple pass.

Step 3—Boom
  A. Cutting and Shaping
    1. Piece 9 cut to 49″ in length.
      a. Drill ⅜″ hole 4″ from one end
      b. Drill ⅜″ hole 2″ from other end for lock bolt 21.
    2. Telescope E cut to 30″
    3. Drill ⅜″ hole 2″ from end.
    4. Piece 10 cut to 13½″
    5. Drill three ⅜″ holes in piece 10

  B. Welding piece 10 to boom.
    1. Electrode—⅛″ dia. Lincoln E 6013
    2. Flat position
    3. Fillet—multiple pass

Step 4—Jack Base Assembly-Refer to Detail Sheet No. 4
  A. Cutting and Shaping
    1. Piece A—⅜″ plate 8″ long by 5″
    2. Piece A flame cut to fit vertical support as shown in detail sheet no. 4.
    3. Piece B—½″ plate 6″ x 5¼″-flame cut to fit.
    4. Pieces C and D—2½″ x 2½″ x ½″ with ⅝″ hole.
    5. Piece E—⅝″ x 5″ steel rod
    6. Piece F—5″ x 5″ x ⅜″ with 2¼″ holes.
    7. Piece G—1½″ ID pipe 2″ long.
    8. Pieces H-I 2″ x 2″ channel.
  B. Layout of Jack Base
    1. Piece A parallel to base.
    2. Other pieces assembled to A.
  C. Joining Parts
    1. Piece A welded to vertical support.
    2. Piece B welded to A and vertical support.
    3. Pin E welded to B.
    4. Piece C welded to F.
    5. Piece C-F assembled to Pin E.
    6. Piece D welded to F.
    7. Piece G assembled to jack with press fit.
    8. Jack bolted to jack base assembly.
      a. Electrode—⅛″ dia Lincoln E 6013
      b. Flat position.
      c. Fillet weld—multiple pass.

Materials

Quantity	Description
20 ft.	2½″ I.D. black pipe
12′ 6″	2″ I.D. black pipe
2′ 4″	¼″ x 6″ flat bar
6″	½″ x 6″ flat bar
1′ 1″	⅜″ x 5″ flat bar
8′ 10″	⅛″ x 1″ x 1″ angle iron
20″	⅜″ x 3″ flat bar
6′ 6″	³⁄₁₆″ x ½″ x ½″
3′	⅜″ proof core chain 2625 wt. lb. limit
1 ea	⅜″ clevis grab hook
1ea	4-ton hydraulic jack
4 ea	6″ swivel caster, 800 lb / caster
5 ea	⅜″ x 1½″ NF bolts
5 ea	⅜″ NF nuts
1 qt.	Zinc chromate primer
1 qt.	Hemi orange paint

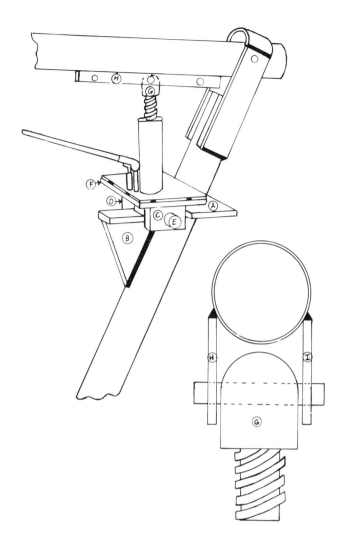

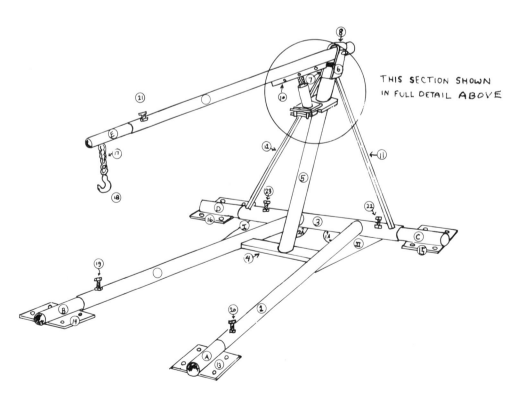

THIS SECTION SHOWN
IN FULL DETAIL ABOVE

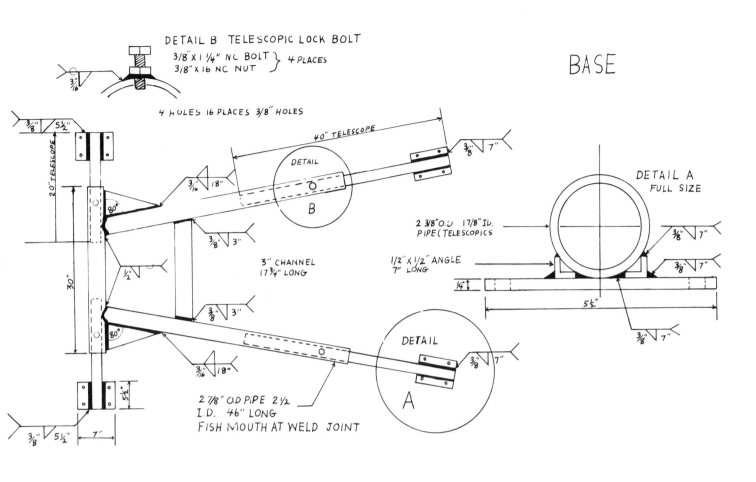

DETAIL B TELESCOPIC LOCK BOLT

3/8" X 1 1/4" NC BOLT ⎫ 4 PLACES
3/8" X 16 NC NUT ⎭

BASE

4 HOLES 16 PLACES 3/8" HOLES

40" TELESCOPE

3/8" 5 1/2"

2.0" TELESCOPE

80°

30"

DETAIL
B

3/16 18"

3/8 3"

1/2"

3" CHANNEL
17 3/4" LONG

3/8 3"

80°

3/16 18"

2 7/8" O.D PIPE 2 1/2
I.D. 46" LONG
FISH MOUTH AT WELD JOINT

DETAIL
A

3/8 7"

3/8 7"

DETAIL A
FULL SIZE

2 3/8" O.D 1 7/8" I.D.
PIPE (TELESCOPICS

1/2" X 1/2" ANGLE
7" LONG

1/4"

5 1/2"

3/8 7"

3/8 7"

3/8 7"

5 1/2"

3/8 5 1/2" 7"

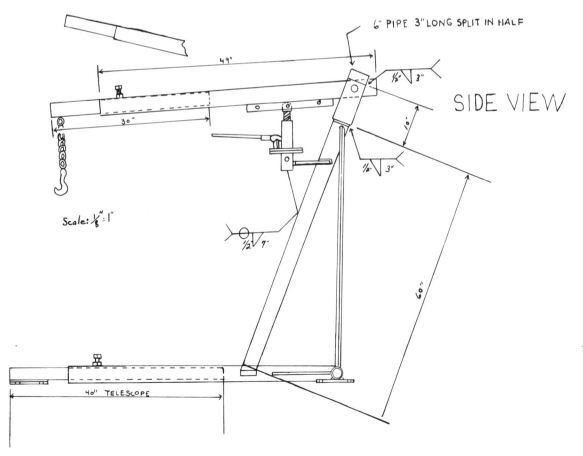

6" PIPE 3" LONG SPLIT IN HALF

49"

1/2 3"

30"

10"

1/8" 3"

SIDE VIEW

Scale: 1/8" = 1"

1/2 7"

60"

40" TELESCOPE

143

Heavy Duty Auto Ramps

Author: Don Werner
Instructor: Paul N. Stevenson
School: Kansas State University
City & State: Manhattan, KS

Requirements of the Auto Ramps:
1. Support over 5 tons
2. Be 12″ tall
3. Separate the ramp from the stand for ease of working under the car
4. Be fairly light weight for easy handling

In designing these ramps to fit the needs and requirements, research was conducted by examining ramps in stores and getting ideas about their material and construction. Measurements of the ramp angle, length, width, and height were taken.

From these measurements and observations preliminary sketches were made of the project, making minor changes in its construction. These basically included relocating some of the structural bracing used on the ramps and stands. The final drawing was then drawn to a scale of 1½″ = 1′. From this drawing the lengths of all metal needed were derived.

Cut the metal to the length specified in the drawing using the power metal band saw. Cut the specific angles as the project is assembled to insure a tight fit.

Tack weld the square tubular metal frame, checking for squareness as each piece is welded. When squaring the entire stand, weld the first support rung into place and tack weld scrap metal on the bottom of the legs of the stand. To square the frame, measure diagonally from corner to corner; then put a bar clamp on the longest diagonal and tighten until the length of the diagonals equal each other. With the frame squared and the bar clamps still in place, tack the cross bracing into place and weld completely. Next, weld the cross support rungs into place. The spacing for these are denoted on the final drawing. Weld the group of four rungs close together to provide extra support where the wheel sits.

Weld the short piece of pipe into place 4″ off the ground on the square tubular frame where the ramp is to join it. Construct both stands the same way.

Construction of the Ramps

Tack weld the square tubular frame first and then check for levelness. Note: All six points of the ramp must touch the ground. Weld the structural bracing into place, but to do this the frame must be square. To square, weld the first and last rung into place and then tack weld some scrap metal on the bottom of the legs of the square tub-

ing. Next measure the diagonals and tighten a bar clamp on the longest diagonal until they equal. Tack weld the cross bracing and weld into place and then weld the support rungs into place all the way up the ramp. Space these as shown in the drawing.

Fabricate the hooks as follows: Bend the 10½″ long, ¼″ rod to resemble that in the drawing. Insert the bent rod into the 3″ piece of pipe to be welded to the ramp and weld a nut onto the long end of the rod to act as a stop when it is lifted. This hook arrangement is then welded onto the ramp 4″ from the ground as shown in the drawing. This completes the construction part of this project. Both ramps are constructed the same.

The ramps maximum capacity should be 10 tons—8 tons safely. There is no provision made to block the wheel from rolling back off the stand after the ramp is removed; however, a block of wood can be put in between the last two rungs or block the wheels still on the ground.

144

MATERIALS LIST

Ramps: for two Ramps)

square tubing 1¼″	quantity
3′ 2″	(4)
1′	(4)
6″	(4)
18′ 8″	total
angle iron 1″	
1′ 3″	(12)
8″	(4)
10″	(10)
26′	total

Stand: (for two stands)

square tubing 1¼″	
1′	(8)
19″	(4)
4″	(4)
10″	(2)
17′ 4″	total
angle iron 1″	
1′ 5″	(8)
10″	(14)
1′ 3″	(4)
28′	total

K.S.U. SUPPLIES

495 count wire
30 min bench grinder
90 min port. grinder
120 min wire wheel
15 min cutting gas
10 min cut-off saw
3 hrs band saw

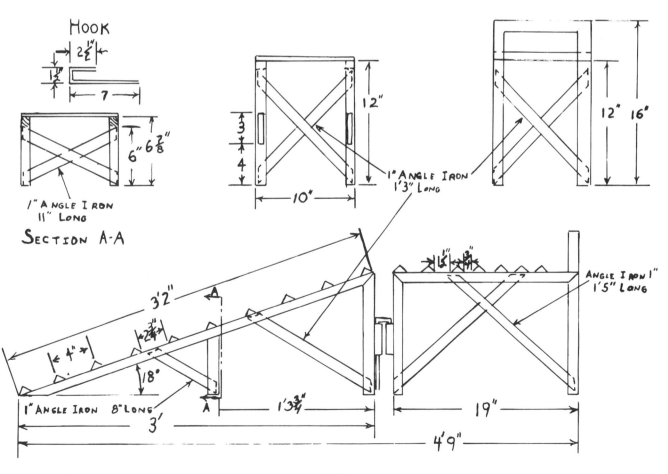

HOOK

2½″

1½″

7

6″ 6⅞″

1″ ANGLE IRON
11″ LONG

SECTION A-A

12″

3

4

10″

1″ ANGLE IRON
1′3″ LONG

12″ 16″

ANGLE IRON 1″
1′5″ LONG

3′2″

A

4″

2¾″

18°

1″ ANGLE IRON 8″ LONG

A

3′

1′3¾″

19″

4′9″

Do It Yourself Anvil

Author: Daryl D. Smith
Instructor: Lee Steinmyer
School: Manhattan Area Vo-Tech School
City & State: Manhattan, KS

The do it yourself anvil consists of heavy plate steel scrap which could be made from a variety of sizes, depending on what is readily available. This particular anvil was assembled from 3 pieces of 2½″ and 1 piece of 1¾″ plate. Because no pieces were available for the correct size base, two pieces of 2½″ plate were double vee cut and welded together. A 10″ x 9″ base was the result. The 3″ radius half circles were flame cut by hand. The holes for fastening the base plate down were drilled with a ⅜″ drill bit and drill press.

Looking up from the base the stem was cut from 1¾″ plate and welded to the base. The stem was 16″ in length and 5¼″ in height. This length could vary about 3″ when the horn and rear of the anvil were shaped. The top and the horn of the anvil was made from 2½″ plate and was welded to the stem. After the top was welded the stem, horn and rear radius of the anvil were flame cut to the desired shape, this could vary to the builders future use. The bottom radius of the horn was ground to give a

finished appearance.

The deck and horn of the anvil were then hard faced with a manganese 3/16″ hard surfacing rod. Stringer beads were individually work hardened by peening as applied. This also helped in keeping the surface flat. Once the entire surface of the horn and deck have one layer of stringer beads lengthwise, another layer of hardfacing was applied, using a weave technique across the anvil. These were individually peened as applied also. This made a surface that was almost smooth, being a necessity, since the hard facing is difficult to grind to a finished appearance. After the surfaces were ground, a ½″ diameter hole was cut through the rear deck of the anvil using bits for hard steel drilling with the drill press. A hardness test on the rockwell scale of the anvil came out 38-41 which should increase to about 50 rockwell as the anvil is used. The desired weight of the anvil was 100 lbs. The end result was 113 lbs.

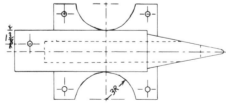

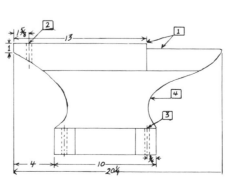

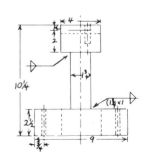

1	HARDFACE WITH MANGANESE ROD AND WORKHARDEN TO (± 5RC. 40 RC.
2	DRILL ½ INCH
3	DRILL ⅜ INCH
4	FLAME CUT TO DESIRED APPEARANCE

Hydraulic Pulling Machine

Author: *Karl W. Halverson*
Instructor: *Robert Durall*
School: *Western Wisconsin Technical Institute*
City & State: *LaCrosse, WI*

The purpose of the Hydraulic Pulling Machine is to exert an external pulling force which is used to bend or reposition automobile body parts or frames. It is portable and easily maneuverable and it requires only one man to operate it. The machine can be floor anchored or it can also be anchored to the auto which is being worked on. In relation to similar pulling devices, the Hydraulic Pulling Machine would probably be rated as a medium duty tool.

The machine is designed around the hydraulic system which utilizes a farm equipment type hydraulic cylinder. The cylinder has a 3″ bore and a 10″ stroke and is rated to operate at pressures up to 4000 pounds per square inch. The machine will exert a pull of 14,000 pounds at 2000 pounds per square inch and has a potential of 28,000 pounds pull at 4000 pounds per square inch. The amount of pull will depend on the operating pressure of the pump used and the pull can be increased by the use of a snatch block and a double line. The power is transferred to the work through a ⅜″ alloy steel chain. Alloy chain is a must and it can be purchased at most auto parts suppliers. A chain of lesser quality could possibly break, causing injury to the operator or damage to the automobile. This chain is hooked to the L-shaped bracket which is attached to the shaft end of the hydraulic cylinder. This bracket slides in a guide track as the hydraulic cylinder extends upward and the purpose of the bracket is to relieve the lateral pressure from the cylinder shaft and seal. A spring is used to retract the cylinder after the pump pressure has been relieved. The entire hydraulic assembly (Power Assembly A) slides onto the vertical tube of Sub-Assembly B. This hydraulic system can be raised or lowered on the vertical tube, depending on whether a low or high pull is required. A light duty winch has been added to aid in raising and lowering since the hydraulic system is quite heavy. Once the assembly is winched into position, it is pinned in place and the tension on the winch is released.

The machine is mounted on three retractable swivel casters. After the machine is in the desired location, the casters on the legs of Sub-Assembly C are retracted by cranking them up. Raising the casters will put any pressure on the legs of the machine and it will also help in keeping the machine from sliding out of position. The swivel caster on the floor beam (Sub-Assembly D) is mounted on a piece of leaf spring which enables the caster to automatically retract as pressures increase. The floor beam can be removed from the machine by removal of a pin. Removing the beam allows ease in transporting, the use of different lengths of beams and the use of the machine as a floor anchored power post type of pulling device. To use it as a power post, the machine is anchored by use of the shackles on its back side, to a floor which has been prepared for this use by embedding some sort of anchoring devices in the concrete floor. When anchoring the machine, the automobile must also be anchored to the floor. When not using the floor anchor system, the automobile must be anchored to the floor beam of the machine. Sub-Assembly E is used for this purpose and it will work in many cases although each pulling situation is unique and sometimes will require custom made anchor brackets.

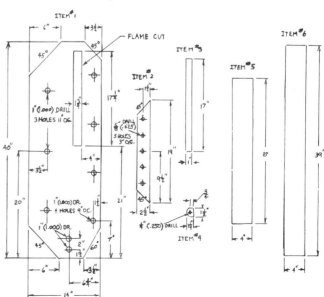

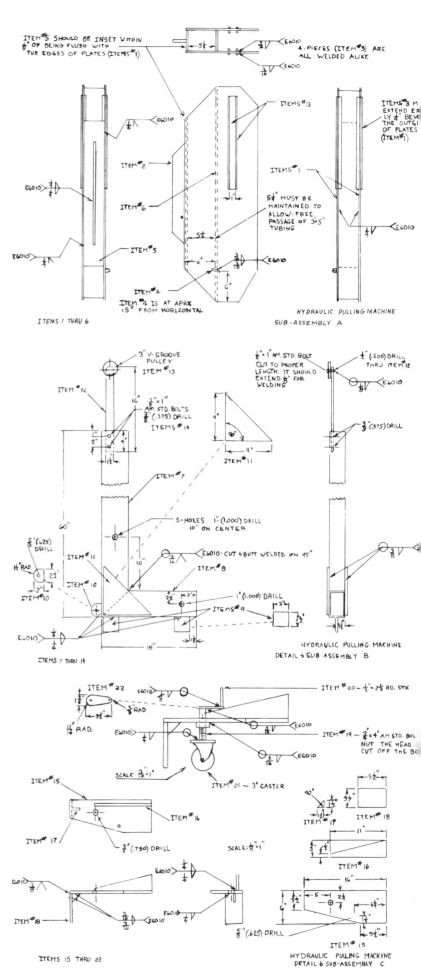

Hydraulic Pulling Machine
Sub-Assembly A

Items 1 thru 6

Hydraulic Pulling Machine
Detail & Sub Assembly B

Items 7 thru 14

Hydraulic Pulling Machine
Detail & Sub-Assembly C

Items 15 thru 22

148

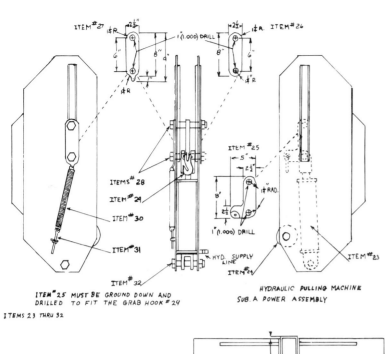

ITEM #27   ITEM #26
1 (1.000) DRILL

ITEM #25

ITEMS #28
ITEM #24
ITEM #30
ITEM #31
ITEM #32

HYD. SUPPLY LINE
ITEM #23

ITEM #25 MUST BE GROUND DOWN AND
DRILLED TO FIT THE GRAB HOOK #29

ITEMS 23 THRU 32

HYDRAULIC PULLING MACHINE
SUB. A POWER ASSEMBLY

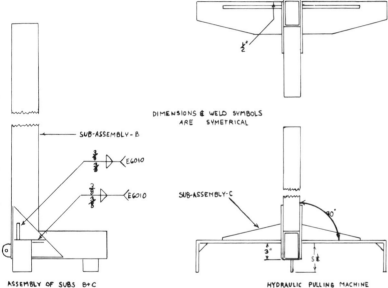

SUB-ASSEMBLY-B

E6010
E6010

SUB-ASSEMBLY-C

DIMENSIONS & WELD SYMBOLS
ARE SYMETRICAL

ASSEMBLY OF SUBS B+C

HYDRAULIC PULLING MACHINE

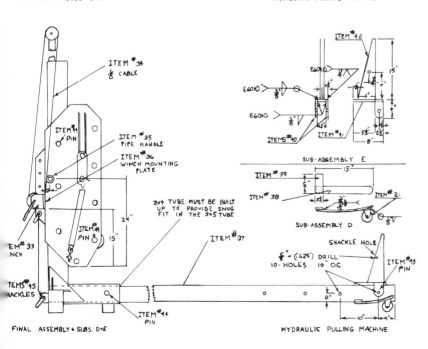

ITEM #34
⅛ CABLE

ITEM #44 PIN
ITEM #35 PIPE HANDLE
ITEM #36 WINCH MOUNTING PLATE

ITEM #42
E6010
E6010
E6010
ITEMS #40   ITEM #41

SUB-ASSEMBLY E

ITEM #39
ITEM #38   ITEM #21

SUB-ASSEMBLY D

2×4 TUBE MUST BE BUILT
UP TO PROVIDE SNUG
FIT IN THE 3×5 TUBE

ITEM #44 PIN

ITEM #33 WINCH

ITEMS #45 SHACKLES

ITEM #37

SHACKLE HOLE

⅝" (.625) DRILL
10 HOLES 10" O.C.

ITEM #43 PIN

ITEM #44 PIN

FINAL ASSEMBLY + SUBS. D+E

HYDRAULIC PULLING MACHINE

Materials

Quantity	Item
2	¼″ x 14″ x 40″ Plate
1	½″ x 2½″ x 19 Plate or Bar
4	¼″ x 1″ x 17″ Plate or Bar
1	¼″ x 1¼″ x 1½″ Plate or Bar
1	⅜″ x 4″ x 27″ Plate or Bar
1	⅜″ x 4″ x 39″ Plate or Bar
1	3″ x 5″ x ¼″ x 60″ Rectangular Tube
1	3″ x 5″ x ¼″ x 18″ Rectangular Tube
2	½″ x 2½″ x 3″ Plate or Bar
1	½″ x 2″ x 2½″ Plate or Bar
2	½″ x 9″ x 9″ Plate (45° Gusset)
1	⅜″ x 1½″ x 16″ Plate or Bar
1	3″ V-Groove Pulley with Bolt to fit center hole
2	⅜″ x 1″ AM. Std. Bolt & Nut
2	½″ x 6″ x 16″ Plate or Bar
2	½″ x 3″ x 11″ Plate or Bar
2	⅜″ x 1½″ x 1½″ Plate or Bar (45° Gusset)
2	½″ x 3½″ x 5½″ Plate or Bar
2	¾″ x 4″ AM. STD. Bolt & Nut
2	½″ x 2½″ Round Stock
3	3″ Swivel Caster (Heavy Duty)
2	⅛″ x 1⅜″ x 3½″ Sheet or Band Stock
1	Hydraulic Cylinder (3″ Bore x 10″ Stroke)
1	4″ Pulley grooved for ⅜″ Chain
1	1″ x 5″ x 8″ Plate or Bar
1	⅛″ x 2½″ x 8″ Sheet or Band Stock
1	⅛″ x 2½″ x 9″ Sheet or Band Stock
2	1″ x 6″ AM. STD. Bolt & Nut
1	⅜″ Alloy Steel Grab Hook
1	Tension Spring with 10″ Extension Travel
1	¼″ x 4″ I-Bolt & Nut
1	1″ x 5″ AM. STD. Bolt & Nut
1	500# Capacity Hand Winch
1	⅛″ x 10′ Steel Aircraft Cable
2	1″ x 5″ Standard Pipe
1	⅜″ x 3½″ x 6″ Plate or Bar
1	2″ x 4″ x ¼″ x 10′ Rectangular Tube
1	Approximately 15″ piece of Light Duty Automotive Leaf Spring
1	⅜″ x 2¼″ x 5″ Plate or Bar
2	½″ x 2½″ x 4″ Plate or Bar
1	½″ x 2″ x 8″ Plate or Bar
1	1″ x 4″ x 15″ Plate or Bar
1	⅝″ x 3″ Hardened Pin
3	1″ x 6″ Hardened Pin
5	½″ Hi-Test Shackle

Universal Vise Mounting

Author:	*Richard E. Scheurer*
Instructor:	*W. E. Whiteker*
School:	*Ohio Mechanics Institute*
City & State:	*Cincinnati, OH*

This mounting supports a universal based vise on a beam which allows it to be used in multiple attitudes and positions.

A quadrant was added to the end of a structural beam (see support beam drawing); and a U-shaped plate fabricated (see Universal Mount drawing) and attached to the beam's end with an axle.

The "Universal Mount" is nearly balanced in its limited rotation about the one inch bolt axle; with the addition of a vise, the operator must then lift this entire weight at the horizontal. By welding ¼ of the weight of the vise to each of the two fly outer surfaces, the effort required to adjust the position near the horizontal is minimized.

A single hand lock can be fabricated by welding a heavy 1½" washer under the head of the 1½" bolt, and adding two blocks to the underside of the washer so as to prevent the assembly from rotating when installed into the slots. Then, by welding a one foot bar the 1½" nut, the position of the "Universal Mount" can be locked by pulling on the bar with one hand.

Assembly Details
Select a massive and rigid mounting location-the average metal work bench is not sufficient. The beam may be mounted by either the top or the bottom flange. After the beam is securely in place, load the "Universal Mount" onto the end of the beam, and align the 1¹⁄₁₆" diameter holes. Install a one inch bolt, with a washer on each side, and a nut (a stud with two nuts may be substituted). This serves as the axle, and the nut is tightened only moderately. Install a 1½" bolt in the slots and tighten sufficiently to prevent motion of the "Universal Mount". If the dimensional stackups are such that it is difficult to lock the "Universal Mount" in any position, locate the low spots and emplace a weld bead to compensate.

Notes on Actual Prototype
Beam was mounted to 12" wide concrete with toe clamps. Anchor bolts are permanently embedded in the concrete. Beam can be moved 11" in and out. "Universal Mount" rotates through a full 90°. Vise jaws can be positioned below the bench top.

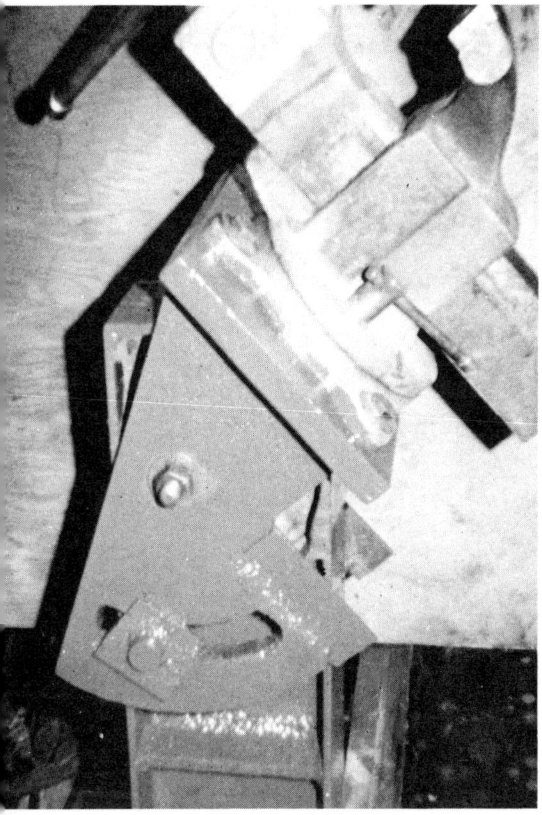

SUPPORT BEAM ORIGINAL DESIGN

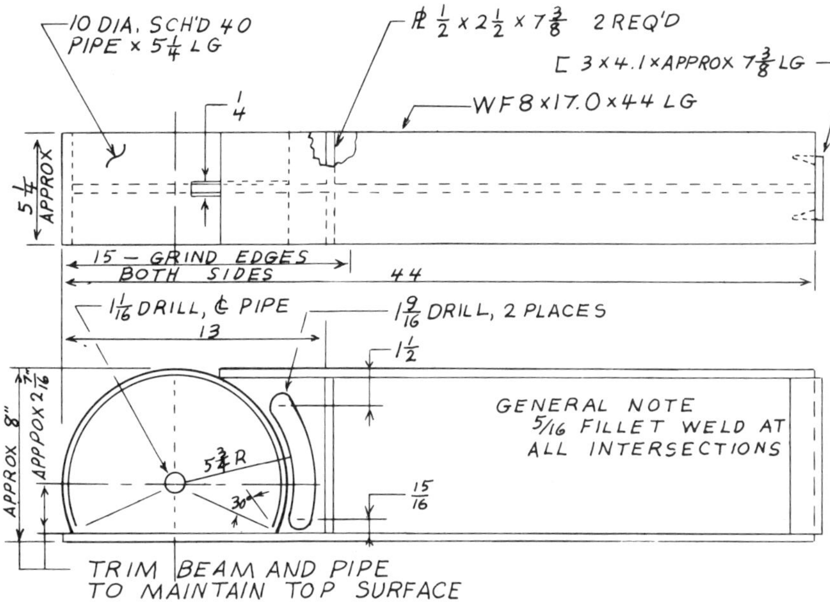
10 DIA. SCH'D 40 PIPE × 5 1/4 LG
PL 1/2 × 2 1/2 × 7 3/8 2 REQ'D
[3 × 4.1 × APPROX 7 3/8 LG
WF 8 × 17.0 × 44 LG
1/4
5 1/4 APPROX
15 – GRIND EDGES BOTH SIDES
44
1 1/16 DRILL, ℄ PIPE
1 9/16 DRILL, 2 PLACES
13
1 1/2
APPROX 8"
APPROX 2 7/16
5 3/4 R
30°
15/16
GENERAL NOTE
5/16 FILLET WELD AT ALL INTERSECTIONS
TRIM BEAM AND PIPE TO MAINTAIN TOP SURFACE

UNIVERSAL MOUNT

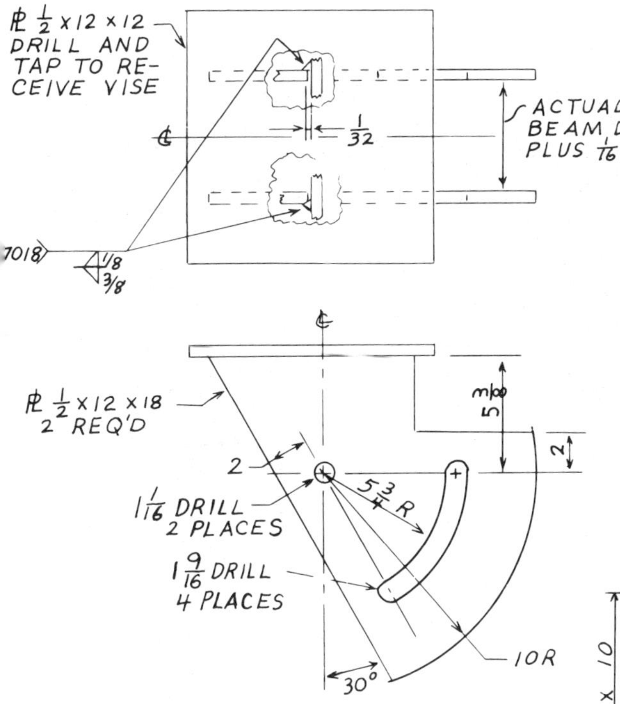
PL 1/2 × 12 × 12 DRILL AND TAP TO RECEIVE VISE
℄
1/32
ACTUAL BEAM DIM. PLUS 1/16
7018
1/8
3/8
PL 1/2 × 12 × 18 2 REQ'D
5 3/8
2
2
1 1/16 DRILL 2 PLACES
5 3/4 R
1 9/16 DRILL 4 PLACES
10R
30°

SUPPORT BEAM – FULLY WELDED, SIZE PER MATERIAL

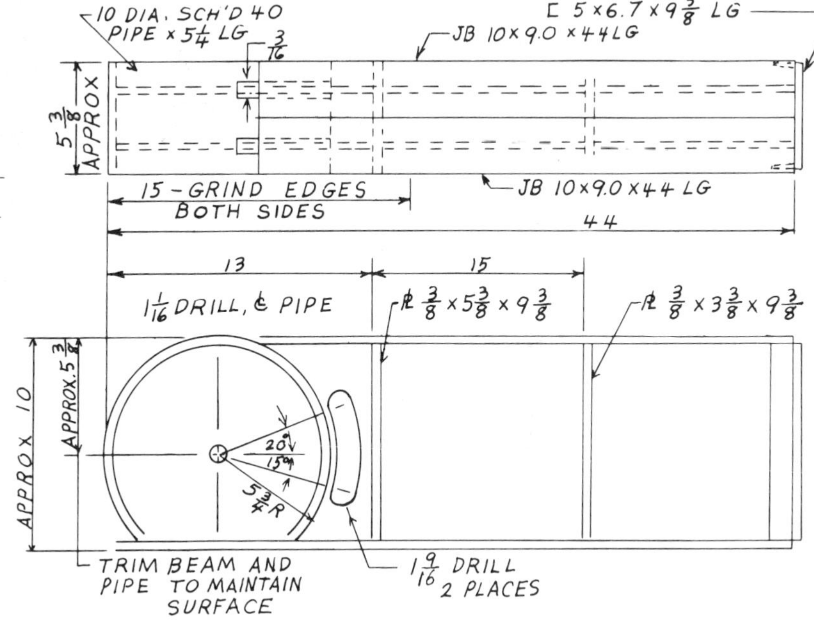
10 DIA. SCH'D 40 PIPE × 5 1/4 LG
3/16
JB 10 × 9.0 × 44 LG
[5 × 6.7 × 9 3/8 LG
5 3/8 APPROX
15 – GRIND EDGES BOTH SIDES
JB 10 × 9.0 × 44 LG
44
13
15
1 1/16 DRILL, ℄ PIPE
PL 3/8 × 5 3/8 × 9 3/8
PL 3/8 × 3 3/8 × 9 3/8
APPROX 10
APPROX. 5 3/8
20°
15°
5 3/4 R
TRIM BEAM AND PIPE TO MAINTAIN SURFACE
1 9/16 DRILL 2 PLACES

Heavy Duty Multi-Purpose Stand

Author: *Raymond Clem*
Instructor: *Odie Price*
School: *N.E.K.A. Vo-Tech School*
City & State: *Atchison, KS*

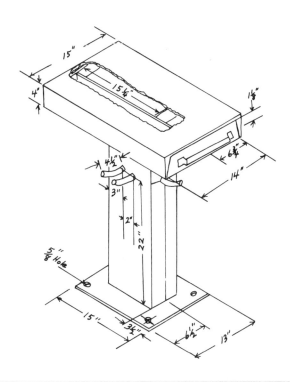

This stand is designed basically for a heavy duty vise, but with minor changes may be adapted to serve as a small welding table, or a stand for a drill press or grinder.

The pedestal has two five-eights inch diameter rods on three of the sides for hanging hammers and a single rod on the fourth side for hanging a hacksaw. The drawer has been laid out to accomodate small, medium, and large files or other small tools. It is designed with a shelf lip on the inside front of the drawer to keep water or oil from getting into the drawer from the top of the stand, when the drawer is closed. The stand is made of steel and the drawer is made of aluminum.

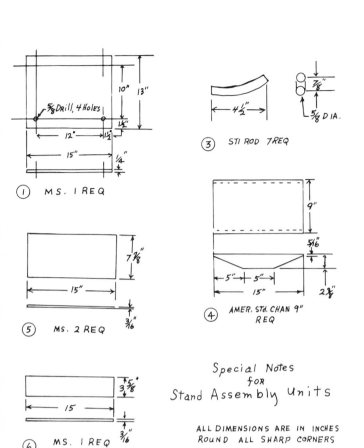

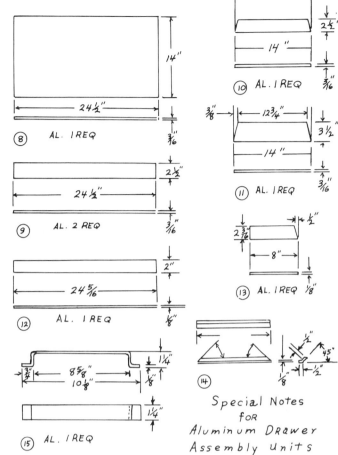

Special Notes for Stand Assembly Units

ALL DIMENSIONS ARE IN INCHES
ROUND ALL SHARP CORNERS

Special Notes for Aluminum Drawer Assembly Units

WELDED EXPLODED VIEW

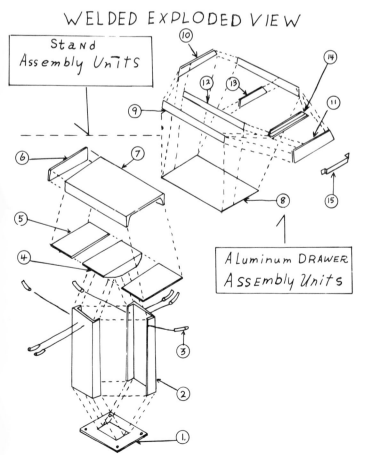

Stand Assembly Units

Aluminum DRAWER Assembly Units

DET	REQ	NAME	DESCRIPTION
		MATERIAL LIST	
1	1	Steel Plate	MS - 1/4" x 13" x 15"
2	2	Chan. Iron	AMER. Std. Chan. 8"U 18.75 x 28"
3	7	Steel Rod	Stl. Rod — 5/8 D. x 5"
4	1	Chan. Iron	AMER. Std. Chan. 9" U 13.4 x 15"
5	2	Steel Plate	MS - 3/16" x 7 7/8" x 15"
6	1	Steel Plate	MS - 3/16" x 3 5/8" x 15"
7	1	Chan Iron	AMER. Std. Chan. 15"U 33.9 x 24 3/4"
8	1	×Al. Sheet	AL. 3/16" x 14" x 24 1/2"
9	2	×Al. Sheet	AL. 3/16 x 2 1/2"x 24 1/2"
10	1	×Al. Sheet	AL. 3/16 x 2 1/2"x 14"
11	1	×Al. Sheet	AL. 3/16" x 3 1/2" x 14"
12	1	×Al. Sheet	AL. 1/8" x 2" x 24 5/16
13	1	×Al. Sheet	AL. 1/8 x 23 3/16" x 8"
14	1	×Al. Sheet	AL. 1/8" x 1" x 13"
15	1	×Al. Sheet	AL. 1/8" x 1 1/2" x 13"
16			
17			Aluminum Sold by pound 11.5 lbs.

Portable Cart For Oxygen And Acetylene Tanks And Accessories

Author:	*Paul E. Rutherford*
Instructor:	*Russell E. Clark*
School:	*Knoxville Reg. Voc. Tech. School*
City & State:	*Knoxville, TN*

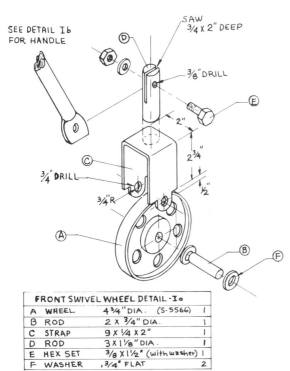

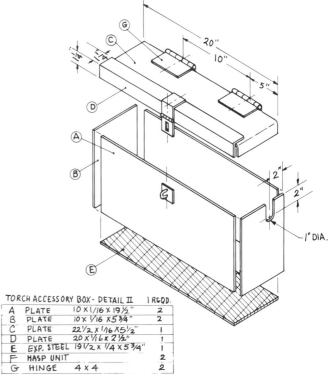

SEE DETAIL I b
FOR HANDLE

SAW 3/4 x 2" DEEP

3/8" DRILL

3/4" DRILL

3/4" R

2"

2 3/4"

1/2"

FRONT SWIVEL WHEEL DETAIL - I a			
A	WHEEL	4 3/4" DIA. (S-5566)	1
B	ROD	2 x 3/4" DIA.	1
C	STRAP	9 x 1/4 x 2"	1
D	ROD	3 x 1/8" DIA.	1
E	HEX SET	3/8 x 1 1/2" (with washer)	1
F	WASHER	3/4" FLAT	2

20"

10"

5"

2"

2"

1" DIA.

TORCH ACCESSORY BOX - DETAIL II			1 REQD.
A	PLATE	10 x 1/16 x 19 1/2"	2
B	PLATE	10 x 1/16 x 5 3/4"	2
C	PLATE	22 1/2 x 1/16 x 5 1/2"	1
D	PLATE	20 x 1/16 x 2 1/2"	1
E	EXP. STEEL	19 1/2 x 1/4 x 5 3/4"	1
F	HASP UNIT		2
G	HINGE	4 x 4	2

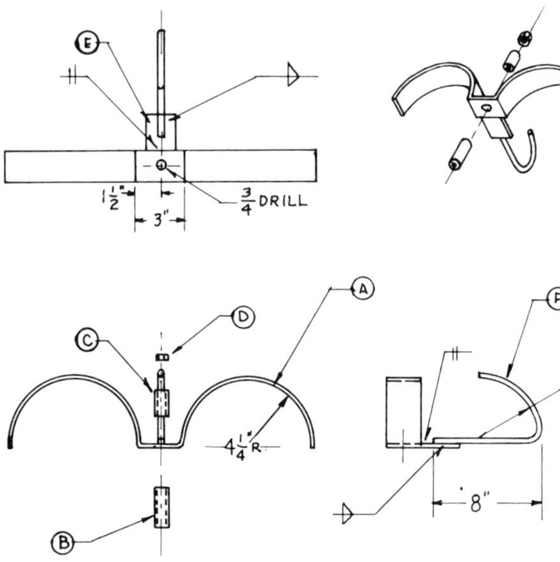

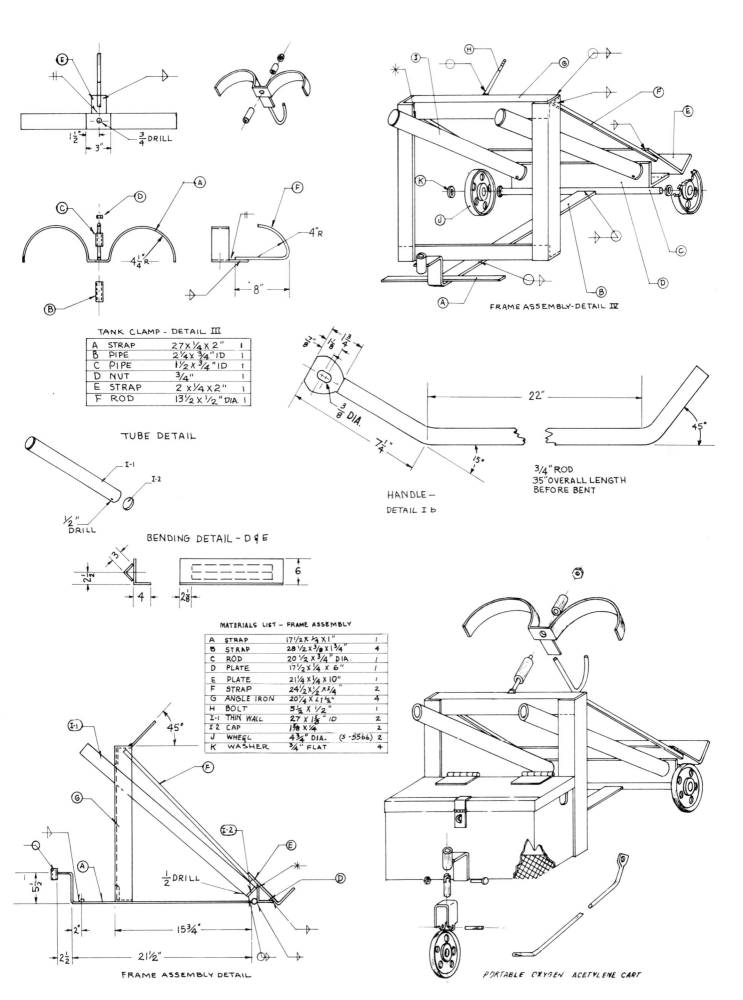

E
1 1/2"
3"
3/4 DRILL
A
C
D
B
F
4 1/4" R
4"R
8"

TANK CLAMP - DETAIL III

A	STRAP	27 X 1/4 X 2"	1
B	PIPE	2 1/4 X 3/4" ID	1
C	PIPE	1 1/2 X 3/4" ID	1
D	NUT	3/4"	1
E	STRAP	2 X 1/4 X 2"	1
F	ROD	13 1/2 X 1/2" DIA.	1

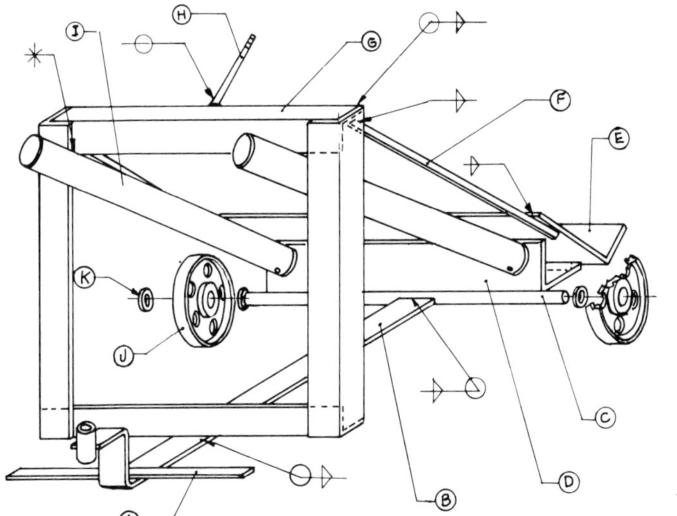

H
I
G
F
E
K
J
C
D
B
A

FRAME ASSEMBLY-DETAIL IV

TUBE DETAIL

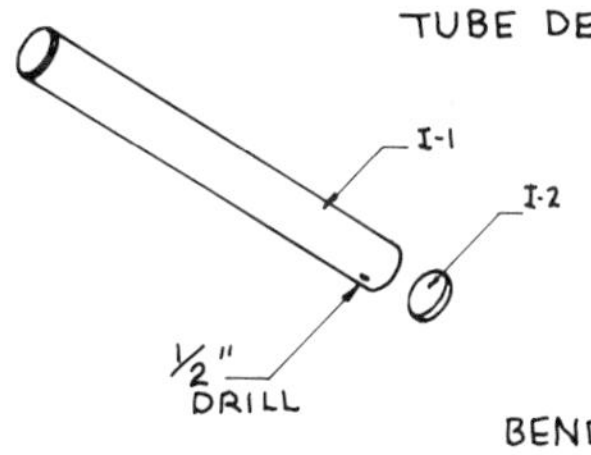

I-1
I-2
1/2" DRILL

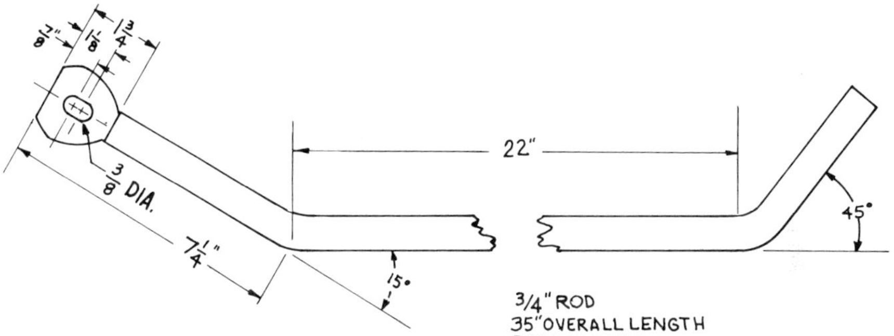

1/2"
1 1/8
1 3/4
3/8 DIA.
7 1/4"
15°
22"
45°
3/4" ROD
35" OVERALL LENGTH
BEFORE BENT

HANDLE - DETAIL I b

BENDING DETAIL - D & E

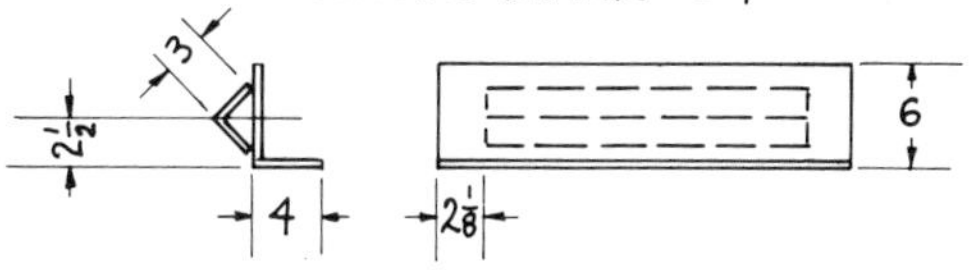

3
2 1/2
4
6
2 1/8

MATERIALS LIST - FRAME ASSEMBLY

A	STRAP	17 1/2 X 1/4 X 1"	1
B	STRAP	28 1/2 X 3/8 X 1 3/4"	4
C	ROD	20 1/2 X 3/4" DIA.	1
D	PLATE	17 1/2 X 1/4 X 6"	1
E	PLATE	21 1/4 X 1/4 X 10"	1
F	STRAP	24 1/2 X 1/2 X 3/4"	2
G	ANGLE IRON	20 1/4 X ∠1 1/2"	4
H	BOLT	5 1/2 X 1/2"	1
I-1	THIN WALL	27 X 1 5/8" ID	2
I-2	CAP	1 5/8 X 1/4	2
J	WHEEL	4 3/4" DIA. (S-5566)	2
K	WASHER	3/4" FLAT	4

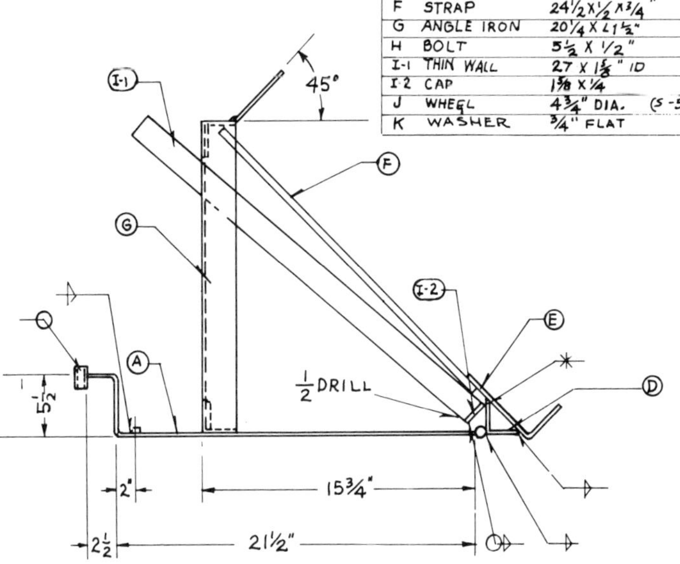

I-1
45°
F
G
I-2
E
A
1/2 DRILL
D
5 1/2
2"
15 3/4"
2 1/2
21 1/2"

FRAME ASSEMBLY DETAIL

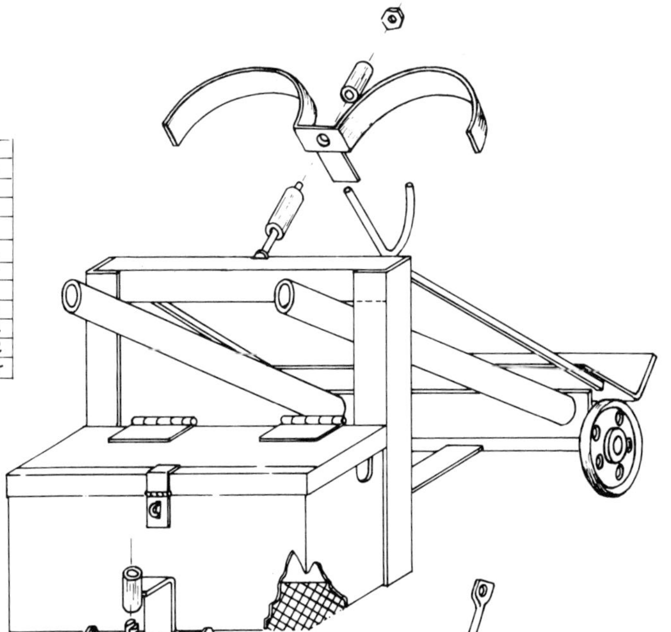

PORTABLE OXYGEN ACETYLENE CART

Fabrication of Field-Unit Welding Truck Bed

Author: *Christopher Lyn Brewer*
                               Robert L. Finley
                               Larry B. Henry
Instructor: *Harry Hill*
School: *Western Nebraska Tech. College*
City & State: *Sidney, NB*

The operator can reach all controls from ground level because of the layout. The oxy-acetylene containers were positioned so minimum lifting is required for a change of the bottles. The outside channels were flanged outward to protect reflectors and lights. The frame was attached to the chassis by angle-iron clips and bolts. If the truck were to become unserviceable, the whole truck bed would be transferred to the chassis of another truck. There is a tool box on each side of the truck, each being completely enclosed to protect against the elements.

Fabrication
The truck bed frame was first fitted on the truck chassis to assure proper fit. As this was done, it was tack-welded. It was then removed and welded with semi-automatic arc welding. This was done very easily by using a crane to turn the truck bed frame. This way, quality welds could be made in the flat position. The decking was then added by skip-welding on the underside. The welds were 1″ long and spaced 6″ apart. It was then turned over and the top welded solid.

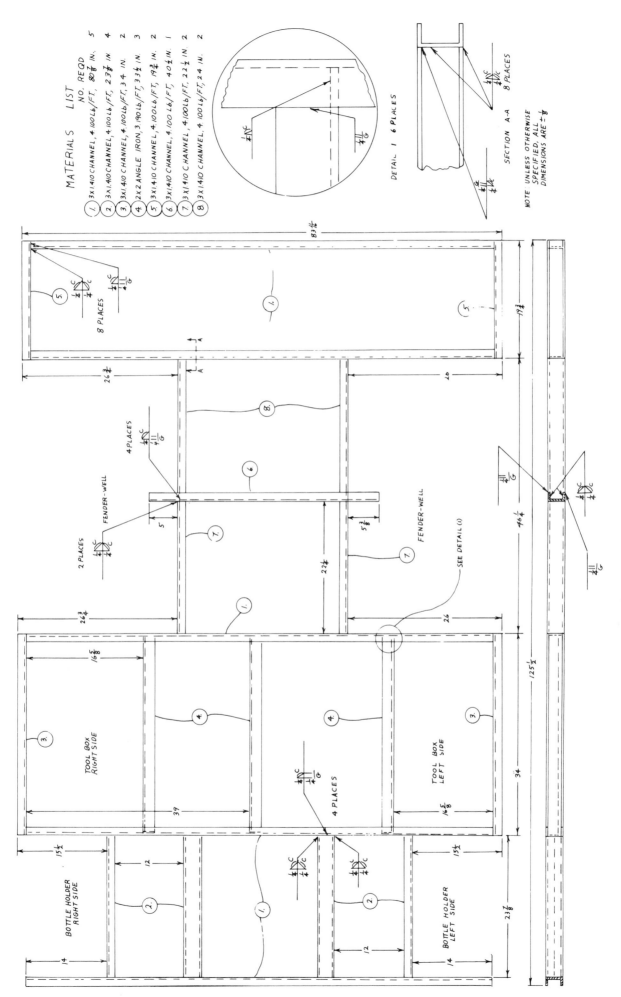

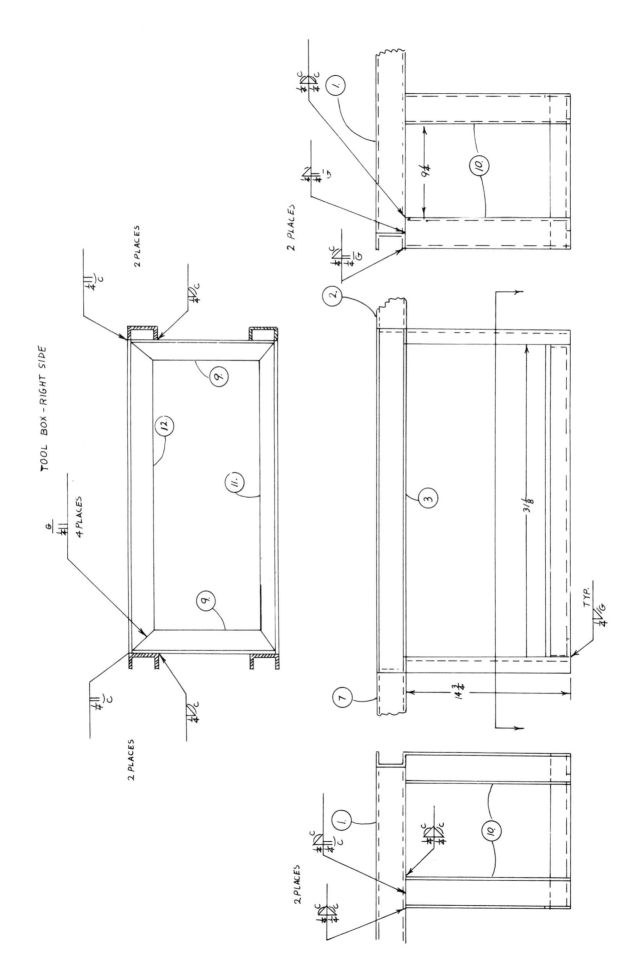

TOOL BOX - RIGHT SIDE

TOOL BOX LEFT SIDE

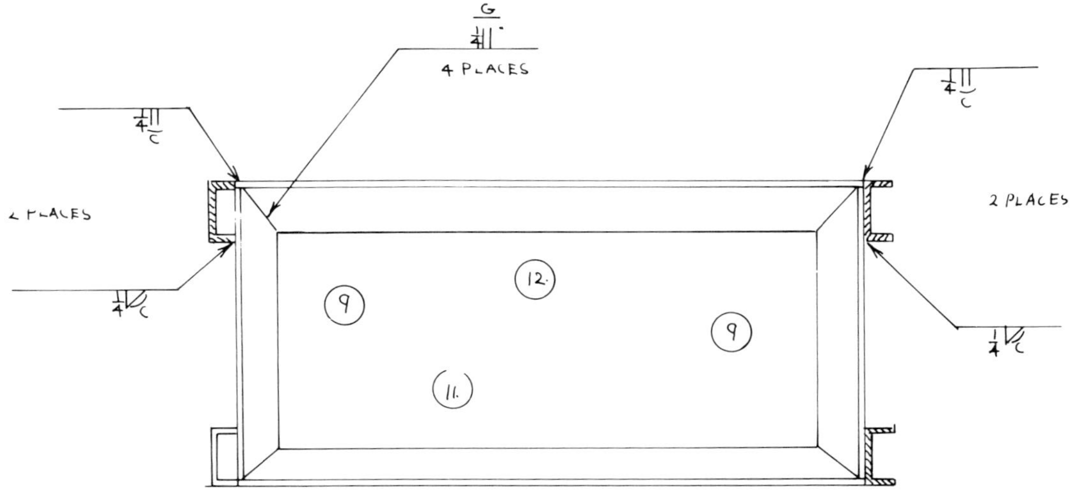

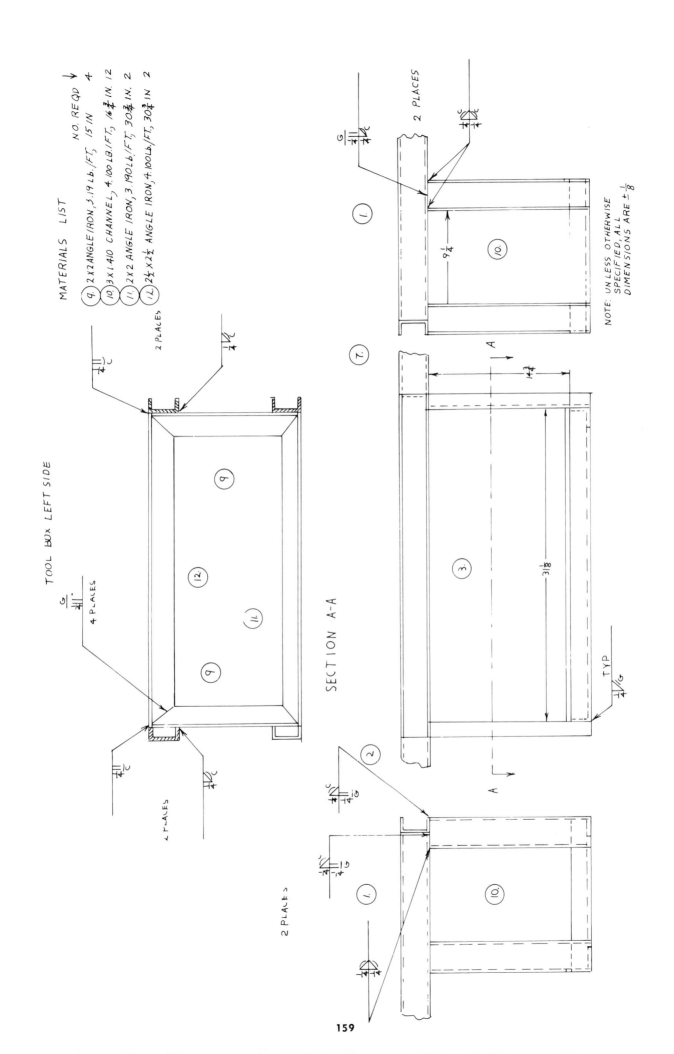

MATERIALS LIST

		NO. REQD
9.	2 X 2 ANGLE IRON, 3.19 Lb./FT, 15 IN	4
10.	3 X 1.410 CHANNEL, 4.100 LB./FT, 16 3/4 IN.	12
11.	2 X 2 ANGLE IRON, 3.190 Lb./FT, 30 3/4 IN.	2
12.	2 1/2 X 2 1/2 ANGLE IRON, 4.100 Lb./FT, 30 3/4 IN	2

SECTION A-A

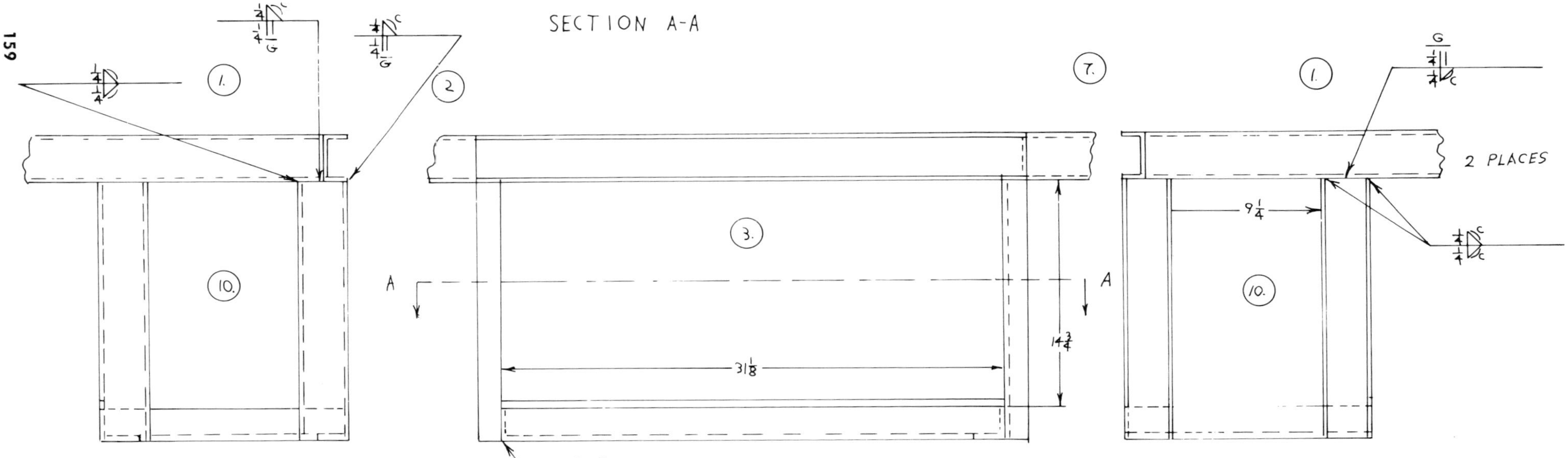

NOTE: UNLESS OTHERWISE SPECIFIED, ALL DIMENSIONS ARE ± 1/8

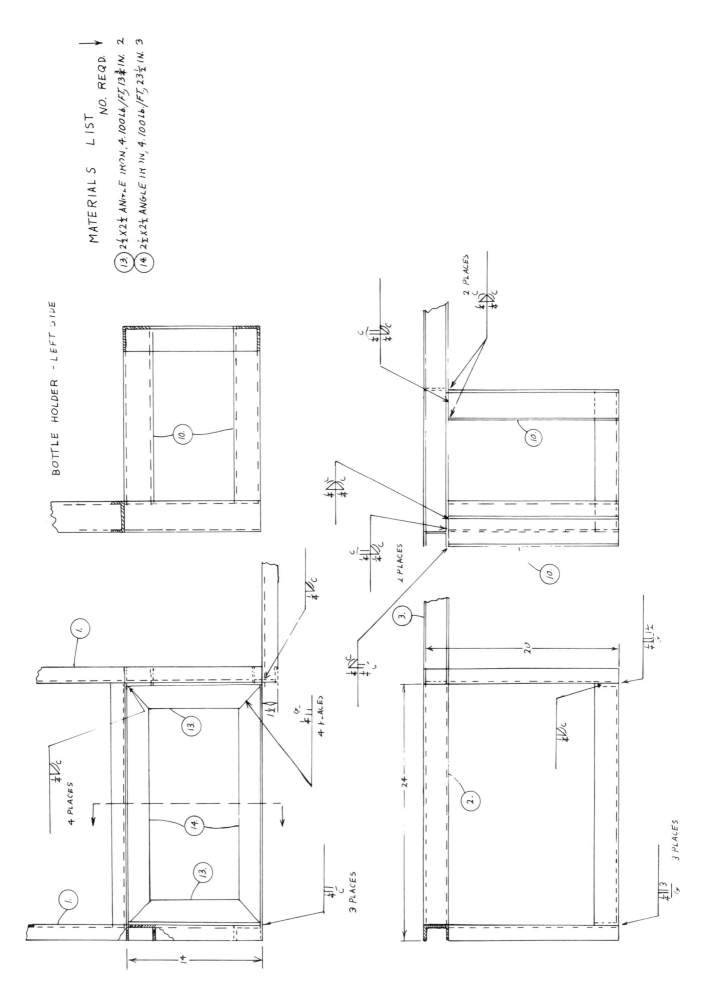

MATERIALS LIST

NO. REQD.

13. $2\frac{1}{4} \times 2\frac{1}{4}$ ANGLE IRON, 4.10 LB/FT, $13\frac{3}{4}$ IN. 2

14. $2\frac{1}{4} \times 2\frac{1}{4}$ ANGLE IRON, 4.10 LB/FT, $23\frac{1}{2}$ IN. 3

BOTTLE HOLDER - LEFT SIDE

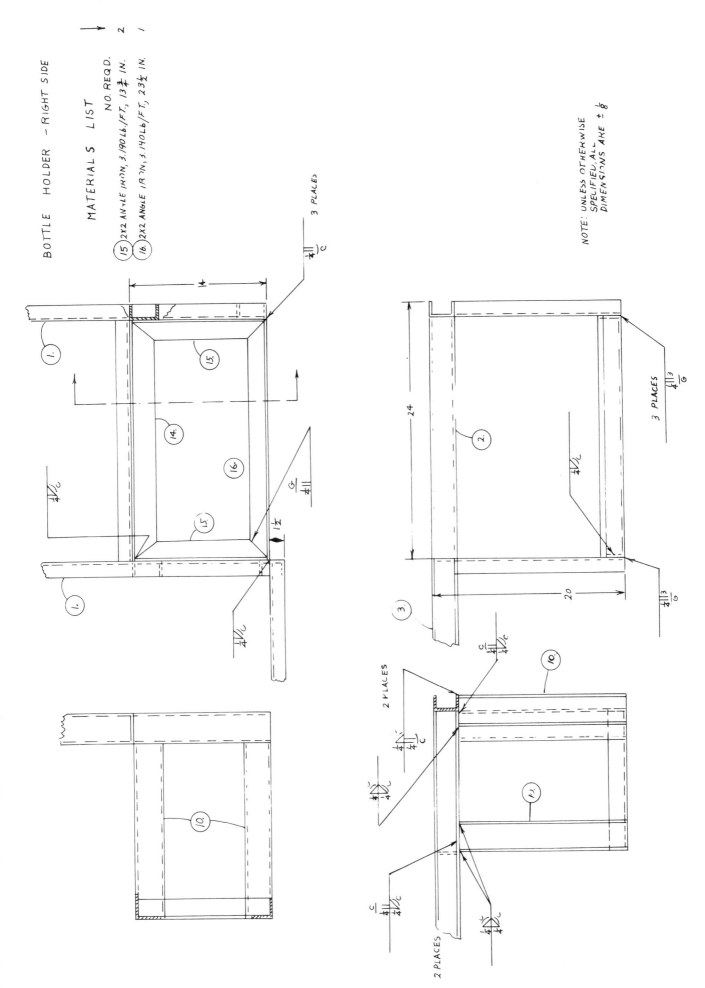

BOTTLE HOLDER – RIGHT SIDE

MATERIALS LIST

		NO. REQD.
15	2X2 ANGLE IRON, 3.190 Lb./FT., 13¼ IN.	2
16.	2X2 ANGLE IRON, 3.190 Lb./FT., 23½ IN.	1

NOTE: UNLESS OTHERWISE
SPECIFIED, ALL
DIMENSIONS ARE ± 1/8

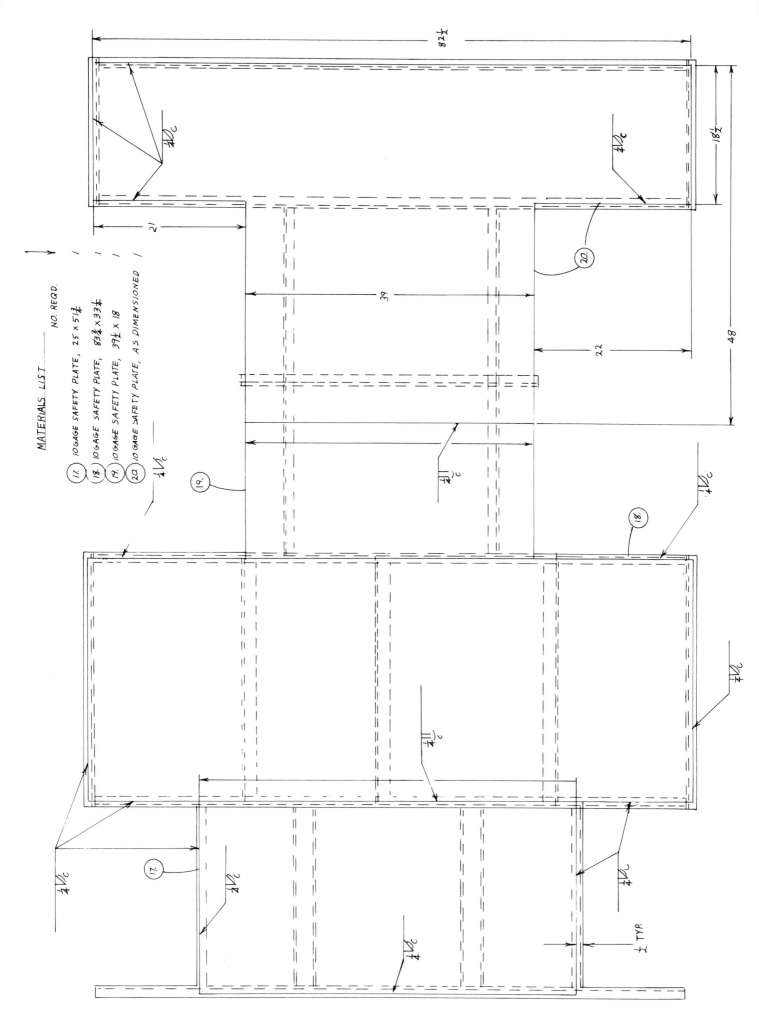

MATERIALS LIST

NO. REQD.

17. 10 GAGE SAFETY PLATE, 25 x 51¼   1
18. 10 GAGE SAFETY PLATE, 83¾ x 33¼   1
19. 10 GAGE SAFETY PLATE, 39½ x 18   1
20. 10 GAGE SAFETY PLATE, AS DIMENSIONED   1

82¼

18½

21

39

22

48

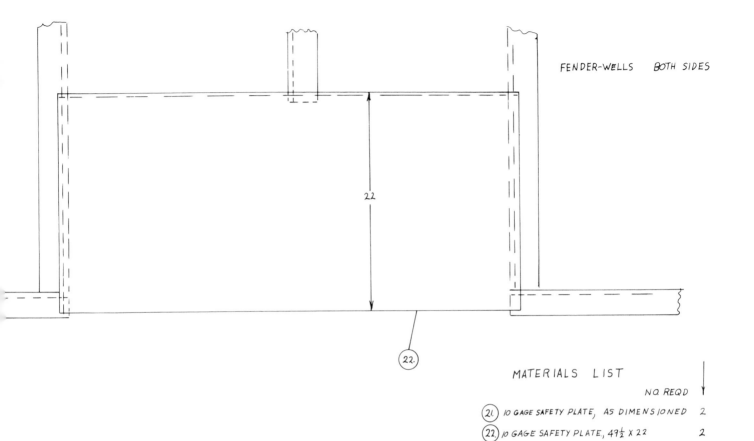

FENDER-WELLS   BOTH SIDES

22

22.

MATERIALS   LIST

NO. REQD

21.) 10 GAGE SAFETY PLATE, AS DIMENSIONED   2

22.) 10 GAGE SAFETY PLATE, $47\frac{1}{2}$ X 22   2

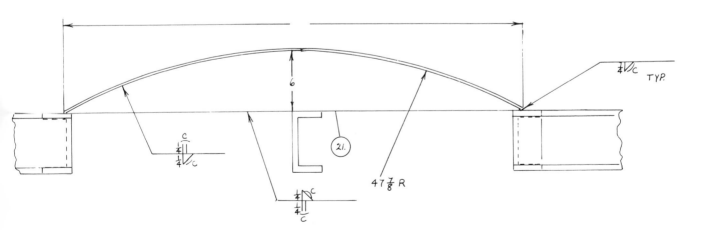

6

$47\frac{7}{8}$ R

21.

$\frac{1}{4}$ / C   TYP.

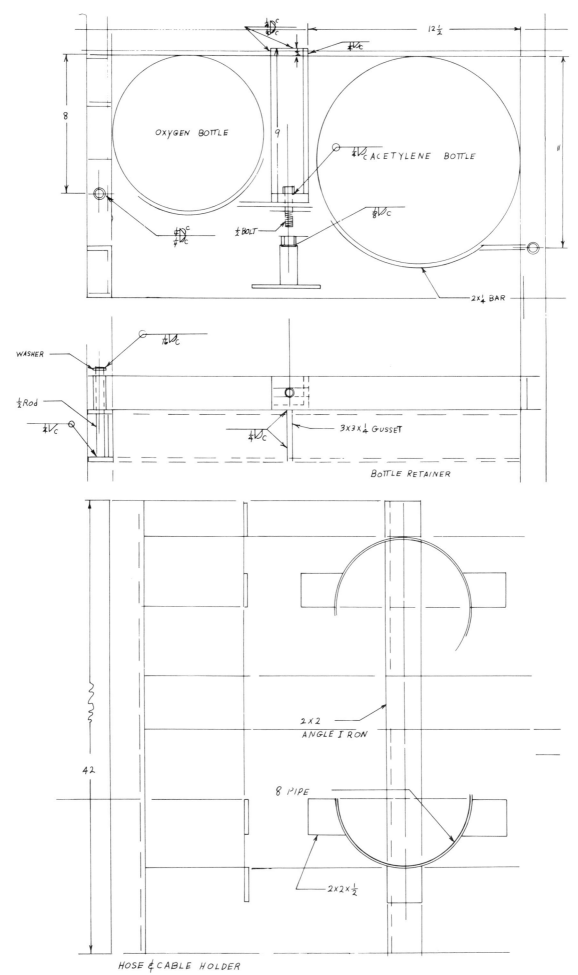

OXYGEN BOTTLE

ACETYLENE BOTTLE

$12\frac{1}{2}$

8

9

11

$\frac{1}{2}$ BOLT

$2 \times \frac{1}{4}$ BAR

WASHER

$\frac{1}{2}$ Rod

$3 \times 3 \times \frac{1}{4}$ GUSSET

BOTTLE RETAINER

2×2 ANGLE IRON

8 PIPE

42

$2 \times 2 \times \frac{1}{2}$

HOSE & CABLE HOLDER

164

An Automotive & Marine Engine Transporter

Author:	*Jim Andrews*
	Dave Holman
	James Keenan
	Charles Haywood
Instructor:	*Albert N. Clark, Jr.*
School:	*Cape May Co. Vo. Tech Center*
City & State:	*Cape May Court House, NJ*

Frame

Cut pipe to proper lengths and radius ends to fit as required. Full size layouts on a flat surface such as a concrete floor are suggested, as an aid to establishing proper angles on the pipe ends and for positioning of pipe for tack welding.

Weld the "A" frame section first and then the top horizontal member with the two semi-vertical sections. Next weld the "A" frame section to the top horizontal rail.

The side rail sections are placed on the floor layout next and welded together. Once this is accomplished the side rails can be welded to each end of the frame.

The ¼" x 2" braces can now be cut to length and welded in place either with the frame in normal position or positioned to accomplish most of the welds as horizontal position welds.

Main Wheel Frames

Cut pieces (see drawing reference "a") of ⅜" x 3" to proper length and weld after drilling 1" axle holes and using 6" long axles to align side pieces properly for welding to top piece "b". Be aware of tendency of the welding to draw side pieces out of parallel.

Next weld Main Wheel brackets to bottom of "A" frame. Use floor layout to keep wheels tracking properly.

Drill ³⁄₁₆" cotter pin holes "c" in one end of each axle and weld a ⅛" x 2" washer "d" to the outside end of each axle.

Cut pieces of ⅜" x 3" stock to proper lengths as indicated by drawing (Scale ⅛" equals 1").

After cutting the 3 pieces "e" of the upper section, layout and drill the one inch holes. Use a small pilot drill bit (⅛" Dia.) to assure accuracy. Drill one inch dia. hole in cross member "f" in which the 1" Dia. vertical steering shaft is inserted and welded on the bottom. Assemble the two ⅜" x 3" x 6" plates (with 1" holes) on the vertical 1" Dia. shaft, clamp up square and weld together to the ⅜" x 3"

x 3" front member. Next weld these upper (⅜" x 3" x 6") sections of the steering assembly to the pipe frame. A radius is cut into the upper plate to receive the 2" I.D. pipe as per isometric drawing.

Weld the ⅜" x 3" x 9" side members to the top cross member (with the vertical 1" Dia. shaft welded in the center) and to the bottom support plate (⅜" x 3" x 10"). Next cut to shape and weld the forward side angle braces "g" in place. Cut the 1" x 2" slot in the front end of this plate to accept the steering handle base "h" (1" x 1½" x 3½").

Cut the steering handle shaft "i" to length, flatten outer bottom areas and drill one of the mounting holes thru the shaft and thru the bottom support plate. Bolt into position to hold for best alignment for drilling remaining bolt hole.

Weld 1" I.D. pipe "J" to bottom of support to serve as steering assembly axle bearing.

Shape handle from ¾" Dia. solid round stock and weld to handle base. Drill 1" Dia. hole in handle base and assemble steering mechanism as per drawing and illustrations.

Chain Hoist Support Bracket

"k" - Shape from ⅜" x 3" steel plate by heating and bending around piece of scrap pipe. Inside radius may be machined on a lathe in order to provide a good bearing surface for top circumference of transporter frame.

Weld temporary brace to end of "U" shaped piece in order to drill 1" hole accurately for ease of insertion of 1" Dia. support shaft.

Lubrication

Grease fittings may be installed if desired at appropriate locations

Painting

1. One coat of rust retardant undercoat.
2. Two coats of automotive enamel.

Materials

Quantity	Description
31 ft.	21″ I.D. x ³⁄₁₆″ wall thickness (pipe)
12 ft.	⅜″ x 3″ steel (flat stock)
11 ft.	¼′ x 2″ steel (flat stock)
2 pc.	14½″ Dia. Wheels
2 pc.	10½″ Dia. Wheels
2 ft.	1″ Dia. Round steel (axle)
6 ft.	3.4″ Dia. round stock (handle)
7 pc.	Washers ⅛″ x 2″ Dia. 1″ hole
5 pc.	³⁄₁₆″ x 2″ cotter pins
1 pc.	1″ x 1½″ x 3½″ steel bar stock (handle base)
20 lb.	#7018 - ⁵⁄₃₂″ welding rod
4 cans	Red spray paint (1 undercoat)
1 can	Blue spray paint

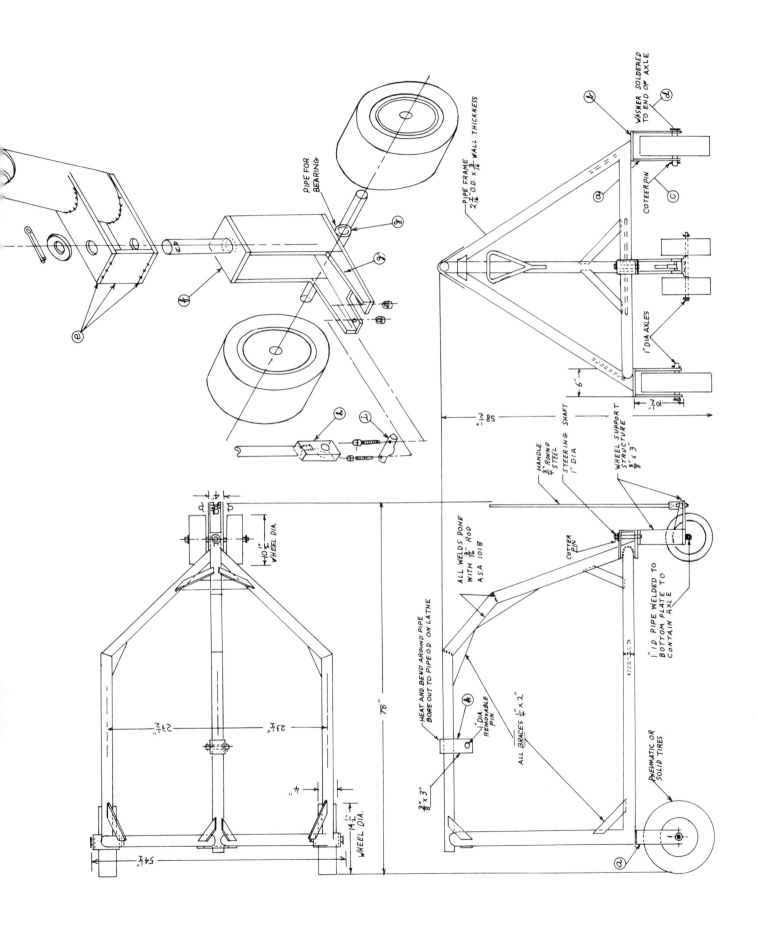

PIPE FOR BEARING

PIPE FRAME 2¼" O.D. x ⅜" WALL THICKNESS

WASHER SOLDERED TO END OF AXLE

COTTER PIN

1" DIA AXLES

6"

HANDLE ¾" ROUND STEEL

STEERING SHAFT 1" DIA

WHEEL SUPPORT STRUCTURE ⅜ x 3"

ALL WELDS DONE WITH ⅛" ROD A.S.A 1018

COTTER PIN

1" I.D. PIPE WELDED TO BOTTOM PLATE TO CONTAIN AXLE

HEAT AND BEND AROUND PIPE BORE OUT TO PIPE O.D. ON LATHE

⅜" DIA. REMOVABLE PIN

ALL BRACES ¼" x 2"

3" x 3"
⅛ x 3"

PNEUMATIC OR SOLID TIRES

40¼" WHEEL DIA.

78"

23½"

23¼"

4"

14½" WHEEL DIA.

54½"

58"

167

Hydraulic Engine Hoist

Author: Richard Leetham
Instructor: Teryl Hunsaker
School: Grantsville High School
City & State: Grantsville, Utah

The hydraulic engine hoist is used to lift engines, pieces of metal and shop machinery as well as raise automobiles to work on them. It has an adjustable boom, adjustable legs and can be easily moved around the shop. This makes it versatile easy to use and easy to store.

Fabrication of Legs

Materials Used

2 pieces of 2 x 2 x ¼″ square rod 6″ long
2 each—1 x 5″ machine bolt
4 pieces 1″ I.D. Sch. 40 pipe, 1″ long
2 pieces 1¼″ I.D. Sch. 40 pipe, 1″ long
2 each 1⅜″ flat washer

Attach Rubber Wheels to Base and Legs

Materials Used

3 each—6″ wheel 1⁹⁄₁₆ tread width—cushion neoprene heavy duty rigid caster (wheel base 5″)
1 each—6″ wheel 1⁹⁄₁₆ tread width—cushion neoprene heavy duty swivel caster (wheel base 5″)
1 piece ½″ plate 5″ x 8″
1 piece ½″ plate 5″ x 12″

Fabrication of Mast

1 piece 3 x 6 x ¼ x 66″ rectangular tubing
1 piece 2 x 5 x ¼ x 16″ rectangular tubing

6 pieces 1 x ¼ x 8″ strap

Fabrication of Boom

1 piece 3 x 6 x ¼ x 12″ rectangular tube
1 piece 3 x 6 x ¼ x 34″ rectangular tube
1 piece 2 x 5 x ¼ x 34″ rectangular tube
2 pieces 2 x 5 x ¼″ plate metal
1 piece 2″ round stock 5″ long
2 x 2 x ⅜″ plate metal

Dolly Assembly

1 piece 2 x 2 x ³⁄₁₆ x 7″ square tubing
2 each 5″ rubber wheels
1 each ⅝″ piece round stock 6″ long
2 each ⅝″ washers
1 each 2 x 2 x ³⁄₁₆ x 4½″ square tubing
1 each 1½ x 1½″ square tubing 4″ long
1 each 1¼″ x 1¼″ x .0937 square tubing 39″ long
2 each ¾″ x ¾″ x .078 square tubing 10″ long
2 each ¾″ x ¾″ x .078 square tubing 4″ long

Assembly of Hydraulic Ram and Reservoir

4 pieces of 3″ x 3″ x ¼″ plate
1 piece 4½ x 4½ x ¼″ plate
1 piece 4½ x 2 x ¼″ plate
1 hydraulic ram 33″ long and 2½″ in diameter
1 1½ quart capacity reservoir
24″ hydraulic hose with couplers on fittings

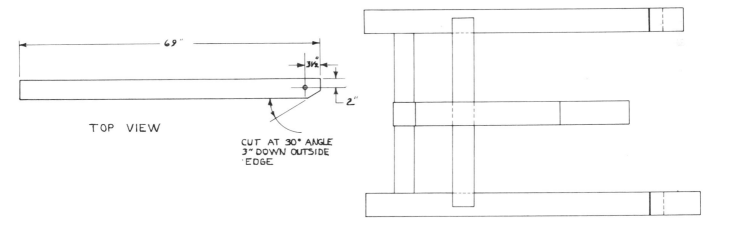

TOP VIEW

69"

3½"

2"

CUT AT 30° ANGLE
3" DOWN OUTSIDE
EDGE

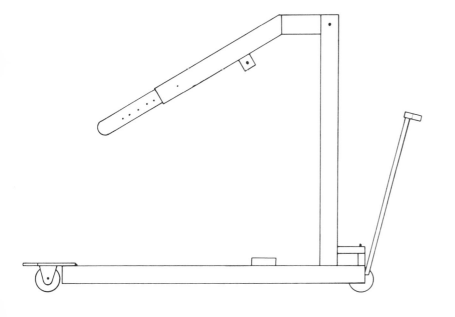

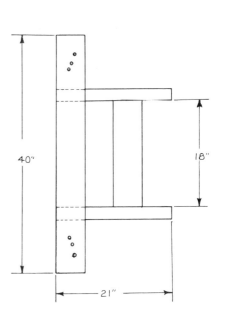

40"

18"

21"

Welding Rod Oven

Author: *Willie Wiley*
                   Johnie Cage
Instructor: *Edward Logue*
City & State: *Newark, NJ*

Basic Description

Because dampness destroys the effectiveness of most electrode coverings, it is important that electrodes be stored in a properly controlled environment.

The purpose of this project was to design and construct a rod oven which would maintain a dry environment for the storage of electrodes in the Welding Shop.

After considering the needs of the shop, it was decided that the oven should be designed to handle 450 lbs. of 18″ electrodes, and should be equipped with an adjustable thermostat ranging in temperature from 100°F to 600°F.

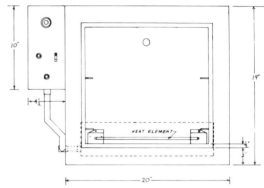

FRONT VIEW

Specifications and Materials

Materials
1—4′ x 10′ sheet of 16GA hot rolled steel
1—1″ x ⅛″ flat bar, 6′ long
  Electrical Parts

Overall Dimensions	19″ high x 20″ wide x 22″ deep
Interior Dimensions	14″ high x 15″ wide x 18″ deep Two shelves, evenly spaced
Electrical Specifications	240 volts Single phase 2 kilowatts Alternating current
Project Features	Heavy 16GA steel interior and exterior 3″ fiberglass insulation Recessed front-opening door Mounted control panel ON/OFF power switch Interior light switch Power indicator switch 100°F-600°F thermostat

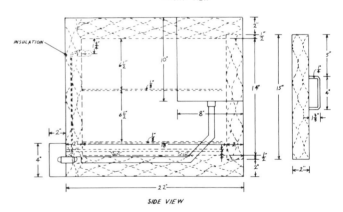

SIDE VIEW

Steps in Constructing the Project

After completing the prints for the rod oven, the following procedures were undertaken:

1. Layout and cutting of materials;
2. Formation of material on hand break;
3. Sub-assembly of parts, using TIG welding;
4. Final assembly of parts, using TIG welding;
5. Grinding and polishing of welds;
6. Wire panel box.

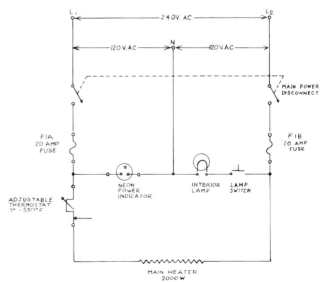

A

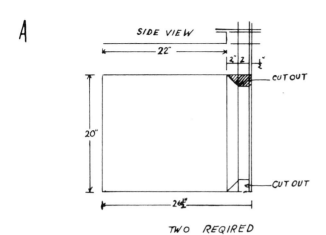

SIDE VIEW

22"

2" 2" ½"

CUT OUT

20"

26½"

CUT OUT

TWO REQIRED

B

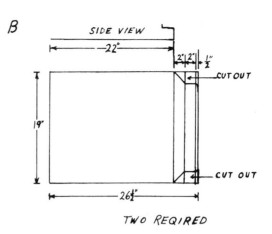

SIDE VIEW

22"

2" 2" 1" ½

CUT OUT

19"

26½"

CUT OUT

TWO REQIRED

C

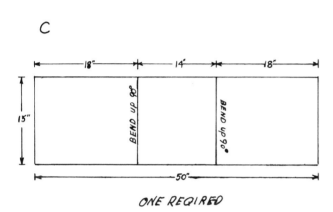

18"   14'   18"

15"

BEND UP 90°   BEND UP 90°

50"

ONE REQIRED

<u>NOTE:</u>

A. TOP & BOTTOM of OUT SIDE SHELL
B. RIGHT & LEFT SIDES of OUT SIDE SHELL
C. IN SIDE SHELL.

OUT SIDE BACK PANEL 19"x20"
TOP & BOTTOM of IN SIDE SHELL 14"x18" PLATES
ALL CUT OUTS 45° ANGLE   A & B

A

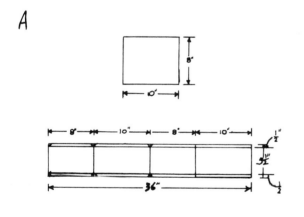

8"

10'

8"   10"   8'   10'

1" ½

5½"

36"

½

B

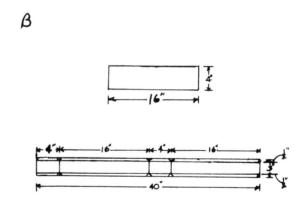

4"

16"

4"   16"   4"   16"

1"

40"

¾"
¼"

C

<u>NOTE:</u>

A. CONTROL BOX
B. HEATING ELEMENT RECEPTACLE
C. DOOR — DOOR HANDLE ¼"x5⅝" ROUND STOCK

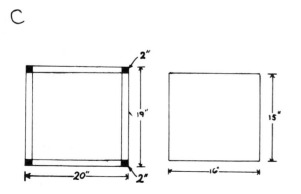

2"

19"

15"

20"   2"   16"

171

Welding Positioner

Author: Ray McDonough
Instructor: Arthur Cambell
School: Mt. San Antonio College
City & State: Walnut, CA

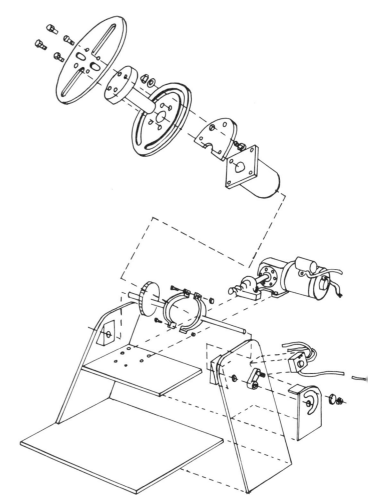

A positioner is a machine that can hold large objects conveniently for the welder and make the job faster and easier.

This positioner can hold a capacity of up to 2,000 lbs. The space it occupies is approximately 24 cubic feet. It features a rotating face plate of 350°.

This positioner consists of the following major parts. The frame consists of a base, side supports, motor support, and axle mounts. The base is a steel plate. The two side supports are angled vertically 30° towards the center. The motor support is a steel plate. The axle mounts are also made of steel. The locking devices are used to lock in the face plate when the desired position is found. The locking devices consist of: Swivel plate, Stationary index, and side locking device.

Caution should be taken when assembling the positioner due to its extreme weight.

Take the base and lay it flat on the table and take the two side supports and weld them at a 30° angle towards the center. The motor support is placed 10″ from the top. The axle mounts are then tack welded on the side supports 4″ down.

The axle clamps are set into the mounts. Then the headstock is placed in and bolted on to the axle clamps. The locking device on the headstock is bolted on. The face is mounted on the swivel lock which is bolted on to the bearing shaft of the headstock. The face is now adapted to the face plate. The side lock is welded onto the side with an arm extended out on the inside of the plate.

The motor is then mounted on the back end of the motor support plate; the gears are meshing with each other and bolt the motor down.

Make sure every nut and bolt is tight. Make a test run without any material or object on it. A word of caution: do not overrun the machine. It does not have a limited stop so you have to watch what you are doing. Don't overload the machine.

To improve this machine, limited stop switches can be incorporated in the side locking devices. To make work easier a motor can be used to drive the headstock instead of being done manually.

Mobile Crane

Author: Brian G. Jepson
Instructor: William T. Stewart
School: Converse County High School
City & State: Douglas, WY

This crane is handy for lifting and moving such items as crankshafts or flywheels off oil field engines. It is hefty enough to lift the front end of a four-wheel drive pickup off the ground, or remove an engine from any vehicle. The boom of this crane will raise high enough that you can easily hang a cow or elk by the hind legs to butcher it and steel castors make it easily moveable.

Base Layer
Material Used

175½″ Schedule 80, 3″ pipe

130″ Schedule 40, 2½″ pipe
16″ 3 x ½″ Strap metal
4—3″ Swivel plate castors
4—½″ nuts
4—1 x ½″ bolts

From a 3″ pipe cut two pieces 61″ long, one 30″ and one 23½″.

Put 30″ piece aside.

Cut a saddle 1″ deep in one end of both 61″ pieces and check for good fit when butted to the 3″ pipe. Cut saddles on both ends of the 23½″ piece.

Measure ¾″ from each end of the 30″ piece and mark. Lay the saddled end of one 61″ piece of pipe next to the 30″ piece with the outside edge of the pipe on the mark. Tack the two pieces together, first on top, on each side, and finally the underneath side.

Then tack the other 61″ piece of pipe on the opposite end of the short pipe using the above procedure. Measure 12″ from the tacked end on the inside of both long legs and mark. Take the 23½″ piece of pipe and place between the long legs even with the two marks. Tack both ends of the brace on the top, bottom and sides in that order and then weld solidly.

Pick one side of the base layer for the top and mark it as such.

Measure in 2½″ on both ends of the 30″ pipe of the base layer and mark with a center punch. The outside ends of the long legs would be marked in the same manner.

Where the pipe has been marked with the center punch, drill ⅝″ holes. Center a ½″ nut over hole and around the edges. Screw a 1 x ½″ bolt into each nut about ¼″. These will be used as set screws to hold the leg extensions in place.

Turn the base layer over so the side marked top is now on the bottom. In the center of the two long legs make a mark 12″ from the outer end of the pipe and another mark 39″ from the same end. Use a straight edge at least

173

28″ long and draw a line from mark to mark lengthwise down the legs. At each end of the lines, measure ¼″ each way and mark. Take the straight edge and draw a line from mark to mark as before. Cut along the outside lines with an Oxy-Acetylene torch so when cut completely out, the slots will be ½″ wide, 27″ long and 12″ from the end of the legs.

Follow the above steps when cutting slots in the 30″ pipe with the exception that the slots will be 8″ long and the cuts will be started 4″ from each end of the pipe.

Cut two pieces of 2½″ schedule 40 pipe 48″ long and another two pieces 17″ long. These will be the extensions.

Insert the two 48″ pieces into the long 3″ pipe legs leaving 4½″ exposed. Measure 40 inches from the exposed end of the 48″ pipe and make a mark on the pipe throught the slot.

Cut four 1″ pieces of ⅜″ rod. Place two pieces inside the slot of the 3″ pipe and on the marks that were made on the 48″ pipe and weld. When this is complete, the inner leg extensions should protrude without turning, 28″ from the end of the legs when fully extended.

Insert one 17″ piece of pipe into each of the 30″ piece of 3″ pipe. Use the above procedure for installing the leg extensions and stops on the 30″ pipe with the exception that the stops need to be welded 16″ from protruding ends of the short extensions instead of the 40″ on the long extensions.

When the welding of the stops and short leg extensions is complete, there should be 12″ protruding from the end of the 30″ piece when fully extended.

Cut four 3 x 4″ plates, drill holes in the center of each and bolt a 250 pound capacity swivel plate castor to each.

Turn the base layer one-half turn so the side marked top is now on top once more. Lay blocks under the end of each leg so when the castor assembly is put under the leg extensions there will be a slight downward pressure to hold them in place.

When putting castors under leg extensions, one of the 3″ sides should flush with the outer end of the extension. Center the apparatus lengthwise under the pipe and tack in place then weld solidly.

When the base layer is turned back over, the wheels should set perpendicular to the floor.

On each 61″ leg, measure 1″ from the saddled ends, mark with a center punch and drill ½″ holes.

With the base layer lying on the floor top side up, measure 8½″ from each end of the 23½″ brace and make two marks. Offset the marks 1″ towards the back of the base layer and mark with a center punch. Drill two ½″ holes where marked.

Turn the base layer over. Measure 8½″ from each end of the same brace as the top side and mark. Offset these marks 1″ towards the front of the base layer and drill two ½″ holes where marked. This completes the construction of Step No. 1.

The Boom

Material Used

51″ Schedule 80, 3″ pipe
48″ Schedule 40, 2½″ pipe
24″ 3 x ½″ strap metal
48 ¾″ 1½″ x ³⁄₁₆″ strap metal
4″ 1½″ pipe
1″ ½″ rod
1—1 x ½″ bolt with nut
1—⁵⁄₁₆″ chain hook
6 links ⁵⁄₁₆″ chain
1—⅜ x 3″ bolt with nut

Cut a piece of 3″ pipe 51″ long, and a piece of 1½″ pipe 4″ long.

Measure 16½″ from one end of the 3″ pipe and mark. Center one side of the 1½″ pipe on the mark and weld.

Cut a piece of 1½ x ³⁄₁₆″ strap metal 48¾″ long. Make a slight bend 2″ from one end of the strap metal. Lay the strap metal on the 3″ pipe with the bent end flush with the end of the pipe. Center the strap metal on the pipe so it can be bent over the 1½″ pipe and welded.

Weld the bent end of the strap metal to the 3″ pipe. It should be welded across the end and along each side of the strap metal for a distance of 2″.

Bend the strap metal over the 1½″ pipe and down to the 3″ pipe again. Keep the strap metal close to the center of the 3″ pipe as possible. Weld the other end of the strap metal to the 3″ pipe in the same manner as the completed end. Where the strap metal is bent over the 1½″ pipe, weld securely.

Cut or drill a ⅝″ hole 2″ from the end of the 3″ pipe and weld a ½″ nut to the pipe. Screw a ½ x 1″ bolt into the nut. This will be used for a set screw. Turn the pipe over so it lays on the flat part of the strap metal. This is the boom. Measure 12″ from the outer end of the boom and mark. Make another mark 39″ from the same end.

Mark and cut out the slot using the same procedures that were used in making the slots in the legs of the base layer.

Cut a piece of 2½″ pipe 48″ long. Slide this pipe into the outer end of the boom, leaving 4″ exposed. Cut a 1″ piece of ⅜″ rod and weld into the slot of the 2½″ pipe to be used as a stop. Follow the same procedure outlined in Step One.

Cut two pieces of 3 x ½″ strap metal 12″ long. Lay one of these pieces flush on top of the other one and clamp. Drill a ⅝″ hole 2″ in from one end and ¾″ hole 1¼″ from the other end.

Measure 2″ from one end of the pieces and mark; then measure 1¼″ from the opposite end and mark. Center the two marks and mark with a center punch. Drill a ⅝″ hole on the end of the pieces that are marked at 2″. Drill a ¾″ hole on the end marked at 1¼″.

Clamp a 2½″ thick block between these two pieces of strap metal keeping them flush on all four sides and letting them stick past the edge of the block about one inch.

Lay the boom on the floor so the slot is on one side and the 1½″ strap metal is on the other side. Place the two pieces that have been clamped together against the slotted side of the boom. Slide the clamped pieces to the back of the boom. Make sure the strap metal pieces are centered on the pipe.

Tack both of these pieces on the outside. Unclamp and slide the block from between them. Weld the pieces on the inside and when fused together well, weld solidly on the outside.

After the two 3 x ½″ strips have been welded, turn the boom so the 1½ x 3/16″ strap metal that has been previously welded on top of the boom will be standing straight up.

On both sides of boom extension measure 1″ from the protruding end and mark. Drill 2 ⅜″ holes.

Purchase a 5/16″ chain hook, six lengths of 5/16″ chain and a 3 x ⅜″ nut and bolt.

Connect the hook to the chain and insert the ⅜″ bolt through one side of the pipe, through the chain and finally through the other side of the pipe. Screw the nut onto the bolt and tighten.

Stand Pipe

Materials Used:

50″ Schedule 80, 3″ pipe
43½″ 3 x ½″ strap metal
6½″ x ¾″ rod
3—4½ x ½″ bolts
3—½″ nuts

Cut a piece of 3″ pipe 50″ long and a piece of 3 x ½″ strap metal 8″ long.

Measure 1⅛″ from each end of the strap metal and mark and drill two ½″ holes.

Lay the strap metal on the floor. Place the 3″ pipe on the strap metal and center it both ways. Weld the 3″ pipe to the strap metal. This is the stand pipe.

Cut another piece of 3 x ½″ strap metal 16½″ long. Measure and mark 2″ and again at 6″ from each end. Drill two ¾″ holes.

Place a square on the strap metal and draw a line where the six inch marks have been made. Put the metal in a vise so one of the lines will be ¼″ above and parallel to

the top of the jaws of the vise. Heat the metal along the line to a cherry red. Bend the metal to make a 90° angle. Repeat on the other end of the strap metal.

When the bending of the strap metal is complete, it should look as shown in Diagram No. 3.

Cut another piece of 3 x ½″ strap metal 19″ long. Measure 7¼″ from each end. Square the marks and procede as outlined above. Lay this piece aside.

Set the stand pipe with the untouched end at the top on the 23½″ brace of the base layer completed in Step one. Match the ½″ holes in the stand pipe to the ½″ holes in the brace of the base layer and bolt together with two 4½″ bolts. The top of the stand pipe should be perpendicular to the back of the base layer.

Measure 3″ down from the top of the stand pipe and mark on each side. Drill ½″ holes where marked.

Take the first piece of strap metal that was cut and bent and set it on top of the stand pipe. Center the strap metal on the stand pipe with the 4½″ solid end down. The 6″ sides should be parallel with the long legs of the base layer. Weld solidly.

Cut two pieces of 1¼″ x ¼″ strap metal 48″ long. These will be used for braces. Measure 1″ from each end of both pieces and mark. Center the marks and mark again with a center punch. Drill ½″ holes where marked.

Hold one of the pieces of strap metal upright along the side of the stand pipe. Place a 4½ x ½″ bolt through the bottom hole of the brace and through the ½″ holes that were drilled on the sides of the long extensions. Repeat with the other brace on the other long leg extension.

Insert a 4½ x ½″ bolt through the ½″ hole in the top of one of the braces, through the two holes drilled at the top of the stand pipe and through the top hole of the other brace. Thread a nut on the bolt and tighten.

Cut a piece of ¾″ rod 6″ long. Center and clamp this rod on the second piece of 3 x ½″ strap metal that was bent. This is the jack stand base.

Measure and mark 30″ from the base of the stand pipe. Make the mark on the front side. Place the above piece of strap metal so both of the 7¼″ sides are even with the mark. Tack it along the top and along each side as far as possible. After tacking, the jack stand base should still be flush with the mark on the bottom and straight with the rest of the crane. Weld solidly.

Jack stand and its components

Materials Used.

8 x 5 x ¼″ Plate metal
19″ 1¼″ x ⅛″ strap metal
5½″ 1½ x 3/16″ strap metal
4″ 2 x ¼″ strap metal
3″ 1½″ pipe

2½" ¾" pipe
1—5¼ x ¾" bolt
1—4 x ⅝" bolt
1—¾" nut
1—⅝" nut
1—Walker 12 ton Hydraulic jack

Cut a piece of ¼" plate metal 5" wide and 8" long. Cut a piece of 1¼" x ⅛" strap metal 19" long.

Lay the piece of 8 x 5" plate metal on the floor. On one of the 8" edges, measure and mark ½ from each end. Take the 19" piece of strap metal and lay it with one edge turned up along the edge of the plate just marked. The end of the strap metal should be even with the mark on the plate metal leaving 18½" of strap metal protruding past the end of the plate metal. Mark this end with an "R". Tack the end of the strap metal to the plate metal. Bend the remaining strap metal around the end of the plate metal so it will look like the jack stand shown in Diagram No. 4 and tack. Turn the jack stand over and weld the strap metal to the plate metal solidly.

Cut two pieces of 2 x ¼" strap metal 2" long. Measure and mark with a center punch 1" from each edge of the pieces. Make sure the marks are centered both ways. Drill ¾" holes where marked.

Measure and mark, on the bottom, 3" from the end of the plate metal that was marked "R". Take a square and square the mark so when a line is drawn it will run from one of the 8" sides of the plate metal to the other 8" side. Place one of the 2 x 2" pieces on edge, on the line just drawn. Center the piece so there is 1¼" of the jack stand on either end of the 2 x 2" piece and tack.

Measure and mark ½" from the opposite end of the plate metal and square as was done on the completed end.

Place the jack stand on the ¾" rod that was welded to the jack stand base in Step Three. The 2 x 2" piece on the bottom of the 8 x 5" plate metal should be on the left side when looking at the crane from the front. Slide the other 2 x 2" piece onto the other end of the ¾" rod. Align with the drawn line, center and weld solidly. Weld the tacked 2 x 2" piece solidly. When completed, the jack stand should look as shown in Diagram No. 4.

Cut a piece of ¾" pipe 2½" long and a piece of 1½" pipe 3" long. Center the ¾" pipe on one end of the 1½" pipe leaving ¾" on each side of the 1½" pipe. Weld solidly.

Cut a piece of 1½ x ³⁄₁₆" strap metal 5½" long. Bend this piece of strap metal so it will fit tightly around the 1½" pipe. Slide the strap metal ¼" past the end of the 1½" pipe and weld solidly. This will be used to set the top of the hydraulic jack in.

Insert a 4 x ⅝" bolt through one of the ⅝" holes that were drilled in the boom completed in Step two, through the ¾" pipe and finally through the other ⅝" hole on the boom. Place a ⅝" nut on the bolt and tighten.

Place the back end of the boom in between the bent strap on top of the stand pipe and align all of the ¾" holes. Insert a 5½ x ¾" bolt through the four holes and tighten. Place a Walker 12 ton hydraulic jack in the jack stand and set the piece bolted to the boom on top of the screw part of the jack.

Paint the Mobile Crane the color desired.

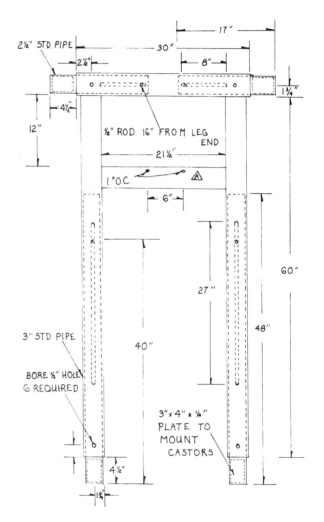

DIAGRAM NO. 1

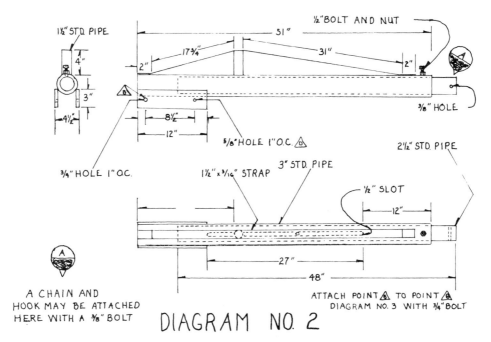

1½" STD. PIPE

4"

3"

4½"

½" BOLT AND NUT

51"

17¾"

31"

2"

2"

3/8" HOLE

¾" HOLE 1" O.C.

8½"

12"

⅝" HOLE 1" O.C. △B

A CHAIN AND
HOOK MAY BE ATTACHED
HERE WITH A 3/8" BOLT

1½" x 3/16" STRAP

3" STD. PIPE

½" SLOT

2½" STD. PIPE

12"

27"

48"

ATTACH POINT △A TO POINT △B
DIAGRAM NO. 3 WITH ¾" BOLT

DIAGRAM NO. 2

DIAGRAM NO. 3

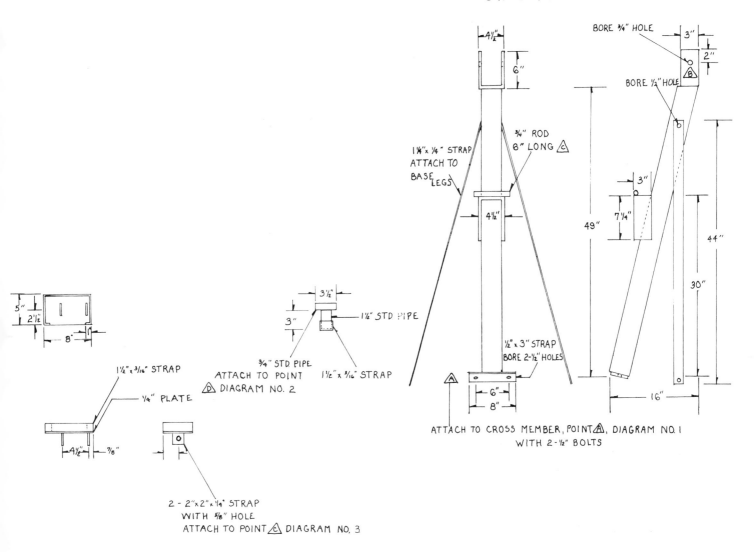

BORE ¾" HOLE

3"

2"

4½"

6"

BORE ½" HOLE

¾" ROD
6" LONG △C

1⅛" x ¼" STRAP
ATTACH TO
BASE LEGS

4½"

49"

3"

7¼"

3"

44"

30"

½" x 3" STRAP
BORE 2-½" HOLES

16"

6"

8"

ATTACH TO CROSS MEMBER, POINT △A, DIAGRAM NO. 1
WITH 2-½" BOLTS

5"

2½"

8"

1½" x 3/16" STRAP

¼" PLATE

3½"

3"

1½" STD PIPE

¾" STD. PIPE
ATTACH TO POINT
△A DIAGRAM NO. 2

1½" x 3/16" STRAP

4½"

7/8"

2 - 2" x 2" x ¼" STRAP
WITH ⅝" HOLE
ATTACH TO POINT △C DIAGRAM NO. 3

DIAGRAM NO. 4

Universal Shop Hoist

Author:	*Mike Massett*
	Jim Hurley
Instructor:	*Thomas E. Fox*
School:	*Helena Vo-Tech Center*
City & State:	*Helena, MT*

This hoist was added to the school shop because we had no way of lifting heavy objects. The hoist is mounted in an existing 8″ wide flange centrally located in the work area. The main extension of the hoist itself is an 8″ I beam 18.4#, 11′ long. The horizontal beam is placed into the existing 8″ wide flange by means of two ½″ thick plates cut to fit inside the wide flange which are placed 13′ from the floor. 5′ above these plates are two more plates also cut to fit inside the wide flange for the brace. The brace, made from 1″ cold rolled round stock, runs from the two plates down to the horizontal beam at a point 7′ 11½″ from the wall. Each plate had a 1″ hole drilled into it, 1″ from its end, for a pin. The pin was made out of 1″ cold rolled round stock which would allow the hoist to pivot. Next the pins were taken to machine shop where two bushings were made for the pins. The bushings had grease zerks placed in the sides of them to allow the hoist to be greased periodically. The bushing for the hoist was then welded to the beam. The one for the brace was temporarily set aside.

Now the mounting of the brace on the beam itself had to be made. The design of the hoist was laid out on the floor with soapstone to its full size scale. The cold rolled round stock for the brace was then cut to length and set aside. Next, three plates were cut for the brace. Each had a 1″ hole drilled into it. Two plates were welded to the hoist, the other one was welded to the cold rolled stock, the bushing was also welded to the cold rolled round stock at this time. A pin was made for the brace at the hoist end. It had a washer welded to it at one end and a hole through it at the other end for a bolt. The other pins for the hoist were made the same way.

Next the plates were put on and the pins were fitted into place to make sure of proper fit. The hoist, completely together, was then lifted up and into the existing 8″ wide flange by a forklift and tack welded. After the welding was finished a Wright 1½ ton chain hoist was mounted on the beam by means of a trolley which would hold it there and also let it roll up and down the length of the beam. All welding was done with low hydrogen E-8018-C3. The hoist was then painted black.

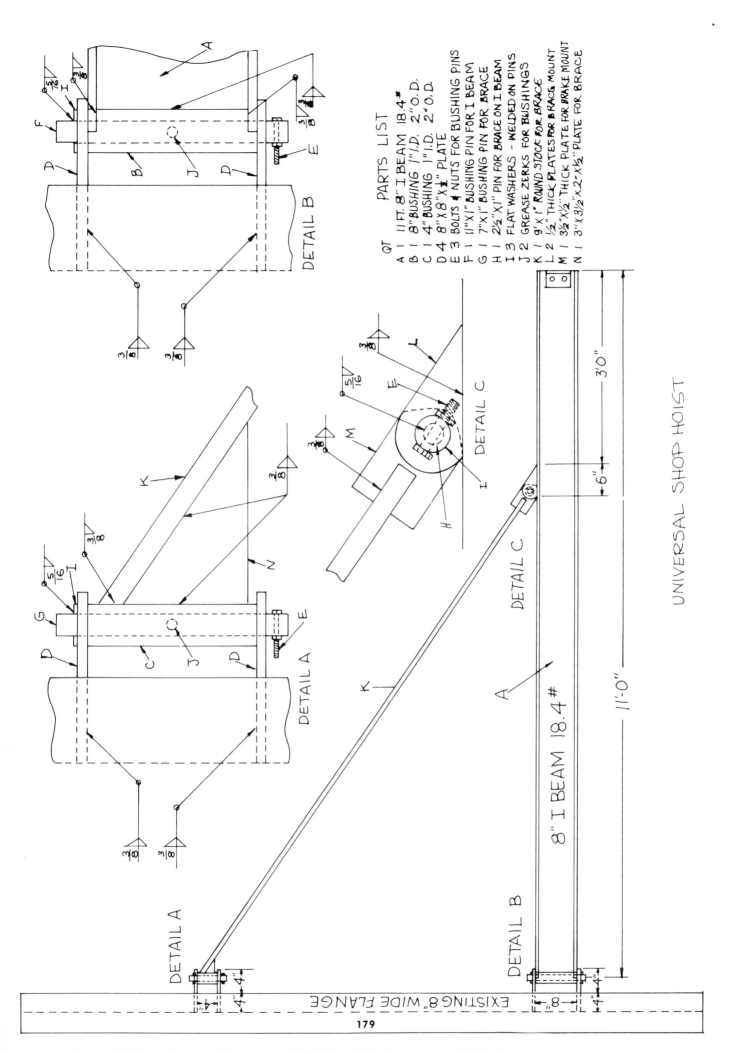

PARTS LIST

QT		
A	1	11 FT. 8" I BEAM 18.4 #
B	1	8" BUSHING 1" I.D. 2" O.D.
C	1	4" BUSHING 1" I.D. 2" O.D.
D	4	8" X 8" X 1" PLATE
E	3	BOLTS & NUTS FOR BUSHING PINS
F	1	1" X 1" BUSHING PIN FOR I BEAM
G	1	7" X 1" BUSHING PIN FOR BRACE
H	1	2½" X 1" PIN FOR BRACE ON I BEAM
I	3	FLAT WASHERS – WELDED ON PINS
J	2	GREASE ZERKS FOR BUSHINGS
K	1	9' X 1" ROUND STOCK FOR BRACE
L	2	½" THICK PLATES FOR BRACE MOUNT
M	1	3½" X ½" THICK PLATE FOR BRAKE MOUNT
N	1	3" X 3½" X 2" X ½" PLATE FOR BRACE

DETAIL B

DETAIL A

DETAIL C

DETAIL B

DETAIL A

8" I BEAM 18.4 #

UNIVERSAL SHOP HOIST

EXISTING 8" WIDE FLANGE

179

Design, Fabrication and Construction of A Hydraulic Press for Bend-Testing Welds

Author: Perry A. Johnson
Instructor: James Poye
School: Wisconsin Indianhead Tech. Inst.
City & State: New Richmond, WI

This bender is used for bending welds that are made to certification standards. This allows students to make welds and test them to find and correct any problem before making the actual certification weld.

The adaptability of this is varied. A metal tensile tester will be mounted on the back above the motor and pump. Different attachments can be put on to do different bending jobs, to make angles, and a table for straightening parts.

The main frame is made of ⅜" x 8" x 3½" channel iron. Two of these, 8' long welded back to back the entire length with 7018 flux core wire feed (GMAW) make a square post 8" x 7" x 8" that everything mounts on.

The post stands on a base that is made of the same ⅜" x 8" x 3½" channel iron. Four of these, one in each direction, extends out 2'. The base is welded to the post.

On the top of the post a 1¼" x 7" x 15" piece of C.R.S. is welded. This holds the top of the hydraulic cylinder and makes a point in which the cylinder can push against. The other end of the cylinder is braced to hold the cylinder parallel to the post.

The male part that makes the bend is attached to the yolk of the ram. A pin keeps this in place and to remove the male part the pin is removed.

The female part is attached to two round bars that go through the square post. These round bars are pinned at the back to keep them in, and there are two wedges in front to keep them straight when pressure is applied. The female part of the bender can be removed by removing two bolts on the front. All the bracing attached to the round bars are welded with 275 All State stainless steel stick electrode because of the 120,000 tensile strength involved.

The holes for the round bars to go through were flame cut larger and pipe that slides over the round bars was welded in with wire feed (GMAW) and ground off flush with the surface of the post.

The power is supplied by a 2 hp. electric motor that drives a automobile power steering pump with a 3" pulley on the motor and a 12" pulley on the pump and a V

belt. The pump pushes the hydraulic fluid to a hydraulic valve that directs the flow to the cylinder or back to the reserve. The hydraulic reserve system was made to cool the oil so continuous operation is possible. A problem came about by not enough oil coming into the pump from the reserve, so a return was made through the top of the pump. The top part of the reserve takes air out of the system and oil is drawn into the top of the pump. The bottom part of the reserve cools the oil and sends it to the top part of the reserve and to the pump. The valve when in neutral position, lets the oil flow through and back to the reserve. In the "up" position the ram goes up and the "down" position sends the ram down. This set-up produces enough pressure to push a ⅜" x 1½" certification weld down into the female radius with approximately 15 ton capacity. The fittings on the reserve were welded with an All State 13 FC, German Silver, which has 80,000 lb. tensile strength, and the reserve tanks were welded together with 7024 stick electrode. The switch box for the motor is just below the hydraulic valve making all the controls in one location and safely away from the bending. This also has a sturdy pulley and belt guard for protection.

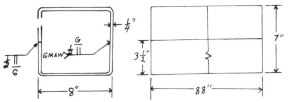

ILLus. #1

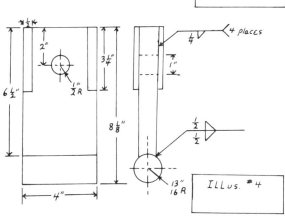

ILLus. #3

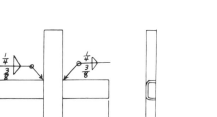

ILLus. #2

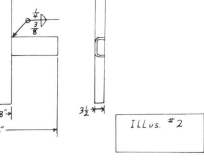

AIR OUT

OIL LEVEL

OIL IN

POWER STEERING
PUMP RESERVE

OIL OUT

COOLING TANK

POWER STEERING
PUMP

ILLus. #5

Pump and Reserve System

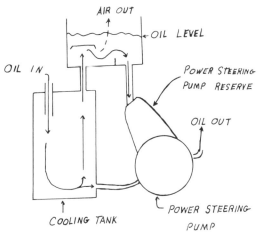

Cutting Table For Welding

Author: Edward E. Drake
Instructor: Everett J. Morris
School: Faribault AVTI
City & State: Faribault, MN

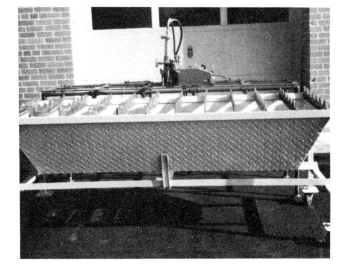

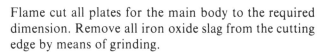

Flame cut all plates for the main body to the required dimension. Remove all iron oxide slag from the cutting edge by means of grinding.

Assemble top of table (#13 and #15), tack welding all weld joints with ⅛" 6010 electrode, setting the amperage higher than normal for a flat tack weld which can easily blend into the finished weld. All tack welds should be done in this manner. Finish weld all tack weld joints using ⅛" 6010 electrodes at normal amperage.

Assemble and tack weld body of table (#5 and #12), fitting corners so that there is a natural vee for vee groove welding. Part #9 should be positioned and tack welded into place at this time. Holding the first one in the center of the small opening and the other four parts at 12" spacings out both ways. Weld in place.

After tacking the main body, the finished weld should be done by back step welding, to minimize distortion. Staggering the welds from one end of the body to the other will also help to minimize distortion. Finish weld #9 by means of fillet weld, both sides. Weld one side and then stagger weld the other side. This will let one side cool and help control distortion.

Next, weld top angle frame to body of table, using staggered intermittent welds to control distortion. Frame should be tack welded to body of table before finish weld is done.

Drill the four holes in each of the #2 plates to fit the #1 casters. Tack and finish weld the plates to the legs, #3.

Assemble and tack weld legs and lower tubular frame members #14 and then tack weld legs to the assembled body and top frame. Tack weld angle drawer slides, #6, to top of tubular cross member #14.

Position support channel #8 and tack in place. Finish weld legs, cross member, drawer slides and channel support by a staggered sequence to control distortion.

Assemble #1 casters to legs. Stand table upright and tack weld #7 plates in position, leaving the space required for the part #11, support bars, which will be removable.

Part #11, support bars, are fabricated from ⅜" plate, using a sheet metal pattern and a shape cutting torch unit. The sawtooth pattern steel plate to be cut for minimum interference with the cutting torch flame.

The two drawers, #4, which are used to catch the slag from the cutting operation, are fabricated from 16 gauge pickled hot rolled steel sheet. They are notched in all four corners to the required dimension and the edges are bent in a box pan brake to form the slag catching drawers.

The corners of the drawers are welded with short circuiting transfer welding with .035 aws 70S3 wire.

The handles for the drawers are fabricated from ½" pipe and 3/16 sheet metal, cut to the required dimension and welded together with gas metal arc welding and then welded to the drawers with the same process.

The steel plate for the body of the table was made from 4-way safety plate, as the plate was available at a nominal cost. The 4-way diamond design of the plate also enhanced the appearance of the finished table.

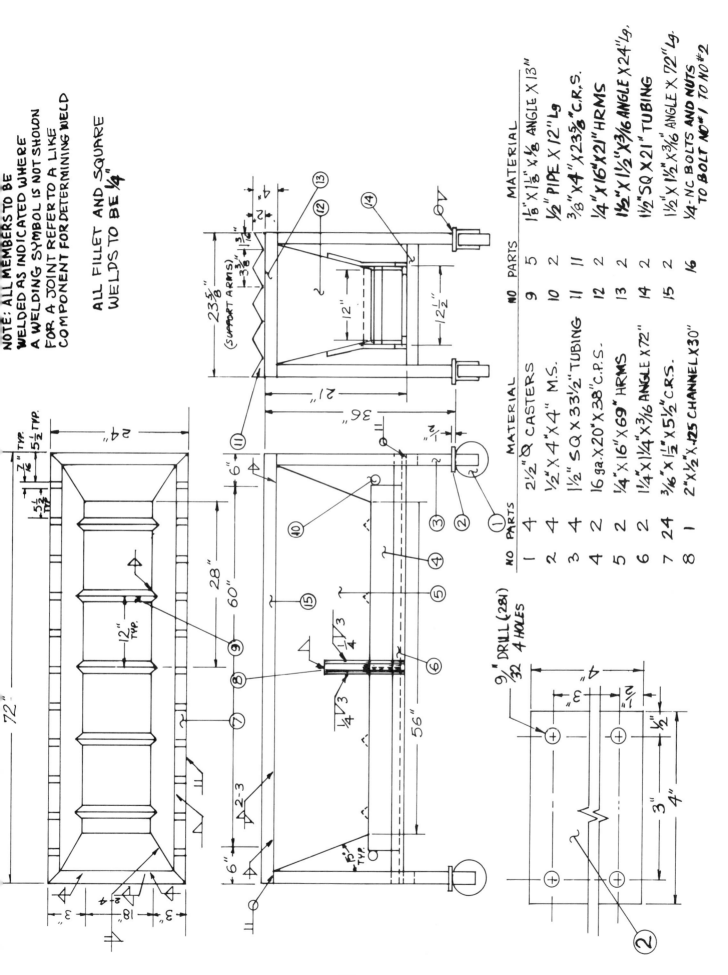

NOTE: ALL MEMBERS TO BE WELDED AS INDICATED WHERE A WELDING SYMBOL IS NOT SHOWN FOR A JOINT REFER TO A LIKE COMPONENT FOR DETERMINING WELD

ALL FILLET AND SQUARE WELDS TO BE ¼"

NO	PARTS	MATERIAL
1	4	2½" Ø CASTERS
2	4	½" X 4" X 4" M.S.
3	4	1½" SQ X 33½" TUBING
4	2	16 ga.X 20" X 38" C.P.S.
5	2	¼" X 16" X 69" HRMS
6	2	1¼" X 1¼" X 3/16 ANGLE X 72"
7	24	3/16" X 1½" X 5½" C.R.S.
8	1	2" X ½" X .125 CHANNEL X 30"

NO	PARTS	MATERIAL
9	5	1½" X 1⅛" X ⅛" ANGLE X 13"
10	2	½" PIPE X 12" Lg
11	11	⅜" X 4" X 23⅝" C.R.S.
12	2	¼" X 16" X 2J" HRMS
13	2	1½" X 1½" X 3/16 ANGLE X 24" Lg.
14	2	1½" SQ X 21" TUBING
15	2	1½" X 1½" X 3/16 ANGLE X 72" Lg.
	16	¼-NC BOLTS AND NUTS TO BOLT NO. #1 TO NO #2

9/32" DRILL (28A) 4 HOLES

183

"Stub Saver"

Author: William J. Hill
Instructor: Alexander Buttner
School: City Community College (Voorhes)
City & State: New York, NY

The usual method of joining filler rod stubs has been to lay stubs on a flat surface and apply flame to fuse rods. This usually results in stubs sticking to the workbench and a good deal of wasted filler rod material. By the use of the "Stub Saver" filler rod stubs can be aligned quickly, held firmly and fused with one pass of the welding flame. The Stub Saver will eliminate burned fingers and gloves, wasted filler rod stubs and scarred work benches. It will also save industry valuable production time lost when an operator must join stubs.

The "Stub Saver" can be made from scrap metal in any welding location. It can be made quickly and economically by a skilled operator. It can also be made by a student welder as a class project. The student who fabricates this device will experience measurement, layout, the use of a flame cutting torch and one of the welding processes to join the parts of this device. The welding process may be Braze welding, Oxy-acetylene welding, S.M.A.W., T.I.G. or M.I.G. depending on scrap being used to fabricate device.

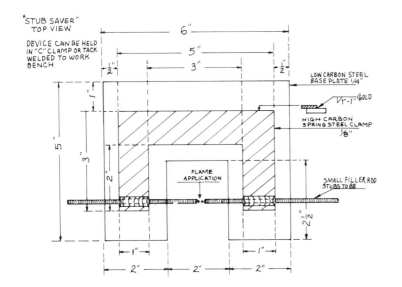

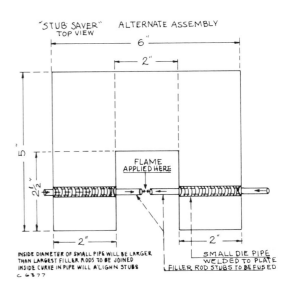

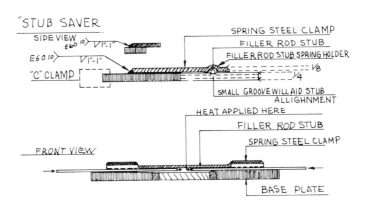

Building a Vise

Author: Gordon Hennen
Instructor: Gary Hambleton
School: St. Cloud Area Voc-Tech Institute
City & State: St. Cloud, MN

This is a rugged, all steel vise; unlike any cast iron one you would purchase. This vise will not break or distort. Maximum opening between jaws is 10½", which is really kind of a treat; since most vises of its size usually have about 8-9" openings between jaws. This makes for a handy width when working on bigger projects that require the use of a vise.

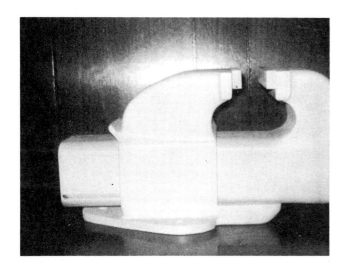
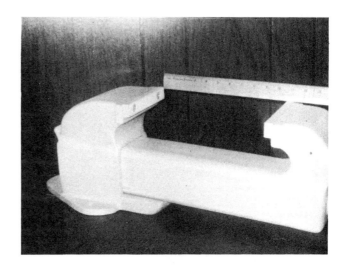

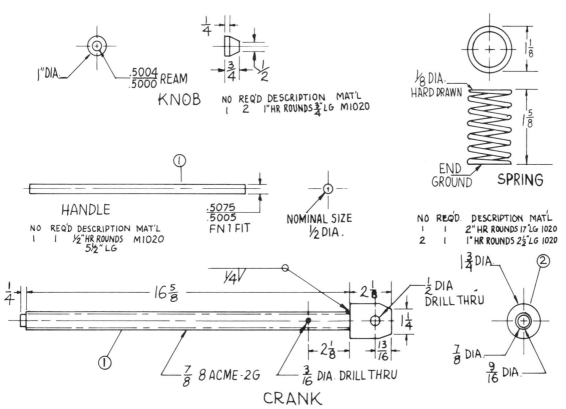

KNOB

NO	REQ'D	DESCRIPTION	MAT'L
1	2	1"HR ROUNDS ¾"LG	M1020

SPRING

⅛ DIA.
HARD DRAWN

END GROUND

NO	REQ'D	DESCRIPTION	MAT'L
1	1	2" HR ROUNDS 17"LG	1020
2	1	1" HR ROUNDS 2½"LG	1020

HANDLE

NO	REQ'D	DESCRIPTION	MAT'L
1	1	½"HR ROUNDS 5½"LG	M1020

.5075
.5005
FN1 FIT

NOMINAL SIZE
½ DIA.

CRANK

16⅝   ¼V

⅞ 8 ACME-2G   ³⁄₁₆ DIA. DRILL THRU

½ DIA DRILL THRU

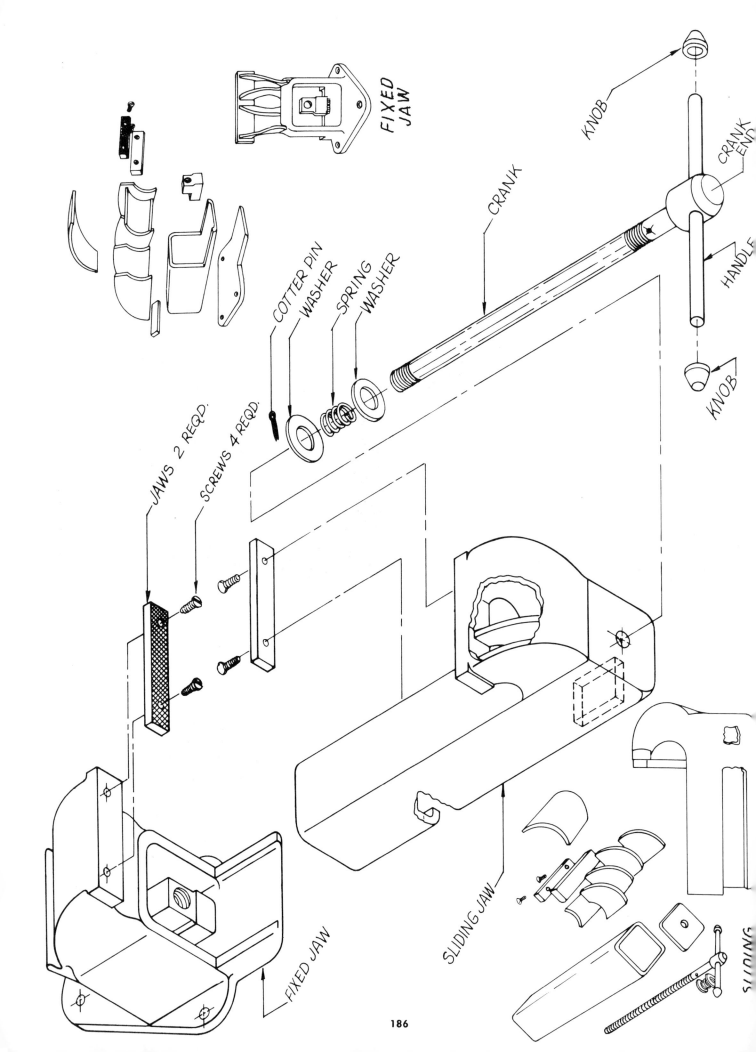

FIXED JAW

KNOB

CRANK END

CRANK

HANDLE

KNOB

COTTER PIN

WASHER

SPRING

WASHER

JAWS 2 REQD.

SCREWS 4 REQD.

FIXED JAW

SLIDING JAW

SLIDING

186

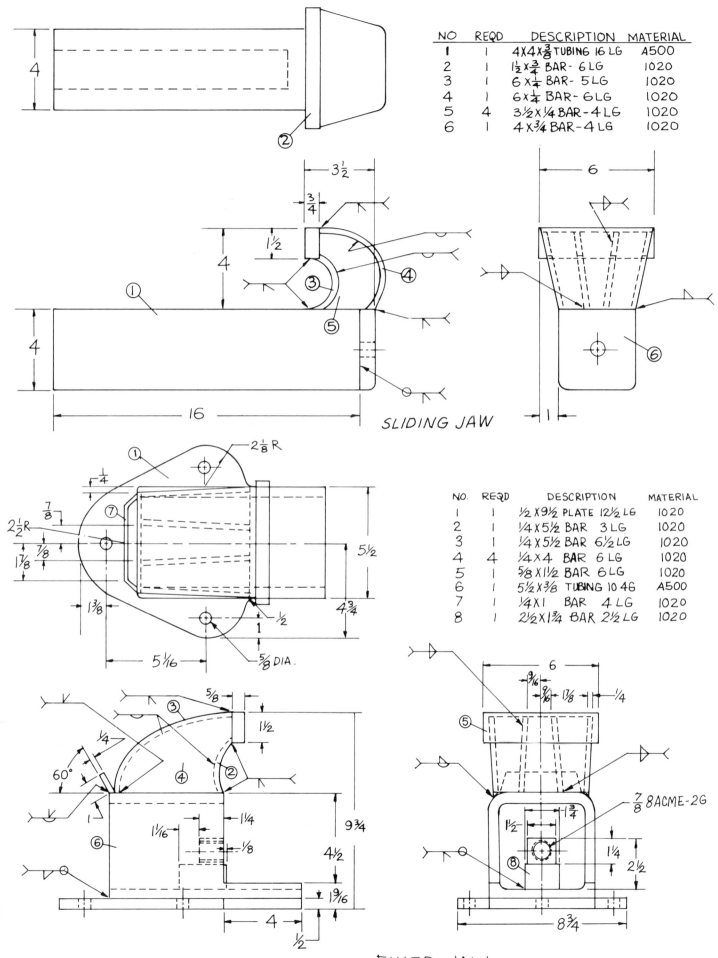

NO	REQD	DESCRIPTION	MATERIAL
1	1	4X4X$\frac{3}{8}$ TUBING 16 LG	A500
2	1	$1\frac{1}{2}$X$\frac{3}{4}$ BAR - 6 LG	1020
3	1	6X$\frac{1}{4}$ BAR - 5 LG	1020
4	1	6X$\frac{1}{4}$ BAR - 6 LG	1020
5	4	3½X¼ BAR - 4 LG	1020
6	1	4X¾ BAR - 4 LG	1020

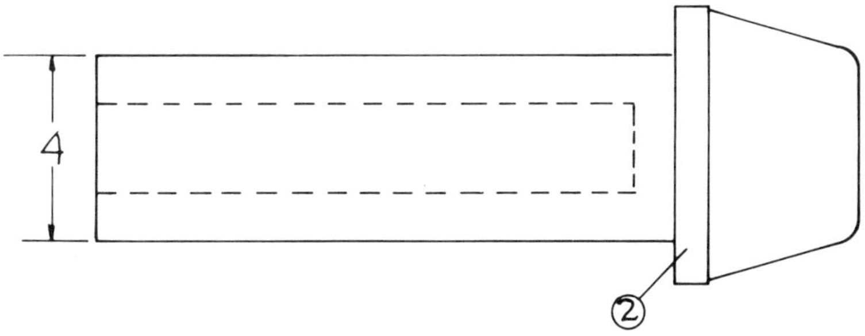

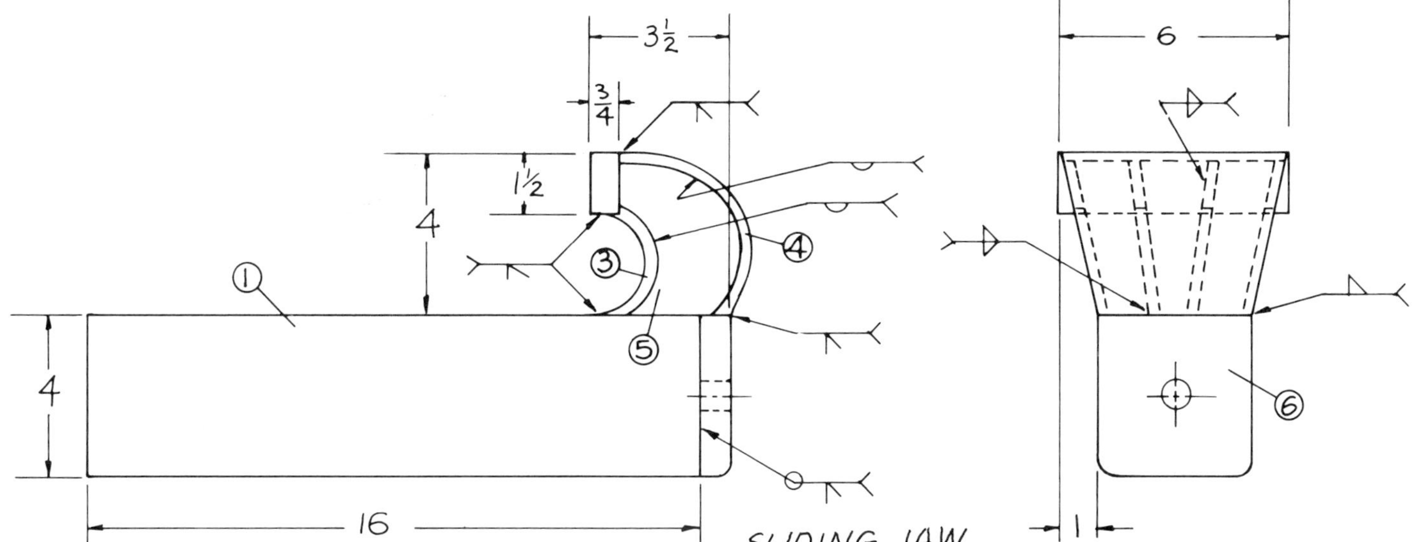

SLIDING JAW

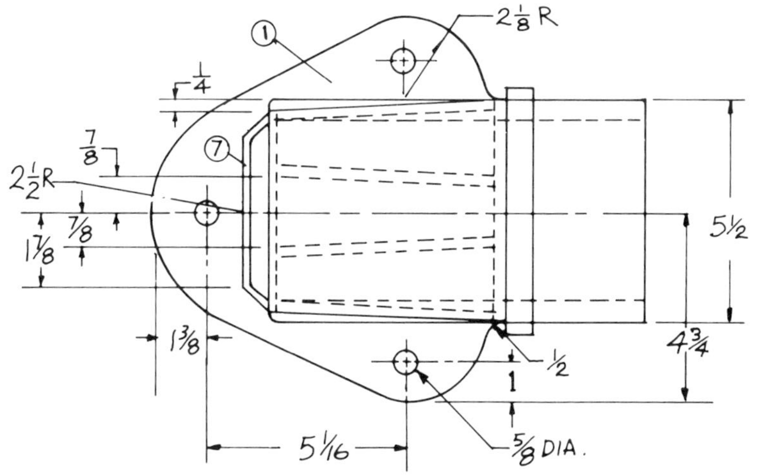

NO.	REQD	DESCRIPTION	MATERIAL
1	1	½ X 9½ PLATE 12½ LG	1020
2	1	¼ X 5½ BAR 3 LG	1020
3	1	¼ X 5½ BAR 6½ LG	1020
4	4	¼ X 4 BAR 6 LG	1020
5	1	⅝ X 1½ BAR 6 LG	1020
6	1	5½ X ⅜ TUBING 10 4G	A500
7	1	¼ X 1 BAR 4 LG	1020
8	1	2½ X 1¾ BAR 2½ LG	1020

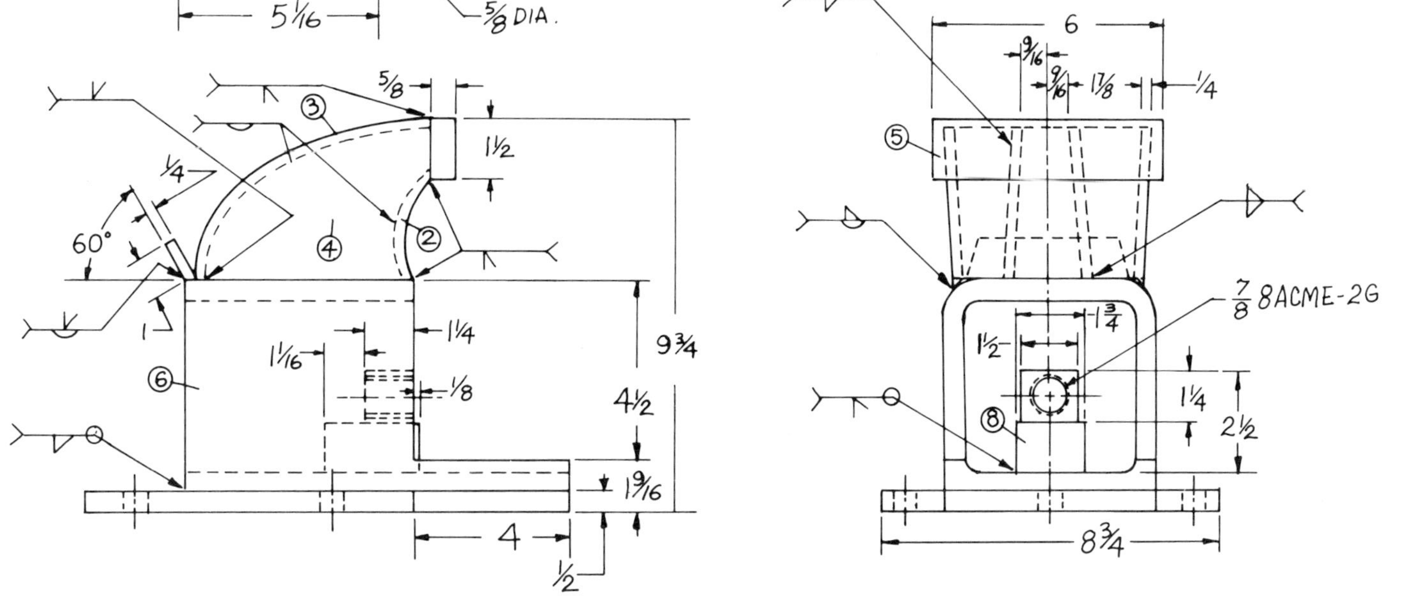

FIXED JAW

Ornamental Support Column And Rail

Author: Rich Christianson
Instructor: Dale Rawlings
School: Butte Vo-Tech
City & State: Butte, MT

The support columns were constructed first. One inch square tubing of .072 inch thickness was used for the vertical members. The short horizontal supports were also one inch square tubing of .072 inch thickness. The large S shaped scrolls were made from ½ inch hot rolled square bar. The scrolls on each curve are made of ⅛ inch by ½ inch flat bar. The end brackets are ¼ inch by 2 inch flat bar. One inch strips of 1 inch angle iron were used for the bolt brackets.

The single faced column was made first. The square tubing was sawed to length, and the cross members were welded on first. On the columns all scrolls are centered on the tubing. The S scrolls were all bent with a small jig and welded in. The smaller scrolls in each curve were then bent and welded. All welds which faced out were ground off flush. The end brackets were drilled with 3 holes ⅜ inch diameter spaced as indicated in the drawing, and then welded on. The end brackets were flame cut round at the corners and ground smooth. The bolt brackets were drilled with 1 hole ⅛ inch diameter centered as in the drawing, and then welded on.

The two faced column was then constructed in the same manner. The only differences were in the end brackets, which had only two ⅜ inch holes on each side, and were flame cut at 45° and welded L-shaped and ground off flush.

The top and bottom of the front rail were made of ½ inch by 1 inch channel iron. The upright pieces are of ½ inch hot rolled square bar. The S-shaped scrolls are also ½ inch hot rolled square bar. The small scrolls are ⅛ inch by ½ inch flat bar. The center scrolls are made entirely of ⅛ inch by ¾ inch equal leg angle iron. The bar under the numbers is made of ½ inch square bar.

After the channel iron was sawed to length, it was drilled with ¼ inch holes on each end as specified in the drawing. Each square bar next to the scrolls was torch heated and twisted ½ turn with the vise clamped 6 inches from the end. A crescent wrench 2 inches from the end worked well and kept the twists fairly uniform. Square holes were punched in the channel iron at each place an upright square bar was to be placed. When the square bar was welded in place the weld on the top channel iron was ground flush. The S-shaped scrolls were then bent and welded on. The small scrolls were then bent and welded

on. The border for the numbers was cut and welded in place, then the numbers were cut and welded. The numbers were filled with braze. The large scrolls under the numbers were then cut, bent, and welded in place.

The ornamental columns were attached with 1 inch lag bolts. The ornamental rail was bolted to the columns with ¼ inch by 1 inch stove bolts. This arrangement permits the removal of the railing when furniture is to be moved in or out.

The side railing top and bottom were made of ½ inch by 1 inch channel iron. The two vertical bars are ½ inch square bar. One inch strips of 1 inch angle iron were used for bolt brackets.

After the channel iron was sawed to length, it was drilled with ¼ inch holes on each end as specified in the drawing. The two vertical bars were twisted the same as the vertical bars on the front were twisted. Square holes were punched in the channel iron at each place an upright square bar was to be welded. When the square bar was welded in place the weld on top was ground off flush.

The rail was bolted to the ornamental support column with ¼ inch by 1 inch stove bolts. Bolt brackets were made of 1 inch strips of 1 inch angle iron drilled with ¼ inch holes on one leg, and ⅜ inch holes on the other leg.

The leg with the ⅜ inch hole was bolted to the wall with a ⅜ inch by 1 inch lag bolt. The rail was bolted with ¼ inch by 1 inch stove bolts to the bolt brackets on the wall, and by ¼ inch by 1 inch stove bolts to the bolt brackets on the ornamental support column.

Bill of Materials

    5 - .072″ x 1″ square tubing 8′ 2″
   12 - .072″ x 1″ square tubing 9″
    2 - ½″ x 1″ channel iron 6′ 8″
    2 - ½″ x 1″ channel iron 2′ 4″
    8 - ½″ x ½″ square bar 28″
   11 - ½″ x ½″ square bar 36″
    1 - ½″ x ½″ square bar 11½″
   22 - ⅛″ x ½″ flat bar 22″
    2 - ⅛″ x ½″ flat bar 52″
    2 - ⅛″ x ¾″ x ¾″ angle iron 6″
    1 - ⅛″ x ¾″ x ¾″ angle iron 6½″
    1 - ⅛″ x ¾″ x ¾″ angle iron 3″
    8 - ⅛″ x 1″ x 1″ angle iron 1″
    6 - ¼″ x 2″ flat bar 14″
    8 - ¼″ x 1″ stove bolts
    8 - ¼″ stove bolt nuts
   16 - ⅜″ x 1″ lag bolts

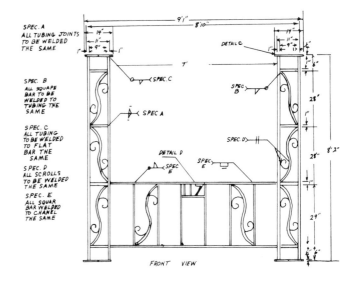

FRONT VIEW

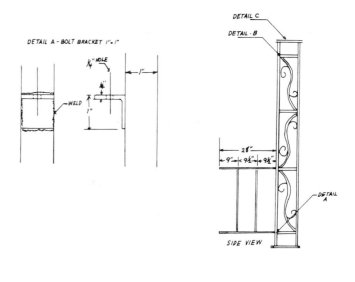

SIDE VIEW

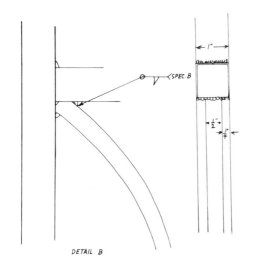

DETAIL B

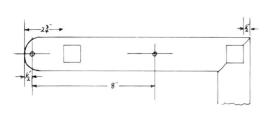

DETAIL A – BOLT BRACKET 1″=1″

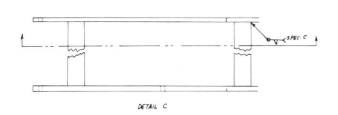

DETAIL C

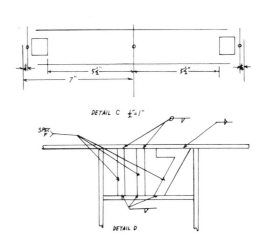

DETAIL C ¼″=1″

DETAIL D

Welding Bench

Author: *Rick Strawn*
Instructor: *Mr. J. C. Sinclair*
School: *Cimarron High School*
City & State: *Cimarron, KS*

To make the top frame cut a piece of 1½" angle iron 16'8" long, long enough for the 6' sides and 28" ends of the bench. Cut small triangles out of one side of the angle iron. After cutting out the triangles fold the angle iron in a rectangle to form the top frame of the bench and weld. Cut 4 legs for the bench 32" long out of 1½" angle iron. Cut rails to support the legs. Two rails 28" long and 2 rails 6'. Since the legs are fitting inside of the top frame trim the rails slightly to make them fit square. Lay the legs on the floor open side of the angle iron facing in toward the center, lay the long rails in place, the top of the rail 4" up from the bottom of the legs and weld them into place. After doing both sides put the end rails in place and weld.

After welding the end rails in place weld the two sides together by welding the free end of the end rail to the other side. Make cutter bars. Cut 9 cutter bars to a length of 27½" long and place them 2¾" apart from each other. Then spot weld these into place underneath the top frame of angle iron with the flat side facing up. After the cutter bars are welded place the top frame on the bottom frame and weld it into place.

From ¼" plate 27½" x 36" cut 4" off of the end to made it the right length. For the welding plate "C" clamp the plate into place and drill two 7½" holes on each side and one on the end spaced evenly apart. Put plow bolt in and put the nuts on and tighten them. From the plate left over cut 4 pieces of plate 4 x 3½" and drill holes in them for ¼" bolts to hold the wheels to the plate. Then weld the pieces of plate to the bottom of the legs. Next, make the shelf for the welder. Cut the bottom shelf 27½" wide by 6' long and spot weld it every 3 to 4" on top of the rails, add supports underneath to keep it from sagging. Use ¾" rod welded underneath every 11" except under where the welder is to sit put them every 9". Then cut four ¾" rods 1' long to use as braces from the corner of the angle iron and wheel plates to the side rails and weld them into place to strengthen the welding bench. Cut a ¾" bar 27½" long and weld across the end of the ¼" plate to keep it from sagging when it is heated. Cut two pieces of 1½" angle iron 28" long to use as supports from the side rails to the top frame. Place the open side of the angle iron toward the side with the plate on it, then weld them into place. Make a chute to prevent hot metal and sparks from falling onto the bottom shelf. Use two pieces of ½" angle iron, 30" long placed 2" down from the top at a 30° angle. Weld ½" angle iron to the legs on the cutter bar end and to the vertical braces. Then put a piece of ten gauge metal 36" x 30" and weld this in place. Put in a divider to keep hot sparks off of the weld. Use ½ of a sheet of 10 gauge metal 19" x 28".

Bill of Material

No. of pieces	width	length	name of part
1 angle iron	1½ x 1½ in	16 ft. 8 in	top frame
4 angle iron	1½ x 1½ in	32 in.	legs
2 angle iron	1½ x 1½ in.	6 foot	side rails
2 angle iron	1½ x 1½ in.	28 inches	end rails
2 angle iron	½" x ½"	30 inches	chute holders
2 angle iron	1½ x 1½ in.	28 inches	vertical braces
1 ¼" plate	27½ inches	30 inches	welding top
1 10 gage metal	27½ inches	6 foot	bottom shelf
½ of 1 ten gage metal	19 inches	28 inches	divider
9 channel iron	1" x ½" x ⅛ in.	27½ inches	cutter bars
7 rods	¾ inches	27½ inches	shelf braces
4 rods	¾ inch	12 inches	leg to rail braces
4 ¼" plate	3¼ inches	4¼ inches	wheel plates
4 wheels	3 inch diameter	4 inches high	wheels
1 ten gauge	30 inches	36 inches	chute metal
1 rod	¾ inch	27½ inches	plate brace
7 plow bolts	½ inch	1 inch	plow bolts

TOP VIEW

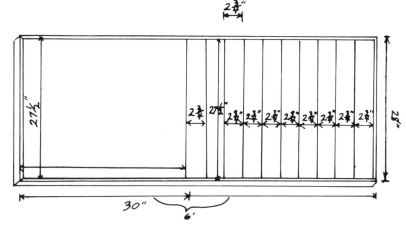

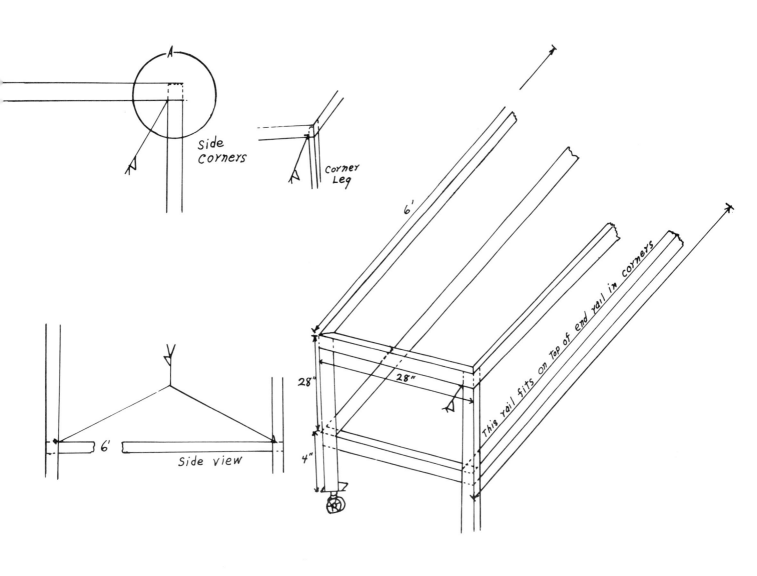

Side Corners

Corner Leg

A

28"

28"

4"

6'

This rail fits on top of end rail in corners

6'

Side view

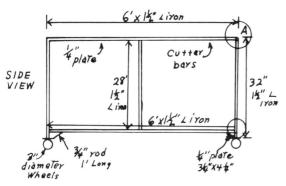

SIDE VIEW

6' x 1½" L iron

¼" plate

28'
1½"
L Iron

Cutter bars

A

32"
1½" L
iron

6' x 1½" L iron

3"
diameter
Wheels

¾" rod
1' Long

¼" plate
36" x 4¼"

28" x 1½" L IRON

10 gage
Metal Devider

28"
x 1½"
L iron

all one
piece

2" down from top
and set at a 30°
angle.

30" x ½"
L iron

chute
36" x 30"

End View

4"
x 1½
L iron

28" x 1½" L-
iron

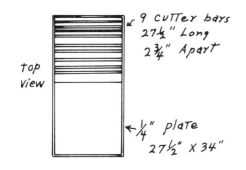

top
View

9 CUTTER bars
27½" Long
2¾" Apart

¼" plate
27½" x 34"

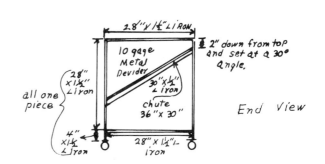

6 ¾" x 27½"
rod used
for support
of the Bottom
Shelf

28"

9" 9" 11¼" 11¼" 11¼" 11½" 11¼"

6'

Bottom
View

Legs

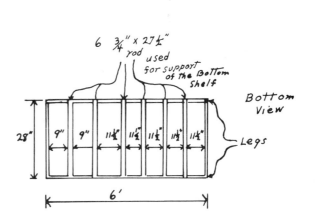

Training School Weldment Safety Holder

The device shown in figure 1, and described by this presentation was designed to prevent injury to welding operator trainees while they absorbed skill-lessons in their craft. The principle components of the fixture consist of a fabricated ring, a piece of chain, a metal bar, and a bolt and nut.

The only critical dimensions for this safety fixture are the length of the chain, and the diameter of the material of which the links are made. Chain stock is ⅜″ diameter, and the chain length is 11″. This length is precisely that which will allow the weldment to be used in all positions while being held in a universal welding fixture.

The clip is burned or drilled so that it has bare clearance over the horizontal arm of the universal jig-fixture. Such clearance allows the clip to be slipped over the pipe and moved along the pipe length at the discretion of the user. The metal bar should be approximately ⅜″ x 1½″ x 6″ mild steel, one end of which is welded by an appropriately sized head to the welding sample configuration.

As shown, the chain is fastened to a bolt that passes through a hole that is burned or drilled through the bar and held by a washer and a nut on the threaded end.

The work piece in this figure (fig. 3) has been photographed in deliberate misalignment from the vertical to illustrate the versatility of this safety device in allowing the weldment to be rotated in any direction of a prescribed plane. The free end of the ⅜″ x 1½″ x 6″ MS bar is inserted between the jaws of the movable holding fixture and held tightly in any pre-determined position by a set screw designed for the purpose.

All items in this design can be cut from scrap material if such is available. Tolerances are general and lend themselves to the ingenuity of the person designing these items for use at their particular facility.

Use of this item during training lessons prevents the weldment from slipping out of the holding fixture and dropping on the hands and feet of the training operator.

Author: Gary Matthews
Instructor: Edward A. Hudson
School: St. John's Welding School
City & State: Jessup, MD

FIG. 1

FIG. 2

FIG. 3

Metal Band Saw

Authors: John Hanson
                    Dan Eide
                    Curtis French
                    Don Grayson
                    Don Myers
Instructor: Daniel C. Scott
School: Western Montana College
City & State: Dillon, MT

The band saw wheels were two 8″ diameter wheels and one 4″ wheel made from cast aluminum. The 8″ drive wheel was designed to have material casted into it for a 9″ diameter pully to be machined later. The patterns for the wheels were made on the wood lathe and used to make the sand molds. The materials we used for aluminum consisted of beer cans, aluminum wire, worn-out motorcycle engines, and any free aluminum we could find.

The wheels were then machined for bearings, band saw blade and pulley. The two 8″ wheels have 2 bearings and the smaller 4″ wheel has one bearing.

The frame construction was arc welded from 1″ square tubing. The jig for the frame was constructed on a metal plate by welding metal tabs in position to hold the square tubing. All of the welding on the frame was done in the jig. The cold rolled steel shafts for the wheels were arc welded to the frame.

12″ channel iron was flame cut to the proper length. a 6″ long x ¼″ plate was welded to the channel to increase the length of the table base. The jig was set up to weld the legs on the table base. The leg material is one square inch tubing.

The vise is designed to cut angles and hold a 12″ wide piece of material. The moveable vise jaw is driven by a threaded rod which moves a hex nut welded to an angle iron on the underside of the table base.

The blade guide assembly was designed to be made from ¾″ square tubing which was to slide inside the 1″ square tubing. To make the fit better between the two tubings, brass shims were welded into the larger tubing with the gas metal arc welder.

The guard was molded from fiberglass. The mold was fabricated from plywood and sheet metal.

The electric motor speed was slowed down by using a jack-shaft with an 8″ pulley at one end and a 1½″ pulley at the other end. Pipe was used to hold the bearings and jack-shaft. The belt tightening mechanism is incorporated into the jack-shaft by sliding it back and forth on the frame.

The blade tightening and tracking mechanism was accomplished by a hinged plate and sliding tubing. The blade guide bearings were designed like other saws with bearings that are adjustable.

Lawn mower wheel shafts were welded to the base legs for mounting old lawn mower wheels.

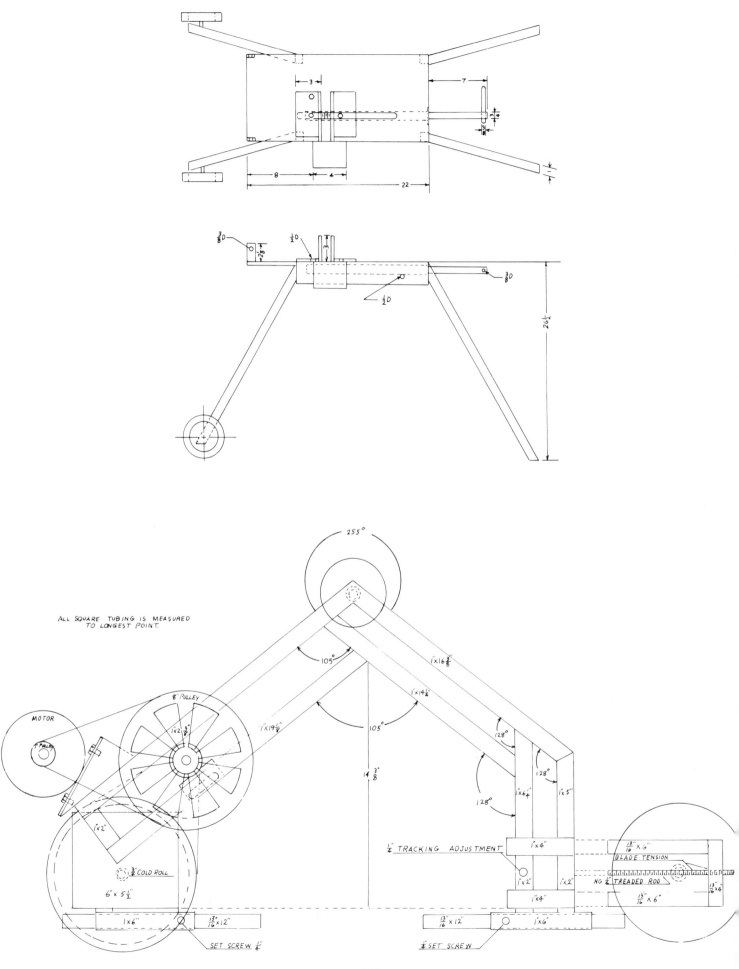

ALL SQUARE TUBING IS MEASURED
TO LONGEST POINT.

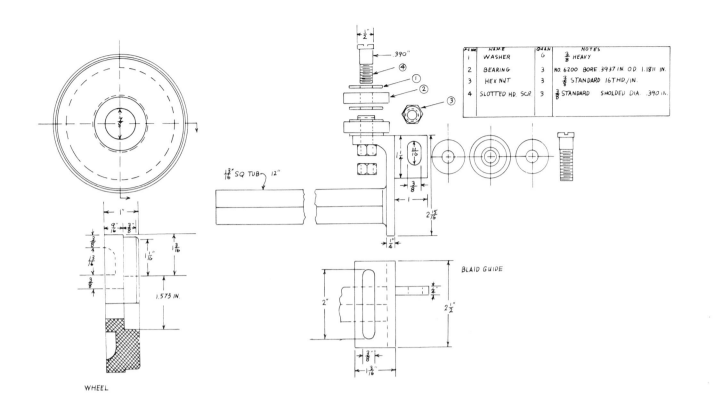

PCM#	NAME	QUAN	NOTES
1	WASHER	6	$\frac{3}{8}$ HEAVY
2	BEARING	3	NO. 6200 BORE .3937 IN. O.D. 1.1811 IN.
3	HEX NUT	3	$\frac{3}{8}$ STANDARD 16 THD./IN.
4	SLOTTED HD. SCR.	3	$\frac{3}{8}$ STANDARD SHOLDED DIA. .390 IN.

WHEEL

BLAID GUIDE

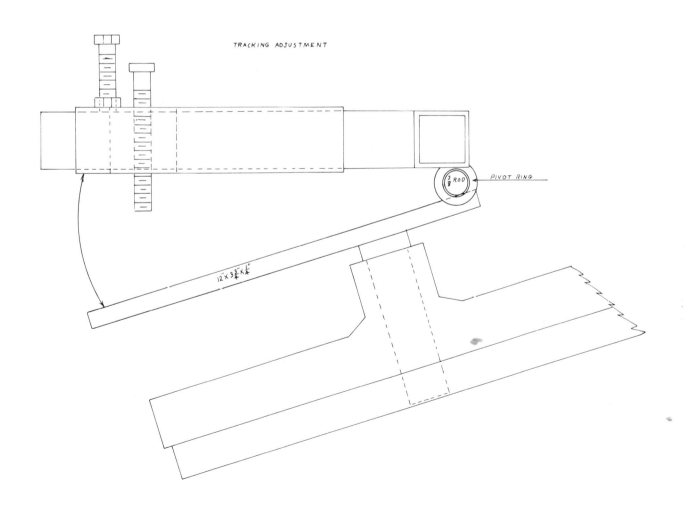

TRACKING ADJUSTMENT

PIVOT RING

Laminated Stylized Steel Anvil

Author: James R. Warkentin, Sr.
Instructor: James Cron
School: Orange Coast Jr. College
City & State: Costa Mesa, CA

The anvil was constructed by laminating heavy steel plates (¾" to 1⅛") welding, building up and grinding contours to an artistic bird like shape that would be a functional tool for use in crafts.

The first step was taking the five pieces of plate, flame cutting the necessary ½" bevels, tacking them together in a backbone configuration, and welding multiple pass fillets with a simple sequence to prevent distortion. The top grooves were filled with 7024 and the rest with 6010. The bottom of the tail was soap stoned, center punched, and cut with a hand flame cutting torch.

Two more pieces of plate were added to either side of the front, edge beveled with air carbon arc, and welded down the top only. The bottom was shaped first into the compound round using air carbon arc, the area ground until the seams shown and burned in with 6010 and reground. The underside of the body was also gouged with carbon arc. Two long rectangular pieces of steel were beveled using a radiograph flame cutting machine and secured to the top side of the tail.

One half inch round stock was cut to length tacked to either end, and shaped by forging with a ball peen hammer, oxygen, and acetylene and a large heating tip.

The leg pattern was drawn at this time, and 5 pieces of plate were cut to get the desired leg width. Four large flame cut bevels were made at the top of the outside two leg plates. The leg was then welded together and joined to the main body.

To attach the anvil to a tree stump, a large reservoir was machined into the bottom center of the leg and a 1½" nut was welded into place. This received a threaded bolt that comes up through bottom. Except for some detailing to the stump the anvil was completed at 155 pounds.

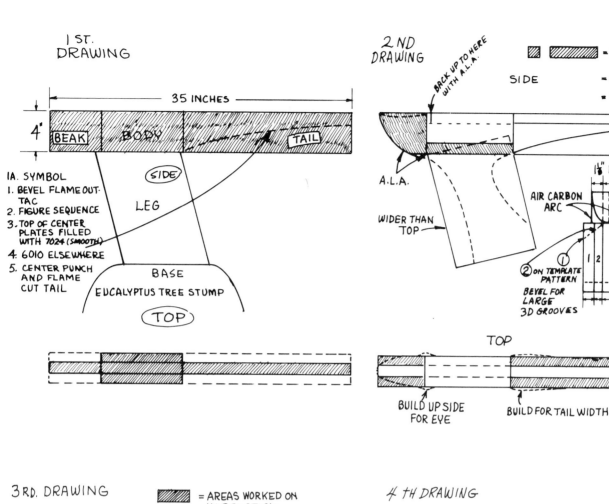

1ST. DRAWING

35 INCHES

4"

BEAK · BODY · TAIL

1A. SYMBOL
1. BEVEL FLAME OUT - TAC
2. FIGURE SEQUENCE
3. TOP OF CENTER PLATES FILLED WITH 7024 (SMOOTH)
4. 6010 ELSEWHERE
5. CENTER PUNCH AND FLAME CUT TAIL

(SIDE)

LEG

BASE
EUCALYPTUS TREE STUMP

(TOP)

2ND DRAWING

BACK UP TO HERE WITH A.L.A.

= PARTS WORKED IN SECOND STEP
= AIR CARBON ARC
= A.L.A.

SIDE

A.L.A.

WIDER THAN TOP

AIR CARBON ARC

FRONT

1⅛" 1" 1⅛"

① ON TEMPLATE PATTERN
② ON TEMPLATE PATTERN

BEVEL FOR LARGE 3D GROOVES

1 2

TOP

BUILD UP SIDE FOR EYE

BUILD FOR TAIL WIDTH

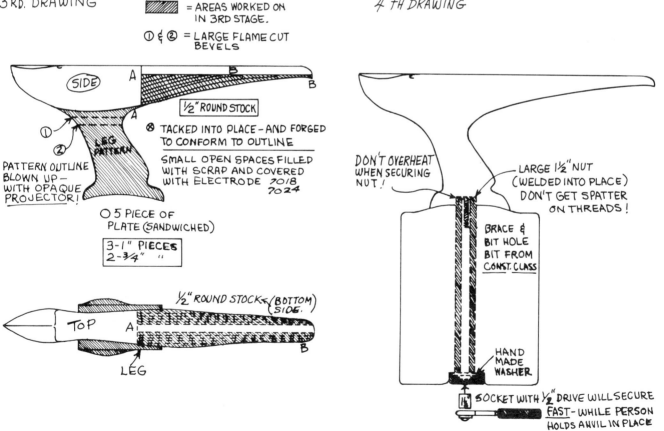

3RD. DRAWING

= AREAS WORKED ON IN 3RD STAGE.
① & ② = LARGE FLAME CUT BEVELS

(SIDE)

A   B

A

①
②

LEG PATTERN

PATTERN OUTLINE BLOWN UP - WITH OPAQUE PROJECTOR!

½" ROUND STOCK

⊗ TACKED INTO PLACE - AND FORGED TO CONFORM TO OUTLINE

SMALL OPEN SPACES FILLED WITH SCRAP AND COVERED WITH ELECTRODE 7018 7024

○ 5 PIECE OF PLATE (SANDWICHED)

3-1" PIECES
2-¾" "

½" ROUND STOCK (BOTTOM) SIDE.

TOP   A

B

LEG

4TH DRAWING

DON'T OVERHEAT WHEN SECURING NUT!

LARGE 1½" NUT (WELDED INTO PLACE) DON'T GET SPATTER ON THREADS!

BRACE & BIT HOLE BIT FROM CONST. CLASS

HAND MADE WASHER

SOCKET WITH ½" DRIVE WILL SECURE FAST - WHILE PERSON HOLDS ANVIL IN PLACE

Welding and Cutting Table

Author: *Mikel Roberson*
Instructor: *Ron Crispin*
School: *Cheyenne East High School*
City & State: *Cheyenne, WY*

Materials

Two 4'' Casters
¼'' Plate—5 square feet
³⁄₁₆'' x 1'' x 1'' Angle Iron 6 feet
¼'' x 1½'' x 1½'' Angle Iron—18 feet
³⁄₁₆'' x 1'' x 1'' strap—3 feet
Legs (2½'' I.D. Pipe) 11 feet
Expanded Metal
    Top Shelf 2' x 3'—6 square feet
    Bottom Shelf 1' x 2'—2 square feet
Handle ½'' rod—2 feet
Positioning Arm and Clamp
Cutting tray
    Hot rolled sheet 2' x 3'—6 square ft.
Cutting rails 5—¼ x 1½'' strap 10 feet
Paint

Upper Frame

Step 1:   Using a metal cutting band saw, cut two ¼'' x 1½'' x 1½'' pieces of hot rolled angle iron 36'' long for the side supports of the table.

Step 2:   Next cut the ends from the same ¼'' x 1½'' x 1½'' angle, 24½'' long. Notch out the ends so they will fit square and still measure 24½'' x

36'' overall dimensions. The entire frame is then tack welded together.

Step 3:   For extra strength tack weld ¼'' x 3'' x 3½'' gussets in each corner. These are cut out of quarter inch plate and ground to fit. Then weld the entire frame and gussets. The frame is welded on both sides, grinding only the corners to maintain a square edge.

Legs

Step 1:   Cut 2½'' I.D. ³⁄₁₆'' wall pipe into two 36'' pieces for the front legs and two 29½'' pieces for the back legs. The casters are 6½'' in height.

Step 2:   Use ¼'' x 5'' x 5½'' plates for the bottoms of the legs. Four plates are needed. Two are tacked and squared to the front legs.

Step 3:   Next take 4'' hard rubber casters measured and lay out ⅜'' holes on the plate and drill. Install the casters to the plate using four ⅜'' x 1'' NC machine bolts with lock washers. The plate is then squared to the bottom of the leg.

Step 4:   After tacking finish weld all the way around the pipe.

Lower Frame

Step 1: Using ¼″ x 1½″ angle iron cut sides 29½″ and ends 18″ long. But to the middle of the pipe legs, 10″ down from the top tack and finish weld adding expanded metal cut 21″ x 33″ and tack to the angle iron to create storage space.

Table Top

Step 1: ¼″ plate is used for a welding to 26½″ x 27½″.

Step 2: Drill four ¾″ diameter holes (one in each corner) to permit changing the positions of the upright clamp. The ⅞″ holes are drilled ⅞″ from the outside edge.

Step 3: For safety the square corners and all edges are ground to a round edge using a side grinder, then smoothed with a file.

Step 4: The top plate was fillet welded in a backstep method offsetting the welds to keep down warpage.

Cutting Area

Step 1: The grate is made of five rails of ¼″ x 1½″ strap cut 23¾″ long.

Step 2: To hold the rails on 1¾″ centers a ½″ x ½″ x 1″ piece of angle iron is placed one on each side of a rail to form a 5⁄16″ slot for the rails to slide in and out of.

Cutting Tray

Step 1: A frame of 3⁄16″ x 1″ x 1″ angle iron is made to hold the tray. The sides are cut 9″ long with an 8″ piece of 3⁄16″ x 1″ strap coming down to form a vertical brace. The angle iron is butted to the leg. The strap is butted to the upper frame. The tray slides in from the back side.

Step 2: The tray is made of 16 gauge hot rolled sheet using the layout below. After bending, the tray is welded using an oxy-acetylene torch.

Lower Shelf

Step 1: The frame is 3⁄16″ x 1″ x 1″ angle iron. Two sides 7½″ long a 22″ piece between forming the back. The front is formed using a piece of angle iron 17¾″ long. A 3⁄16″ x 1″ strap, 15″ long is used on the inside corners as a vertical brace.

Step 2: Expanded metal cut 7¼″ x 22½″ form the bottom.

Positioning Arm

Step 1: The upright for the arm is 1¼″ O.D. ⅛″ wall pipe cut 30″ long. A ¾″ diameter bolt is welded to the end to fasten it to the table. The head of the bolt is ground flush with the pipe.

Step 2: A 1½″ O.D. ⅛″ wall sleeve is cut 3″ long. This slides up and down on the upright.

Step 3: A piece of ¾″ diameter pipe for the extension arm is cut 8″ long. A ⅜″ diameter hole is drilled on a 1½″ center. A ⅜″ nut is welded over the hole. The pipe is then welded to the sleeve.

Step 4: A ½″ diameter rod cut 9″ long is an extension arm. 4″ C-clamp at the end of this rod holds the work. The rod is welded to the center of the clamp.

Step 5: A ⅜″ diameter hole is drilled on the 1½″ center of the sleeve. A ⅜″ nut is welded to the sleeve. Two pieces of ¼″ diameter rod are cut 4″ long. These are then welded to each of the bolts as in diagram:

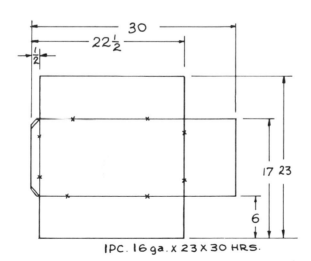

IPC. 16 ga. x 23 x 30 HRS.

Car Ramps

Author: Jim Poffenbarger
Instructor: Robert J. Madsen
School: Burlington Community High School
City & State: Burlington, Iowa

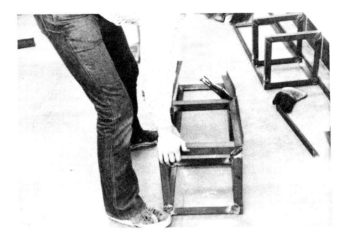

Clamping top runners to meet bottom runners.

Using power hacksaw, cut four pieces 1½″ x 1½″ x ⅛″ angle iron 60″ long. Using angle iron notcher, notch out every 15 inches and at ends of metal to form 15″ square. Weld square together using ⅛″ E-6013 electrodes, 95 to 100 amps and AC current.

Cut four pieces of the same angle iron 50″ long for runners of car ramp. Using vise grips or clamps, clamp runners to square frame and tack in place using ⅛″ E-6013 electrodes, 95 to 100 amps and AC current.

Next cut four pieces 52″ long. Using angle iron notcher, notch out a piece 14″ from the end. Put 52″ angle iron in place on top of the squares and clamp them down. From the notched-out piece, bend it down to meet the bottom runner. Weld into place with ⅛″ E-6013 electrodes, 95 to 100 amp., and AC current.

Fitting deck plate into place.

Next cut braces, two for each side: two 9½″ and two 5″. Place braces 10″ apart between the end and the back square. Weld them in place using ⅛″ E-6013 electrodes at 95 and 100 amp. on AC current. Flame cut six pieces 14″ x 12″ from deck plate 96″ x 14″ x ⅛″. Fit these sections in place on the two ramps. Fit the two top sections. Weld the deck plate in with E-7024 electrode at 135 to 140 amps. on AC current.

Cut two 6″ pieces of ¾″ steel rod and using 5 lbs. P.S.I. of oxygen and 5 P.S.I. Acetylene, heat pieces to a cherry red 2″ in from each end, with a 205 welding tip. Take two pieces of shop metal 14″ x 4″ x ¼″ and with the gas torch round two corners. Weld the two handles on the middle of the shop metal with ⅛″ E6013 electrodes at 95 to 100 amps on AC current. Place this piece on the front of ramps for wheel stops. Weld with ⅛″ E-6013 electrodes at 95 to 100 amps on AC current.

Completed project.

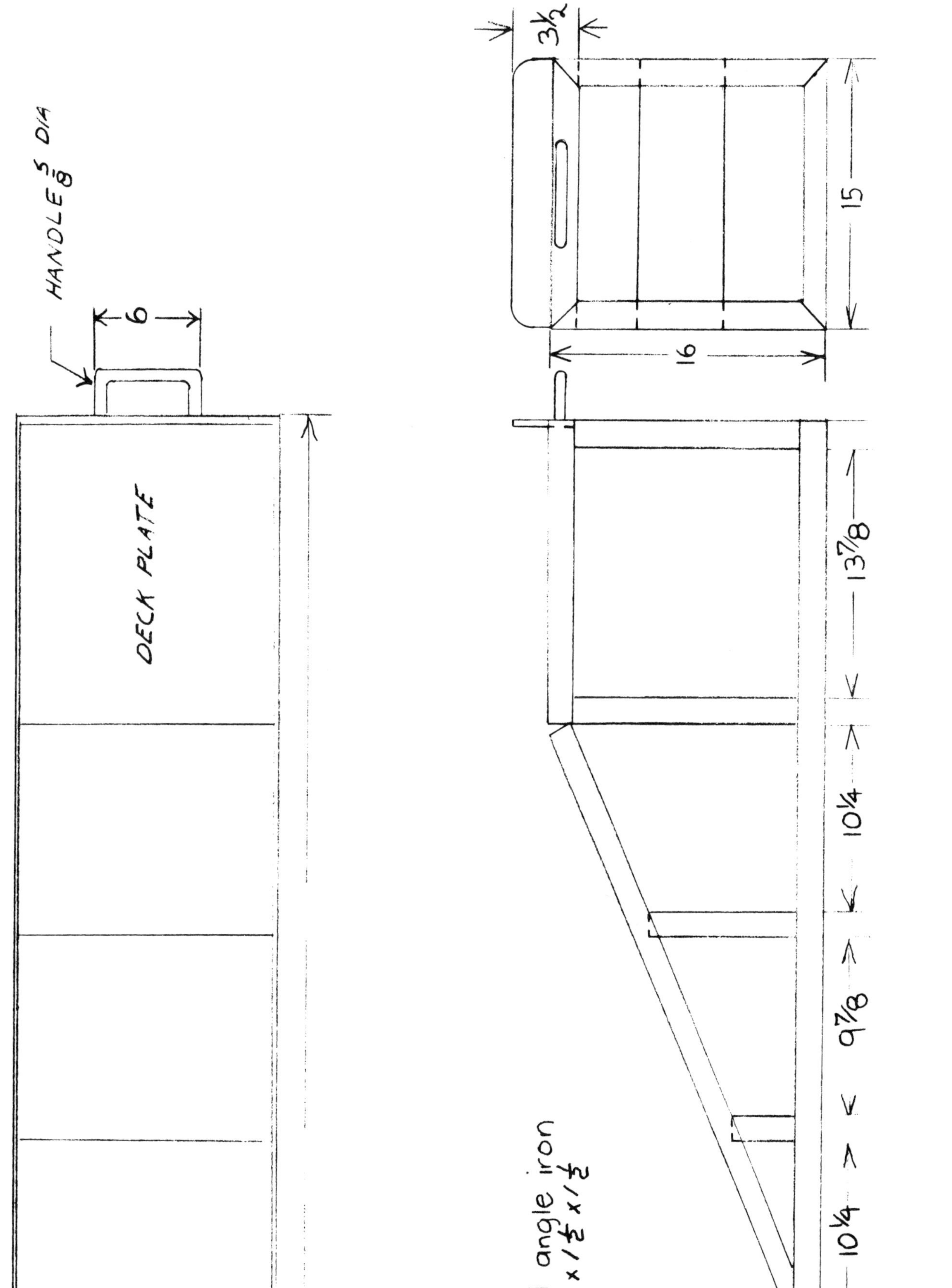

HANDLE $\frac{5}{8}$ DIA

6

DECK PLATE

$3\frac{1}{2}$

15

16

13⅞

10¼

9⅞

10¼

All angle iron
$\frac{1}{8} \times 1\frac{1}{2} \times 1\frac{1}{2}$

CAR RAMPS

Abrasive Cut-Off Saw

Author: Dino J. Migliazzo
Instructor: Norman Mellow and Bob Williams
School: Merced High School
City & State: Merced, CA

Materials

Motor: 3 phase, 3500 RPM
Starter for motor
Bearings-ER 16 (2)
Belts-½″ x 55″ (2)
Pulleys - AX 35 (2)
16 gauge sheet metal (4 x 8)
¼″ plate 32 x 22 ⅛
½″ plate 18 sq. inches
2 x 3 Angle Iron 11.7 ft. needed
2 x 2 Angle Iron 15 ft. needed
1½″ x 1½″ Angle Iron - 9ft.
10″ channel - 15″ needed
2″ channel - 10″ needed
1¼″ shaft - 11.625″ needed
1″ shaft - 9″ needed
½″ shaft - 1 foot needed
1″ galvanized pipe - 18″ needed
3″ diameter thick wall tubing - 7.37″
1 - 45° elbow 1″
2 - ¾ x 1½ bolts, nuts and washers
4 - ½ x 1 bolts, nuts and washers
1 - 1″ left hand thread nut (for blade)
1 - 5″ spring for pipe clamp
40° Honda chain and sprocket (used)
1—10″ blade

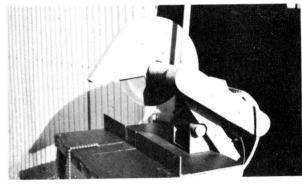

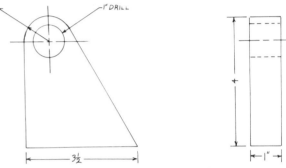

MOTOR MOUNT HINGE—TWO NEEDED

PLATFORM HINGE

WORKING TABLE

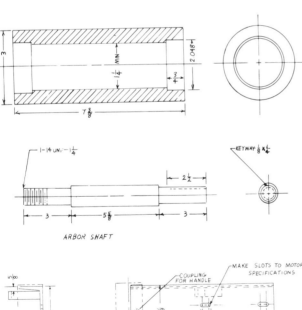

ARBOR SHAFT

MOTOR AND ARBOR MOUNT

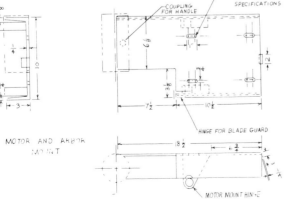

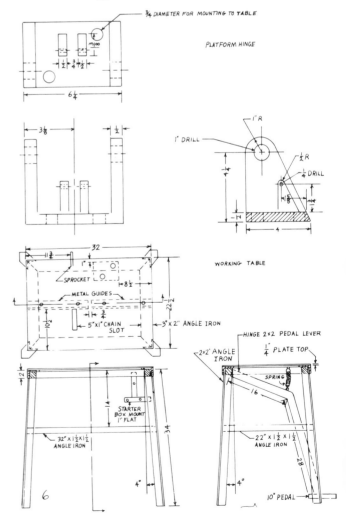

6

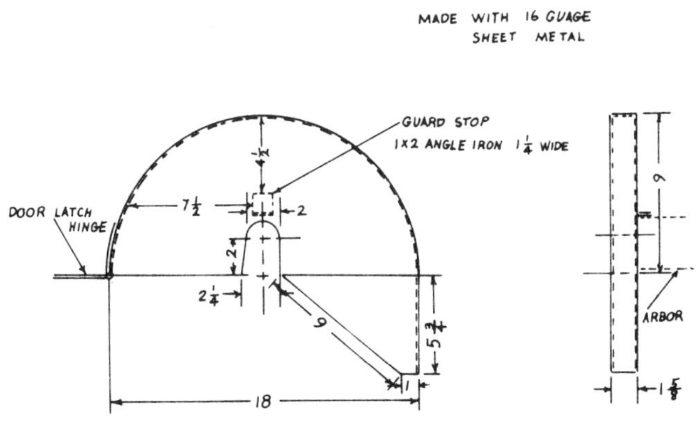
MADE WITH 16 GUAGE SHEET METAL
GUARD STOP 1x2 ANGLE IRON 1 1/4 WIDE
DOOR LATCH HINGE
7 1/2
2
2
2 1/4
9
5 3/4
1
18
6
ARBOR
1 5/8

BLADE GUARD

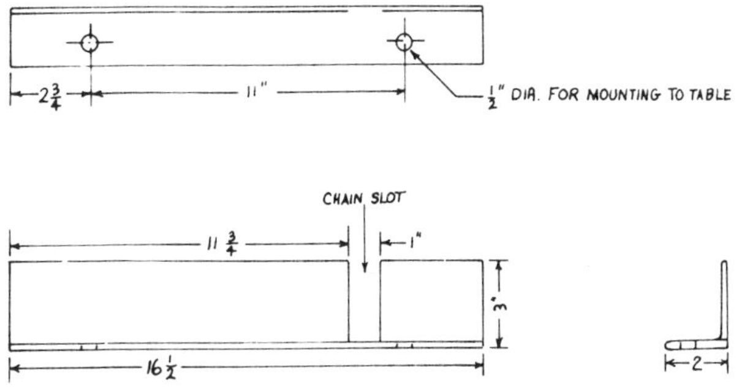
2 3/4
11"
1/2" DIA. FOR MOUNTING TO TABLE
CHAIN SLOT
11 3/4
1"
3"
16 1/2
2

GUIDE FOR BENCH
LEFT SIDE

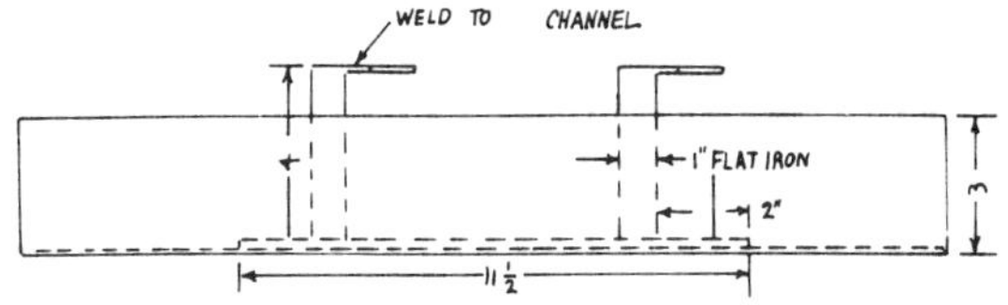
WELD TO CHANNEL
4
1" FLAT IRON
2"
3
11 1/2

BELT AND PULLEY GUARD

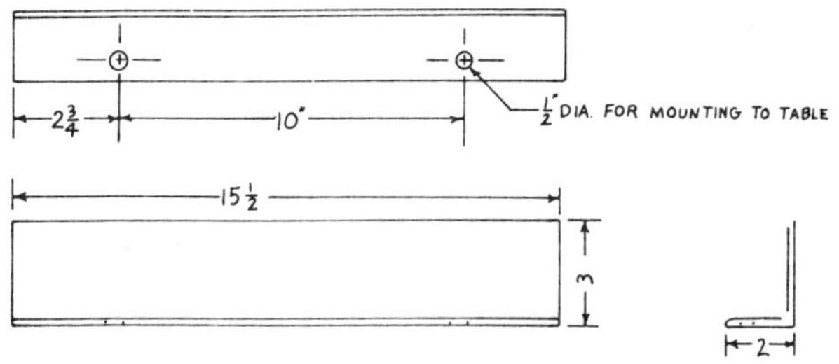
2 3/4
10"
1/2" DIA. FOR MOUNTING TO TABLE
15 1/2
3
2

GUIDE FOR BENCH
RIGHT SIDE

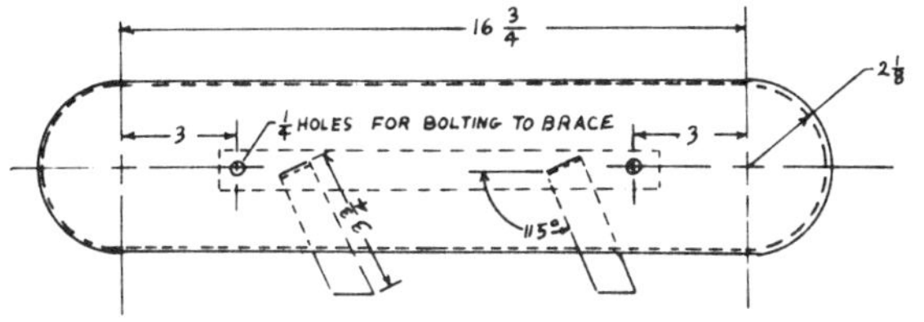
16 3/4
2 1/8
3
1/4 HOLES FOR BOLTING TO BRACE
3
115°

MADE WITH 16 GUAGE SHEET METAL

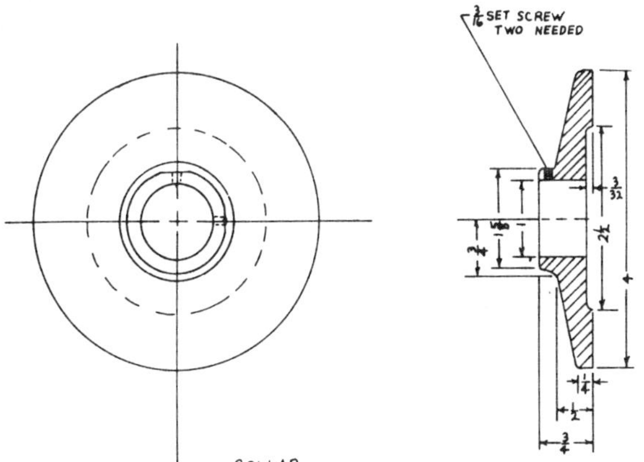
3/16 SET SCREW TWO NEEDED
3/32
2 1/2
4
1/4
1/2
3/4

COLLAR

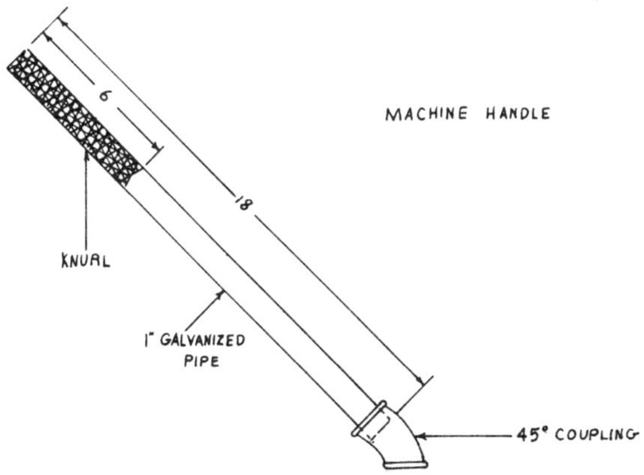
6
18
KNURL
1" GALVANIZED PIPE
45° COUPLING

MACHINE HANDLE

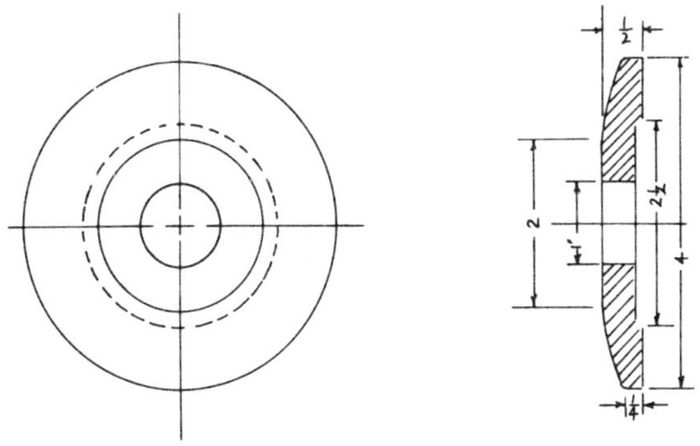
1/2
2
1"
2 1/2
4
1/4

COLLAR

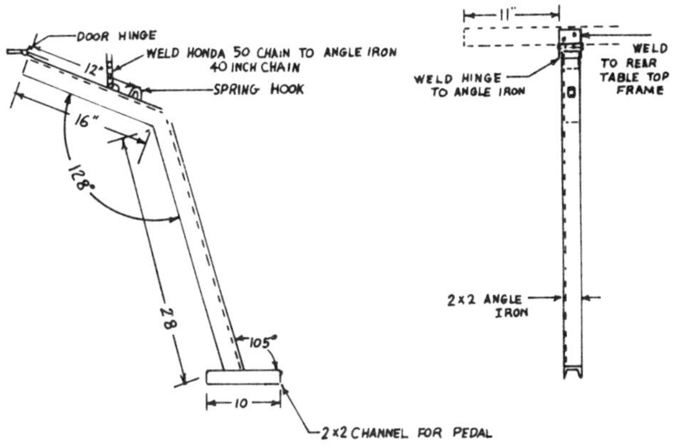
DOOR HINGE
WELD HONDA 50 CHAIN TO ANGLE IRON
40 INCH CHAIN
12"
SPRING HOOK
16"
128°
28
105°
10
2x2 CHANNEL FOR PEDAL
11"
WELD
WELD HINGE TO ANGLE IRON
TO REAR TABLE TOP FRAME
2x2 ANGLE IRON

CLAMP PEDAL

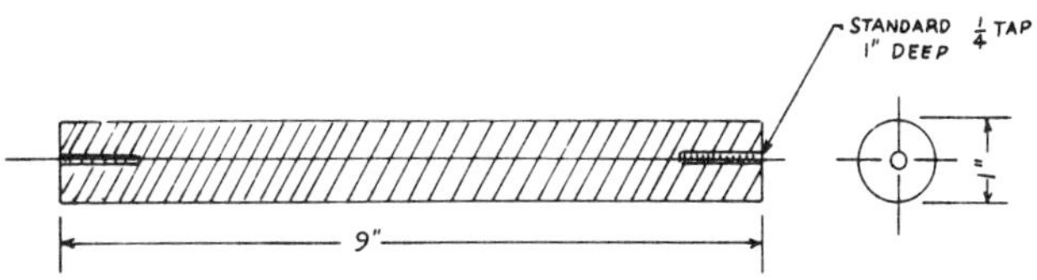
STANDARD 1/4 TAP
1" DEEP
9"
1"

PIN FOR HINGE BETWEEN PLATFORM HINGE AND MOTOR MOUNT HINGE

A Portable Oxy-Acetylene Cutting and Welding Table

Author:	Tom McLaughlin
Instructor:	Hugh E. Doane
School:	North County Tech
City & State:	Florissant, MO

The features of this welding table include: slab bin, cutting table, welding table, tray to contain tool box, three rod holders, two flux holders, a cabinet for storage, and shelves under the table. It is mounted on casters for easy movement. The portability allows for its use in other locations, and its versatility includes all of the functions of a regular welding station.

For materials and dimensions are as follows:
Material 1/8" x 1 1/2" Unless Specified
1/4" = 1" Scale

Frame		1/8" x 1 1/2" angle x 80'
Legs	4	1/8" x 2" angle x 37"
Firebricks	12	standard
Flux Holder	2	1/8" x 4" std. pipe x 4"
Rod Holder	3	1/16" x 2" std. pipe x 15"
Cabinet Door	1	1/16" x 22" x 25"
Cabinet sides	3	1/16" x 20 1/2" x 27"
Cabinet bottom	1	1/16" x 9 1/2" x 26"
Drawer sides	2	1/16" x 9 1/2" x 26"
Drawer front	1	1/16" x 10" x 22" (cut to size)
Drawer back	1	1/16" x 8 1/2" x 22" (cut to size)
Drawer bottom	1	1/16" x 20" x 26"
Drawer handle	1	1/8" x 1" std. pipe x 5"
Drawer handle Mounts	2	1/8" x 1" x 2 1/2" (cut to size)
Drawer Runners	2	1/16" x 2" x 24" (bend to size)
Table top tray	1	1/8" x 8" x 27"
Cutting top	7	3/8" x 2 1/2" x 24"
Center Table top	1	1/8" x 8" x 27"
Flux holder support	2	1/8" x 5 7/8" x 5 7/8" (cut to size)
Hinges	2	Butt 1"
Lock latch	1	
Casters	4	2 1/2" swivel heavy duty

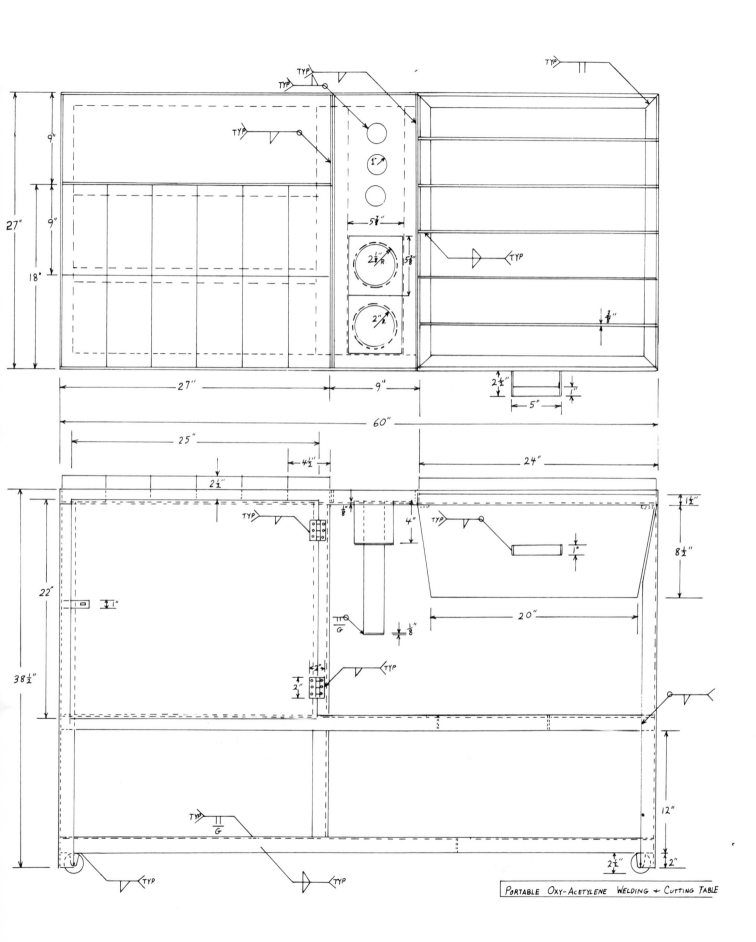

PORTABLE OXY-ACETYLENE WELDING + CUTTING TABLE

Construction of A Deluxe Tire Bead Breaker

Author: Robert C. Engelmann
Instructor: G. J. Choyce
School: Woodlawn Senior High School
City & State: Baltimore, MD

Start with two, 22 x 3 x ¼″ pieces of stock to be the upright members U_1 and U_2 of the bead breaker. Cut two pieces of 1½″ x ¼″ angle iron to 26″. Cut two lengths of cold rolled steel 1½ x ¼″ to 26″. Clamp one of these (A) to a steel plate using vice grip clamps. Beside it, clamp one of the angle iron pieces, (B) making a butt joint as seen in sketch #2. Make sure both are clamped tightly and weld them together using a V-groove type weld. Then flip it over and weld the other side using the same type weld. Prepare a second identical to this. These are parts A_1 and A_2 of the base. Cut three more pieces of 1½ x ¼″ cold rolled steel, two 10″ long and one 3″ long. Weld the two 10″ pieces together using a V-groove butt joint, and assemble the base by tacking each member in place. Inspect angles and positions and weld corner joints with V-groove welds. This completes the base.

Next, make the Foot. Cut two pieces of 1½ x ¼″ cold rolled steel to 15″ and two pieces to 13″. Set these 1″ from one end and the edge joint with a V-groove weld. Label F_1 and F_2 as seen in sketch #3. Bend the protruding ends at 106° and 169°. The third part foot is a forged piece of 1″ x ⅛″ cold rolled angle iron. Round the corners, and forge a 25″ radius. To hold F_1 and F_2 the proper distance apart use a short piece of the same material used for the handle, clamping it between them. Vice grip clamps will hold F_1 and F_2 and F_2 and F_3. See sketch for positioning. Weld the lap joints using V-groove welds.

Locate the position of each upright U_1 and U_2 on the base against the sides A_1 and A_2 and mark them respectively 3″ from the back of the base. Since the base tapers in two directions arrive at the angles by marking the uprights at spots where the pieces meet. Measure down from the top of each upright 6″ in the back and 7½″ in the front. This gives an angle sufficient to bring the top sections of U_1 and U_2 together making an edge joint. Weld the uprights to the base after clamping the three places of contact. Next, locate two holes on the upper part of the uprights and step drill two ½″ diameter holes located 1½″ from the front edge.

For the handle cut a 1¼″ pipe to a 30″ length and cut a 3¾″ slot ½″ wide, down the middle of one end.

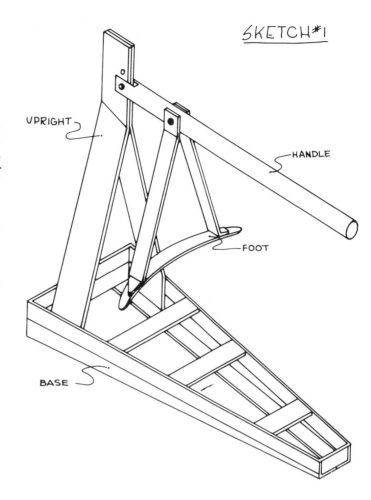

SKETCH#1

UPRIGHT

HANDLE

FOOT

BASE

Step drill a ⅜″ diameter hole through the foot and the handle while held in the assembled position. This hole is located 8″ from the end the slot is cut in. Move down to the slotted area and drill a ½″ hole, 1″ from the end of the pipe perpendicular to the slot.

Using one ⅜″ cap screw (2″ long), and one ½″ cap screw, (1½″ long) attach the foot to the handle and bolt the handle to the upright.

To aid in supporting the wheel, weld three strips of cold rolled steel across to the middle of the base. They are located at random spots and welded to make a flush surface with the base parts A_1 and A_2.

SKETCH#2

BASE & UPRIGHT

A_2
A_1
10″
3″

SKETCH#3

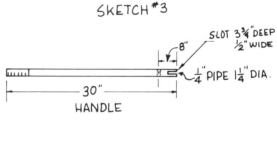

SLOT 3¾″ DEEP ½″ WIDE
8″
¼″ PIPE 1¼″ DIA.
30″
HANDLE

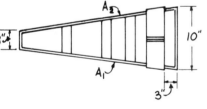

1½″
7″   6¼″
22″
1½″
¼″
26″

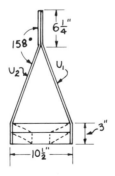

6¼″
158°
U_2 U_1
3″
10½″

DOUBLE THICKNESS

169°
F_2 F_1
13″
106°
11¼″

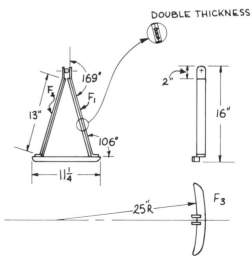

2″
16″

25″R F_3

ORTHOGRAPHIC PROJECTION OF FOOT

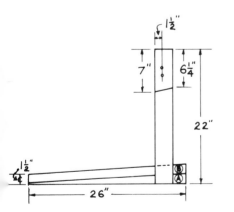

207

Abrasive Cut-Off Saw

Author:	*David McGee*
Instructor:	*Tom Daniel*
School:	*Lexington High School*
City & State:	*Lexington, OK*

Step 1—Take 4 pieces of 1½" pipe, 31" long, and cut them at approximately 25° angles on each end. For leg braces, use ½" pipe, cut to 15" for the top braces and 19" for the bottom. Weld the braces to the legs. Take 1 piece of heavy steel, 2 foot in diameter and ¼" thick, and weld securely to legs.

Step 2—Take 1 piece of channel iron ½ x 4" and cut 20½" long. Weld this to table underneath, leaving 1 foot sticking out from under the table. Make sure flat side is turned up. This piece serves as the brace for the motor, etc.

Step 3—Take ¼" metal and cut 2 pieces, each 16½" long and 10" wide and cut in a semi-circle. Cut another piece 55" long and 4" wide. Weld one of the semi-circles to this piece, then the other making sure they are set in the exact same place. After welding, cut a hole 4" wide and 4" high in each side. The holes need to be rounded at the top. The arbor is to fit through these holes.

Step 4—Take 1 piece of 4" x 6" tubing and cut 8" long. Cut sides down 4" to fold over bearing bar. Take 1 piece of ½" sucker rod and fold sides of tubing over it. The bar needs to be 12" long. Weld bar to folded sides, making sure bar sets level. Then weld remaining cuts. Next, attach whole thing to brace on table, making sure everything sets square and level. Then place 1 pillow back bearing to each side of bar. This is to hold motor plate.

Step 5—Take piece of ¼" thick metal and cut 4 by 8". Set bearings accordingly and mark where bolts need to be set. Cut holes in metal and weld top of bolts to metal. Next, take 2 pieces of 2 x 8 tubing and weld together. Then weld plate with bolts to this. Set motor plate on bearings and measure where blade cover needs to set. It needs to set where blade will be in center of table. Cut hole in each side (top and bottom) of motor plate, 10-12" wide and 17" long. Then set motor plate on bearings and bolt down securely.

Step 6—Take piece of 2 by 8 tubing and cut 2 pieces 12" long and 1" high out of sides. Cut slots in each, approx. 3" long on each end. They need to be just slightly wider than the bolts to be used to hold the motor. To find where slots need to be, measure bolt holes on motor. Then weld brackets to motor plate, again measuring motor to see how far they need to be set apart.

Step 7—Attach arbor to motor plate in the front. The arbor needs to be set so the blade will be lined up with the center of the table. When this is done, attach the blade cover to the motor plate.

Step 8—Attach motor to brackets just enough to hold it in place. Measure the distance between the motor pulley and the blade pulley. Then take a piece of ¼ metal and cut to make a cover for the belt 28" long and 7" wide on one end and 4" on the other end. One side will need to be left open. Attach belt to pulleys and tighten motor. Make braces for belt cover and attach to saw. Weld to the side of the motor plate, using small pieces of thin metal as the braces.

Step 9—Take 1 piece of ½" pipe and cut 15" long. Then close off one end and weld to motor plate next to blade cover. This serves as the handle.

Step 10—Attach "spring back" to motor plate and the table, making the distance between each end of the spring long enough to give the spring enough tension so the motor plate will spring back.

Step 11—Take 2 pieces of ½" pipe and cut 14" long. Angle off each end accordingly and to brace on table and back legs of table to help support the motor.

Step 12—Cut slot in center of table so the blade will fit down through it without scraping either side of the slot or the front or the back. Then take 1 piece of angle iron and cut out 2 pieces, each 23" long. Then measure where they need to set and either weld to table or bolt them. The flat side needs to be facing forward. This is to serve as a vice to hold the metal to be cut in place. For the front of this "vice", use any big screw type object with a flat end on it. Weld this piece to table.

Materials Used:

- 1 5 horse electric motor
- 12 feet 2 x 8 tubing
- 1 foot 4 x 6 tubing
- 24 feet ½" tubing
- 5 feet ¼" tubing
- 2 feet angle iron
- 1 round metal plate (2 feet dia., ¼" thick)
- 6 feet ¼" light steel
- 1 piece channel iron 20½" long
- 1 heavy auto spring
- 1 arbor
- 1 foot ½" sucker rod
- 2 pillow block bearings
- 1 qt. paint
- 1 belt 54" long
- 1 breaker box

FRONT VIEW

LEFT-SIDE VIEW

RIGHT-SIDE VIEW

Welder's Dream Machine

Author: David L. Streicher
Instructor: Ted Moses
School: North County Technical School
City & State: Florissant, MO

"A portable Air Compressor and Alternator with Work Bench, Vice and Bench Grinder"

Materials Used

18" dia. x 40" tank
5 hp. horizontal shaft engine
Automobile air conditioning compressor
Automobile alternator
Bench grinder
Bench vise
Two 10" wheels
Two 3" caster wheels
⅛" x 1" x 1" angle iron—total 14'
One ⅛" PL x 12" x 40"
Twelve 44" 2 x 4's
Two ⅛" PL x 3" x 40"

Specifications and Dimensions

Overall length 44"
Overall width 24"
Overall height 36"
Overall weight 250 lbs.

Steps

1. Start with the faceplate. Cut two ⅛" PL x 3" x 44" and one piece of ⅛" PL x 12" x 44".
2. Fit the two 3" pieces to the 12" piece to form a piece of channel and square them together.
3. Then weld
4. Next, mount the engine about 2" from the end and 1" from the side. Use four 1" pieces of ½" pipe for spacers.
5. Use a ⅜" drill and ⁵⁄₁₆" bolts.
6. After the engine is tightened down, mount the compressor 7" away from the engine.
7. Make the legs to the table next. They are made out of 1" x 1" angle iron and 13" long. Weld the four pieces to each corner of the faceplate, then take two more pieces of angle iron 20" in length and weld them to the top of the legs to support the bench.
8. Cut the material for the wheel supports. For the front cut one ⅛" PL x 3" x 16" and two ⅛" PL x 3" x 5". Put them together to form a channel, square, then weld.
9. Measure 7" from the front of the tank, then tack weld.

10. Cut the metal for the rear wheel support—two ⅛″ PL. x 6″ x 6″ and one ⅛″ PL 3″ x 16″. Debur metal.
11. Fit together like front support to form channel, square and weld.
12. Measure 8″ from the rear of the tank and set the support on so that the web of the channel lies in the same plane. Tack weld.
13. Check fit up and weld to tank.
14. Take two 3″ swivel wheels and bolt on either side of the front wheel support.
15. Cut a piece of ⅝″ dia. round stock 24″ long.
16 Center on rear wheel support and weld on.
17. Take two ¹¹⁄₁₆″ washers and put on the round stock 4″ from each end so the wheels have something to rest on.
18. Drill a ⅛″ hole on each end of the round stock to hold the cotter pin in.
19. Mount wheels and insert cotter pins.
20. Next, make the table.
21. Cut one ³⁄₃₂″ PL 24 x 44″, and two ⅛″ PL 2″ x 44″ and two ⅛″ PL x 2″ x 24″. Debur material.
22. Fit the two 44″ long pieces to the side of the table top, tack weld and square up.
23. Fit the two end pieces on, tack weld then square up.
24. Square the corners, then tack weld.
25. Cut two pieces of 1″ x 1″ x 35″ angle. Fit them between the two leg supports and weld.
26. Set the table on top of the leg supports and center it. Drill a ¼″ hole on each corner where the bench touches the angle. Bolt the bench down with 4 bolts.
27. After the bench is mounted, mount the alternator. It is mounted just above the engine and compressor. Take a two-belted pulley and mount it on the engine flywheel. Make a bracket for the alternator. It is made out of ³⁄₁₆″ PL, 1″ x 6″ and is bent at a 90° angle on each end. It has two ½″ holes on the bent

pieces and two ¼″ holes drilled through the unbent piece to bolt it to the bench.
28. Line the two pulleys up on the alternator and the engine. Mark the holes for the bracket and drill two ⅜″ holes and bolt the bracket to the bottom side of the table. Mount the alternator.
29. Make an adjustable bracket for tightening the bolt. Use ³⁄₁₆″ PL and cut a piece ¾″ x 12″ and drill a ⅜″ hole at one end, and a ⅜″ wide by 5″ long slot at the other.
30. Cut another piece ³⁄₁₆″ x 1″ x 3″ and bend it in the center at a 90° angle. Drill two ½″ holes at either end.
31. Bolt the two bracket pieces together and bolt the slotted end to the alternator. Tilt the alternator up and mark the hole where the bracket will be held. Drill with a ½″ hole and bolt to the bottom of the bench.
32. Mount the vise on the bench.
33. Mount the bench grinder, but first mount the gear box. The gear box is used because you have to change the direction and slow down the speed of the grinder. Mount it right over the pulley to the engine, then mount the grinder right over the gear box pulley. Cut a hole in the bench for the belt to go through.
34. Build the cabinet according to the detail and mount it under the bench.
35. Put in the pipe for the air and run it through the safety switch. Check the detail.
36. Now put in the wiring.
37. Make brackets for the handle and weld to front wheel support.
38. Make hanger for hoses and attach hoses and regulator.

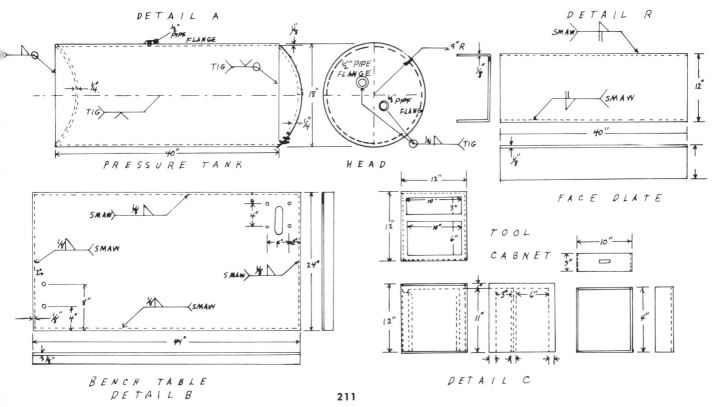

DETAIL A

PRESSURE TANK   HEAD

DETAIL R

FACE PLATE

TOOL CABINET

BENCH TABLE
DETAIL B

DETAIL C

211

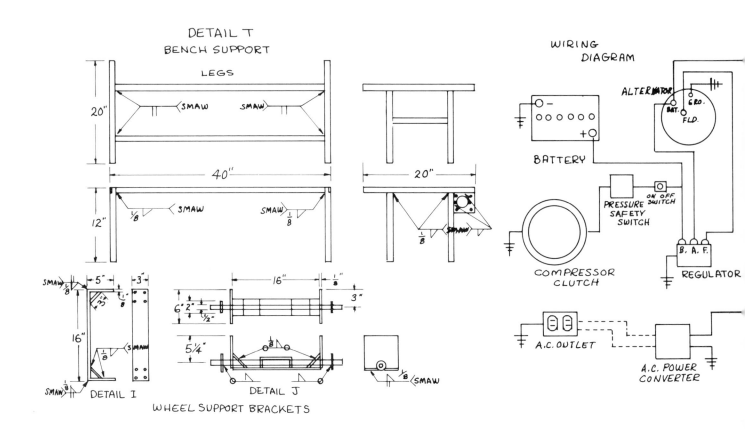

DETAIL T
BENCH SUPPORT

LEGS

WIRING DIAGRAM

DETAIL I

DETAIL J

WHEEL SUPPORT BRACKETS

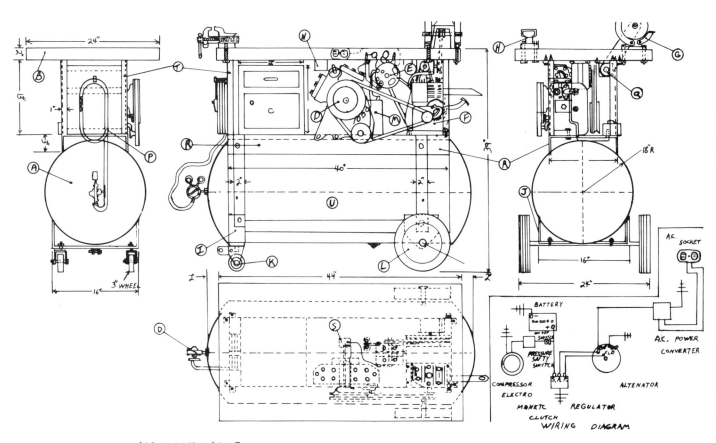

A	TANK	H	BENCH VISE	O	AIR REGULATOR
B	BENCH	I	FRONT WHEEL SUPPORT	P	AIR HOSE
C	TOOL CABNET	J	REAR WHEEL SUPPORT	Q	2:1 GEAR BOX
D	AUTO AIR COMPRESSOR	K	FRONT WHEELS	R	FACE PLATE
E	AUTO ALTENATOR	L	REAR WHEELS	S	PRESSURE SAFTY SWITCH
F	5 HORE POWER ENGINE	M	BATTERY	T	TABLE LEGS
G	BENCH GRINDER	N	A.C. POWER CONVERTER	U	TANK HOLD DOWN STRAPS

ASSEMBLY PRINT

Wood Burning Stove

Author: *Juergen Eisele*
Instructor: *Floyd D. Cotton, Jr.*
School: *Albert I. Prince Technical School*
City & State: *Hartford, CT*

To begin with I had two tanks each 14″ in diameter and 4′ in length. The difference came in the thickness of the cylinder walls; one of which was ⅛″ thick and the other ¼″ thick. Due to this difference in thickness it was easy to decide to use the ¼″ tank on the bottom.

The first step was to make sure the tanks were empty and washed out to prevent any kind of explosion or fire. I started with the heavier cylinder and cut the top off (Figure 1). The top was to be my door. I tilted the cylinder horizontally and cut a 34″ x 13″ rectangle out of the side. After cutting this opening I built a box out of ⅜″ mild steel and welded it over the opening (Figure 1). This addition increased both the diameter and the volume which would allow for more fuel space. Specifically the bottom cylinder was built up for the following reasons. It seemed the 14″ diameter would not have had adequate volume to support a fire which would have to produce enough heat for all the metal I was to use. This extra area of metal would also radiate more heat. Aside from increasing the area the rectangular box provided an added bonus. It could also serve as a fine hot plate to cook on.

The next step was to cut a hole in the back of the cooking plate and weld a 6′ connector pipe to this plate (Figure 2). This pipe would eventually slide into a larger connector pipe that was attached to the top cylinder.

Next came the bottom stand for the unit (Figure 2). It was made out of two angle iron bed supports which had a support advantage to them. On each end of the angle iron were cast iron squares which were easily ground down to make ideal legs. Next, thinking transportability I cut 4″ support pieces of larger angle iron. I took these pieces and welded a triangular shape in the center of each support. Each piece was then welded exactly the same distance from the floor with the open side of the angle iron facing the cylinder (Figure 2 inside view). These pieces gave support to the bottom stand and since these supports were separated by the triangular inserts they were ready to accept the upper structure.

213

The next step was to make four more angle supports, each only 2″ long with a triangular shape welded to the top of the angle iron. These four angle supports were then welded to the top cylinder directly in line with the lower angle supports (Figure 3). Once again I took some smaller angle iron which would fit inside the support slots and made two H shaped supports with the cross angles coming to rest on the edge of the cooking plate (Figure 3). These cross supports added stability and strength which would become important in latter assembly. Two people can handle it easily, but I have also assembled it myself.

The next step was to roll a cylinder which would fit snugly over the 6″ connector pipe attached to the cooking plate. For a cylinder I rolled a flat piece of ³⁄₁₆″ sheet metal so it fit snuggly around the pipe coming out of the cooking plate. I then welded the seam and marked the underside of the top cylinder and cut the appropriate size hole for the connector pipe. The connector pipe was then welded to the top cylinder (Figure 3). The final exhaust stack had to be rolled. I rolled a stack which was welded to the top front of the upper cylinder which would eventually connect to the chimney (Figure 3).

At this time I went back to the door (Figure 4). Taking the top that had been cut from the tank I first cut away the valve and safety cap threads. After grinding the rough edges I welded a round plate over the valve stem opening. I moved then to the air vent at the base of the door. After drilling approximately a dozen ¹¹⁄₁₆″ holes, I continued on the back side of the door and welded a couple of guides for the vent door. The vent door was cut to size, then heated red hot and hammered to conform to the rounded edge of the stove door. A slot was then cut vertically through the middle of the vent holes. A key was made and inserted through the vertical slot and also through a rectangular hole in the base of the vent door. The vent door could now be opened and closed.

With the vent completed I added a handle made from ¼″ flat stock. The hinge I used was a large steel hinge which was tacked into place. The hinge was heated and hammered to conform to the shape of the cylinder and finally completely welded. Even though the hinge was heated and bent, the pin still comes out and it works perfectly. A stationary latch was added which would catch because of the play there is in the hinge.

The last thing left to do on the door was to weld a metal strip around the inside edge of the door which would give it a smoke tight fit. About an inch inside the cylinder is the original backing strip. When the door is closed the two strips just about meet which also helps create a good seal.

The stove would now be complete except for the valve stem opening in the top cylinder. But I decided that I would incorporate the fireplace heat exchange principle in the top cylinder (Figure 5). The top cylinder was meant to help radiate the heat before it goes up the chimney. Adding more pipes in the top cylinder would make the stove even more efficient. I took the top cylinder and cut four 2″ holes in the front and five 2″ holes in the back or bottom of the cylinder. Then cut the threads of the valve stem and safety cap away and ground the rough edges which left me with the fifth hole in front. I passed five pieces of pipe through these holes and welded all around each end. Then I cut off the excess pipe and ground away the rough edges. In the rear of the cylinder I welded a box which covered all five openings with one large opening coming off to the side, where a blower can be attached.

I added the finishing touches by burning the old paint off with a heating torch and wire brushing the ash and paint away. Washing away the dust and giving the entire stove a couple coats of quality heat-proof black paint completed the project.

FIG.-1

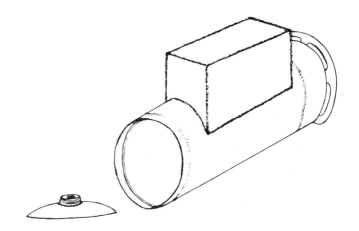

FIG.-2

FIG.-3

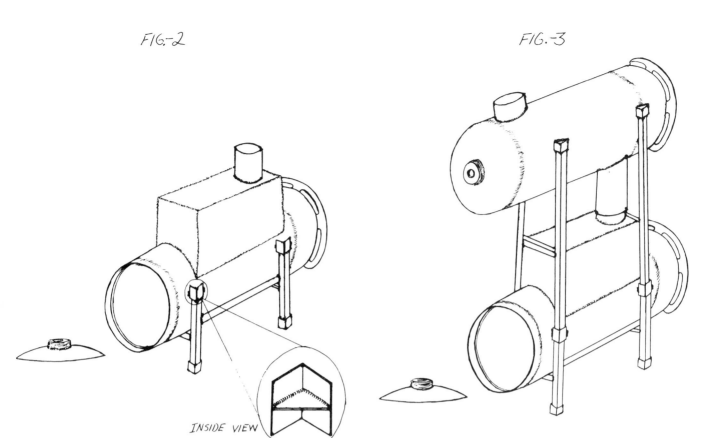

INSIDE VIEW

FIG.4-F

FIG. 4-B

FIG.-5

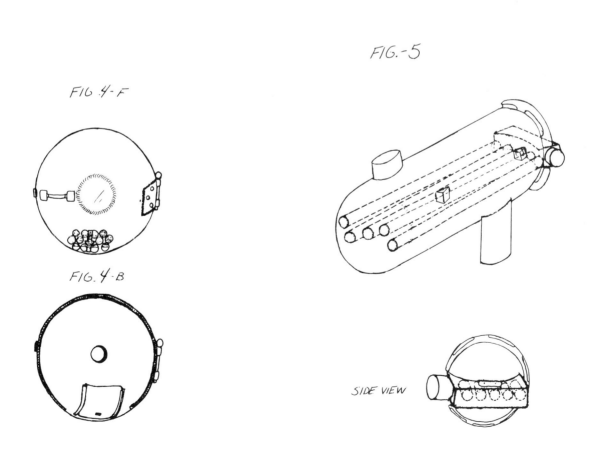

SIDE VIEW

215

Air Tank-Bumper

Author: Larry Rodriguez
Instructor: Manuel Quintana
School: New Mexico Technical
                  Vocational School
City & State: Espanola, NM

The air tank hose is 25′ long for inflating tires, rafts, tubes, etc. It does not, nor was it made to take the place of a compressor. It was designed to have readily available compressed air where it is not available—in emergency situations—such as a flat occurring on a narrow bridge, a driveway, a dangerous high traffic area or on back country trips. The flat tire could be inflated and driven a short way without damaging the tube or tire. It has also been used to inflate tires which have gone flat over a period of time and are not necessarily punctured. Another place it can be used is in the back country where you would lower the pressure in the tires for traction in sand or soft dirt.

Materials

One 6′ x 5″ x 3/16″ pipe
One 10¼′ x 5″ x 3/16″ mild steel plate
One 2″ trailer ball with 1″ shank
One 25′ x ¼″ I.D. hose
One hose coupler assembly
One inflator valve

Assembly procedure:

1. Cut pipe to 5′ 11¼″ long and bevel ends.
2. Flame cut two mounting brackets from ½″ mild steel, and drill holes for mounting on frame.
3. Weld brackets to pipe and test for fit.
4. Mark three holes for gauge, coupler and valve in a convenient place where they cannot be easily broken or pulled off but are readily accessible when needed.
5. Bevel and weld 5″ diameter x 3/16″ round end plates.
6. Fabricate and weld trailer hitch out of ½″ mild steel.
7. Weld guard for fittings and allow to cool before installing fittings.
8. Install fittings and pressurize to check for leaks using soap and water.
9. Paint desired color and install.

Pipe Bending Machine

Author: Paul J. Sukowaty
Instructor: Mr. Nicla
School: North High School
City & State: Sheboygan, WI

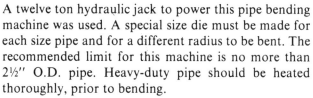

A twelve ton hydraulic jack to power this pipe bending machine was used. A special size die must be made for each size pipe and for a different radius to be bent. The recommended limit for this machine is no more than 2½″ O.D. pipe. Heavy-duty pipe should be heated thoroughly, prior to bending.

If thin wall pipe kinks, put plugs in the ends of the pipe and pack it full of moist sand. The moist sand will give it more support for a better bend. All drawings have been numbered and placed in the order that should be followed in building this machine. Also, each part in the drawing has been given a number. Make these parts in this order. Drawing No. 1 shows all of the dimensions for the frame. All of the parts are to be welded together to form a very rigid structure. All pieces must be put in the exact right place or other parts may not bolt up correctly. Drill holes in part No. 3 after one piece has been welded on each side. Then drill the holes all the way through.

Drawing No. 1
This part has been put here to help support the front bearing where most of the load is.

Drawing No. 2 holds the hydraulic jack and die in position. 8″ springs are used to collapse the jack and bring

the die away from the shoes so that the pipe can be placed in the shoe easily. Bars of steel can be put behind the die to help support it against all of the pressure.

Drawing No. 2
Parts no. 5 and 6 together make a clamp to hold this completed piece to the frame.

Drawing No. 3 shows the assembly that holds the shoes in position. The springs are attached also, to keep the shoes and die snuggly around the pipe at all times. The main bearings are shown at the bottom of the page. Parts No. 6 can not be welded to the shaft until all bearings have been bolted down and everything is in its correct position. All welds must be perfect to withstand all of the pressure.

Drawing No. 3
Remember that a left hand and a right hand shoe holder assembly must be made.

Drawing No. 4 shows the rams that hold the spring in position. They also offer adjustment for spring tension. The springs that are used are out of the front end of a car. They are 18″ long when fully extended. They have a 3¾″ I.D. and a 5″ O.D.

Drawing No. 6

Die

Size 2″ with Radius of 7″

Use 1″ x 4″ N.C. bolt to fasten

Blocks can be placed behind the die to give it more support and also to keep it straight.

Drawings No. 6 and 7 shows die and shoes. The shoes are made out of H.D. pipe cut in half. Than a square backing is welded on to them. The die is turned down on a lathe. The groove must be cut very accurately to the dimensions. Using this basic idea, any size die or shoe can be made.

Drawing No. 7

Shoe

Size 2″

Use ½″ x 3½″ N.C. bolt to fasten

Be sure to pound off all edges to allow the pipe to slide through without catching.

Materials

I Beam	12″ x 4″ x 4′
Channel	6″ x 2″ x 21″
Flat Stock	5″ x ¼″ x 32″
Flat Stock	4″ x ¼″ x 23¾″
Flat Stock	3″ x ¼″ x 6″
Flat Stock	1″ x ¼″ x 5½″
Flat Stock	1½″ x ¾″ x 3″
H.D. Pipe	¾″ I.D. x 1″ O.D. x 3½″
Flat Stock	4″ x 1″ x 6″
Flat Stock	6″ x ½″ x 46½″
Flat Stock	¾″ x ¼″ x 33″
Flat Stock	1½″ x ¼″ x 33″
Flat Stock	6″ x ¾″ x 18″
Flat Stock	3″ x ½″ x 15¾″
Flat Stock	3″ x ⅜″ x 28″
H.D. Pipe	2″ I.D. 3″ O.D. x 16″
Water Pipe	2″ x 22″
Water Pipe	1½″ x 24″
H.D. Pipe	¾″ I.D. x 4″
Flat Stock	2″ x ¼″ x 20″
Flat Stock	6″ x ¼″ x 12″
Flat Stock	4″ x ¼″ x 8″
2 Car Springs	
2 8″ Springs	

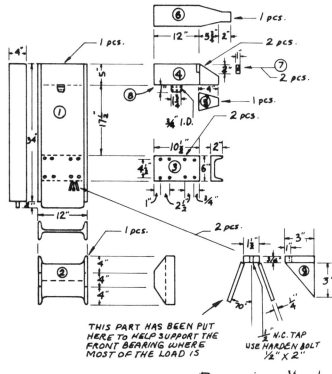

THIS PART HAS BEEN PUT HERE TO HELP SUPPORT THE FRONT BEARING WHERE MOST OF THE LOAD IS

½″ N.C. TAP
USE HARDEN BOLT
½″ X 2″

Drawing No. 1

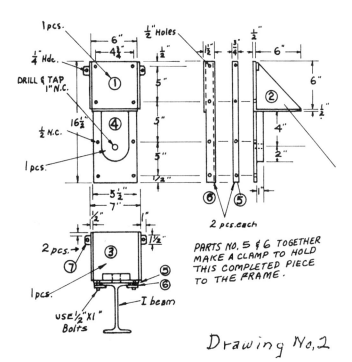

PARTS NO. 5 & 6 TOGETHER MAKE A CLAMP TO HOLD THIS COMPLETED PIECE TO THE FRAME.

USE ½″ X 1 Bolts

Drawing No. 2

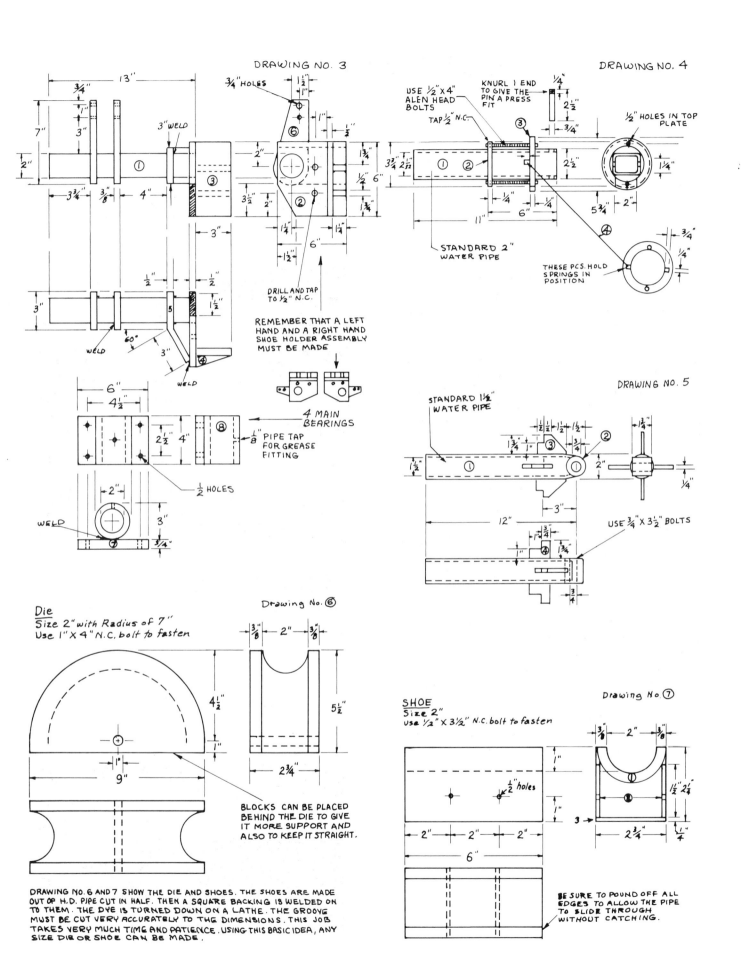

DRAWING NO. 3

DRAWING NO. 4

3/4" HOLES

3" WELD

USE 1/2" X 4" ALEN HEAD BOLTS

KNURL 1 END TO GIVE THE PIN A PRESS FIT

TAP 1/2" N.C.

1/2" HOLES IN TOP PLATE

STANDARD 2" WATER PIPE

THESE PCS. HOLD SPRINGS IN POSITION

DRILL AND TAP TO 1/2" N.C.

REMEMBER THAT A LEFT HAND AND A RIGHT HAND SHOE HOLDER ASSEMBLY MUST BE MADE

4 MAIN BEARINGS

1/8" PIPE TAP FOR GREASE FITTING

1/2 HOLES

WELD

DRAWING NO. 5

STANDARD 1 1/2" WATER PIPE

USE 3/4" X 3 1/2" BOLTS

Die
Size 2" with Radius of 7"
Use 1" X 4" N.C. bolt to fasten

Drawing No. 6

BLOCKS CAN BE PLACED BEHIND THE DIE TO GIVE IT MORE SUPPORT AND ALSO TO KEEP IT STRAIGHT.

SHOE
Size 2"
Use 1/2" X 3 1/2" N.C. bolt to fasten

Drawing No. 7

1/2 holes

BE SURE TO POUND OFF ALL EDGES TO ALLOW THE PIPE TO SLIDE THROUGH WITHOUT CATCHING.

DRAWING NO. 6 AND 7 SHOW THE DIE AND SHOES. THE SHOES ARE MADE OUT OF H.D. PIPE CUT IN HALF. THEN A SQUARE BACKING IS WELDED ON TO THEM. THE DYE IS TURNED DOWN ON A LATHE. THE GROOVE MUST BE CUT VERY ACCURATELY TO THE DIMENSIONS. THIS JOB TAKES VERY MUCH TIME AND PATIENCE. USING THIS BASIC IDEA, ANY SIZE DIE OR SHOE CAN BE MADE.

Truck Mounted Hoist

Author: Kenneth Kerfoot
Instructor: Steve Vinter
School: American River College
City & State: Sacramento, CA

The boom has four positions ranging from 40 inches to 6 feet. The mast can turn in a 360 degree arc. The base of the hoist is bolted to the bed of the truck utilizing existing holes in the bed which contained bolts to secure the wooden boards. The base can be mounted without welding or without any major modification to the truck. The drilling of two ⅜″ holes into the side rail are the only necessary alteration to the truck itself. Within moments the mast and boom can be easily removed when the hoist is not needed. The mast is simply unplugged from its base, the base can be left in the vehicle.

The first section of the hoist to be constructed is the base. After cutting the ⅜″ plate to size, it is fitted into position and tacked while in the truck. The 4″ inside diameter pipe is butt welded to the base plate which acts as a sleeve for the mast. Next to be built is the mast, which is 3½″ inside diameter pipe. Welded to the pipe are the gussets used to support the jack. These are cut from ⅜″ plate. A ¾″ bolt and a section of ¾″ pipe and 6″ C clamps are used to hold these gussets in position while being welded. The hinge at the top of the mast is made of ½″ plate. A ¾″ hole is drilled into which a ¾″ bolt is inserted to support the boom. The plates were bolted to the boom while being welded to minimize distortion. The two pieces of box tubing which are used for the boom are drilled to accommodate ⁹⁄₁₆″ bolts. The support brackets for the ram of the jack are made of ⅜″ plate drilled with ¾″ hole. The brackets are welded into position using a "C" clamp, a ¾″ bolt with a piece of ¾″ pipe 3″ long is used for a spacer while welding the plates to the boom.

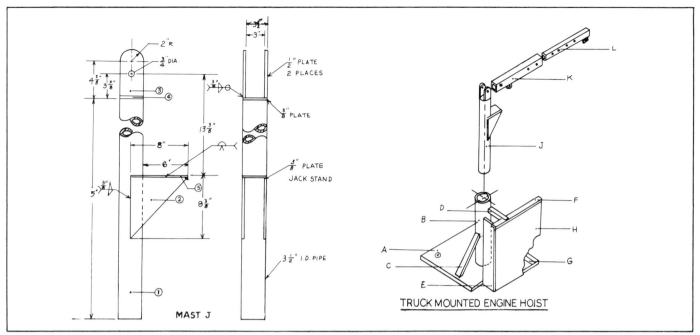

MAST J

TRUCK MOUNTED ENGINE HOIST

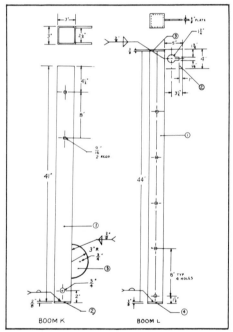

BOOM K   BOOM L

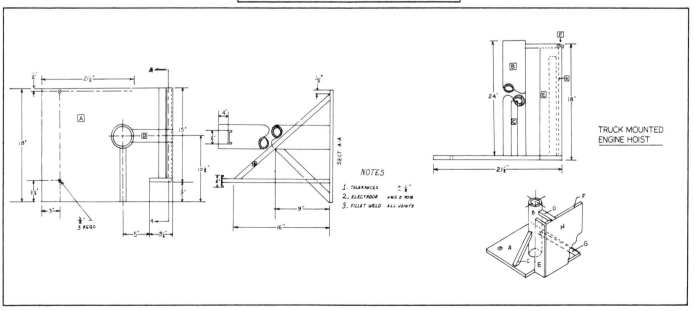

SECT A-A

NOTES

1. TOLERANCES   ± 1/8"
2. ELECTRODE   AWS E 7018
3. FILLET WELD   ALL JOINTS

TRUCK MOUNTED
ENGINE HOIST

Welding & Cutting Bench

Author: Gary Rackliffe
Instructor: Roger F. Kennedy
School: Ferris State College
City & State: Big Rapids, MI

Top Frame: Legs and frame are made of 1½″ x 1½″ x ⅛″ angle. The frame for the top of the bench is made from one piece of angle 148″ long. A 90° notch is cut in the piece at 14″, 42″, 88″ and 116″ from one end. The notches can be flame cut or made with a power hack saw and shear. Cut through the angle radius so that when the piece is bent 90° at each corner a tight joint is made. These joints are welded from the outside, welding towards the vertical leg of the angle.

Legs: Legs are positioned at the corners of the brick section to give stability along with good support for the center. The left side cutting area is supported by 45° angle braces welded to the table edge and the legs. A brace for the legs made from angle is mitred and folded to fit inside the legs on three sides. A front brace, 10½″ from the floor is set back 6″ for welder comfort. A leveling screw can be added to one leg if desired.

Brick Surface: Fire bricks, 4½″ x 9″ x 2½″, are placed on a 16 ga. steel sheet that is put into the top frame, supported by two angle iron ribs under the sheet. Shims driven between the bricks hold them tightly in place.

Cutting Surface: Bar stock ⅜″ x 1½″ spread 3″ apart starting 1″ from the bricks forms the cutting surface. Bars, mounted individually for easy removal, are held in place by 2½″ high by 1¼″ wide pieces of ⅛″ sheet metal welded to the angle frame. If needed the height of the bar can be raised by welding spacers to the frame angle.

Cutting Table Skirt & Drawer: A 16 ga. steel skirt with sides slanting inward, welded underneath the cutting

surface, catches slag and scrap, and collects them in a metal drawer. The skirt can be skip welded at 3″ intervals joining the bottom and sides, and to the angle frame and legs. The drawer edges are welded continuously to prevent leakage of sand with which it is filled. The drawer slides on angle runners.

Overhead Fixture & Tool Box: A fixture is placed on the back of the bench for use in out of position welding and holding large objects. It is adjustable, horizontally, vertically, and rotates 360°. Details are shown in the draw-

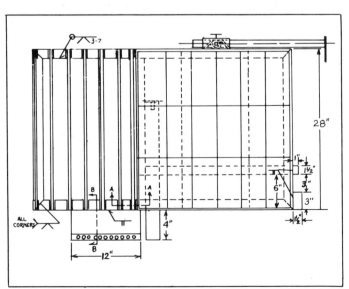

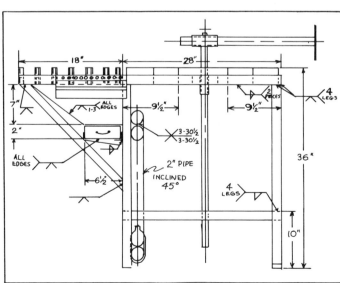

ing. A tool box for tips, striker, tip cleaner, soapstone and other tools is put at the left side of the bench. The box is lower in front than in back and has a ¼″ space in its bottom for dirt to fall through. The tip holder is wood angled at 45°. Torch holder and rod holder are made from pieces of 2″ pipe.

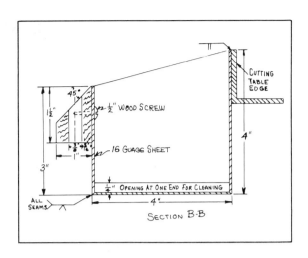

SECTION B-B

Bill of Materials

Material	Part	Size
1½″ x 1½″ x ⅛″	Top Frame	19′ 4″
Angle	Legs	11′
	Cutting Table Braces	4′ 5″
	Drawer Slides	4′ 8″
⅜″ x 1½″ Bar Stock	Cutting Table Bars	16′ 2″
	Spacers	1′ 2″
2″ Pipe	Rod Holder	5′ 8″
1½″ Pipe	Horizontal Overhead Fixture	5″
	Vertical Overhead Fixture	3″
1¼″ Pipe	Vertical Overhead Arm	3′
	Horizontal Overhead Arm	2′
	Torch Holder (Split in Half)	3″
16 Gage Sheet	45¼″ x 46″ x ¾″	
	(see layout for parts)	14.8 Sq. ′
⅛″ Sheet	7½″ x 18½″	
	(see layout for parts)	.97 Sq. ′
⅝″ Threaded Rod	Screws	10″
⅝″ Nuts	Four for above	
⅝″ Tube	Screw Handles	6″
¼″ x 1″ Bolt and Wing Nut	Rod Holder Bottom	
¾″ Hex Head Screws	2 for Tip Holder	
Hardwood	12″ x 1½″ x 1″ Tip Holder	
Firebricks	18—9″ x 4½″ x 2½″	

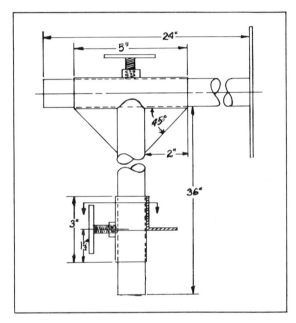

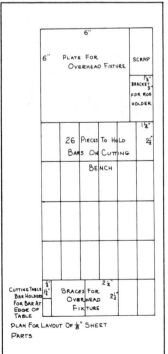

PLAN FOR LAYOUT OF ⅛″ SHEET PARTS

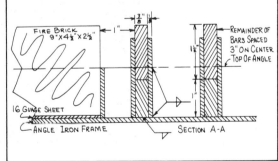

SECTION A-A

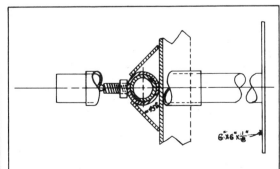

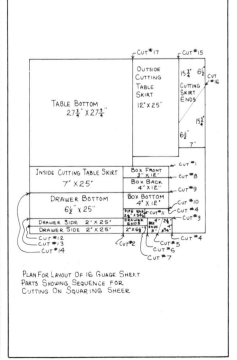

PLAN FOR LAYOUT OF 16 GUAGE SHEET PARTS SHOWING SEQUENCE FOR CUTTING ON SQUARING SHEER

A Weld Tester

Author: Charles Ray Bringman
Instructor: Dr. S. Joseph Freeze
School: Indiana State University
City & State: Terre Haute, IN

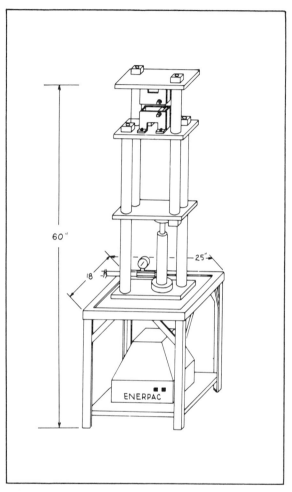

Weld Tester

This tester subjects welds to opposing forces until a fracture occurs. By observing the amount of force required to fracture and the position of the fracture, welds made under varying conditions can be compared. The tester can be used to determine yield point, elongation and ductility of a welded specimen. It was built for a total cost of $500.

An Enerpac model PER 1321 hydraulic pump having a maximum pressure of 10,000 p.s.i., coupled to an RC-106 cylinder, having an effective cylinder area of 2.236 sq. inches, is used to provide the required force. A remote control switch allows the operator to stand a short distance away.

Applied force is measured by adding an Enerpac GF-105 pressure gauge to the system. The gauge is calibrated to the RC-106 cylinder so that the readings observed are directly related to the applied force. A stationary pointer hand records the reading after fracture occurs.

The gripper for holding test specimens uses a hardened steel rubbing block and a hardened knurled cam. Side plates are fabricated from angle iron. Welds had 100% penetration. Tester frame, floorplate and guide rods were welded and machined as shown on the drawings.

The tester can also perform guided bend tests by placing appropriate dies between the center and lower plates which move closer together as the cylinder is extended.

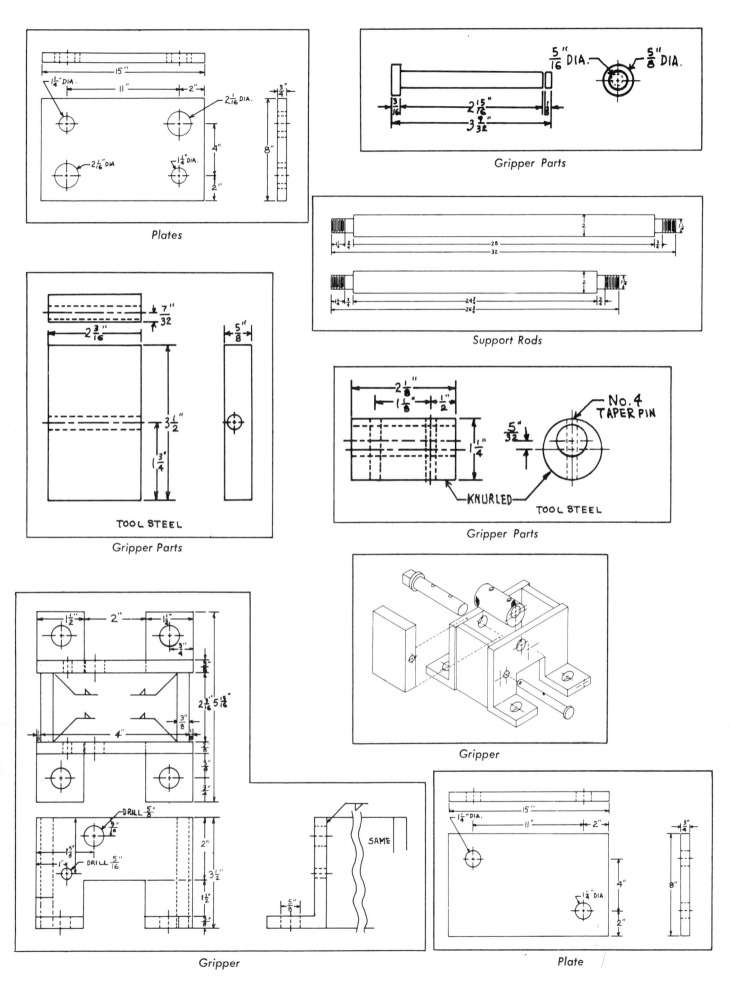

Plates

Gripper Parts

Support Rods

Gripper Parts

Gripper Parts

TOOL STEEL

Gripper Parts

Gripper

Gripper

Plate

Automotive Engine Stand

Author: James T. Seliskar
Instructor: Jesse H. Wilder
School: University of Dayton
City & State: Dayton, Ohio

Rigidity is achieved by using 3″ x 3″ square stock instead of the usual round or rectangular stock. Long front leg adds stability. A 2″ x 2″ square tubing gusset prevents heavier engines from bouncing when being moved. The rubber wheels lock to hold the stand in position.

The adjustable head has four arms that can be adjusted with set screws to hold several sizes of engines. The arms are slotted for adjusting. The entire head can be rotated around a center shaft to maintain balance.

A drag technique was used on all fillet and lap welds in the horizontal or downhand position. The electrode was AWS class E6013.

Parts list:
1) 2 pieces 3″ x 3″ (OD) by ⅛″ wall hot rolled structural steel tubing (38″ long).
2) 1 piece 3″ x 3″ (OD) by ¼″ wall hot rolled structural steel tubing (30″ long).
3) 1 piece 2″ x 2″ (OD) by ⅛″ wall hot rolled structural steel tubing (15″ long).
4) Mild steel plate (10″ x 6½″) by ¾″ thick.
5) Bar stock (2¼″ x 7″ long).
6) 2 (non-swivel) locking 3 inch rubber casters.
7) 1 (swivel) locking 3 inch rubber caster.
8) Misc. bar stock (1″ x 1″ x 20″ long), 1″ hex stock (12″ long).
9) 2 cans of epoxy red spray paint.

SECTION D
TABLE OF CONTENTS
TRAILERS

Athletic Trailer

Author: *Robert Patton*
Instructor: *Robert J. Madsen*
School: *Burlington Community High School*
City & State: *Burlington, IA*

Arc welding braces to frame

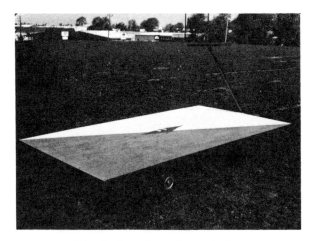

Finished project after painting

This trailer is used to move high school track team equipment from the school building to the track area.

1. Purchase 60 ft. of 1¼″ x 1¼″ x ⅛″ steel tubing.
2. Using power hacksaw, cut two 9 foot lengths and - two 5 foot lengths.
3. Weld rectangular frame together.
4. Cut two pieces of steel tubing 57½″ long for braces of frame.
5. Weld braces to frame using same machine settings as above.
6. Cut three pieces 34¾″ to run parallel to frame and weld as above.
7. Cut two pieces of steel tubing 28¼″ and weld 9¾″ from center brace.
8. Using cutting torch, cut three plates for wheels to be mounted on. Plate size two back wheels 10¼″ x 8¾″ x ¼″, on front wheel 10¼″ x 7¼″ x ¼″.
9. Using power drill press, drill four holes in each plate ½″ in size.
10. Weld plates to frame of trailer.
11. Take a piece of 1¼″ x 1¼″ x ⅛″ tubing, 46″ long, and make a T using another piece 30″ long.
12. Take an 8″ piece of 1¼″ x 1¼″ x ⅛″ tubing and weld in between one set of wheels.
13. Take two pieces of metal (6″ x 1¼″ x ¼″) and weld an 8″ piece on both sides.
14. Drill one hole one-quarter through both the 6″ piece of metal and the 46″ piece of tubing.
15. Bolt together with ¼″ bolt.
16. Mount wheels on frame with ½″ bolts.
17. Cut plywood to fit frame.
18. Bolt plywood to frame using ½″ bolts.
19. Paint trailer.

Materials
60 ft. 1¼″ x 1¼″ x ⅛″ steel tubing
2 steel plates 16″ x 12″ x ¼″
3 sets of wheels (surplus)
2 sheets of plywood 4′ x 8′ x ½″
3 cans of paint
12 ½″ bolts (for wheels)
30 ¼″ bolts (for plywood)

ATHLETIC TRAILER

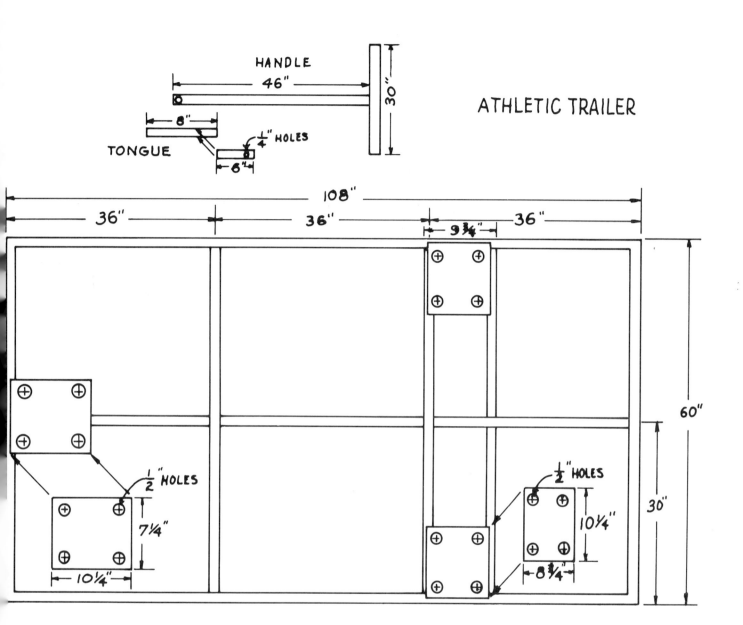

HANDLE

46"

30"

TONGUE

8"

6"

$\frac{1}{4}$" HOLES

108"

36"   36"   9¾"   36"

60"

$\frac{1}{2}$" HOLES

7¼"

10¼"

30"

$\frac{1}{2}$" HOLES

10¼"

8¾"

DIAGRAM OF WHEELS

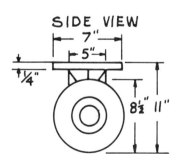

SIDE VIEW

7"

5"

¼"

8½" 11"

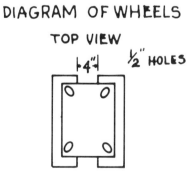

TOP VIEW

4"   ½" HOLES

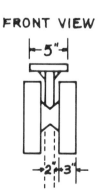

FRONT VIEW

5"

2" 3"

Tandem Livestock Trailer

Author: *Robert Foshee*
Instructor: *Willis Bell*
High School: *Red Level High School*
City & State: *Red Level, AL*

This livestock trailer is designed to be efficient, versatile and practical. It has an open front end which provides better visibility when backing up to chutes and gives more room. A middle gate allows better balance of the load in the front and rear compartments and separation of large and small animals. The front gate enables unloading the front compartment without having to disturb the rear compartment. While unloading the rear compartment a small sliding gate can be used. The rear gate as well as the middle gate can also be removed if wished.

Materials Used:

24′ ¼″ x 1½″ x 1½″ Angle Iron
60′ ¼″ x 3″ x 3″ Angle Iron
80′ ³⁄₁₆″ x 1½″ x 1½″ Angle Iron
33′ ½″ x 1¼″ Angle Iron
1 Set Straight Fenders
79 sq. ft. 16 gauge sheet metal
15 pcs. 1″ square tubing 20′ long
10′ ½″ Steel Rod
13′ ¾″ Steel Rod
22′ 1″ Black Pipe
8′ ¾″ Black Pipe
1′ ½″ Black Pipe
3′ ³⁄₁₆″ x 1″ Flat Iron
6   4″ x ½″ Bolts and Nuts
2 gals. Lacquer and Enamel Thinner
2 qts. Lacquer Primer
1 gal. Dupont Enamel
Spring and Equalizer Hangers
caster, Coupler, Jack and Ball
3   ⅜″ x 1½″ Bolts and Nuts
2   Dietz Lights
16 gauge Electrical Wire
147′ 2 x 8 Penta Treated Lumber
1 set hubs, axle springs, rims, tires

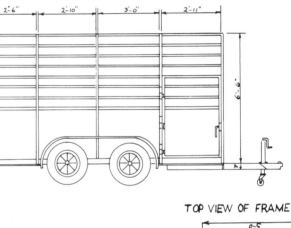

LEFT SIDE VIEW

TOP VIEW OF FRAME

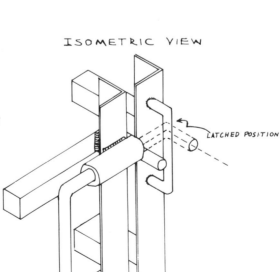

ISOMETRIC VIEW

LATCHED POSITION

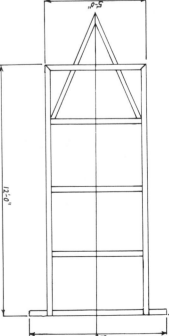

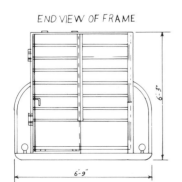

END VIEW OF FRAME

230

The Design and Construction of A Tandem-Axle Automobile Transporter

Author: Terri A. Foley
Instructor: J. Vezey
School: Billings Vo-Tech Center
City & State: Billings, MT

The tandem-axle assembly, complete with electric brakes and leaf springs, was purchased from a house-trailer manufacturer. The axles originally measured 77" from center to center on the spring-hangers, and were cut to 74" as specified on the prints.

The axles were shortened by removing a 3" section from the center of each, fitting them with chill-rings, and tacking them together in an angle-iron jig to maintain alignment. Wheel alignment was carefully checked with a tape before the final welding.

The frame of the trailer was then cut, laid out, squared, and tacked together. The 4 longitudinal sections were 2" x 4" x .095 rectangular tubing and the 2 end pieces were 4" x 4" x .250 square tubing.

12 spring hangers were made from 2" x ⅜" flat bar, measuring 8" in length overall, and 7" to the center of the ⅝" hole. This length allows 3" travel space for springs and axels. The bottom end of each hanger was rounded off with a torch and ground smooth.

The blueprints specified that the center of the spring-axel assembly will be 6" back from the actual center of the frame to insure proper balance when the trailer is loaded.

The center pairs of hangers were welded to the frame at this mid-point and the front and back pairs were welded to align with spring mounting holes. ⅝" bolts were used to mount springs.

The cross-supports were placed directly in front of the front hangers and directly behind the back hangers. The top supports, made from 2" x 4" x .095 tubing fit between the two inside longitudinal pieces and flush with the frame. The bottom supports made from 2" x 2" x .095 tubing, extend to the outside edge of the frame and tie into the spring hangers to support the whole structure.

One additional 2" x 2" x .095 cross-support was welded under the frame to help support the ramps and also the rear wheels of the automobile.

The frame was then suspended and leveled on blocks for the construction of the tongue.

The tongue was designed so that the distance from the front edge of the 4" x 4" crossmember to the center of the ball would be 3 feet. Since a standard pick-up bed is about 6 feet wide, a diagonal measurement of slightly over 3 feet was needed for clearance, so that the truck could be turned in excess of 45°.

The tongue was constructed from 4" x 5.4 standard channel with the two long sections welded to the underside of the frame and the two short sections welded flush with the frame. The front of the tongue was cut and beveled to fit the forged steel V-type coupler purchased for the trailer. The hitch had a 2 inch ball and a 5,000 pound capacity.

³⁄₁₆" deck plate was then sheared to 1 foot widths and notches for the spring hangars were flame-cut. The plate was then leveled, tacked, and welded to the rectangular tubing with #7018 in a staggered intermittent sequence for minimum distortion.

A slight camber occured during welding of the underside and was corrected by flame-heating the top of the curve and allowing contraction to correct the camber.

The fenders, constructed of 14 gauge steel, were designed to be functional as well as attractive.

The fender design was fairly complex, using triangulation to determine angles and requiring a right and left side. The back of each fender extends 4" below the frame to eliminate the need for mud flaps. Triangular gussets were attached front and back to reinforce the fenders vertically and also horizontally.

The steel was sheared, notched, and the longitudinal bends were made on a cornice brake. Fabrication of a 9" male die for the press brake was necessary to make the four lateral bends.

The back piece was spot-welded to the fenders and micro-wire was used for finishing and to attach the fenders to the frame.

The ramps were 1' x 5' x ³⁄₁₆'' deck plate welded to 3'' x 1½'' x ³⁄₁₆'' angle iron, using the staggered intermittant sequence. The corners were rounded off for extra clearance and for good appearance.

The ramp hanger assembly consists of a 1 foot section of 2'' x ³⁄₈'' flat bar welded to 1'' x 3'' x ½'' plate, ground to 45'' and welded to the back of the trailer, and a 11'' section of 1½'' x ³⁄₁₆'' angle iron welded to the underside of the ramps.

The ramp carriers attached to the back cross-support were 1' x ⅝'' round stock. Eye bolts and wing nuts were used to secure ramps to frame when travelling.

A ³⁄₁₆'' plate box was constructed to house rear light fixtures. The rear lights are combination stop-brake and tail lights and the side lamps are for clearance.

A license plate carrier was also fabricated from ³⁄₁₆'' plate and a license plate light installed.

A piece of ¼'' plate was cut and welded to the tongue to provide a base for the section of 3'' pipe used to support the winch. A winch was needed to help load cars that are not in running condition, and also to anchor automobiles in transit. A pulley was installed under the frame as a cable-guide.

A 14 gauge box was constructed to house the battery that powers the electric break-away switch required by state law for vehicles more than 3,000 pounds.

Materials

84 feet of 2'' x 4'' x .095 rectangular tube
19½ feet of 4'' x .250 square tube
43 square feet of ³⁄₁₆'' deck plate
20 feet of ³⁄₈'' by 2'' flat bar
20 feet of 4'' by 5.4 standard channel
1 sheet 4' x 10' x 14 guage
16 feet of 2'' by .095 square tube
4' x 4' x ³⁄₁₆ plate
2 breaking axles
4 wheels and tires
1 hammerblow 2B8 hitch
1 hammerblow 155 jack and wheel
30 feet of ¼'' 17 x 19 galvanized aircraft cable
1 #590 fulton winch
2 ³⁄₈'' x 5'' eye bolts
3 ⁷⁄₁₆'' x 1¼'' cap screws
12 ⅝'' washers
6 ⅝'' lock washers
6 ⅝'' nuts
2 ³⁄₈'' wing nuts
2 ¼'' cable clamps
1 ¼'' thimble
1 ¼'' slip hook
1 - 686 whitaker boom
50 feet of 923 whitaker ¹⁶⁄₃ wire
10 - 840 whitaker clips
2 - stop/tail lights
4 - marker lights
1 - breakaway switch
1 - connector plug socket
1 - license plate light
1 - hotshot battery
1 - 3'' pulley sheave
Assorted bolts

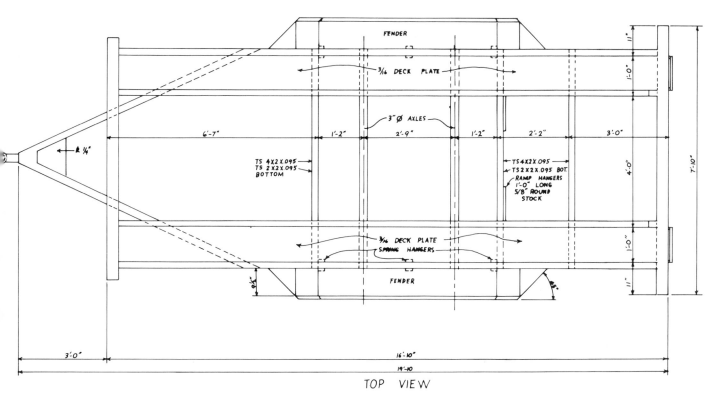

FENDER

3/16 DECK PLATE

3" Ø AXLES

6'-7"   1'-2"   2'-9"   1'-2"   2'-2"   3'-0"

TS 4X2X.095
TS 2X2X.095
BOTTOM

TS 4X2X.095
TS 2X2X.095 BOT.
RAMP HANGERS
1'-0" LONG
5/8" ROUND
STOCK

3/16 DECK PLATE
SPRING HANGERS

FENDER

11"   1'-0"   4'-0"   1'-0"   11"

7'-10"

R 1/4"

3'-0"   16'-10"

19'-10"

TOP VIEW

ALL ENDS OF TUBES TO
BE CAPPED WITH 14 GAUGE

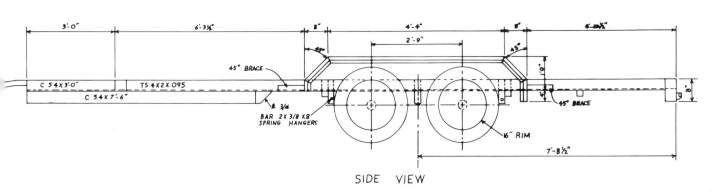

3'-0"   6'-3 1/4"   8"   4'-4"   8"   4'-10 1/2"

2'-9"

45° BRACE

C 5.4X3'-0"   TS 4X2X.095

C 5.4X7'-6"

R 3/16
BAR 2X 3/8 X8
SPRING HANGERS

45° BRACE

16" RIM

7'-8 1/2"

1'-0"   8"

SIDE VIEW

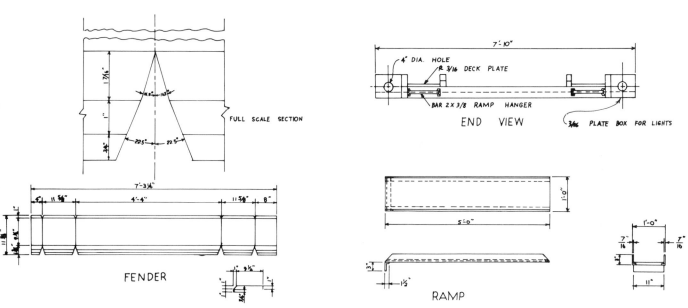

1 7/16"

1"

3/4"

14.5°   14.5°

22.5°   22.5°

FULL SCALE SECTION

7'-3 1/4"

4"   11 5/8"   4'-4"   11 5/8"   8"

1"   1"   11 3/8"   3/4"

FENDER

1"   9 1/2"   3/8"

7'-10"

4" DIA. HOLE

R 3/16 DECK PLATE

BAR 2X3/8 RAMP HANGER   3/16 PLATE BOX FOR LIGHTS

END VIEW

1'-0"

5'-0"

3"

1 1/2"

1'-0"

7/16"   7/16"

11"

RAMP

233

Design and Fabrication of Heavy-Duty Utility Trailer

Authors:	John Swanbom
	Michael Flynn
	Jerry Tracey
Instructor:	E. Papy
School:	City Center for Learning
City & State:	St. Petersburg, FL

The trailer is 14'7" long, 7'2" wide. The trailer box is formed of 10 Ga. H.R.S. The chasis is made of 4" cold form channel. A set of used mobile home axels with electric brakes were used. Total weight of the unit is 1465 pounds and can be easily moved about by one man.

Careful loading of the trailer will maintain the weight ratio so that the automobile and trailer maintain a level attitude when loaded.

A load of 6500 pounds has been hauled, using a 1972 Ford LTD. There was no noticeable load on the automobile, and stopping was no problem, due to the electric brakes on the trailer.

Following is a step-by-step explanation

Step 1 Cut two (2) pieces 4" cold from channel, 14'6" long.

Step 2 Cut two (2) pieces 4" cold from channel, 5'8" long.

Step 3 Cut one (1) piece 4" channel, 10' long.

Step 4 Cut eight (8) pieces 4" channel 28¼" long and cope to fit.

Step 5 Lay out all pieces, using framing square and rule, as shown in top view. Tack weld all points, taking care to maintain squareness. Measure diagonally across frame to check square of frame.

Step 6 Find center of front and rear member and center punch.

Step 7 Frame will be easier to work on if placed on stands at this point. Notch 14'6" channel, as indicated. Stretch chalk line, across center line punch marks. Extend line well past form of frame.

Step 8 Taking care to maintain line on center-bend notched channel iron until they touch center line. Using a piece of scrap angle iron, tack weld across channel irons to hold them in place.

Step 9 Cut one (1) piece 4" channel iron 11" long. Trim 4" channel for close fit, as shown. Tack item #7 in place.

Step 10 Using ⅛" E6010, or other suitable electrode, complete welding of frame, using caution to maintain all measurements.

Step 11 Cut all gussets, as shown, and weld into frame.

Step 12 Grind all welds on top sides of frame flush.

Step 13 Cut 1" x 1" x ⅛" angle iron supports, and install, as shown. Grind top side of welds flush.

*Step 14 Shear two (2) pieces 10 Ga. U.S.S., 10' x 20²³⁄₃₂" and form, as shown in Section "B-B".

*Step 15 Shear two (2) pieces 10 Ga. U.S.S., 58' x 16³⁄₁₆" and form, as shown in Section "B-B".

Step 16 Install two (2) sides, as shown. Tack weld in place.

Step 17 Install front end of box and tack into position.

Step 18 Check box for correct measurement. When all measurements are correct, weld all corner joints of box and weld to frame, as shown.

Step 19 This step requires fitting axles to frame. Determine length of axles by measuring distance across frame, center to center. Cut axle and remove excess. Weld spring hangers into place and install springs and axles.

Step 20 Align axles by clamping a 3' piece of angle iron on two (2) sides of axle. Tack weld together.

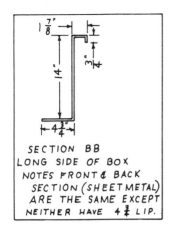

SECTION BB
LONG SIDE OF BOX
NOTES FRONT & BACK
SECTION (SHEET METAL)
ARE THE SAME EXCEPT
NEITHER HAVE 4¾ LIP.

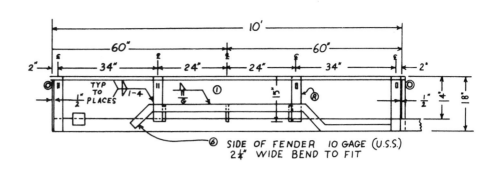

SIDE OF FENDER 10 GAGE (U.S.S.)
2¼" WIDE BEND TO FIT

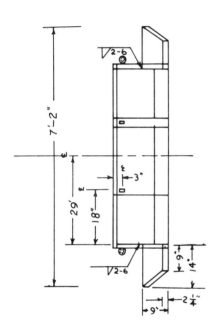

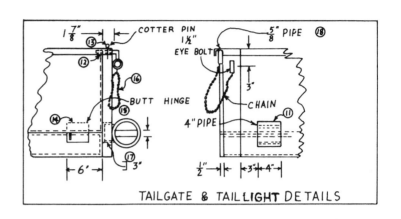

TAILGATE & TAILLIGHT DETAILS

NO.	PARTS REQUIRED	ITEM
1	⅝" PIPE 10"	18
2	COLD FORMED] 3"X4"	17
2	CHAIN X 2'	16
2	⅜ Ł 1' X 4"	15
1	COMBINATION BRAKE & TAIL LIGHT	
1	BRAKE LIGHT	
4	REFLECTORS 2 RED / 2 ORANGE	
3	3" BUTT HINGES	14
2	COTTER PINS	13
1	½" ROUND X 14"	12
2	4" PIPE X 4"	11
3	1½" EYE BOLTS	10
6	⅜ Ł X 1" X 13"	9
4	COLD FORMED] 3" X 15"	8
6	COLD FORMED] 3" X 18"	7
2	10 GAGE (U.S.S) 2¼" X 8"	6
2	10 GAGE (U.S.S.) 9" X 24"	5
2	10 GAGE (U.S.S.) 14" X 72"	4
3	10 GAGE (U.S.S.) 14" X 58"	3
1	10 GAGE (U.S.S.) 48" X 9' 11⅞"	2
2	10 GAGE (U.S.S.) 14" X 10' (WITH 4½" 90° BEND AT BOTTOM)	1
	10 GAGE (U.S.S.)	

TRAILER BOX DETAIL

Step 21 Using ⅛" E 6010, weld axle, taking care to get 100% penetration on root pass. Complete welding, using accepted pipe welding techniques.

*NOTE: Material Thickness—.125; Inside Radius—.125; Bend Deduction—.219.

Step 22 Begin fabrication of fenders by shearing two (2) pieces—72" x 14" x 10 Ga. H.R.S. Flame cut to shape, as shown on print detail #6. (Item #4) Cut two (2) pieces—24" x 9" x 10 Ga. and cut to shape. (Item #5).

Step 23 Bend fenders, as indicated, keeping in mind you are making one right side and one left side.

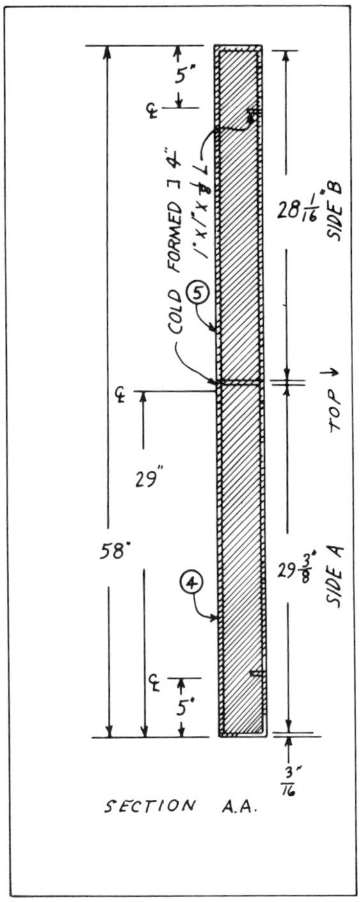
COLD FORMED] 4" 1"X1"X⅛ L
5"
28 1/16" SIDE B
TOP
29"
58"
29 3/8" SIDE A
5"
3/16"
SECTION A.A.

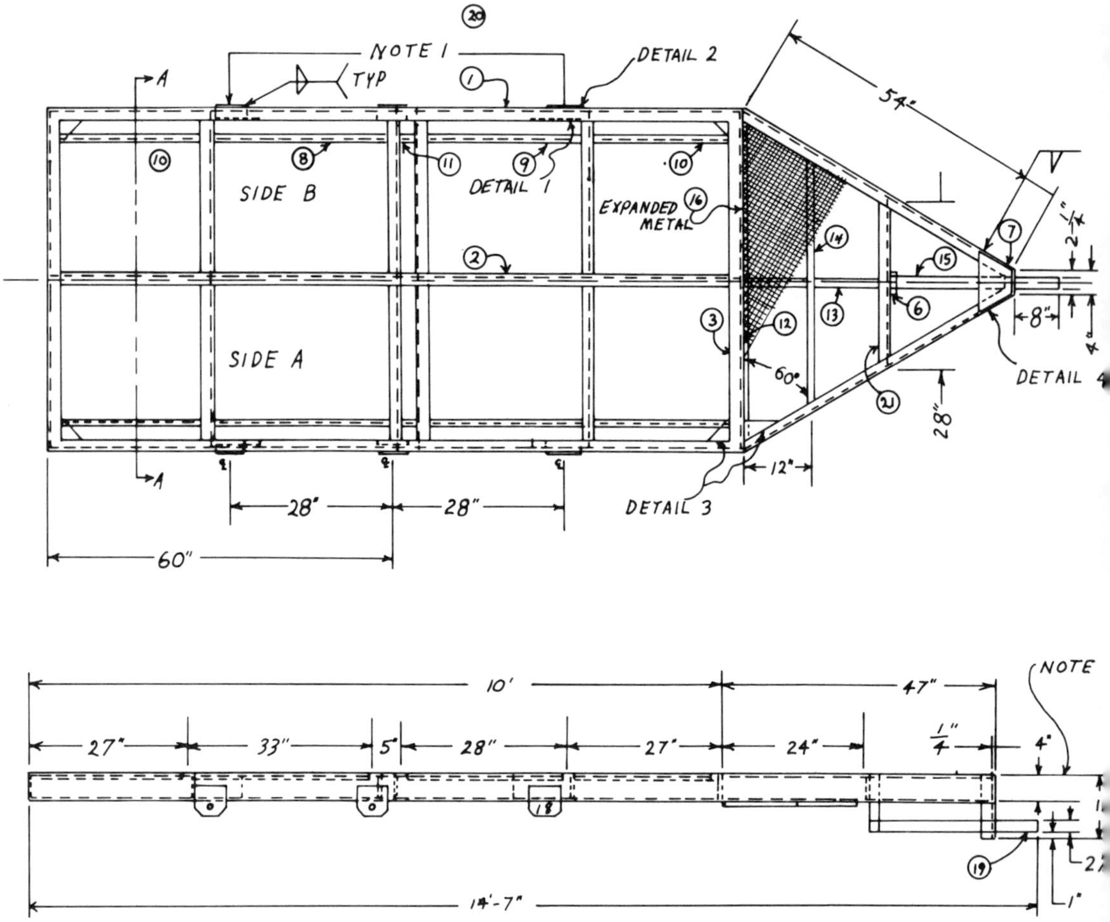
NOTE 1
DETAIL 2
TYP
SIDE B
DETAIL 1
EXPANDED METAL
SIDE A
54"
DETAIL 4
DETAIL 3
28"
28"
60"
12"
10'
47"
NOTE
27"
33"
5"
28"
27"
24"
14'-7"

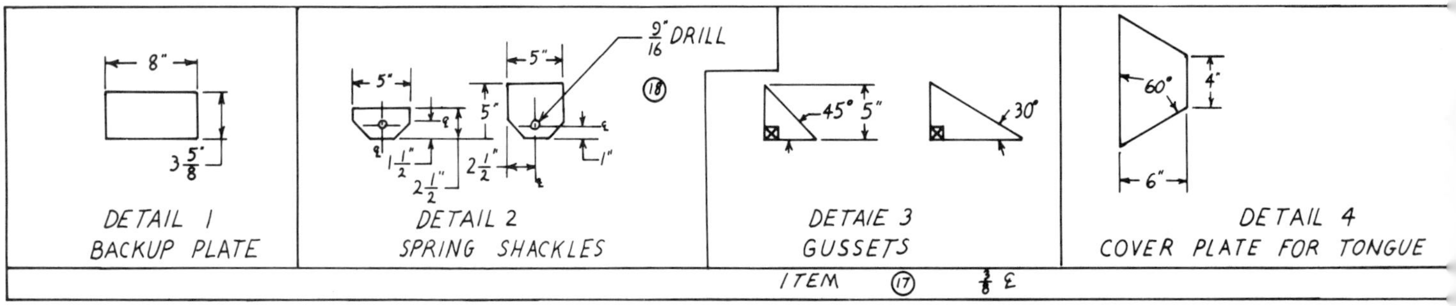
8"
3 5/8"
DETAIL 1
BACKUP PLATE
9/16" DRILL
5"
DETAIL 2
SPRING SHACKLES
45°
30°
DETAIE 3
GUSSETS
60°
4"
6"
DETAIL 4
COVER PLATE FOR TONGUE
ITEM (17) 3/8 E

1	BALL COUPLING	19
6	½" N.C. 5" 5 POINT BOLTS	18
1	⅜ LP 30"X40"	17
1	EXPANDED METAL 24"X58"	16
1	SQUARE TUBING 2¼X2¼X30"	15
1	" ∠ X 43"	14
1	" ∠ X 24"	13
1	" ∠ X 54½"	12
2	" ∠ X 3¼	11
4	" ∠ X 25⅜"	10
2	" ∠ X 26¼"	9
2	1"X1" ⅛ ∠ X 31¾"	8

1	"] 4"X11"	7
1	"] 3"X 10"	6
4	"] 4"X 28 1/16"	5
4	"] 4"X 29⅜"	4
2	"] 4"X 58"	3
1	"] 4"X 10"	2
2	COLD FORMED] 4" X 14'16"	1
NO.	PARTS REQUIRED PAGE 1	ITEM
1	STANDARD TANDEM TRAILER AXLE & SPRINGS WITH SHORTENED AXLE.	21
1	COLD FORMED] 4" X 28"	21

Step 24 Notch fender to accept 3″ channel on sides of box.

Step 25 Shear strips of 10 Ga. 2¼″ wide to form outside lip of fenders.

Step 26 Tack weld fender parts together. When all parts are assembled, weld entire length of all joints-outside only.

Step 27 Install 3″ channel side braces, as indicated. (item #8).

Step 28 Fabricate fender braces. Cut six (6) pieces ⅜″ x 1″ x 18″—flat bar and form, as shown. (Item #9) Weld in place, allowing 4″ clearance from top of tire. Set fenders in place and weld, as indicated.

Step 29 Fabricate stop-tail light brackets and install. Fabricate clearance light brackets and install.

Step 30 Trailer should be set on its wheels at this time and should sit level.

Step 31 Weld butt hinges to tailgate and to trailer.

Construct locking device, using ½″ x 1″ pipe and ½″ round stock, as shown in tailgate detail. Weld locking device into place.

Step 32 Using bare ³⁄₁₆″ electrodes, form tie down rings. Rings are 2″ circles. Weld rings to box, as shown.

Step 33 Cut and install expanded metal in tongue of trailer, as shown (item #16).

Step 34 At this point it must be determined what height trailer coupling must be. Standard ball height is 18″ to 21″. Fabricate trailer coupling to this height with trailer level.

Step 35 Grind all welds in preparation for painting. All surfaces should be treated before painting with Metal Preparation #S717. Prime paint entire unit with Red oxide 808, and finish with Centari #42813-AM.

Step 36 After paint is dry, wire in all lights and install safety chain, according to state regulations.

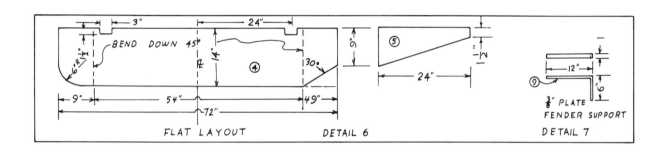

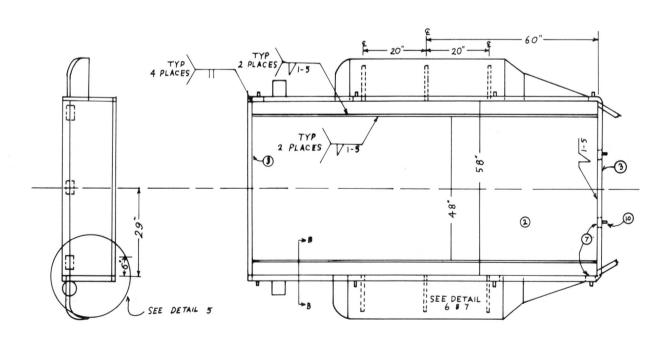

Heavy-Duty Fifth Wheel Agricultural Trailer

Author:	Fred Bjorklund
	Pat Bleskey
Instructor:	C. Cramer
School:	Helena Vocational-Technical Center
City & State:	Helena, MT

The trailer design has provisions for a 16 foot, hydraulic hoist-equipped, grain type box to be installed at a later date.

The trailer was constructed in sections to keep the amount of out-of-position welding necessary to a minimum.

The E 6010 electrode was used primarily for positioning of parts.

All weldments were made with a E 7018 low hydrogen electrode of various sizes.

Axle and hitch assemblies were supplied by the client.

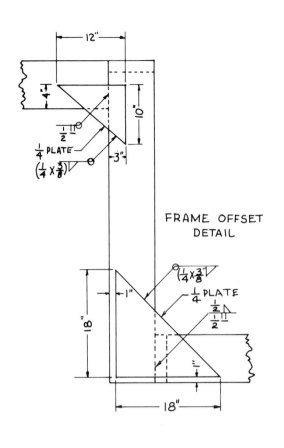

FRAME OFFSET
DETAIL

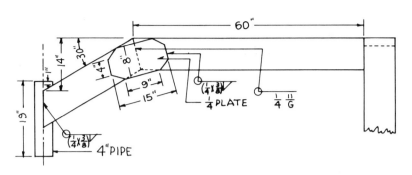

TONGUE DETAIL

4" PIPE

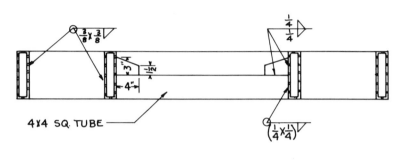

4X4 SQ. TUBE

SECTION A-A

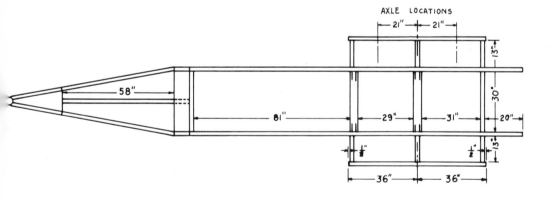

AXLE LOCATIONS

MATERIAL LIST

75 LIN. FT. 2"X8" 15.42#
    RECT. TUBING
5 LIN. FT. 4"X4" 12.02#
    SQUARE TUBING
18 INCHES 1/4"X4" FLAT
19 INCHES 4" SCH. 40
    PIPE
4 PLATES 1/4"X8"X15"
1 PLATE 1/4"X10"X12"
1 PLATE 1/4"X18"X12"
1 PLATE 1/4"X8"X9"

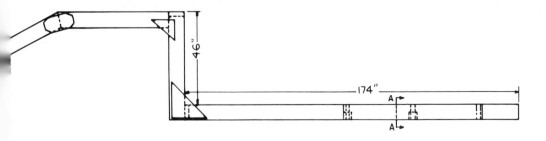

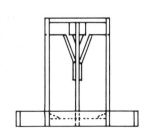

The Combination Machinery and Hay Trailer

Author: *Michael D. Steffen*
School: *Garden City Community Junior College*
Instructor: *Gale Seibert*
City & State: *Garden City, KS*

The first step in construction was to build the wheel and axle assembly of the tandem axle trailer. Purchased spindles, hubs and rims were used to make the axle assembly stronger and straighter. An 80″ piece of 3″ x 6″ x ⅜″ rectangular tubing was used to serve as the walking beam. A hole was drilled the right size of the spindle in the walking beam so the wheels would be straight. The spindles were welded to the rectangular tubing at every location that could be reached. The walking beam and a 4″ x 3′ x ¼″ section of pipe were welded together. A 4½″ x 9″ x ¼″ OD pipe was used for the main axle. Into this was slipped the 3′ section and walking beam to serve as the wearing surface of the tandem axle. The OD of the 4″ pipe and the ID of the 4½″ pipe were only a ¹⁄₁₆″ difference in size. With this tight fit the axle will wear much longer and remain free of play. A ¾″ rod with threads on it was slipped through the center of the two pipes so it would hold the axle assembly together and also it could be taken apart if needed.

For the frame guide rails and rollers 3″ x 5″ x ⅜″ angle iron was welded for the frame to slide in. A 1″ pipe was put in front to hold it square. This was all welded on the axle assembly. A hole was cut 30″ from the front of the angle iron and a 2″ x 3″ roller put on both sides. On both sides of the back end of the angle iron, was mounted a 4″ x 2″ roller. The rollers make the frame roll on and off the axle assembly easily. Also on the roller frame are the tie down chains to hold the frame to the axle.

Tandem axle assembly. Also shown is tie downs. these go around frame guide angle iron to tie down.

Rollers on back of frame and also on axle assembly so frame rolls easily.

The next step in construction was the frame. The side pipes available for the frame were 7' too short, so a 24" piece of pipe was cut to fit on the inside of the joint and was welded to splice the joint as illustrated. The side pipes were 4½" OD.

Next the end, front, and middle bars. 2" x 3" x ¼" angle iron were put in. Bolt holes were punched in the angle iron before welding. These holes were for attaching the floor boards. The punch machine saved time and labor. On the back end of the trailer were two more 4" x 2" rollers, so it could roll up and down the frame guides. An angled extension was added to the hitch tongue to bring it down to the level of the pick-up, so the trailer would ride level.

After painting the flooring of 3" x 12" x 7' rough fir was bolted to the frame.

The hayback was made of ¾" sucker rod. It was attached with 4 bolts. When using the trailer for hay, it serves as a support back for the baled hay.

The trailer is 9' wide by 28' long with four 7' sections in it to give it more strength.

Crank Jack.

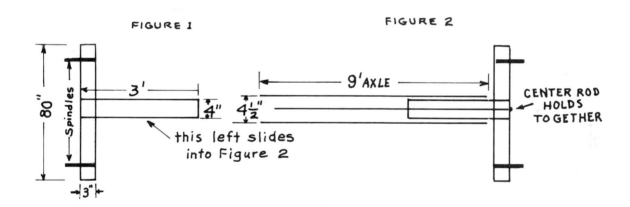

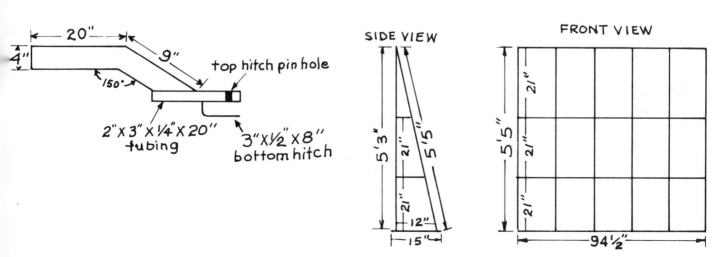

The trailer in position to load machinery. Drive across and pull into place.

The tandem axle with frame guide angle irons shown. This is all behind the trailer when trailer is down.

Wheel locks into position for road travel.

Wheels locked in position to pull forward to let trailer ground. Also used when pushing frame back on axle

Two Horse Trailer

Author: G. Kegel
Instructor: C. Nystrem
School: Northern Montana College
City & State: Haure, MT

Specifications

length:
   Overall - 12' 10"
   Body - 7' 10"

Height:
   Overall - 7' 10"
   Inside - 4' 11"

Width:
   Overall - 7' 1½"
   Inside'-'4' 11"

Axle Capacity - 7,000 lbs.

10" electric brakes

Hitch Capacity - 2,000 lbs.
Total trailer weight - 2,200 lbs.

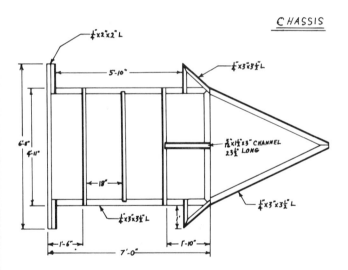

CHASSIS

The trailer is one foot longer than the conventional trailer, flat inside walls with 10 inch foam padding, a removeable divider for a more versatile trailer and completely enclosed for added protection.

The chassis is constructed completely out of ¼" angle iron with a 2" length of black pipe welded to the rear cross member to prevent snagging. The sides and front of the frame are made from ¼" x 3" x 3½" angle iron while the cross members are constructed out of ¼" x 2" x 2" angle iron.

The shackles for the axles were carefully positioned on the frame so that their width was exactly 5' apart and their distance had to be exactly 29" apart and perfectly centered. With the axles bolted in place the whole structure was flipped over and placed on jacks so that it could be leveled.

The skeleton tubing had to be placed at shoulder height to the animals, and the distance between the top length and the second length had to be 9½" so that sliding windows would fit inbetween them. Also the escape door had to be big enough for an adult to get in and out conveniently.

The breast plate was made from a piece of ³⁄₁₆″ x 2″ x 2″ piece of angle iron. This piece connected the two sides together and helped stabilize them. After the piece was welded the sides, front and the roof were fabricated from 16 gauge sheet metal which was heavy enough to withstand stress or impact and not too heavy to weigh the trailer down. The sheet metal was welded to the tubing on both sides of the tubing at a distance of about 6″ apart.

The hitch coupler had to be a standard 18″ off the ground. After figuring out the position, the ¼″ x 3″ x 3½″ angle iron hitch was welded to the coupler first and then cutting the lengths to a width of 4′ 11″ the assembly can be easily welded to the front uprights. The hitch assembly was welded about 3½″ above the bottom of the frame and a 5½″ x 10″ gusset was welded underneath for added strength. The bows for the top were made from .083″ x 1″ x 1″ tubing and cut in half in the center so that a center piece could be added in for strength.

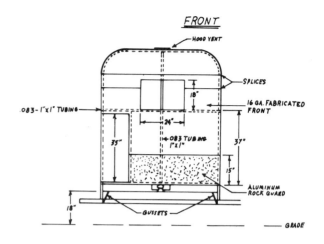

SHACKLE PLACEMENT

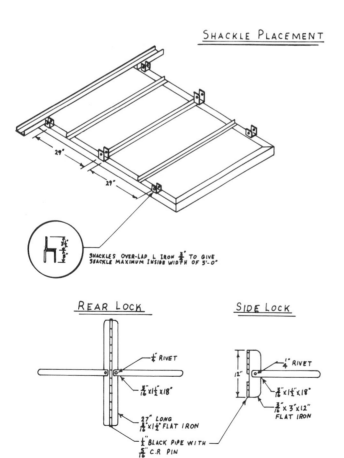

SHACKLES OVER-LAP L IRON ¾″ TO GIVE
SHACKLE MAXIMUM INSIDE WIDTH OF 5′-0″

REAR LOCK   ### SIDE LOCK

The front assembly was the most complicated because it had to meet up perfectly with the top and the side walls. The 3 bows were made out of .083″ x 1″ x 1″ tubing and bent around an old rack wheel. Their diameter had to be exactly 5′. The rack wheel was almost the correct size. After Welding the bows to the front uprights pieces of ½″ black pipe were welded between the bows where the saddle compartment door and front door were to be cut out. The floor were added to the saddle compartment and the feed area. The 16 gauge sheet metal was formed to the bows using a rope and a comealong to bend the metal around the bows. After all the metal was in place, a sabre saw was used with a metal cutting saw blade in it to cut out the two doors. By trimming the pieces cut out they were bowed and welded to a ³⁄₁₆″ x 2″ piece of flat iron and then welded them back in place using heavy duty piano type hinges. The windows were cut out so that they would be in line with the rear sliding windows.

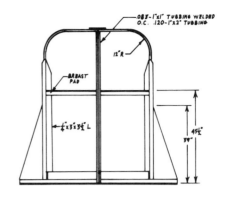

.083-1"x1" TUBING WELDED
O.C. .120-1"x2" TUBING

12" R

BREAST
PAD

¼"x3"x3½" L

45½"

39"

REAR DOORS

.083-1"x1" TUBING

16GA. X-ED TO ADD
STIFFNESS

.120-1"x2" TUBING

23"

51½"

27"

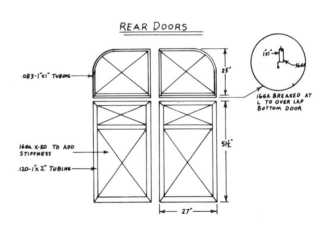

1"x1"
16GA.

16GA. BREAKED AT
L TO OVER LAP
BOTTOM DOOR

LEFT SIDE

56"

.120"-1"x2" TUBING
SKELETON

¼"x3"x3½" L

3/16"x2x2 L

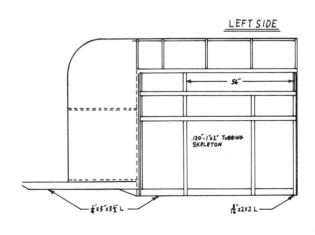

245

6 Ton Flat Bed Equipment Trailer

Author: John Hill
Instructor: Joseph Hill
School: Queen Anne's County High School
City & State: Centreville, MD

One	5'10'' four inch channel	Cross Member at Bend
One	8' nine inch channel	Head Board
One	7'9''	4 x 9'' Tail I Beam
Two	¼'' x 12'' x 18'	Diamond plate
Two	¼'' x 6'' x 18'	Flat Iron—Sides
Four	¾'' x 6'' x 12''	Gussett for Nose Plate
Two	5'' x 8'' x 14'	Main I Beams
Two	4' x 8'' x 5''	Beaver Tail I Beams
Two	8'' x 5'' x 5'	Front End I Beams
Nine	7' x 9'' x 5'' Channel	Cross members
Eight	¼'' x 3''	Gussetts for Head Board Support
One	5'10'' x ¼'' x 2''	Angle for End Cut of Boards
Two	½'' x 5'' x 10''	Diamond Plate Gussetts to Support Head Board
Two	½'' x 8'' x 4''	Flat Stock
One	5' x ¼'' x 2''	Flat Stock for Hanger Support
Four	12'' x 5'' Channel	Fish Plates and Rubboard Support
One	4'' x 18'' x 34''	Nose Plate
One	5'10'' x ½'' x ½''	Angle
Two	4' x 2'	Sheets of Expanded Metal
Four	¼'' x 1'' x 12''	Flat Stock for Gussetts on Rub-Rail
One	¼'' x 2½'' x 36''	Flat Stock to Box in Head Board and Tail Board
One	12'' x 36''	Channel to Support Jack
Two	¼''	Gussetts to fill in Tail Board to Sides
Six	U-shaped	Angle Hangers
Two	Mobile home trailer axles	
Thirty	⅛'' x ½'' x 2''	Wire harness Tie Downs
Eight	½''	Semi Round Tie Downs
One	2⁵⁄₁₆''	Trailer Ball and Coupler
One	Heavy Duty Adjustable Trailer Jack	
Two hundred	⁵⁄₁₆'' x 2½''	Carriage bolts, lock washers, square washers & nuts
12	6'' x 1¾'' x 18'	Oak Planks for Decking
One	10' x 14/6	Gauge trailer cord
One	14 gauge	Wired Harness to wire trailer
Four	Round Trailer tail lights	
Four	Red Reflectors	
Two	Half-Round Orange Running Lights	
Two	Half-Round Red Running Lights	

1. Cut two 8 x 5 I Beams into 14 feet lengths.
2. Pierce each beam at two foot intervals to accommodate the 5" channels.
3. Pierce each beam 1½" from top to give ample clearance for planking.
4. Insert channel into pierced I beams and set the frame square. Beams must have a center distance of 6'3".
5. Tack each channel to I beams and then weld in a vertical upward position.
6. Cut two 8 x 5 I beams 60" on center with 36° angle on one end and a 54° angle on the other for front of trailer.
7. Box off the 54° cut with a 8" x 4" x ½" flat stock.
8. Weld 18 x 4 x 1" flat stock into position by centering the plate into the I beam.
9. Pierce 2 x 2" square holes equally down the whole stock.
10. Cut two 5 x 8" I beams four feet in length with 13° angles on each end for the beaver tail.
11. Pierce holes in beaver tail I beams for 5" channel spaced 4" from rear and 2' from that point leaving a space of 1½" from top of 5 x 8" I beam.
12. Weld beaver tail I beams to main frame of trailer. Weld securely and reinforce inside of I beam with a 5" channel 12" long at the angle.
13. Weld 7'9" long x 4" x 9" I beam to rear of Trailer for back bumper. Cut suitable size holes for desired size of lights.
14. Insert 5" channel through pierced holes. Tack the channels and then weld securely in a vertical upward position.
15. Notch 9" channel 8' long for head board to fit front of deck to fit over 5 x 8" I Beam and extend above 5 x 8" I Beam five inches.
16. Turn trailer upside down and find center of bed of the trailer. The front axle center should be located at that point. The axle hanger should be mounted at the respected point according to where the springs land.
17. Mount axles on hangers.
18. Turn trailer right side up.
19. Cut the fifth and seventh cross-members ends off to 10" to clear the wheels. Weld ¼" x 6" x 14' long rubrails on ends of remaining channel and cut out for wheels.
20. Follow same procedure for the other side of the trailer. Weld ¼" x 12" Diamond Plate on outside edge of bed.
21. Box the ends of the head board with ¼" x ½" x 4" plate and weld vertically in a downward position. Do the same with rear bumper using ¼ x 4 x 9".
22. Weld gussets the size of axle hangers to support them. Weld them in a vertical upward position.
23. Use 12" channel 36" cut to fit front of trailer for suitable jack stand.
24. Use expanded metal to box entire front of trailer for carrying chains, tires, tools, etc.
25. Deck trailer with 1¾" lumber. Use 5⁄16" x 2½" carriage bolts with square washer, lock washers and nuts.
26. Weld two tie downs to top of head board 2" from the ends. Paint trailer with suitable under coat paint and follow with a suitable over coat paint. Weld four tie downs under 5 x 8" I Beam. At the beaver tail bend 1" in front of front axle hanger.
27. Use fourteen gauge wire to harness wire. Run wire to all lights. Fasten all lights to designated area.

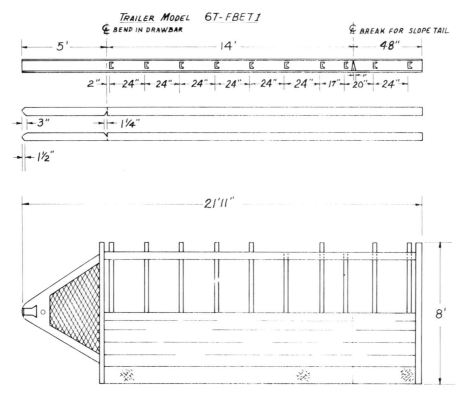

TRAILER MODEL 6T-FBET1

247

Heavy Duty Goose-Neck Trailer

Author: Theodore Nelson
Allen Brewer
Instructor: Thomas E. Fox
School: Helena Vo-Tech
City & State: Helena, MT

Dimensions & materials:

For our main frame, which was 24 feet long by 6 feet wide, we used 58 feet of 8″ channel.

For the goose-neck and outside frame, 105′ of 6″ channel was used.

To support the wood deck, 115′ of 4″ channel was used. In this operation, care had to be taken to make sure there was enough wheel clearance so boxing around the wheels was accomplished.

A 2″ x 2″ x ¼″ x 31′ piece of angle iron was used for support against twisting and gave more rigidity to the long span of 8″ channel in the main frame.

6 sq. ft. of ¼″ plate was used for gussets on the 8′ channel main frame and goose-neck.

2 sq. ft. of 16 gauge mild steel was used for light pockets at the front and rear of the trailer.

A 1½″ x ¼″ by 16′ piece of flat stock was used for trim. To house the tail lights, 8″ of 5″ pipe was used.

We salvaged one semi-pedestal jack from a local trucking firm. This was used for lifting the trailer on and off the truck.

All steel such as 8″, 6″, and 4″ channel were all coped together when possible to give it a better strength and appearance.

Two trailer axles measuring 8′5″, and with a load capacity of 3 ton per axle were used but as our trailer was 8′ wide the axles had to be shortened to 7′ 1″. To maintain the permanent camber 8″ was cut off each end. Before spindles could be reassembled, machining was accomplished. One set of wheels had electric brakes that were used for the trailing axle. Strings, shackles, axles, and wheels were assembled and tacked in place. The line-up was then completed, allowing for ⅛″ tow in front of the wheels.

In order that the goose-neck wouldn't hit the box of the trailer it was laid out to allow for plenty of room for short turns.

Other items added to our trailer were; stake pockets, to give the trailer more versatility and load handling capability; four tie down loops on each side, to enable loads to be anchored down; six clearance lights were installed at front, center, and rear. Conduit was used for wiring to prolong the life and to prevent shorts in the wiring.

After the trailer was completed, we took the time to clean the welds of all slag and spatter.

Parts list		
Qt	Description	Des
58′	8″ channel	A
105′	6″ channel	B
115′	4″ channel	C
31′	2″x2″x¼″ angle	D
6⁵ᵈ	¼″ plate	E
2⁵ᵈ	16 gauge sheet metal	F
16′	1½″x¼″ flat stock	G
8″	5″ T.D. pipe Sch 40	H
1	Semi pedestal jack	I
1	Trailer Hitch	J
6	Clearence Lights	K
14	Stake Pockets	L
8	Tie downs	M
2	Tail lights	N
4′	1″ Pipe	O
2	Axles Not Shown	P

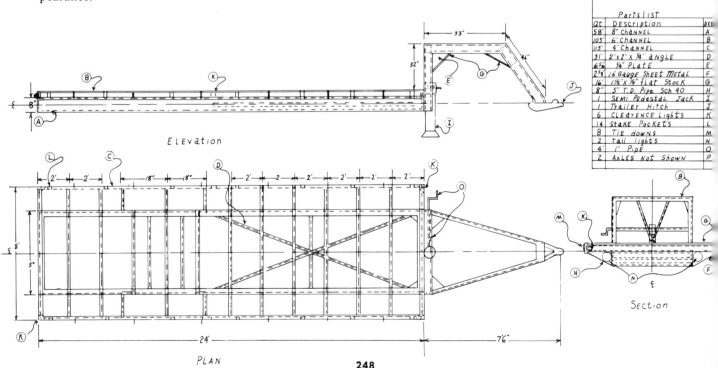

ELEVATION

SECTION

PLAN

Building a Stock Trailer

Author: Tommy Christopher
Instructor: Farrell Warwick
School: White County Voc. High School
City & State: Cleveland, GA

113'4" of 1½ x 1½ x ¼" angle iron
175' of 1" channel iron
864 sq. ft. of sheet metal
94" of 3 x 3 x ⅜" box tubing
27' of 2 x 4 x ¼" box tubing
140" of 2 x 2 x ⅛" box tubing
490" of 2 x 2 x ¼" angle iron
1 set trailer axles

Frame

The side pieces of the frame are 2 x 4 x ¼" tubing, 162" long. The cross rails for the back and front are 2 x 2 x ⅛" tubing 70" long. The front is rolled out of 2 x 4 x ¼" tubing. Place the tubing together and weld vertically and horizontally.

The cross pieces are 7 pieces of angle iron 2 x 2 x ¼" spaced on two foot centers and welded vertically and horizontally on each side.

The tung 3 x 3 x ⅜" tubing 94" long, is welded to three of the cross rails and to the front roll. The tongue braces of 2 x 2" tubing are welded from the front cross rail, at each side and to the tongue.

After completing the bottom frame, the axles should be mounted. To get the best pulling trailer, the back axle should be located 46" on center from the rear of the trailer. The front axle is located 31" on center from the back axle. This gives the trailer more weight on the front, which is better for pulling.

Sides

Vertical pieces or standards, 1½ x 1½ x ¼" angle iron are

the first to be welded. It takes 22 pieces of angle iron 68" long for the side standards. The standard should be welded on the side rail as shown. The sheet metal pieces are 32" wide and 162" long. They need to be welded at each side standard.

The top pieces are made from channel iron 1 x ⅛" and 162" long. It takes 5 pieces for each side. The channel should be welded at each standard on each side with overhead and flat welds.

On the left side is an escape door made out of 1½ x 1½ x ¼" angle iron, and 5 pieces of channel iron 1 x ⅛ x 8" long.

Front

The front is a piece of sheet metal 63" high, with a 15" open space at the top and a piece of 1" channel iron around the top. The 1" channel iron is supported by 4 pieces of vertical 1' channel iron 15" long. The wench on the front is 2" wide and 20" long.

Back

The door frames are made out of 1½ x 1 x ¼" angle iron. The sheet metal is 30", the horizontal bars are 1" channel 30" long. A brace runs from the top down to the 2 pieces of 1" channel iron letting them cross each other in the middle on each door. The side walls are 10" wide.

Top

The top is made of 6 pieces of 1" channel iron, 6" high with a radius of 35" bend in the middle of each one. This is for spreading a canvas.

Fenders

The fenders are 10" wide with a piece of 1½ x 1½ x ¼" angle iron around the outside. The floor of the trailer is made out of wood.

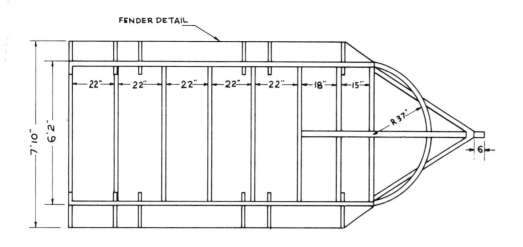

FENDER DETAIL

22" 22" 22" 22" 22" 18" 15"

R 37"

7'10" 6'2"

6"

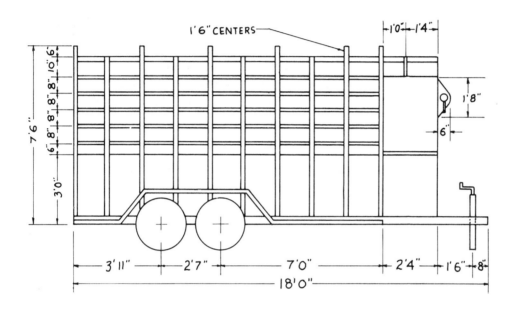

1'6" CENTERS

1'0" 1'4"

7'6" 6" 8" 8" 8" 8" 10" 6"

3'0"

1'8"

6"

3'11" 2'7" 7'0" 2'4" 1'6" 8"

18'0"

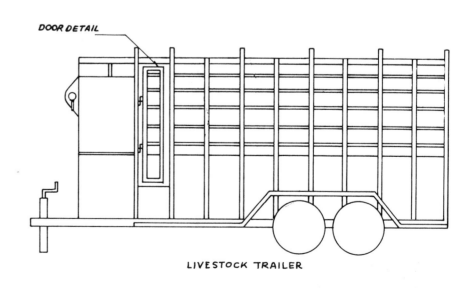

DOOR DETAIL

LIVESTOCK TRAILER

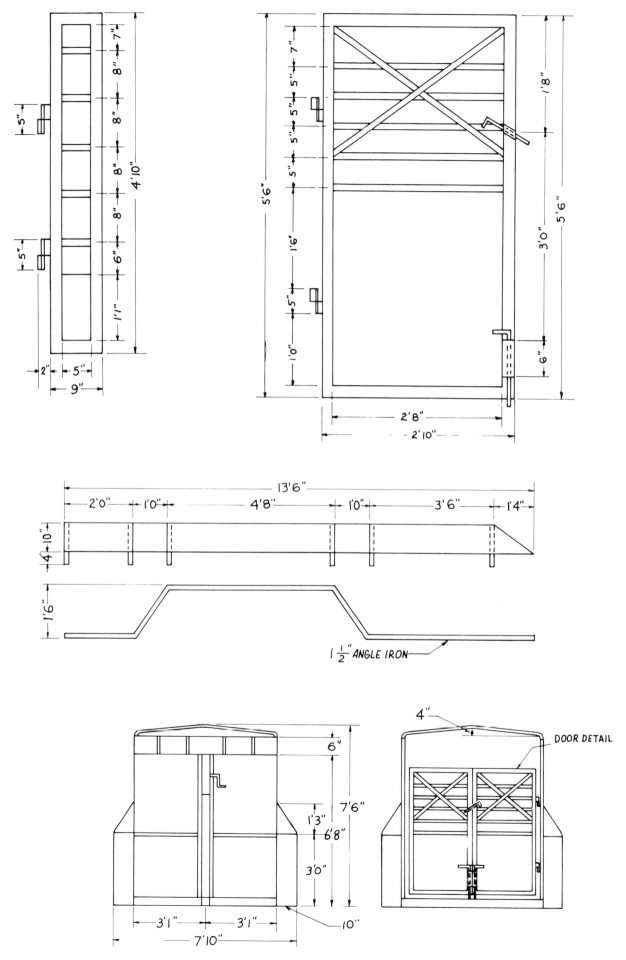

1 ½" ANGLE IRON

4"

DOOR DETAIL

A Trailer For Hauling Carpentry Tools

Author: Alan R. Armstrong
Instructor: Arthur Monroe
School: Pasadena City College
City & State: Pasadena, CA

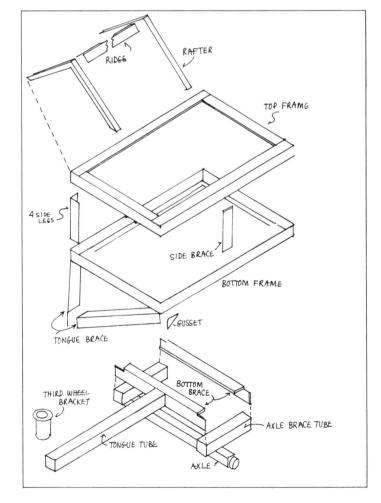

Step-by-Step Trailer Construction Notes

Step 1 CONSTRUCTION OF THE TOP AND BOTTOM ANGLE IRON FRAMES.

Materials for BOTTOM FRAME:

Two-2" angle x ³⁄₁₆" x 72"

Two-2" angle x ³⁄₁₆ x 47⅝

Materials for TOP FRAME:

Two-2" angle x ⅛" x 72"

Two-2" angle x ⅛" x 47¾"

Outside dimensions of both frames are 48" x 72"

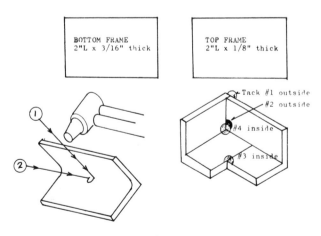

Method of notching angle iron with a hand torch

Placement of tacks to lessen distortion

a) Make tracks #1 & #2 at all four corners of BOTTOM FRAME.

b) Make tack #3, check for square. If under 90 degrees Peen tack until square. If square, make tack #4 at inside corner. Repeat for other corners.

NOTE: THE FOLLOWING DRAWINGS ARE NOT NECESSARILY TO SCALE NOR ARE THEY IN THE PROPER PERSPECTIVE.

NOTE: UNLESS OTHERWISE STATED USE ⅛" 6013 D.C. REVERSE.

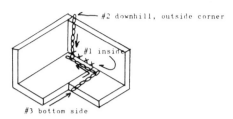

Welding sequence: Make welds #1, 2, 3 on all four corners of BOTTOM FRAME then go back and weld remaining seams top and bottom.

To make sure The BOTTOM FRAME is square, measure it diagonally corner to corner. If it is square both diagonal measurements will be the same. This is much more accurate than using a framing square.

To insure that both the TOP and BOTTOM FRAMES have the same outside dimension (48" x 72"), the BOTTOM FRAME is completed first, then the sections that comprise the TOP FRAME are clamped to it and welded.

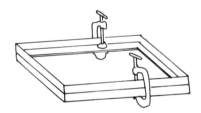

Step 2 Attach the four LEGS to the BOTTOM FRAME
Materials: Four-LEGS each 2" angle x ³/₁₆" thick x 18" long.

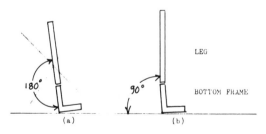

Don't assume that the BOTTOM FRAME is parallel to the floor. Don't align the LEG at 180 degrees to BOTTOM FRAME (a). Instead square the LEG at 90 degrees to the floor (b).

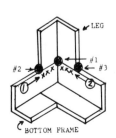
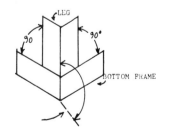

Placement of tacks: Tack #1 on outside corner. Tacks #2 & 3 on outside edge.

Welding sequence: Welds #1 & 2 outside from edge to corner. Welds #3 & 4 inside from edge to corner.

When checking for square don't forget the outside angle.

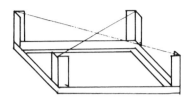

Check to make sure that the diagonal measurements between the LEGS are equal.

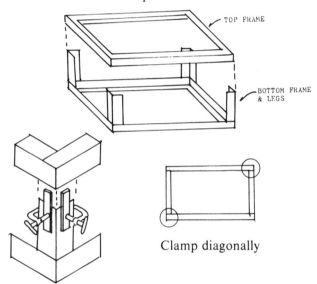

Clamp diagonally

Step 3 Attach the TOP FRAME to the BOTTOM FRAME and LEGS.

The outside edges of the FRAMES and the LEGS must be flush.

Use clamps to obtain a good fit up.

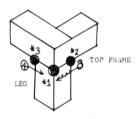

Placement of tacks: Tack #1 on all four inside corners of FRAME. Tack #2 & 3 on all four outside edges.

Welding sequence: Welds 1 & 2 outside from edge to corner on all four LEGS of FRAME. Welds #3 & 4 inside from edge to corner.

Step 4 Attach the two SIDE BRACES
Materials: Two pieces of flat bar 2" x ³/₁₆" x 14½" long. The SIDE BRACES must be the same length as the LEGS to prevent distortion of the frame.

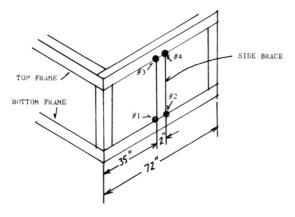

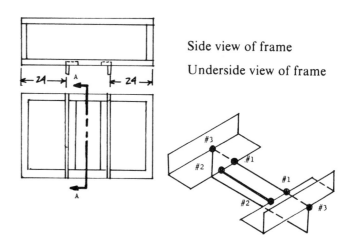

Side view of frame

Underside view of frame

Placement of tacks: Tack #1 & 2 on bottom corners.
Tack #3 & 4 on top corners.
Welding sequence: Weld top and bottom outside then do inside.

Placement of tacks: Make tacks #1 & 2, check to make sure it's square, then make tacks #3.

Step 5 Correcting warpage by heating and cooling. Because the frame is being fabricated on a cement slab and without the use of proper clamps and fixtures, warpage must be expected. A straight edge or a line from corner to corner will tell which areas of the frame are warped. You should be more concerned with warpage on the sides of the trailer then on the front and rear at this time.

The frame after welding

Heat this area to a dull red, then quickly cool with a wet rag.

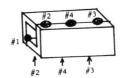

Welding sequence: Weld #1 on top side. Weld #2 & 3 in opposite directions as shown. Weld #4 other side of weld #1.

Step 7 Fabrication of square tube from angle iron.

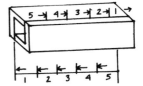

Steel contracts more than it expands. To correct warpage the idea is to get the steel to contract more on one edge than on the other, causing it to warp in the desired direction. It may be necessary to repeat this process in several areas to straighten a badly distorted area.

Placement of tacks: Tack as shown alternating between top and bottom of tube.

Welding sequence: Alternate step welds from the top to the bottom of the tube.

Step 6 Attach two-BOTTOM FRAME BRACES to the frame.
Materials: Two-BOTTOM FRAME BRACES 2" angle x 3/16" x 48" long. Notch angle as indicated.

Step 8 Fabricate two-AXLE BRACE TUBES 23⅝" long.
Materials: Four-2" angle x 3/16" x 23⅝" long. Fabricate tube as per Step 7. Use ⅛ 7018 electrode.

Step 9 Attach AXLE BRACE TUBES to BOTTOM BRACE.

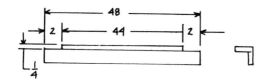

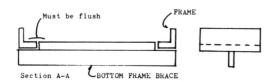

Section A-A   BOTTOM FRAME BRACE

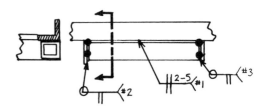

254

Placement of Tack as shown on both outside and opposite side of AXLE BRACE TUBE. Weld sequence: Weld as shown using ⅛ 7018 electrode. The tube when welded should be water tight.

Step 10 Fabricate TONGUE TUBE 60″ long.
Materials: Two-2″ angle x ³⁄₁₆ x 60″ long. Fabricate as per Step 7. Use ⅛″ 7018 electrode.

Step 11 Attach TONGUE TUBE to BOTTOM FRAME.

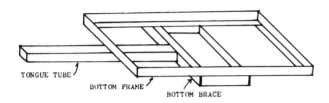

Proper fit up is very important, the TONGUE TUBE must be at a perfect right angle to the BOTTOM BRACE.

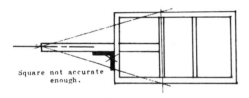

Using a framing square to determine this angle is not accurate enough. Instead, measure from the tip of the TONGUE TUBE to the outside centers of the AXLE BRACE TUBES. These two measurements must be equal.

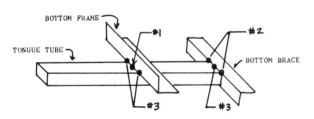

Placement of tacks: Tack #1 center of TUBE. Tack #2 center of TUBE on BOTTOM BRACE. Tack #3 edges of TUBE.

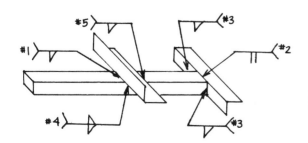

Weld sequence: Weld as shown. Use ⅛″ 7018

Step 12 Attach the TONGUE BRACES
Materials: Two-2″ angle x ³⁄₁₆″ x 33″ long

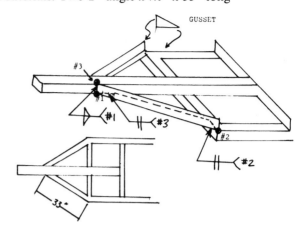

Cut off ends of TONGUE BRACES to fit TONGUE TUBE and BOTTOM FRAME.
Placement of tacks: as shown.
Weld sequence: as shown. Use ⅛″ 7018.

Step 13 Fabricate two GUSSETS
Materials: Two-2″ x 3″ x ³⁄₁₆″ plate cut diagonally

See Step 12 for location.

Step 14 Attach AXLE to AXLE BRACE TUBE
Materials: one-TRAILER AXLE
The AXLE must be perfectly centered on the AXLE BRACE TUBE and it must be at perfect right angle to the TONGUE TUBE. Check this by measuring.

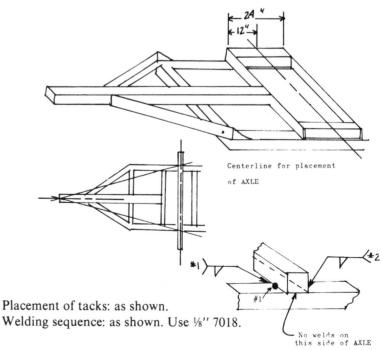

Placement of tacks: as shown.
Welding sequence: as shown. Use ⅛″ 7018.

Step 15 Fabrication of RAFTERS
Materials: Four-2″ angle x ⅛″ thick x 33⅞″ long.

255

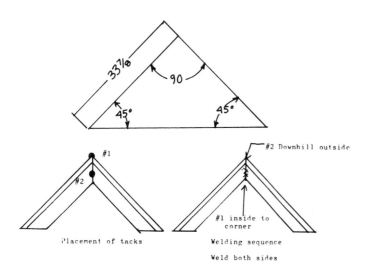

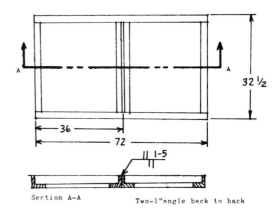

Fit up, tack and weld as per Step 1.

Step 19 Drill and bolt hinges on to DOORS and RIDGE. Drill and bolt lock hasps in place. These items could also be welded in place for greater strength and durability.

Step 20 fabricate and weld in place FENDER BRACE
Materials:
Two-1" square tubing x 12" long
Two-1" square tubing x 9" long.

Center FENDER BRACE over wheel and weld in place onto SIDE BRACE and BOTTOM FRAME.

Step 21 Weld FENDER in place.
Materials: Two-FENDERS
Position FENDER over wheel and weld in place to FENDER BRACE.

Step 22 Attach THIRD WHEEL to trailer. Position in corner of TONGUE TUBE and TONGUE BRACE.

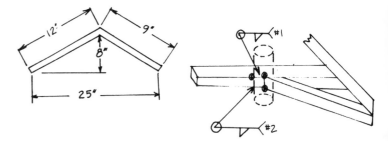

Tack as shown, use ⅛" 7018 rod.

Step 23 Plug end of TONGUE TUBE to make water proof and attach Trailer hitch.
Materials: One-2" x 2" plate ¼" thick
One TRAILER HITCH

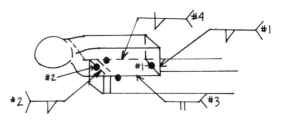

Placement of tacks and weld sequence as shown

Step 16 Attach RAFTERS to TOP FRAME.
The peak of the rafters must be on the trailers center line. Use a straight edge as shown. Do not use a square as the TOP FRAME could be warped.

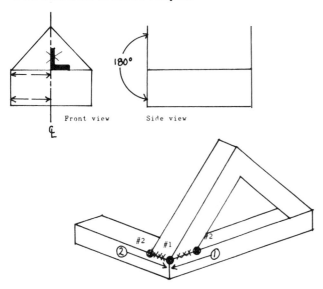

Placement of tacks: as shown
Welding sequence: as shown, start at toe and work toward heel.

Step 17 Attach RIDGE between the two RAFTERS.
Materials: One-2" angle x ³⁄₁₆ thick x 68" long.

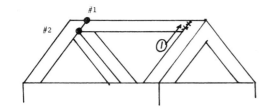

Placement of tacks: As shown.
Welding sequence: As shown, run from corner to top of RIDGE.

Step 18 Fabricate two-DOORS.
Materials:
4-1" angle x ⅛" thick x 72" long.
8-1" angle x ⅛" thick x 32½" long.

Double-Axle Flatbed Trailer

Author:	*Martin Hodge*
Instructor:	*James Shore*
School:	*Mt. Hood Community College*
City and State:	*Gresham, OR*

The trailer turned out to completely suit the needs for which it was intended. Not only did the Auto Club have the trailer which it needed, but the welding class had the benefit of making a useful product as a learning exercise. This gave us experience in drawing and reading blueprints, and fabricating from these prints. We also learned about squaring and alignment and controlling warpage. This was a most interesting and fun project for the welding class to participate on.

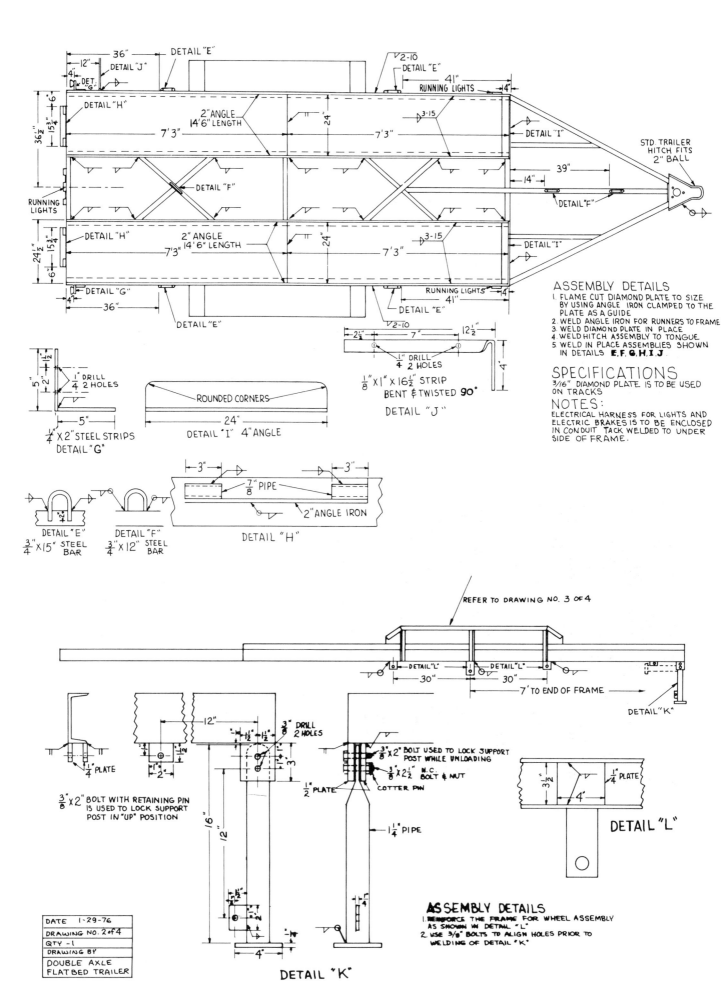

ASSEMBLY DETAILS

1. FLAME CUT DIAMOND PLATE TO SIZE BY USING ANGLE IRON CLAMPED TO THE PLATE AS A GUIDE
2. WELD ANGLE IRON FOR RUNNERS TO FRAME
3. WELD DIAMOND PLATE IN PLACE
4. WELD HITCH ASSEMBLY TO TONGUE
5. WELD IN PLACE ASSEMBLIES SHOWN IN DETAILS **E,F,G,H,I,J**

SPECIFICATIONS

3/16" DIAMOND PLATE IS TO BE USED ON TRACKS

NOTES:

ELECTRICAL HARNESS FOR LIGHTS AND ELECTRIC BRAKES IS TO BE ENCLOSED IN CONDUIT TACK WELDED TO UNDER SIDE OF FRAME.

DETAIL "E"
3/4" X 15" STEEL BAR

DETAIL "F"
3/4" X 12" STEEL BAR

DETAIL "G"
1/4" X 2" STEEL STRIPS

DETAIL "H"
7/8" PIPE
2" ANGLE IRON

DETAIL "I" 4" ANGLE
ROUNDED CORNERS

DETAIL "J"
1/8" X 1" X 16 1/2" STRIP BENT & TWISTED 90°

REFER TO DRAWING NO. 3 OF 4

DETAIL "K"

DETAIL "L"

3/8" X 2" BOLT WITH RETAINING PIN IS USED TO LOCK SUPPORT POST IN "UP" POSITION

3/8" X 2" BOLT USED TO LOCK SUPPORT POST WHILE UNLOADING
3/8" X 2 1/2" N.C. BOLT & NUT
COTTER PIN
1 1/4" PIPE

ASSEMBLY DETAILS

1. REINFORCE THE FRAME FOR WHEEL ASSEMBLY AS SHOWN IN DETAIL "L"
2. USE 3/8" BOLTS TO ALIGN HOLES PRIOR TO WELDING OF DETAIL "K"

DATE	1-29-76
DRAWING NO. 2 of 4	
QTY -1	
DRAWING BY	
DOUBLE AXLE FLATBED TRAILER	

258

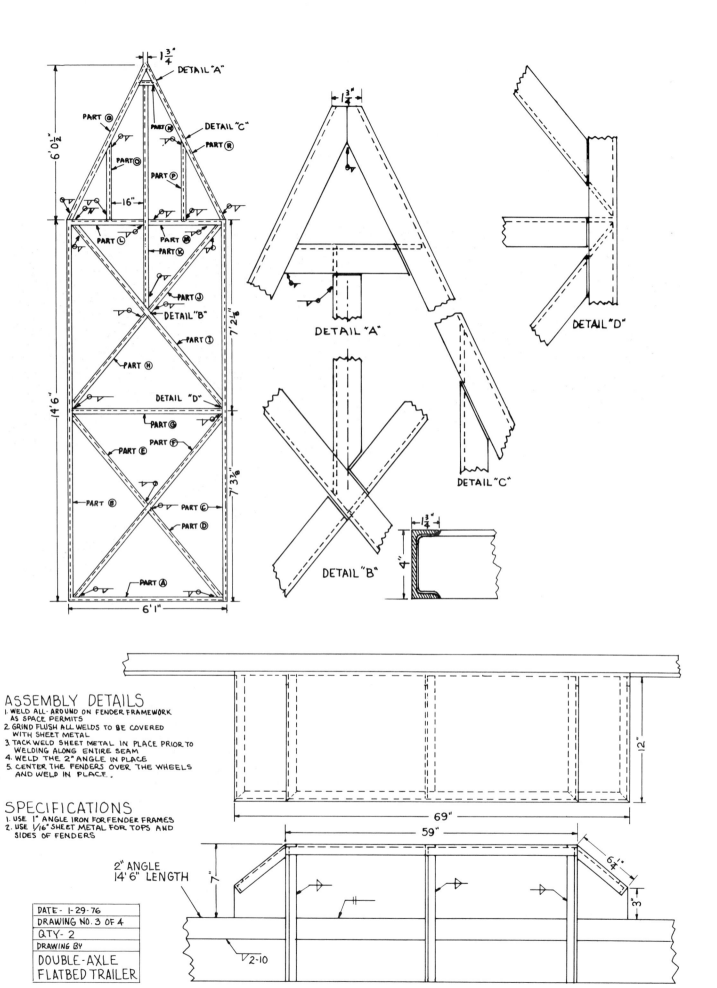

ASSEMBLY DETAILS

1. WELD ALL-AROUND ON FENDER FRAMEWORK AS SPACE PERMITS
2. GRIND FLUSH ALL WELDS TO BE COVERED WITH SHEET METAL
3. TACK WELD SHEET METAL IN PLACE PRIOR TO WELDING ALONG ENTIRE SEAM
4. WELD THE 2" ANGLE IN PLACE
5. CENTER THE FENDERS OVER THE WHEELS AND WELD IN PLACE.

SPECIFICATIONS

1. USE 1" ANGLE IRON FOR FENDER FRAMES
2. USE 1/16" SHEET METAL FOR TOPS AND SIDES OF FENDERS

DETAIL "A"

DETAIL "C"

DETAIL "D"

DETAIL "B"

| DATE- 1-29-76 |
| DRAWING NO. 3 OF 4 |
| QTY- 2 |
| DRAWING BY |
| DOUBLE-AXLE FLATBED TRAILER |

2" ANGLE 14'6" LENGTH

Tandem Axle, Boat/Utility Trailer

Author:	*Keith D. Trembath*
	David A. Finstrom
Instructor:	*Richard W. Halley*
School:	*Dunwoody Industrial Institute*
City & State:	*Minneapolis, MN*

A flat, box type frame, 19' long, 77" wide with a 5' tongue extension, is made from 3" x 2" x 14 ga. rectangular tubing with 2½" x 2½" x 3/16" square tubing for the tongue.

Weld rectangular framework working from center joints to outer ends, welding joints first one side then its opposite to minimize distortion. Use 3/32" E7018 electrode. After completing framework, layout tongue, angular frame extensions and braces; weld with procedure same as for frame.

To compensate for difference in material thickness between frame and tongue, ¼" plates are added to each joint area. Plates are longer than the joint area to more evenly distribute load stresses. Also two braces of rectangular tubing are added between the first cross member and the forward frame tube member to allow frame to flex vertically without excessive stress on weld joints.

To make the trailer adaptable for different size boats a subframe is used for the spring and axle assembly. Two pieces of 3" x 2" x ¼" angle iron are put against the frame on either side, squared, and clamped. Two cross pieces are laid in place and welded. Front spring mounts are spaced equidistant from the tongue and the remaining mounts positioned according to the spring manufacturer's dimensions. All this is accomplished with the subframe still clamped in place.

To provide wheel and tire clearance and a drop to the frame for level riding, a 3/8" plate is formed to give a 3" offset and 7" drop. These are welded to the ends of the axles, made from lengths of 2½" x 2½" x 3/16" square tubing extending the width of the subframe. Welds are 3/8" multi-pass welds, welded all around. After checking for 3/8" plate alignment, remove wheels and weld reinforcements to the extension as shown.

Drawings show other details of the design and welding.

Tandem Trailer Materials List

Quantity	Part Number	Description
24'		2½" x 2½" x ³⁄₁₆" sq. tube
96'		2" x 3" x 14 ga. sq. tube
1 each		Surge Unit
3 each		Tandem Fenders
2 sets		1600# Springs w/ Shackles
1 each		Tandem Equalizer Set
1 each		Recessed Lite Kit (comp)
1 each		Brake Kit
10'		³⁄₁₆" Steel Brake Line
1 each		Hand Winch 2500# (comp)
		3½" x 8' x ⅛ m.s. plate
5 each		½" x 6" Cap Screws
10 each		⅜" x 2¾" Cap Screws
18 each		2½" U-bolts 5½" long
1 can		Wheel bearing grease
20 each		Rambler Lug Nuts
25'		2" x 3" x ¼" angle iron
10 each		½" x 2¾" Cap Screws

Quantity	Part Number	Description
		¼" x 5" x 50" MS Plate (21#)
		³⁄₁₆" x 13: x 45" MS Plate (30#)
		¼" x 9" x 21: MS Plate (14#)
		¼" x 1½" x 18" MS Plate (2#)
		⅛" x 12" x 18" MS Plate (8#)
		⅜" x 2" x 16" MS Plate (3#)
80"		3" Channel Iron (28#)
		⅜" x 4" x 7" MS Plate (3#)
		¼" x 4" x 5" MS Plate (2#)
4 each		2" x 5" U-bolts ½" dia.
1	1457-2	Lee Brake Clip
4 each	B21 L	³⁄₁₆" Brake Fitting
27 each	11190	Brake Hose (flex)
1	18167	Brake Hose (flex)
1	35550	Brake Hose (flex)
16 each		⅜" x 3" bolts with nuts & washers
2 sets		Rambler Bolt on Front Spindles (Used)
4 each		15" Rims with tires
5 each		Keel Rollers

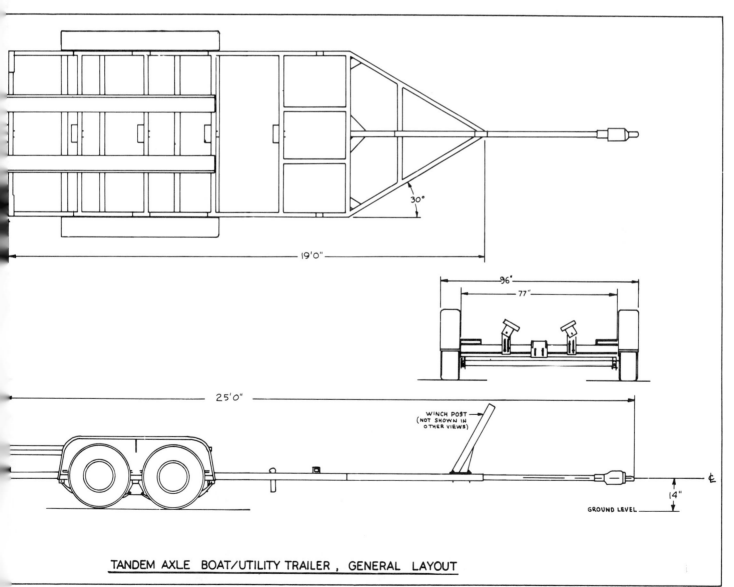

TANDEM AXLE BOAT/UTILITY TRAILER , GENERAL LAYOUT

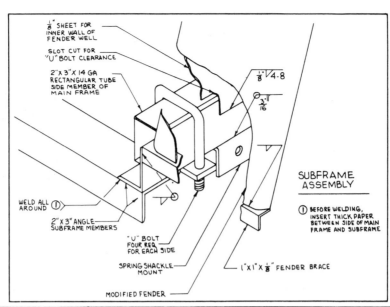

⅛" SHEET FOR INNER WALL OF FENDER WELL

SLOT CUT FOR "U" BOLT CLEARANCE

2" X 3" X 14 GA RECTANGULAR TUBE SIDE MEMBER OF MAIN FRAME

$\frac{1}{8}$ / 4-8

$\frac{3}{16}$ - 11

WELD ALL AROUND ①

2" X 3" ANGLE SUBFRAME MEMBERS

"U" BOLT FOUR REQ FOR EACH SIDE

SPRING SHACKLE MOUNT

MODIFIED FENDER

1" X 1" X ⅛" FENDER BRACE

SUBFRAME ASSEMBLY

① BEFORE WELDING, INSERT THICK PAPER BETWEEN SIDE OF MAIN FRAME AND SUBFRAME

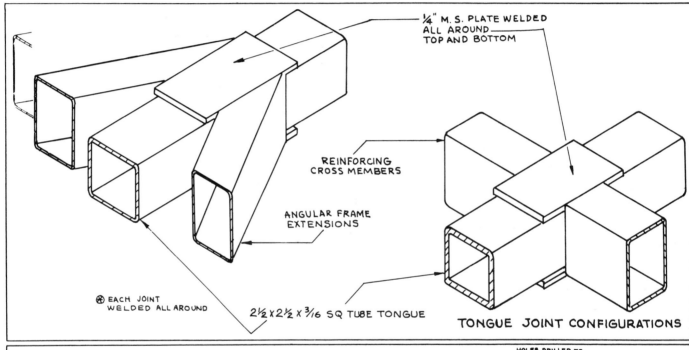

¼" M.S. PLATE WELDED ALL AROUND TOP AND BOTTOM

REINFORCING CROSS MEMBERS

ANGULAR FRAME EXTENSIONS

⊛ EACH JOINT WELDED ALL AROUND

2½ X 2½ X 3/16 SQ TUBE TONGUE

TONGUE JOINT CONFIGURATIONS

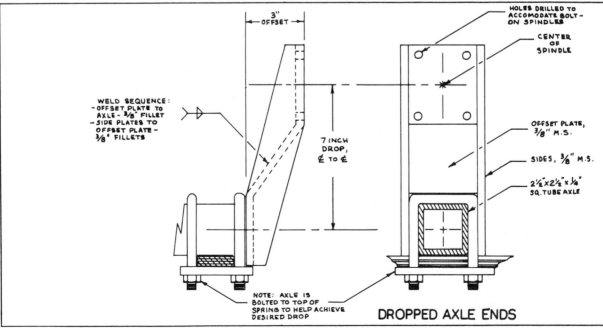

3" OFFSET

HOLES DRILLED TO ACCOMODATE BOLT-ON SPINDLES

CENTER OF SPINDLE

WELD SEQUENCE:
- OFFSET PLATE TO AXLE - ⅜" FILLET
- SIDE PLATES TO OFFSET PLATE - ⅜" FILLETS

7 INCH DROP, ₵ TO ₵

OFFSET PLATE, ⅜" M.S.

SIDES, ⅜" M.S.

2½" X 2½" X ⅛" SQ. TUBE AXLE

NOTE: AXLE IS BOLTED TO TOP OF SPRING TO HELP ACHIEVE DESIRED DROP

DROPPED AXLE ENDS

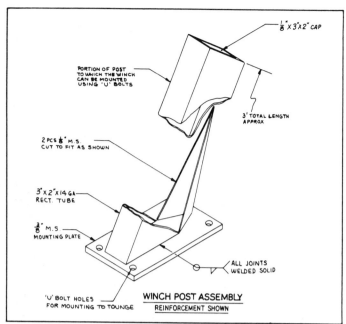

$\frac{1}{8}$" X 3"X 2" CAP

PORTION OF POST
TO WHICH THE WINCH
CAN BE MOUNTED
USING 'U' BOLTS

3' TOTAL LENGTH
APPROX

2 PCS $\frac{1}{8}$" M.S.
CUT TO FIT AS SHOWN

3" X 2" X 14 GA.
RECT. TUBE

$\frac{3}{8}$" M.S
MOUNTING PLATE

ALL JOINTS
WELDED SOLID

'U' BOLT HOLES
FOR MOUNTING TO TOUNGE

WINCH POST ASSEMBLY
REINFORCEMENT SHOWN

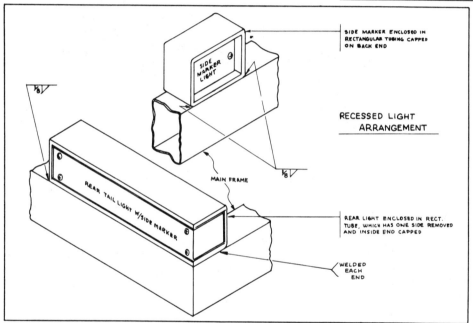

SIDE MARKER ENCLOSED IN
RECTANGULAR TUBING CAPPED
ON BACK END

SIDE
MARKER
LIGHT

$\frac{1}{8}$

RECESSED LIGHT
ARRANGEMENT

$\frac{1}{8}$

MAIN FRAME

REAR TAIL LIGHT W/SIDE MARKER

REAR LIGHT ENCLOSED IN RECT.
TUBE, WHICH HAS ONE SIDE REMOVED
AND INSIDE END CAPPED

WELDED
EACH
END

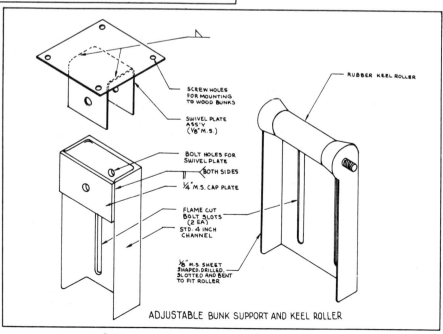

SCREW HOLES
FOR MOUNTING
TO WOOD BUNKS

RUBBER KEEL ROLLER

SWIVEL PLATE
ASS'Y
($\frac{1}{8}$" M.S.)

BOLT HOLES FOR
SWIVEL PLATE
BOTH SIDES

$\frac{1}{4}$" M.S. CAP PLATE

FLAME CUT
BOLT SLOTS
(2 EA)

STD. 4 INCH
CHANNEL

$\frac{1}{8}$" M.S. SHEET
SHAPED, DRILLED,
SLOTTED AND BENT
TO FIT ROLLER

ADJUSTABLE BUNK SUPPORT AND KEEL ROLLER

General Utility Trailer

Author:|Leonard A. Whitcanack
Instructor:|James E. Tripp
School:|Central Florida Community College
City & State:|Ocala, FL

Materials and total cost

1. Springs and axle—used
2. Rims (2)—used
3. Tires (2)—used
4. Hitch—New
5. Square tubing—39′ of 2″ x 2″ x ³⁄₁₆″
6. Square tubing—60′ of 1″ x 1″ x 16 ga.
7. Square tubing—8′ of 1¼″ x 1¼″ x 14 ga.
8. Floor Plate—1 sheet of 4′ x 10′ x 14 ga.
9. Smooth Plate—1 sheet of 4′ x 10′ x 14 ga.
10. Latches (3)
11. Smooth Plate—1 sheet of 2′ x 4′ 6″ x 14 ga.
12. Safety chain—6′
13. Lights, tail (2)—stop-turn signal
14. Primer—2 qts.
15. Yellow paint—1 qt.
16. Orange paint—1 pt.

Layout and Fabrication:

Top View: Cut chassis member from 24 foot lengths of 2″ x 2″ x ³⁄₁₆″ square tubing using hacksaw. The 45° mitred angles at the 4 corners can be made with a carpenter's square. Measure carefully so that members will fit tightly and squarely against each other to give a good fit-up for welding. Layout cuts parts as shown on a table or the floor. Clamp together and tack weld all joints. After all joints are tacked, position the frame so that final welding of joints on all four sides of tubing can be made in the downhand position. Use a ⁵⁄₃₂″ E6010 with DC or an E6013 with AC at approximately 150 amperes. Grind flush the welds made on the top of the frame against which floor plate will be welded. Cut tongue and tongue braces to dimensions shown from 4″ x 2″ x ¼″ square tubing and weld joints all around. Raise and support finished frame to allow positioning angle and springs. Weld frame to the underside of the frame as shown in the photograph. These butt welds will be made in the horizontal position. Cut trailer floor plates to size from 4′ x 10′ x 14 ga. studded flooring plate. Leave ⅛″ space between plates when positioned on frame. Weld plates together and to frame member in one operation. Weld 3″ sections of ¼″ square tubing to the side frames. These are for holding side frame support members. Be sure they are square with frame.

Side View: Cut side frame support members with dimensions and angles as shown from a 24 foot piece of 1″ x 1″ x 16 ga. square tubing. Layout and weld frame members. Tack weld all joints then up-end the frame so that final welds of side member to top members can be made downhand. Cut side panels from 14 ga. plate, position and weld intermittently to the side frame support members. The support members will be showing on the outside of the trailer. Cut fenders from left over floor plating. Weld to the side panels. A 1″ x 1″ angle iron is welded the entire length of the side panel at the bottom on the inside.

Front View: Make frame members from 1″ x 1″ x 16 ga. square tubing. Weld square tubing 1½″ x 3″ to floor for holding frame members. Cut front panel from 14 ga. plate and tack weld to frame members. Flare panel slightly at bottom so that it won't interfere with tube holders when assembled. Front panel is secured to the side panel with a bolt latch. Latch is made from a short piece of angle welded to side panel and drilled to receive bolt. Holes for bolts are drilled through front end frame members.

End View Gate: Frame members of 1″ x 1″ x 16 ga. tubing and panels of 14 ga. plate are cut, clamped and welded as other side frames. Holes are drilled in floor for ½″ x 3″ round pipe that receives latches. Bolts ⁵⁄₁₆″ x 3″ are welded to bottom of frame members. These fit into tubing on frame members and make the gate hinges. Bar brace is used to prevent sides from swaying when gates are removed.

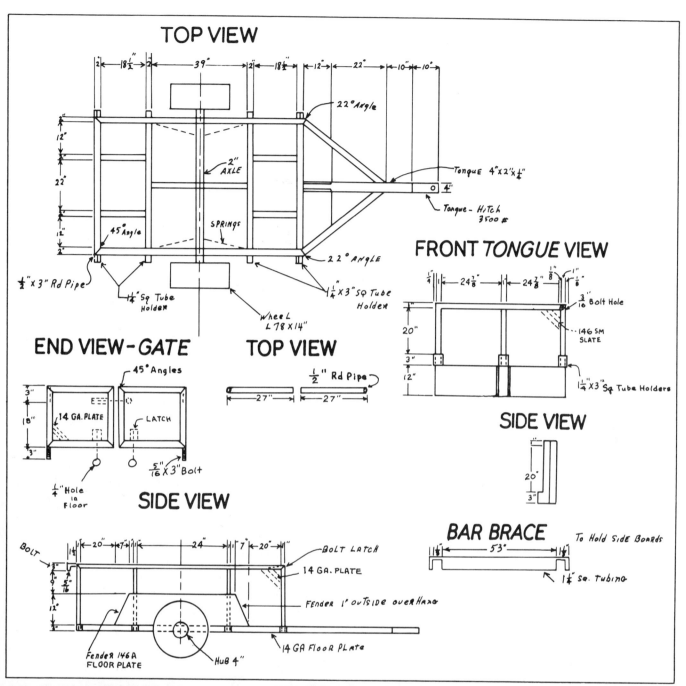

TOP VIEW

2" | 18½" | 2" | 39" | 2" | 18½" | 12" | 22" | 10" | 10"

22° Angle

2" AXLE

12"

22"

12"

45° Angle

SPRINGS

½" X 3" Rd Pipe

1¼" Sq Tube Holder

Wheel L 78 X 14"

22° Angle

1¼" X 3" Sq Tube Holder

Tongue 4"x2"x¼"

4"

Tongue - Hitch 3500 #

FRONT TONGUE VIEW

¼" | 24⅞" | 24⅞" | ⅛" | 1" ⅛"

20"

3"

12"

³⁄₁₆" Bolt Hole

146 SM Slate

1¼" X 3" Sq Tube Holders

END VIEW - GATE

45° Angles

3"

18"

3"

14 GA. PLATE

LATCH

5⁄16" X 3" Bolt

¼" Hole in Floor

TOP VIEW

½" Rd Pipe

27" | 27"

SIDE VIEW

1"

20"

3"

BAR BRACE

53"

1¼" | 1¼"

To Hold Side Boards

1¼" Sq. Tubing

SIDE VIEW

BOLT

1¼" | 20" | 7" | 24" | 7" | 20"

3"
9"
5⁄16

12"

BOLT LATCH

14 GA. PLATE

Fender 1" outside over Hand

14 GA Floor Plate

Fender 146A FLOOR PLATE

HUB 4"

Gooseneck Trailer

Author: Allen C. Riech
Instructor: Timothy Holtquist
School: Lake Preston High School
City & State: Lake Preston, SD

Materials Used:

No. of Pieces	Description
2	15' x 8'' x ¼'' structural (st.) channel iron — frame
2	50'' x 8'' x ¼'' channel iron— gooseneck arm
70 lbs.	7014 welding electrodes
4	10'' x 8'' x ¼'' st. channel — perimeter box
1	10'' x 8'' x ¼'' st. channel — inside perimeter box
2	6' x 8'' x ¼'' st. channel — side of perimeter box
5	34'' x 8'' x ¼'' st. channel — cross members
2	88'' x 8'' x ¼'' st. channel — horizontal neck
1	3½'' x 33½'' pipe neck brace
1	33½'' x 8'' x ¼'' st. channel
1	29¼'' x 4'' x ⅛'' square tube hitch part
6	10'' x 10'' x ¼'' triangle corner neck bracings
1 kit	axle tubes, spindles, brake switches, brakes springs, "U" Bolts, wheel rims
1 kit	hoist, battery, pump valve, hoses, diverter, valve reservoir.
2	33½'' x 5'' x ¼'' st. channel — hoist "I" beam
4	7.00 x 15% tires, radials
1	33½'' x 24'' x ¼'' plate, steel — pump mounting
4	3'' x 2'' x ⅜'' pipe — rear hinge
1	33½'' x 5'' x ¼'' st. channel — rear brace
1	1¼'' x 40'' shaft rear hinge
2	2' x 3'' x 10'' x ¼'' angle iron
1	3½'' x 30'' x ¼'' square tube
2	4'' x 4'' x ¼'' iron with 2 corners 1'' x 2''
1	3'' x 1½'' x ¹¹⁄₃₂'' pipe ball socket
1	3'' diameter x ¼'' cap on hitch
1	3½'' x 8'' hydraulic cylinder
1	1⅛'' nut
1	6'' sand shoe
2	4'' x 4'' x 1'' jack mounting
1	1'' x 6'' x 34'' steel

Materials Used:

No. of Pieces	Description
1	12'' x 12'' x ½'' plate top of pickup hitch
1	2⁵⁄₁₆'' ball with 1⅜'' shank
5	30' pieces of 14 ga. wire
1	29' garden hose
1	16' x 7'10'' combination box with mud flaps
1½ gal.	black paint
3 pints	1 pt. of each — orange, red, white
2 lbs.	wheel bearing grease

1. Sides
   a. Take 2 pieces of 8″ structural channel iron 15′ long and cut 1 end off each at a 45° angle using a tri-square.

2. Arms—for gooseneck
   a. Cut 2 pieces of 8″ structural channel iron 50″ long with opposite 45° angles. See figure 2.
   b. Spot weld the arms and sides than weld fully around.

3. Perimeter—for box frame
   a. Cut 4—10″ pieces of 8″ structural channel iron with 1 end square and the other at a 45° angle.
   b. Cut 2—10″ pieces of 8″ channel with 1 end to be cut down to fit inside the perimeter channel iron.
   Tongue pattern—so tongue will fit properly inside the channel, cut 1″ off 1—8″ wide channel piece. Place it on end over the end of another channel piece intended to fit inside the tongue. Cut around the inside of the 1″ channel. Going from the front of the frame to the rear of it.
   c. Spot weld the 6—10″ pieces to the frame—3 on each side.

For one side placement proceed as follows: (Measurement from front to rear).

1. Measure off 90¾″ and spot weld the 10″ piece with the 45° angle on it with the open end facing toward the rear.

2. Measure 36″ from the outside of the first 10″ piece and spot weld the middle channel. Place this channel also facing the rear of the frame.

3. Measure 36″ from the outside of the middle channel and place the 10″ piece with the 45° angle on it there. The open ends must all be facing toward the front of the frame.

Perimeter Side

Cut 2—8″ channels 6′ long with opposite 45° angles on the ends. Place this perimeter side on the other 3 channel irons that are already spot welded. Square it up and spot weld. Once everything is square, weld fully all around.

4. Welding the 2 sides of the frame together.
   a. Cut 4 pieces of 34″ long 8″ channel iron.
   b. Cut tongues on both ends of each so that they will fit inside the 2 frame sides. The final length should be 33½″ because the 8″ channel is ¼″ thick.
   c. Place 3 of these in the perimeter box frame and square off with the outside perimeter that is already welded.
   d. Place the fourth piece 2″ from the arms of the gooseneck facing the rear of the frame. The front end of the box will rest flush with this.

5. Welding of the neck.
   a. Cut 2—88″ long pieces of 8″ channel providing

** All channels must be placed as shown. The front of the box must have 2″ of clearance from the back of the frame.

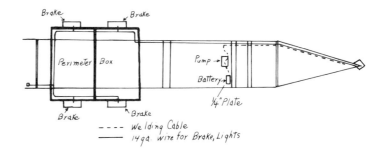

Brake   Brake

Perimeter   Box   Pump →   Battery →   ¼″ Plate

Brake   Brake

- - - - Welding Cable
———— 14 ga. wire for Brake, Lights

Pickup Box

Rear   Front

Under Pickup   Pickup Floor
Under Pickup Floor
Top of Floor

Starter

Pickup Wiring harness

- - - Welding Cable ——— 14 ga. wire for Brakes Lights

a 45° angle on one end. Cut straight across on the opposite end.
   b. Mark at 20″ with chalk the channel with the 45° angle. At that mark make a "V" shaped slit with a ½″ on the wide end. This will make it possible to bend the neck inward.
   c. Spot weld the arms together matching the 45° angles together. Immediately weld both inside and outside the channel.
   d. Cut a 3½″ O.D. pipe 33½″ long and place over the welding on the inside of the channel arms. Grinding may be necessary for the pipe to fit and weld properly.
   e. Spot weld pipe in place.
   f. Cut 1 piece of 8″ channel iron 33½″ long with the ends to fit inside the webs. Place the channel iron 19¾″ ahead of the 45° angle just welded and spot weld them into place.
   g. Bend the 2 neck channels toward the center till they both meet evenly.
   h. Cut 1 piece of square tubular steel measuring 4″ on the outside. Cut off squarely at 29½″.
   i. Drill 1—¾″ hole in the center of the length of the square tube. Drill from an upper corner of the tube through the opposite lower corner at a 45° angle.
   j. Set the piece of tubular steel on the top of the channel irons to mark and cut. After cutting the channel weld the steel together.
   k. All parts previously spot welded are to be welded securely.

6. Installing the neck bracings.
   a. To strengthen the 3—90° angles, corner bracings are required.
   b. Bracings should be in a straight line. Using ¼" steel cut 6 triangular pieces measuring 10" x 10" x 14" each. These pieces are to fit into the corners of the neck. Two bracings fit snuggly into the corners of the arms and neck frame. Finally 2 bracings will fit between the 2 horizontal neck frames and tubular pieces. Fit them squarely.
   c. Place the upper 4 triangular pieces into the corners of the frame and spot weld into place. The final 2 triangular pieces are placed at the corners on the outside of the frame and arms to provide a 10" clearance between the box and front end of the frame.

7. Mounting the spring brackets
   a. The spring brackets are to measure 31" from hole to hole.
   b. Measure 126¾" from the front of the frame to the back. This is the center point of the frame for the spring mounting. The hole of the center should be in line with the center point, the frame, and the opposite spring bracket. To figure axel placement, measure 60% of the way back on the load not the frame.
   c. Spot weld the center bracket after squaring up the 2 brackets with each other and the frame.
   d. Place the other 4 brackets, measuring 31" each way from the center hole to the center of each bracket.
   e. Spot weld all brackets and recheck for squareness with all other brackets and frame to prevent later wearing of the tires.
   f. Complete welding.

8. Axle Assembly
   a. Cut square axle tubes to 59¼" long.
   b. Make 1—2" slit on the top side 2" from each end of the tube, then cut a piece 2" x 2" x 1½" from each end of the tube. Insert the axle and spot weld into place. Take special note that the brake shoe mounting bracket bolts line up with the axle so all bolts can be used.

9. Mounting springs and axles.
   a. Using "U" bolts and axle mounting brackets, put parts together but don't tighten the "U" bolts.
   b. Place the axle and springs under the frame and insert the bolts through the brackets and equalizer.
   c. After placing and mounting the axle and springs tighten all bolts. An impact wrench is the best choice for tightening the "U" bolts but care must be taken that they are tightened evenly for even load distribution.

10. Installing brakes, bearings, hubs and wheels.
    a. Using bolts supplied with the axle kit, install the brakes with magnets on the bottom.
    b. Tighten bolts evenly and securely.
    c. Grease the inner bearing. Apply lubricant to the bearing and hub, then turn the bearing to work it in evenly.
    d. Install the bearing into the hub using a rubber hammer to tap the bearing.
    e. Work a generous amount into the outer bearing and place over the spindle inside the hub.
    f. Install the washer inside the hub followed by the nut. Install the cutter key. The wheel should be able to turn easily.
    g. Install the wheel bolts, torquing them between 75-80 ft/lb.

11. Installing the hoist and hydraulic system.
    a. Cut 2—5" pieces out of the first crossmember of the perimeter box located at the front of the frame. Locate the center of the frame and measure 9¾" behind and ahead of the center mark. At these locations mark 3" down the side of the crossmember and 5" adjacent to the measured 9¾" mark.
    b. Cut 2—5" structural channel iron 33" long. These are to fit flush with the bottom of the frame.
    c. Weld the 2 pieces back to back so that an "I" beam will be formed. Weld only every other 1½" to prevent cracking of the welds.
    d. Weld inside the frame with the center weld at 69" from the front of the frame.
    e. Cut 2—3" x ¼" angle iron 2" long. Set this over the shaft of the hoist.

12. Mounting pump and control.
    a. Cut a piece of ¼" plate 33½" x 24" to mount the valve, pump and battery on.
    b. Fasten the pump, valve, reservoir, and battery securely to the ¼" plate. Attach the hoses to these controls as shown in the instructions received with the hoist.

13. Installing the rear hoist hinge.
    a. Cut 4—2" pipe at 3" length. The pipe must have ⅜" walls and 1¼" diameter.
    b. Cut 1—5" piece of channel at 33½" length.
    c. Center this channel vertically and weld into place at 176" from the front of the frame. (This will be the rear crossmember.).
    d. Cut 1—2" hole centering at 177¾" from the front of the frame and ¼" from the top of the frame.
    e. Cut 1—1¼" shaft 40" long.
    f. Place 2 of the 4—3" x 2" pipes on the shaft. Place them through the holes.
    g. Slide the pipes on the shaft. They are to fit flush with the outsides of the frame.

h. Weld the pipes securely inside and outside of the frame. Recheck for it fitting squarely with the frame.

i. Take out the shaft and grind off any excess weld from the outside of the frame to make it fit squarely.

j. Cut 2—10″ pieces of 3″ x 2″ x ¼″ angle iron. Cut 1—1¼″ hole in the angle iron on the 3″ side.

k. To make sure that the pipe fits squarely, weld it on the 2″ side of the angle iron.

14. Trailer hitch

a. Cut 1 piece of 3½″ tubular 30″ long. Drill 8 holes at each end measuring ¾″ in diameter. Start drilling the holes nearest the middle and work outward. The total number of holes is 16 with 8 on each of the 2 tubular corners. The holes are to be drilled in straight alignment through the opposite side.

b. Cut 2—4″ x 4″ pieces of ¼″ plate with 2 of 4 corners extended 2″ beyond the 4″ point. These corners which are opposite each other are to be 1″ wide. Drill holes in the newly cut plate.

c. Cut 1 piece of 3″ pipe with ¹¹⁄₃₂″ wall and 1½″ length.

d. Cut ¼″ plate 3″ in diameter.

e. Set ¼″ plate on top of the pipe and weld securely into place to form the ball socket.

f. Set the ball socket on the ¼″ plate. This must be centered over the hole and welded securely.

g. Place the socket and plate on 1 end of the cut tubular pipe. This also is to be centered on the opposite end of the previous 2 sets of 8 holes drilled.

h. One corner of each plate should have a ½″ bolt inserted in the ½″ hole of the ¼″ socket plate. The front middle hole can have a padlock instead of a bolt for theft protection.

15. Hydraulic jack.

a. Remove the clevis on the 1 end of the shaft.

b. Weld a 1⅛″ nut to the center of the top of the 6″ diameter sand shoe.

c. Cut 2 pieces of 1″ plate 4″ x 4″ for mounting cylinder onto the framework.

d. Drill 1—1″ hole in the 1″ x 4″ metal. It should be centered at 3¼″ out and 1½″ down.

e. Hook the cylinder to the diverter valve supplied with the hoses from the hoist and pump kit.

16. Pickup hitch

a. Cut 1—1″ x 6″ plate 34″ long.

b. Cut 1—1⅜″ hole in the plate to accommodate the ball shank. This must be centered.

c. Loosen the pickup box bolts on 1 side. On the same side raise the box enough to insert the 1″ x 6″ plate under the box floor.

d. Place the 1″ x 6″ plate in the correct position

having the center of the hole lying 6½″ ahead of the axle. Spot weld to the frame. The 1″ x 6″ steel plate must be square with the rear axle of the pickup. Also due to the close location of the gas tanks extreme care must be taken while welding.

e. Cut 1 ½″ steel plate 12″ square with rounded corners for better appearance. Also cut 1—1⅜″ hole in the center to accommodate the shank of the ball.

f. Weld the 1″ x 6″ plate to the pickup frame.

g. With a ¼″ drill bit drill up through the floor of the pickup. This is to be in the center of the hole in the lower corner of the plate.

h. Assemble the hitch with the 12″ plate under the ball and above the floor.

17. Mounting the box

a. Using 2 tractor loaders and 2—⅜″ thick chains carefully lift the box on each end. Then place onto the frame with slow motion.

b. The box is to be 10″ from the front end of the frame. Then place squarely on the frame.

c. Weld the 2 hinges in the rear of the trailer squarely to the box frame.

d. Place the upper hoist mounting bracket with the hoist in lowered position directly over the 5″ bottom mount "I" beam. Spot weld the upper bracket only.

e. Raise and lower the hoist to check if the box will raise straight and that there is no binding.

f. Weld the upper bracket securely.

18. Wiring the trailer

a. Cut 5—30′ pieces of 14 ga. wire.

b. Using an old 50′ garden hose, reduce its length to 29′.

c. Thread the wires through the garden hose.

d. Put the 7-way plug connector on the end of the hose and thread the hose to the back of the trailer.

e. Bolt a 2″ x 2″ x ³⁄₁₆″ angle iron 40″ long on the back of the trailer box frame.

f. Wiring procedures can be done easiest with the use of a circuit breaker.

19. Mounting Mud flaps

a. Using holes and bolts provided with the mud flap kit mount the mud flaps 3″—4″ from the ground and 1′ from the most rear tire.

20. Painting

a. Clean the rust and oil from the frame to be painted. Then with a paint sprayer and recommended respirator spray the frame at 40 psi.

Fabrication of a Tilt-Bed Trailer

Author: Sidney Schmitt
Instructor: Fred D. Goldman
School: Southeastern Community College
City & State: West Burlington, IA

House trailer axles that were 8'5'' in overall length were used. These were shortened to 7' by sawing 1'5'' out of the center of each and welding the remaining halves back together. This was accomplished by measuring the amount to be taken out, drawing a straight line between the marks and then center punching just outside the marks. This was done for the purpose of retiming the axles when ready to weld back together. The axles were then sawed, removing the piece. After that, the halves were placed together and affixed with a pipe clamp and timed by the center punches.

Next the pieces for the subframe were cut. The subframe and tongue are fabricated entirely out of 5'' channel iron—two pieces 15' long, two pieces 8' long, and three pieces 5'4'' long. These seven pieces were welded together—the two 15' pieces being the length and the three 5'4'' pieces fitting between the 15' pieces at the following dimensions: one flush with one of the 15' ends, the next at the 4' line, and the third at the 8' line, leaving the rear open for the tilt bed. This was welded completely in the fixed position.

Four feet from the end with the flush crossbar, the 8' pieces are mounted, going out to form the tongue. These are angled in until there are 3'' between the ends and then welded. Where the 8' pieces pass under the front crossbar, 3/8'' x 5'' x 9'' piece of flat bar is welded into the channel to box the channel. This is for strength in this spot as it will be a main stress point for the trailer.

With the subframe welded together, the axles were mounted. At 13' from the front crossbar, the rear axle was mounted. Leaving 6'' between the two axles, the front axle was mounted to the sub-frame. After mounting the axles, the hitch and jack were mounted. This was done by bending the channels for the tongue until the hitch fit over them and then the hitch was welded. The jack was located in its place in the hitch and welded in. This completed the subframe assembly.

After finishing the subframe, the next step was the tilt-bed assembly. The four main runners for the bed were started with 20' long pieces with 59'' between the two middle runners. Five crossbars, each 58⅞'' long were welded at the following positions: one at 39'' from one end, the next 39¾" on center, the 40¼" on center, and two at 35¼" on center. The ends of the crossbars were prepared to fit the channel by cutting the corners to fit into the channel of the runners. Two pieces were cut 7'9". One of these pieces was welded on the end with the channel facing out. These six pieces were welded in their fixed position.

16' from the front a 22 degree bevel was cut from the four 20' pieces. This was done to make the bend for the angled portion of the bed. At these points, the channels were heated and bent down. These places were then welded.

Eight pieces were then cut 16⅞" long. One end of each was prepared to fit the channel as were the other crossbars. Four of these were welded into their positions of 39", 39¾", on center, 6'8" on center, 29¾" on center. To the outside of these, the other two 20' channels were welded on.

At 31" from the angle portion of the bed, runners were cut off at the 22 degree angle leaving the ends at a 90° angle to the ground. The other 7'9" piece was welded to the rear.

The flooring was reinforced with 2½" x 2½" x ¼" angle iron. Four lengths, one each 38¾", 39⅝", 34¾", and 33" were cut. The 33" piece had the ends beveled 22° to fit the angle bed. The one lip on each was cut to fit the channel so as to be flush with the tilt bed when completed. These were welded into their respective positions.

The pivot point was then determined. This was done by using a round stock between the underframe and the tilt bed and moving it forward or backward until the point of balance preferred was found. This point of balance can vary to suit the fabrication. At this point a hole was drilled in each side of the subframe. The diameter was 2½" to accomodate the pivot pins. Two plates were made, ⅜" x 5" x 9" to box the inside of the channel and matching holes in these plates were drilled. These plates were welded to the subframe. The pins were inserted and welded.

Two plates ½" x 3" x 5" were cut for the pivot pads. A 2½" hole was drilled ½" from one end of the pivot pad. These were mounted on the pins and the plates were welded to the tilt bed. Four ½" x ½" sq. pieces were cut and two were welded to the outside of each pin to prevent the tilt bed from slipping.

In the center of the front, the channels were boxed in. A piece of ½" x 1" x 12" was cut and 2" from one end, a 90° bend was made. This was then welded at a 90° angle to the tilt bed in the center of the front. Two pieces, ⅜" x 5" x 9" were placed parallel with the ½" x 1" x 12" piece with the nut of the 1" diameter bolt between them so

fixed that when the bolt was screwed into the nut, the bolt would come to rest on the lip of the ½" x 1" x 12" piece. The nut was then welded into its position. With this done a safety chain was added behind the tie-down. This was done by welding the middle of the chain to the tilt bed. With a hook on each end, it could then be fastened down for safety.

To strengthen the flooring, 2" x 1½" x ³⁄₁₆" formed angle iron in between all of the channel iron. The following sizes were needed: 16 pieces, 3' long, 4 pieces, 3'3" long, 2 pieces, 2'7" long, 4 pieces 3'2" long, 12 pieces 1'4" long, 6 pieces, 2'6" long, and 2 pieces 3'4" long. These pieces were welded in their respective positions according to the requirements in the channel spacing. Where angles were fastened to the channel iron, each was notched to fit into the channel so as to leave a flat surface. Also, where these angles crossed they were notched to fit flat. Where these angles were mounted over the wheels, the angle goes to the middle of the two wheels.

Next chain tie-downs were added. These were made from 5" channel iron from which 20 pieces were cut— each piece being 2" long. These were placed as follows: two in the front 1'6" each side from the center, and the rear the same; then down the sides, every 2' except for angled portion of the bed.

Next, the flooring was added. One full sheet was placed on the side where the 2½" x 2½" x ¼" angle iron was four feet on center and tacked into place with a MIG welder. Then another sheet was placed next to it, as side overhang. It also was tacked into place. From the ends of these sheets to the beginning of the angled deck, the distance is 6'. The last two sheets were sheared to 6'. These were placed and tacked in alignment with the first two sheets. From what was left of the last two sheets, 32" were cut from each. These covered the angled deck. They were tacked into place. This completely covered the bed. An automatic torch was set up and used to cut off the overhang. This cut was ground flush and then the sheets were completely welded on using a MIG welder with 75% Argon, 25% CO_2 shielding gas and using .035 wire. The flooring was stitch welded—4", weld, skip 4". With the scraps of the flooring the tongue was covered.

This completed the fabrication of the trailer. The entire trailer was buffed in preparation for painting. The trailer had two primer coats using Rustolium. It then had three coats of light blue on all the visible surfaces.

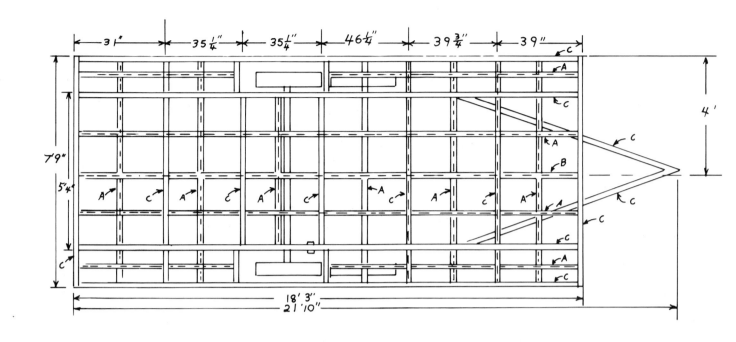

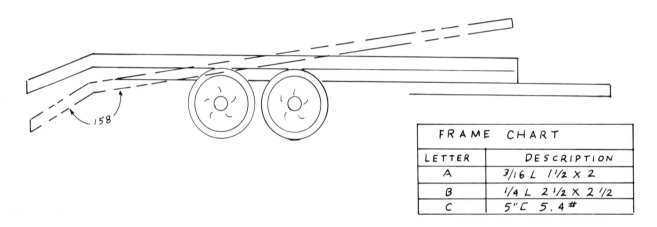

FRAME CHART	
LETTER	DESCRIPTION
A	3/16 L 1½ X 2
B	¼ L 2½ X 2½
C	5" C 5.4 #

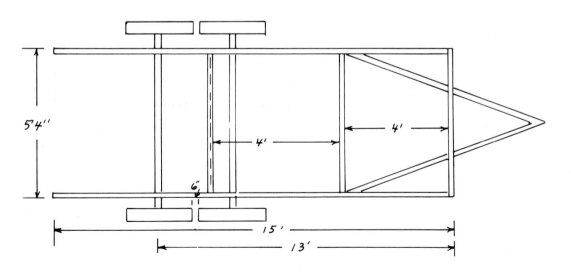